ANTHONY MUNDAY

The Historie of Palmendos

TEAMS

VARIA SERIES

The publication of this volume has been assisted by a subvention from the Spanish Ministry of Science and Innovation (ref. FFI2011–22811)

A list of the books in the series appears at the end of this book.

Medieval Institute Publications is a program of
The Medieval Institute, College of Arts and Sciences

Western Michigan University

Anthony Munday
The Honourable, Pleasant and Rare Conceited Historie of Palmendos

A Critical Edition

by

Leticia Álvarez-Recio

TEAMS

MEDIEVAL INSTITUTE PUBLICATIONS
Western Michigan University
Kalamazoo

Library of Congress Cataloging-in-Publication Data

Names: Munday, Anthony, 1553-1633. | Alvarez Recio, Leticia, editor.
Title: The honourable, pleasant, and rare conceited historie of Palmendos : a critical edition with an introduction, critical apparatus, notes, and glossary / [translated by] Anthony Munday ; edited by Leticia Álvarez-Recio.
Other titles: Primaleón (Romance). Selections (Polendos). English. (Munday)
Description: Kalamazoo : Medieval Institute Publications ; Western Michigan University, [2022] | Series: Teams varia | Includes bibliographical references. | Summary: "This volume contains the first critical edition of The Honourable, Pleasant and Rare Conceited Historie of Palmendos (London, 1589), a chivalric romance translated into English by Anthony Munday. Munday's translation is based on a Spanish original entitled Primaleón de Grecia I (Salamanca, 1512). This Spanish romance, the second book in the Palmerin cycle, soon became a best-seller in the Spanish market, with several editions published between 1512 and 1588. The work was also translated into many continental languages. Anthony Munday translated his Palmendos from the French version by François de Vernassal late in 1588. The Historie of Palmendos comprised the first thirty-two chapters of the French text and focused on the adventures of Palmendos on his journey to Constantinople. It was reprinted in 1653 and 1663 with slight alterations from the 1589 version. This is an original-spelling edition that produces a most reliable text, as close as possible to the author's original manuscript"-- Provided by publisher.
Identifiers: LCCN 2021052299 (print) | LCCN 2021052300 (ebook) | ISBN 9781580444811 (paperback) | ISBN 9781580444828 (hardback) | ISBN 9781580444835 (pdf)
Subjects: LCGFT: Romances.
Classification: LCC PQ6419 .P513 2022 (print) | LCC PQ6419 (ebook) | DDC 863/.3--dc23/eng/20220103
LC record available at https://lccn.loc.gov/2021052299
LC ebook record available at https://lccn.loc.gov/2021052300

Printed and bound by CPI Group (UK) Ltd, Croydon, CR0 4YY
ISBN hardbound: 9781580444828
ISBN paperbound: 9781580444811
eISBN: 9781580444835

In Memoriam

to my father,
Enrique Álvarez García,
1937–2017

Contents

Acknowledgments

THE PRESENT EDITION IS the result of longstanding research in the course of which a fair number of colleagues contributed with invaluable advice and help. I must thank Jordi Sánchez-Martí, who first enticed me to access the amazing world of the Iberian chivalric romances in English. I always found his vast knowledge in the field, together with his meticulous textual editing methods, inspiring and most helpful. I am also greatly indebted to Rafael Portillo and Juan Antonio Prieto-Pablos, who carefully revised the manuscript, providing sensible, constructive advice on the editing process.

Heartfelt thanks go to Manuel José Gómez-Lara for his bibliographical recommendations and to Ana Pérez Vega for her kind help in the translation of the Latin dedication into English. I must also acknowledge Rachel E. Holmes's generous disposition to answer numerous questions regarding early modern notions of marriage, abduction, and rape. I must also thank all members of the Iberian chivalric literature in English research team, as well as various other experts on the topic with whom I have held in-depth discussions at numerous academic meetings and conferences: they include María Beatriz Hernández-Pérez, José Manuel G. Fernández de Sevilla, Alejandra Ortiz-Salamovich, Rocío G. Sumillera, Louise Wilson, Helen Cooper, Donna Hamilton, Helen Moore, Joyce Boro, Elizabeth Evenden-Kenyon, Timothy D. Crowley, Alexander Samson, and Nandini Das. Great thanks to all members of the English Literature department at the University of Seville, and also to Wolfson College, at Cambridge University, as they kindly accepted my membership and always provided me with practical assistance during my research stays. Mercedes Salvador Bello's and David Morris's effective aid in Oxford and Cambridge must be credited too. Finally, I would like to thank the librarians at the rare book collections at Cambridge University, the Bodleian, and the British Library for their kindness, patience, and valuable advice, as well as Shannon Cunningham, at Medieval Institute Publications, for believing in this project.

And last but not least, I express my deepest gratitude to my children and, most of all, to my mother, whose wholehearted support made this work possible. The book is dedicated to them.

Research for this edition was conducted within a project funded by the Spanish Ministry of Science and Innovation (ref. FFI2011–22811), whose financial support is herewith gratefully acknowledged.

Earlier versions of sections 2 and 3 in the Introduction were previously published as articles in *Cahiers Élisabéthains* and *Atlantis*.

Abbreviations

adj. adjective

adv. adverb

Barley *The Delightful History of Celestina the Faire*. Trans. William Barley. London: Adam Islip for William Barley, 1596.

chap. chapter

EDIT16 *Censimento nazionale delle edizioni italiane del XVI secolo*. Roma: Istituto centrale per il catalogo unico delle biblioteche italiane e per le informazioni bibliografiche (ICCU). http://edit16.iccu.sbn.it/web_iccu/ihome.htm.

EEBO *Early English Books Online*. Chadwyck-Healey. ProQuest LLC, 2003–2018. http://eebo.chadwyck.com.

EM English Early Modern English

FB *French Vernacular Books: Books Published in the French Language before 1601*. Ed. Andrew Pettegree, Malcolm Walsby, and Alexander Wilkinson. Leiden and Boston: Brill, 2007.

Fr. in French

IB *Iberian Books: Books Published in Spanish or Portuguese or on the Iberian Peninsula before 1601*. Ed. Alexander Wilkinson. Leiden and Boston: Brill, 2010.

Índice y Motivos Ana C. Bueno Serrano. "Índice y estudio de motivos en los libros de caballerías castellanos (1508–1516)." PhD diss., Universidad de Zaragoza, 2007.

It. in Italian

Marín Pina *Primaleón (Salamanca, 1512)*. Ed. María del Carmen Marín Pina. Alcalá de Henares: Centro de Estudios Cervantinos, 1998.

ME Middle English

Motif-Index Stith Thompson. *Motif-Index of Folk Literature: A Classification of Narrative Elements in Folktales, Ballads, Myths, Fables, Mediaeval Romances, Exempla, Fabliaux, Jestbooks, and Local Legends*. Bloomington: Indiana University Press, 1955–1958. Reprint, 2005.

Mustanoja Tauno F. Mustanoja. *A Middle English Syntax: Parts of Speech*. Helsinki: Société Néophilologique, 1960. Reprint, Amsterdam and Philadelphia: John Benjamin, 2016.

n. noun

no. number

ODP *Oxford Dictionary of Proverbs*. Ed. Jennifer Speake. 6th ed. Oxford: Oxford University Press, 2015.

OED *The Oxford English Dictionary*. Oxford: Oxford University Press. http://dictionary.oed.com.

om. omitted

P1 first edition of *Palmendos* (1589)

P2 second edition of *Palmendos* (1653)

P3 third edition of *Palmendos* (1663)

P1H Huntington Library copy of *Palmendos* (1589)

P1Bod Bodleian Library copy of *Palmendos* (1589)

P1BL British Library copy of *Palmendos* (1589)

phr. v. phrasal verb

ppt. past participle

prep. preposition

prep. phr. prepositional phrase

pron. pronoun

Sp. in Spanish

SR *A Transcript of the Registers of the Company of Stationers of London: 1554–1640*. Ed. Edward Arber. 2 vols. New York: P. Smith, 1950.

STC *A Short-Title Catalogue of Books Printed in England, Scotland, and Ireland and of English Books Printed Abroad, 1475–1640*. A. W. Pollard and G. R. Redgrave. 2nd. ed. rev. W. A. Jacobs, F. S. Ferguson, and Katherine R. Pantzer. 3 vols. London: Bibliographical Society, 1976–1991.

Tilley Morris P. Tilley. *A Dictionary of the Proverbs in England in the Sixteenth and Seventeenth Centuries: A Collection of the Proverbs Found in English Literature and the Dictionaries of the Period*. Ann Arbor: University of Michigan Press, 1950.

USTC *Universal Short Title Catalogue*. Arts and Humanities Research Council, Iberian Books, Brill, Proquest, ICCU, GLN1516, STVC, and STCN. St. Andrews: University of St. Andrews. https://www.ustc.ac.uk/index.php.

v. verb

Introduction

Anthony Munday, Early Modern Prose Fiction, and European Chivalric Romance (1577–1603)

Anthony Munday died in 1633 at the age of seventy-three. He left behind a longstanding career as a poet, playwright, author of civic pageantry, chronicle writer, pamphleteer, and translator that made him one of the most versatile and prolific authors of his age. A controversial figure in his own time, he worked as a spy for Elizabeth's government and wrote or translated works of religious controversy as well as pamphlets on contemporary European politics. He was a playwright and a member of the Admiral's Men in the 1580s and, paradoxically, he also participated in a campaign against the theater. In spite of his middling-class extraction, he was regarded as a gentleman by some of his contemporaries;[1] he was sympathetic to Catholics but persecuted Jesuits, a hack writer who cared about the quality of his works. Munday's mysterious figure poses a considerable challenge to twenty-first-century critics, who have recently explored his connections with the City and his role in late Elizabethan debates on foreign and domestic religious policies.[2]

His work as the leading English translator of European chivalric romance has drawn scholarly attention since 2004, when Helen Moore published her critical edition of Munday's *Amadis de Gaule*. Since then, a considerable quantity of articles and essays on Munday's chivalric translations has been published, thus enhancing Munday's contribution to the

[1] See Thomas Middleton, *The Triumphs of Truth*, D3[r]. Nevertheless, Tracey Hill states that Munday held some "liminal status between artisan and gentry" (*Anthony Munday and Civic Culture*, 26) and Naomi Conn Liebler goes even further as she argues that Munday never "repudiated his working-class origins" (*Early Modern Prose Fiction*, 11).

[2] See Hamilton, *Anthony Munday and the Catholics*; and Hill, *Anthony Munday and Civic Culture*. Munday's religious ambivalence is explored in Lockey, *Early Modern Catholics, Royalists and Cosmopolitans*, chap. 2; and in Highley, *Catholics Writing the Nation*, chap. 5.

market demand for translations in late sixteenth-century London.[3] The significance of his translations and original prose works in the development of English prose fiction has been scarcely explored, though.[4] Such lack of interest is difficult to understand, considering that the rise in book sales of native prose fiction went hand in hand with that of English chivalric translations. Such a coincidence may be explained in terms of the new demands in the Elizabethan book market.[5]

Anthony Munday can be an illustrative case in this regard since he wrote prose fiction and translated French and Spanish chivalric romances almost simultaneously and quite successfully. Yet, as a translator, his larger popularity rests with the twelve chivalric translations he produced between 1588 and 1602, which were then reprinted from 1609 to 1619. By means of such an extraordinary output, he almost monopolized the

[3] For most recent critical studies on Munday's chivalric translations, see Álvarez-Recio, *Iberian Chivalric Romance*, "Anthony Munday's *Palmendos* (1589) in the Early Modern English Book Trade," and "Spanish Chivalric Romances in English Translation"; Hamilton, "Anthony Munday's Translations of Iberian Chivalric Romances"; Moore, "Ancient and Modern Romance" and "The Eastern Mediterranean in the English Amadis Cycle Book V"; Phillips, "Chronicles of Wasted Time"; Ortiz-Salamovich, "Anthony Munday's *Palmerin d'Oliva*"; Sánchez-Martí, *Los libros de caballerías en Inglaterra, 1578–1700*, "*Zelauto*'s Polinarda and the *Palmerin* Romances," and "The Publication History of Anthony Munday's *Palmerin d'Oliva*"; and Wilson, "Fictions of Book Production in Anthony Munday and Henry Chettle's Paratexts," "The Publication of Iberian Romance in Early Modern Europe," and "Playful Paratexts."

[4] Traditionally, continental chivalric books in English translations have been disregarded in most monographs or anthologies of early modern English prose fiction. Only a recent volume edited by Andrew Hadfield, *The Oxford Handbook of English Prose*, contains a chapter by Helen More on *Amadis de Gaule* and John Barclay's *Argenis*.

[5] According to Alan B. Farmer and Zachary Lesser, the market share of poetry and the arts underwent a dramatic rise especially in the 1590s, when this category was second only to religion in the retail trade. From 1559 to 1591, 48.1% prose fiction first editions (2.1% of the market share) sold well and were reprinted subsequently. In the last decade of Elizabeth's reign, they increased to 4.0% of the share; publishers tripled then the number of first editions issued each year. J. G. Ebel reckons that translations amounted to a quarter of the yearly publications in the Elizabethan trade ("A Numerical Survey of Elizabethan Translations," 125). As Gordon Braden observes, literary translations published in the last thirty years of the sixteenth century amounted to 3000, 200–400 being produced each decade. For further details, see Farmer and Lesser, "What Is Print Popularity?"; and Braden and Gillespie, *The Oxford History of Literary Translation in English*, 3, 5, 47.

genre in the market. There were, however, other translators[6] and authors who, clearly inspired by the rise in European chivalric narratives, issued successfully their own native English romances too.[7]

Munday's double role as an author of prose fiction and translator of chivalric romances is explored here. He had strong links with relevant prose narrative writers and collaborated with publishing agents specialized in native or translated prose fiction at a time when writers were becoming professional, and a new reading public was emerging. The three sections below examine those connections and offer a detailed account of Anthony Munday's work in three different stages: (1) in the late 1560s and 1570s, when he produced his earliest narratives and was deeply involved in contemporary debates on the value of fiction; (2) in the 1580s, when he began his translations of the Iberian chivalric cycles; and (3) in the 1590s and early 1600s, when he completed his chivalric translations as he was writing for the theater. The impact of his experience as a writer of fiction on his pamphleteering activity is considered as well. These three sections approach Munday's narrative practices in close relation to those of other contemporary authors, thus enhancing his contribution to the development of prose fiction in late sixteenth-century England.

Munday's Earliest Narrative Experiments: The 1570s

In the 1570s, Munday was long acquainted with the publishing industry, as his father, a member of the Draper's Company, had worked as a stationer, and Munday himself had been an apprentice to printer and bookseller John Allde (active 1555–1584),[8] whose trade flourished in the 1560s and 1570s. Munday must have soon been aware of the new market

6 Among them, Margaret Tyler, R. P. (identified in the EEBO as Robert Parke or Robert Parry), and L. A. (not identified), who translated the nine books of the Spanish *Espejo de príncipes y cavalleros* under the title *The Mirrour of Princely Deeds* (Book 1, 1578, 1580, 1599; Book 2, 1585, 1599; Book 3, 1586, 1599; Books 4–5, 1583; Books 6–7, 1598; Book 8, 1599; Book 9, 1601). William Barley published his own translation of the Spanish *Primaleón de Grecia* under the misleading title *The Delightful History of Celestina the Faire* in 1596, and L. A. translated Geronimo Fernández's *Don Belianis* as *The Honour Chivalry* in 1598.

7 Paul Salzman cites Emanuel Forde, Henry Roberts, or Richard Johnson as clear examples of such influence. See *English Prose Fiction*, 98–101.

8 The *British Book Trade Index* has been consulted for the dates of the professional activity of the publishing agents mentioned in this introduction.

trends when compiling verse anthologies—that is, *A Gorgious Gallery of Gallant Inventions* (1578) and *The Paine of Pleasure* (1580)[9]—and writing such volumes of short stories as *The Mirrour of Mutabilitie* (1579). Those prose and verse collections had had an extraordinary appeal in England since the 1560s, when they had been advertised as volumes that combined poetry and prose, comedy and tragedy, continental and classical authors, thus targeting a wide reading public.[10] Thomas Fenton makes it clear when addressing his *Certaine Tragicall Discourses* (1567) "to all sortes of people" (*2^{r}), and William Painter refers to gentlemen and women, merchants and yeomen, as the readers of his second edition of *The Palace of Pleasure* (1575, A4^{v}). Other collections such as George Pettie's *A Petite Pallace of Pettie his Pleasure* (1576), the short narrative by Barnabe Rich, *Riche his Farewell to the Militarie Profession* (1581), and the popular *Euphues and His England*, by John Lyly (1580, 1^{r}–2^{v}), were explicitly addressed to gentlewomen, by this time an important sector of the reading public.[11] Young noblemen were also considered potential readers of this early fiction, intended to instruct the "unstayed youth" on good conduct, as George Whetstone and Barnabe Rich suggest in their prefaces to *The Rocke of Regard* (1576, 2^{r}) and *The Straunge and Wonderfull Adventures of Don Simonides* (1581, A3^{r-v}), respectively. Munday had addressed the aforementioned *Gorgious Gallery of Gallant Inventions* (1578) and *Mirrour of Mutabilitie* (1579) to "all yong Gentilmen," who were enticed to read those works with a recreational purpose (1578, A2^{r}).[12]

9 Sara Smith is probably right when arguing against Munday's authorship of the *Paine of Pleasure*. Smith acknowledges, however, Munday's involvement in the compilation of the volume ("A Reattribution of Munday's *The Paine of Pleasure*").

10 On the different styles and genres of these collections, see Rhodes, "Italianate Tales: William Painter and George Pettie." On the connections between short-story volumes and poetic miscellanies, see Salzman, "Placing Tudor Fiction." In Andy Kesson's view, such miscellaneous nature was "a defining feature of early prose fiction publications that were sold in terms of their assortment and diversity" (*John Lyly and Early Modern Authorship*, 45).

11 Helen Hackett suggests in *Women and Romance Fiction* that such addresses to women could be part of advertising techniques intended to attract male readers.

12 As Alex Davies argues, those works were "recreational in the sense of being pleasant works which prepare and refresh one for one's real 'work,' even whilst, for their detractors, they represent mere profitless 'amusement'" (*Chivalry and Romance in the English Renaissance*, 19).

The aims of recreation and didacticism were soon employed to advertise fictional works in a highly competitive and prejudiced market. Despite their obvious appeal, the fact that most prose fiction published between the late 1560s and the early 1580s was originally foreign[13] posed a serious problem, as authors had to deal with the threat of censorship.[14] That is why prefaces in those works dwell on the didactic value of this type of literature, which should be associated with such authoritative genres as history.[15] Yet, as Katherine Wilson observes, "the writers of Elizabethan fiction are keen to pose as their readers' moral tutors and masters of ceremonies. But it is often hard to know how seriously to take their claim."[16] Whether they were really serious or not, authors actually regarded their narratives as both "profitable and pleasant," a stock-phrase used in para-

[13] Thirty-two out of the forty-one prose fiction works published from 1566 to 1579 were translations, mainly of continental origin. See O'Dell, *A Chronological List of Prose Fiction in English*; Salzman, *English Prose Fiction*, 351–55; Scanlon, "A Checklist of Prose Romances in English"; and the databases Renaissance Cultural Crossroads and Spanish-English Translations 1500–1640.

[14] Cyndia Susan Clegg states that "the state's most rigorous censorship efforts during the reign of Elizabeth were directed first at preventing the importation and dissemination of those Catholic texts that 'treated of the State and the Queen's majesty.'" Pursuivants were hired by the Privy Council to search for Catholic writings. The Archbishop of Canterbury and the Bishop of London did also have their own prerogatives, while the Stationers' Company monopolized the market of print also establishing their own rules according to the dictates of the monarch (Clegg, *Press Censorship in Jacobean England*, 20–21; Chiari, *Freedom and Censorship in Early Modern English Literature*). Since many of the works of fiction translated into English came from Catholic countries, translators had to do their best to protect their writings from the Elizabethan regime's "repressive mechanisms of control" mostly by resorting to self-censorship. It was not always easy. For instance, printer John Charlewood registered the translation of *Palmerin of England* on February 13, 1581. The stationer licensed it but "upon Condicon that if there be aniethinge founde in The booke when it is extante worthy of Reprehension. That then all the Bookes shalbe put to waste and Burnte" (*SR*, II, 383). On the problems regarding censorship of early modern English fiction texts, see also Maslen, *Elizabethan Fictions*, 8–9.

[15] Thomas Underdowne describes his translation of Heliodorus's romance as a "wittie historie" and insists that "of al knowledge fit for a noble gentleman . . . the knowledge of histories is the most seeming" (*An Aethiopian History*, 1569, 2^{r}). See other examples in Painter, *Palace of Pleasure* (1580), A3^{v} and Fenton, *Certaine Tragicall Discourses* (1575), 2^{r}.

[16] Wilson, *Fictions of Authorship in Late Elizabethan Narratives*, 8.

texts of fiction works translated in the 1570s and 1580s.[17] Anthony Munday, in his early works, had already participated in the debate on the value of fiction, which in his view should be read "advisedlie" and "with regarde" (*The English Romayne Lyfe*, 1582, A4^{r}). In addition, he insists on its entertaining potential to readers and authors alike, for he wishes in his *Zelauto* (1580) that his "woorkes may prooue as profitable to you in the reading: as they were delightfull to me in the writing" (8).[18]

Munday appeals then to an important leitmotif in early fiction: that of writing or translating as an act of pleasure to be shared with readers. All those works and particularly the translations are described as liberal, patriotic deeds that make it possible for English readers to be entertained at quite reasonable prices. They are presented as being socially, scholarly, and financially profitable. The author of one of the dedicatory poems in Whetstone's *Rocke of Regard* (1576) insists on this same idea: "Reader, reward, this gallant gift with thankes,/ Whose worth is much, although the price is small" (2^{v}), which is also supported by Margaret Tyler, as she attacks the prejudices of gentle readers who refuse to share their privileged position with other audiences: "I perceive some may be rather angry to see their Spanish delight turned to an English pastime, they could wel alow the story in Spanish, but they may not afford it so chepe, or they would have it proper to themselves" (*The Mirrour of Princely Deedes*, 1578, A3^{v}). Translations did indeed help widen the English readership of prose fiction.

Despite all arguments in favor of prose narrative, writers were often anxious about their role in the book market. Such established authors of prose fiction as Lyly, Rich, or Whetstone still described their works as "pamphlets," "trifles," "toys," or "trash" in the late 1570s and early 1580s,

[17] See Pedro de Mexías, *The Forest*, trans. Thomas Fortescue (1571, 1576), a3^{v}; Thomas Paynell, *Treasurie of Amadis of Fraunce* (1572), 2^{v}, 4^{r}; Margaret Tyler, *The Mirrour of Princely Deedes* (1578), A3^{r}; Painter, *The Palace of Pleasure* (1575), A4^{r}; Fenton, *Certaine Tragicall Discourses* (1575), 3^{r}; and Pettie, *A Petite Pallace of Pettie his Pleasure* (1576), A2^{r}. There are other examples in Thomas Underdowne, *The Aethiopian Historie* (1577), 3^{r}; Whetstone, *The Rocke of Regarde* (1576), 2^{r} and *An Heptameron of Civill Discourses* (1582), A3^{v}–A4^{r}; and Rich, *The Straunge and Wonderfull Adventures of Don Simonides* (1581), A2^{v}.

[18] As Helen Moore has demonstrated in her analysis of Paynell's *Treasurie of Amadis*, "profitable" became a "polyvalent term" that stressed the social and private benefits of romance as it can signify both "beneficial" but also "curative and remedial" ("Gathering Fruit," 50–54). Her remarks can be extended to other non-romance works of prose fiction of the same period.

thus undervaluing their own products. Authors very often pretended that their own texts had been handed to them by friends, or that they had written or translated what someone else had suggested, hence avoiding full responsibility for their work.[19]

Anthony Munday, for instance, presents his authorial self in quite equivocal terms in his early works. In the preface to the second part of *Zelauto*, he mysteriously argues that "you can haue no more of a Catte but her skyn: nor of me more then I am able to doo" (62). According to Tracey Hill, this implies "that there might be a difference between the "skyn" or the outside (that is, the readable text, that which Munday "does") and the "inside" (that is, the person himself, the enigmatic "Catte" who remains unknowable").[20] Munday's metanarrative displays of the narrator/author ambiguity, quite noticeable in *Zelauto* but equally present in his subsequent chivalric translations, exemplify the experimental nature of his early fiction, thus anticipating the narrative innovations of English native fiction in the 1590s.[21]

The paratextual material of parts one and two of *Zelauto* also points to Munday's authorial position, caught up between two different but coexisting literary production systems. He dedicates his work, as he does in other early fiction writings, to the Earl of Oxford, thus assuming his patronage. On the other hand, there is a growing awareness of his new role in the book trade. Munday's intertextual references to contemporary pieces, by himself or by other authors, place his early fiction in the context of an increasing demand for narrative works. In his epistle to Oxford

[19] See Pettie, *A Petite Pallace of Pettie his Pleasure* (1576), A3^{r}, A4^{r}; Lyly, *Anatomy of Wyt* (1578, 1579), A3^{v}, A4^{v} and *Euphues and His England* (1580), A2^{r}, 6; Whetstone, *The Rocke of Regard* (1576) 2^{r}; Tyler, *The Mirrour of Princely Deeds* (1578) A2^{r}; Rich, *Riche his Farewell to the Militarie Profession* (1581), C2^{r} and *The Straunge and Wonderfull Adventures of Don Simonides* (1581), A2^{r}. Lori Humphrey Newcomb understands such "toys" and "trifles" as coded terms employed to recommend the circulation of these works within coterie circles (*Reading Popular Romance in Early Modern England*, 37). In Juliet Fleming's view, those terms were used by male authors to address their pieces to women ("The Ladies Man and the Age of Elizabeth"). In both cases, writers appeal to their being sources of entertainment, which suggests that they are now accessible to a wider reading public.

[20] Hill, *Anthony Munday and Civic Culture*, 50.

[21] For Jack Stillinger, "a similar narrative complexity does not appear in Elizabethan fiction until Nashe's *The Unfortunate Traveller*, fourteen years later" (*Anthony Munday's Zelauto*, xii).

in *The Mirrour of Mutabilitie* (1579, ℭ2^r–ℭ3^v), he advertises this work as the sequel to *The Mirrour for Magistrates* (whose second part had been published in 1578) and sums up the first seven pages of chapter 1 of his *English Romayne Life* (first published in 1582). In *Zelauto*, he alludes to Aesop's *Fables* (the most recent edition had been published in 1570) and to Lyly's *Euphues: The Anatomy of Wyt* (1579), which had also been dedicated to Oxford and is presented here as a standard of excellence. In addition, he announces the immediate publication of his *Palmerin of England* (6).[22]

The woodcuts used in *Zelauto* show the extent of its intertextual connections with earlier fiction. Thirteen out of the twenty woodcuts employed in that work had been taken from Stephen Bateman's *The Travayled Pilgrime* (1569), a translation of the late fifteenth-century chivalric book *Le Chevalier Délibéré* by Olivier de la Marche, while three came from Thomas North's translation *The Morall Philosophie of Doni* (1570), a collection of Eastern fables translated from the Italian.[23] Munday's letter to the reader in the second part of *Zelauto* describes the use of woodcuts as a marketing device of his printer's own making, even if he finds it useful too: "The Printer (you will say) hath painted it full of pictures, to make it bought the better: and I say the matter is more meritorious, and therefore you should buy it the sooner. So, if you wyll be ruled by the Printer and me: you shall at no tyme want any of the Bookes" (61). He seems to regard his work as the result of a fruitful collaboration between author and printer, for he was soon aware of the possibilities of efficient marketing and advertising devices. His apparent prejudice against his printed works could then be interpreted as a deliberate pose, as a means of linking his fiction with that of more educated authors like John Lyly.

When announcing future volumes in his prefaces, he was only following in the footsteps of previous writers, as self-advertising had been a common practice since the early 1570s. Painter announces the publication of the second tome of his *Palace of Pleasure* in his 1575 edition of the first tome (A4^r); John Lyly promises a second book on Euphues in his 1580

[22] *Palmerin of England* was entered to John Charlewood on February 13, 1581. The earliest known edition of this book dates back to 1596, though there must have been some previous ones in the early 1580s (Thomas, *Spanish and Portuguese Romances of Chivalry*, 251).

[23] On these intertextual references, see Hamilton, "Anthony Munday and *The Merchant of Venice*," 91–92.

edition of *Euphues: The Anatomy of Wyt* (B1ᵛ) and Munday alludes to his other works in his prefaces to the different parts of *Zelauto*. In the second part, he insists on the need to read the whole sequence to understand the apparent "deformednesse" of his work (61). Such sequential mode of reading, which would also be supported by Painter in his 1580 edition of the second tome of *The Palace of Pleasure* (A4ᵛ), would become a general practice in the late 1580s and 1590s, largely thanks to the translations of the main Spanish chivalric cycles.

Romance and Native Prose Fiction: Munday's Chivalric Translations in the 1580s

The sale of chivalric romance achieved a central role in the 1580s prose fiction market. Medieval English romances had enjoyed great popularity from the late fifteenth century, but by the late 1570s publishers were already looking for other, more satisfactory sources of romance material. The success of short-story volumes in English translation very likely enticed publishers and translators to seek new products by drawing from either the classical tradition or continental chivalric literature. Translations of classical poetry and drama had already proved successful, but prose fiction was a different matter. Thomas Underdowne's translation of Heliodorus's *The Aethiopian History*, first published in 1569, which he dedicated to the Earl of Oxford, was the first in a long series of translations that would be published over many years, for Angel Day's version of Longus's *Daphnis and Chloe* was published in 1587, and William Burton's *Clitophon and Leucippe*, by Achilles Tatius, came out in 1597. Underdowne's book became so popular that it had three editions, published in 1569, 1577, and 1587.

Translators of Greek romances very soon regarded the chivalric books as their main rivals in the book market, as Underdowne observes in the second edition of his *Aethiopian History*:

> If I shall compare it with other of like argument, I thinke none commeth neere it. *Mort Darthure*, *Arthur of Little Britaine*, yea, and *Amadis of Gaule* &c. accompt violente murder, or murder for no cause, manhoode: and fornication and all vnlawfull luste, friendlie loue. This booke punisheth the faultes of euill doers, and rewardeth the well liuers. (¶3ʳ)

The translator acknowledges some thematic similarities between Greek and chivalric romances, just as he shows his concern about the reception of his own book. At the same time, he seems to be aware that chivalric works are considered some sort of pulp fiction devised for non-educated readers, whereas Greek romance should appeal to a more sophisticated audience.[24] Greek and chivalric romance, however, shared a common, wide readership comprising craftsmen, middling-class people, and even the nobility.[25] Underdowne's attempts at vindicating his translation were probably a self-defense move to protect his work from the overwhelming presence of chivalric fiction in the contemporary book market.

Thirteen editions of chivalric books came out in the 1580s. Ten of them were of continental, mostly Spanish, origin;[26] the other three were reprints of English medieval romances.[27]Another seven titles, including translations of European works and native English medieval books of chivalry, were entered in the Stationers' Register.[28] Despite the persistence

[24] Steve Mentz has interpreted this strategy as a common practice in Elizabethan times, as authors and publishers tried to ensure their products in the book market by distinguishing them from their generic rivals (*Romance for Sale in Early Modern England*, 35).

[25] Lori Humphrey Newcomb has considered these "hierarchies of taste" as strategies undertaken by wealthy and educated readers who "seeing that the experience of reading for pleasure was no longer exclusively theirs, attempted to subdivide the genre of romance along lines of social class." However, she adds, "only a few romance texts were granted elite literary status; the rest came to be scorned as merely popular" (*Reading Popular Romance in Early Modern England*, 8–9).

[26] See Jean de Cartigny's *The Wandering Knight*, trans. William Goodyear (1581, 1584); Pedro de la Sierra, *The Second Part of the Myrror of Knighthood*, trans. Robert Parke or Robert Parry (1583); Parts II and III of Diego Ortúñez de Calahorra, *The First Booke of the Myrrour of Knighthood* (1585, 1586); and Munday's translations *Palladine of England* (1588), the first part of *Palmerin d'Oliva* (1588), and *Palmendos* (1589). Munday must have published the two parts of *Palmerin of England* early in this decade (see note 22).

[27] See *Arthur of Little Britain* (*Le Morte Darthur*) (1582), *Syr Bevis of Hampton* (1585), and Richard Robinson's translation *The Auncient Order, Societie and Unitie Laudable of Prince Arthure* (1583).

[28] Among them, *Oliver of Castile* (entered to Thomas East in 1581), *The Foure Sons of Aymon* (entered to East in 1582), *King Pontus* (entered to John Charlewood in 1582), *Paris and Vienna* and *Valentine and Orson* (both entered to Purfoot in 1586), Juan de Flores's *Historie of Aurelio and Isabelle* (entered to Aggas in 1588), and *Amadis de Gaule*, Books I–IV (entered to Edward Allde in 1589).

of medieval works in the bookshops of London, translations of European material soon overshadowed them, as publishers showed a growing interest in early sixteenth-century continental works.

A decisive bet for chivalric romance was made by three important men in the book trade: Thomas East (active 1565–1608), John Charlewood (active 1553?–1593), and Edward Allde (active 1584–1627). Interestingly enough, two of them had strong connections with Anthony Munday, who, at this stage, became the most prolific translator of continental romance, thanks to the aforementioned titles. Edward Allde, who was son to John Allde, Munday's master in the 1570s, had worked with Munday in his father's business. He would print many of Munday's works in the late 1590s and early seventeenth century, especially civic pageantry.[29] On the other hand, John Charlewood had printed the majority of Munday's work from 1580 up to his own death in 1593—mostly political treatises, news pamphlets, and fiction.[30]

Munday and Charlewood were both involved in the publication of news. By that time, news had become a very important genre which depended to a great extent on translated material.[31] The threat allegedly posed by Spain and the Jesuits, Mary Stuart's imprisonment and execution, and the religion wars in France allowed for a vast amount of political news to circulate in England. Cecil's anti-Spanish campaign launched in the mid-1580s prompted this news boom, especially in the peak years

[29] Allde, Charlewood, and Munday were neighbors in Cripplegate (Hill, *Anthony Munday and Civic Culture*, 32).

[30] Among them, *The Paine of Pleasure* (1580), *A View of Sundry Examples Reporting Many Straunge Murthers, Sundry Persons Periured, Signes and Tokens of Gods Anger towards Vs* (1580), *The True Report of the Prosperous Successe Which God Gave unto our English Souldiours in Ireland* (1580), *The Arraignment and Execution of a Vilful and Obstinate Traitor* (1581), *A Brief Discourse of the Taking of Edmund Campion* (1581), *A Courtly Controversie between Looue and Learning* (1581), *A Brief and True Reporte of the Execution of Certaine Traytour at Tibourne* (1582), *A Breefe Answer Made unto Two Seditious Pamphlets* (1582), *A Discoverie of Edmund Campion* (1582), *The English Romayne Life* (1582, 1590), *A Watchword to England to Beware of Traytours* (1584), the translation of the Italian play by Luigi Pasqualigo *Fedele and Fortunio* (1585), a revised edition of John Ryckes's *The True Image of Christian Love* (1587), *A Banquet of Daintie Conceits* (1588), *The Masque of the League and the Spanyard Discouered* (1592), and the translations of the treatises *Axiochus* and *Archaioplutos* from the Greek (1592). For this list, see Donna Hamilton, *Anthony Munday and the Catholics*, 199–202.

[31] Barker, "European News Books in English Translation," 231.

1589–1590, when seventy translations from French, Dutch, Spanish, and other languages reached the market with clear propagandistic purposes.[32] Munday and Charlewood, doubtlessly aware of the potential profit of this genre, produced many of these pamphlets just as they were working on *Zelauto* and the first translations of the Palmerin cycle.[33]

Munday was by no means the sole fiction author to make money out of translated news, since William Philip, Arthur Golding, and George Gilpin did too,[34] while Robert Greene, probably the most popular fiction writer at the time, just noticed the potential in Cecil's propaganda when writing his *Spanish Masquerado* (1589). Munday and Greene were also involved in a parallel campaign led by the Archbishop of Canterbury and the Bishop of London against a series of pamphlets that attacked the Church of England under the pseudonym Martin Marprelate. Thomas Nashe, John Lyly, Robert Greene, and Anthony Munday were hired to produce pamphlets supporting the government.[35] Prose fiction became thus associated with pamphlet literature, a genre that could easily reach a wide audience. The irenic response of these writers, intended to counteract Marprelate's threat, dwelled on ideas already proposed by Munday in his translations of Spanish chivalry books, as he openly advocated for the need of a united Christendom.[36] The fact that Lyly, Nashe, Greene, and Munday, together with various young wits of the 1570s such as Thomas Lodge, were suspected of holding links with the Catholic faith, may explain not only

[32] Griffin, "Copying *The Anti-Spaniard*: Post-Armada Hispanophobia and English Renaissance Drama," 193; Parmelee, *Good Newes from France*, 31.

[33] Munday also worked with John Wolfe, the main printer of political news at the time, who issued two anti-Spanish tracts translated by Munday—i.e., *The Coppie of the Anti-Spaniard Made at Paris* (1590) and *The Masque of the League and the Spanyard Discovered* (1592). Wolfe registered Books 2–5 of *Amadis de Gaule* on April 10, 1592 (*SR*, II, 607). These were translated by Munday subsequently.

[34] Barker, "European News Books in English Translation," 239.

[35] For a more detailed analysis of these authors' role in the Marprelate controversy, see Hutson, *Thomas Nashe in Context*, 66–67; Nicholl, "Nashe, Thomas"; and Wilson, "Anthony Munday, Pamphleteer and Pursuivant," 488–90.

[36] Brian C. Lockey has explored Munday's cosmopolitan view of late Elizabethan and Jacobean English Catholicism alongside other translators such as John Harington and Richard Farshawe in *Early Modern Catholics, Royalists and Cosmopolitans*, chap. 2. Donna B. Hamilton adopts a similar view in her analysis of Munday's histories and translations of Iberian romances in her essay "Anthony Munday, Romance Translations, and History Writing."

their willingness to collaborate with the church authorities, but also the widespread prejudiced view of romance—and fiction, in general—as a subversive, potentially Catholic, genre.[37] The alleged sympathy those writers had for Catholicism—most of them had been protégées of the Earl of Oxford and the Earl of Southampton, both of them Catholic—may have been a common link between them. As a matter of fact, the main printers of chivalric romance in the 1580s—that is, the aforementioned East, Charlewood, and Allde—had problems with the Stationers for printing Catholic material, and both East and Charlewood were themselves suspected of Catholicism.[38] In spite of everything, Munday, who could not be considered himself a university wit, had reached by the late 1580s the same status as other relevant fiction writers.

Prose narrative, still as innovative as in previous decades, was by the 1580s more prone to single works than to short-story collections.[39]

[37] On those authors' alleged Catholic sympathies and the association of early modern English fiction with Catholic practices, see Wald, *The Reformation of Romance*, 1–29; Das, *Renaissance Romance*, 130; and Maslen, *Elizabethan Fictions*, 1–18. In Tiffany Jo Werth's view, "the fascination with romance lay precisely in its contested use of successful motifs drawn from a discredited Catholic heritage." As she argues, it was precisely "its supernaturalism, its affective force over readers—especially those deemed most vulnerable—and ultimately the entire aspect of the 'marvelous'" which came to be identified as superstitiously Catholic (*The Fabulous Dark Cloister*, 4).

[38] Most of those authors shared their publishing agents: two of the six works by Greene published in this decade were printed by Charlewood—i.e., *Morando* (1584) and *Arbasto* (1589)—while Edward White, the main publisher of Robert Greene, acquired the rights on Munday's *Banquet of Dainty Conceits* in 1588 and published four of his news pamphlets in 1591–1592. Charlewood also produced two issues of Nashe's *Pierce Penniless* in 1592, while the writer still lived with and worked for John Danter. Both Danter and Charlewood would collaborate in the publication of Munday's *Axiochus* that same year.

[39] Lyly's *Anatomy* was apparently the first book to advertise itself as a narrative unity (rather than a miscellany). According to Andy Kesson, no previous work had been organized as a single story that far (*John Lyly and Early Modern Authorship*, 48). Short-story volumes were still quite popular, though. Up to six collections were published in this decade. Three of them were reprints of Apuleius's *The Golden Ass* (1582) and Pettie's *A Petite Pallace of Pettie his Pleasure* (1585), while the other three were new editions—Whetstone's *Heptameron of Civill Discourses* (1582), Des Périers's *Mirrour of Mirth* (1583), and William Warner's *Pan His Syrinx* (1584). Other works, such as Thomas Lodge's *An Alarum against Usurers* (1584), William Averell's *A Dyall for Dainty Darlings* (1584), and Robert Greene's *Planetomachia* (1585), *The Myrrour of Modestie* (1584), and *Perimedes* (1588), contained short stories as well. Two short

Lyly and Greene, in their turn, promoted the sequels of *Euphues* and *Mamillia*, respectively, for Lyly's *Euphues: The Anatomy of Wyt* (1578) was soon followed by *Euphues and His England* (1579), while the two parts of Greene's *Mamillia* (comp. 1580) were published in a single volume in 1583. Greene's romance, consisting only of thirty-seven leaves printed on both sides, apparently encouraged fiction writers to issue shorter works that might bring them better profit.[40] Robert Greene produced four more short romances in 1584–1588, thus offering his readers good quality entertainment for little money.[41] As R. W. Maslen explains, though the short length of his works had been imposed on him by the market's needs, it soon became a distinguishing feature of his narrative production.[42]

Anthony Munday followed in Greene's footsteps when producing his early works in prose (*Zelauto* and *The English Romayne Life* consisted of only 156 and 84 pages respectively), and many of his chivalric translations were shorter than those by other authors. The different English versions of *The Mirrour of Princely Deedes* published in the 1580s contained 179 (1578, 1580), 334 (1583), 258 (1585), and 252 (1586) leaves. Munday's *Palladine of England* (1588) had 92 and *Palmendos* (1589), 99 leaves, whereas *Palmerin d'Oliua*, Part I (1588) had 176 pages. Munday, in his preface to *Palmerin d'Oliua* (1588), argues in favor of this procedure and explains his reasons for introducing divisions into what had been just a single book in other languages: "A booke growing too bigge in quantitie, is profitable neither to the minde nor the pursse: for that men ar now so wise, and the world so hard, as they looue not to buie pleasure at unreasonable price . . . [since] a man grutcheth not so much at a little mony, payd at severall times, as he doth at once" (*4^r).

Such explicit reference to his translations as mere commodities in the book trade may explain why, from the late 1580s, Munday begins to regard himself as a professional writer. In his view, translating is a hard, laborious task, and he refers to it as being "so long a labour"

stories by Boccaccio and Bandello—*Ammorous Fiammetta*, trans. Bartolomew Young (1587) and *The Tragical Historie of Romeus and Iuliet*, trans. Arthur Brooke (1587)—were issued as short novels, without being included in any larger volume.

[40] Authors were only paid once for their work and never benefited themselves from subsequent reprints.

[41] See his *Arbasto: The Anatomie of Fortune* (1584; 54 pages), *Gwydonius: The Carde of Fancie* (1584; 78 leaves), and *Pandosto: The Triumph of Time* (1588; 56 pages). His *Morando* (1584), a fictional dialogue on love, had only 48 pages.

[42] See his chapter on Robert Greene in *The Oxford Handbook of English Prose*.

(*Palmerin d'Oliva*, 103, line 22)[43] or a "painfull and laborious" activity (Maisonneufve, *Gerileon of England*, 1592, A2^{v}), while he presents himself as a simple agent in the literary production, one who has to comply with the requirements of his publishing agents. In his Epistle Dedicatorie of *Gerileon of England* he complains that he has to combine both his work as a professional writer and his duties as a messenger to the queen, while he apologizes for the quality of his translation, which "should haue been better, if more respite had been graunted me" (A2^{v}). In his letter "to the corteous and freendly readers" in *Palladine of England* (1588), he explains that "being often absent, and the Printer carefull to end his worke by appoynted time, haue beene the cause of all these escapes" (4^{r-v}).

Munday's words echo those by such professional writers as Greene, Nashe, Lodge, and Dekker, who created their own authorial *personae* as "brand names" in the literary market.[44] Such professional self-consciousness became, then, a distinguishing feature in native prose fiction writers. However, and even if the translation of chivalric romance was becoming increasingly popular in England, the only translator who made a similar claim about his professional activity was Anthony Munday. The different translators of the *Mirrour of Knighthood* cycle (of which eight editions were issued from 1578 to 1601), *The Honour of Chivalrie* (1598), and Montemayor's pastoral romance *Diana* (1598), all presented their books as self-entertainment pieces not intended for publication.[45] Munday clearly differs from them by posing as a professional prose writer.

Nevertheless, like other translators of Spanish chivalric romance, he tried to offer a unified narrative that could be followed throughout the various volumes of the sequels. Such concern is patent at a very early stage, when the translator of the second part of *The First Booke of the Myrrour of Knighthood* (1585)—identified as Robert Parke or Robert Parry—addressed his readers thus:

[43] References to *Palmerin d'Oliva* throughout the text have been taken from Jordi Sánchez-Martí's critical edition.

[44] Steve Mentz has studied the notion of literary labor in his essay "Day Labor." See also Phillips, "Chronicles of Wasted Time."

[45] See the second part and the sixth and seventh books of *The Mirror of Knyghthood* (1583, 1598), A2^{r}, A2^{r}, A4^{v}, respectively; *The Honour of Chivalrie* (1598), A3^{r}, A4^{r}; *Diana* (1598), a3^{r}. This strategy was also employed by such authors of native chivalric romance as Emanuel Forde. See his dedications and letter to the reader in *Parismus* (1598) and *Parismenos* (1599).

> I haue (good Reader) according to my forepassed promise, prosecuted the second part of the first Booke of the mirrour of Knighthood: after which likewise (before the second part alreadie printed) followeth another booke, which is entituled in the Spanish worke, the third part of the first booke &c. which, with as much expedition as may be, shalbe published: whereby both the quaint beginning, and the quoy abruption, *shall be brought to a concord, though no conclusion*: Yet shall the whole storye be concluded with diligent spede, if thou accept with thy wonted curtesie, these passed impressions. (A4[r]) (The editor's emphasis)

One year later, he issued a third part (1586) that concluded "the Hystories of these three partes of the first booke, following orderlie one after another: after which three partes before mentioned, foloweth the seconde part of the *Mirror of Knighthood*, which booke is divided into two partes: so that now is extant in the English tongue fiue bookes" (A3[r]).

Munday holds a similar view in the Epistle Dedicatorie of his *Second Booke of Primaleon of Greece* (1596), in which he feels that his readers may be at a loss because he has not followed a correct sequential order; hence, he tries to help them relate the events of this book to those found in other books of the Palmerin series and ensures a unified narrative of the cycle in the near future:

> After I had sent vnto your Worships, the first part of my translated *Palmerine of England*, and considered withall, that the same tooke his original from the third Part of this present *Historie of Primaleon*, which I am now translating, and purpose (by Gods leave) shortly to publish: I thought it necessarie to make you both my Patrones of this likewise, and the third, when it shall be finished, that yee maye see the whole Chronicle of these famous Princes in their full perfection. (A2[r])[46]

[46] In the same vein, Adam Islip (active 1585–1639), the printer of *The Fift Booke of Amadis de Gaule* (1598), signs the letter to the readers and explains why he had been unable to publish the Amadis books in a sequential order. He seems to point to his difficulty in achieving the rights on this material: "Gentlemen, I present you here with the fift book of Amadis de Gaule, of whose delectable history you haue already perused the first and second books: wherefore it may bee, you rather expect the third and fourth bookes to come forth in due course, then that *the fift should thus vntimely appeare before the rest*. The cause of which *vnorderly proceeding*, grew from this occasion: I hauing only interest in this and the following bookes of Amadis, haue already set out this fift booke, being the first of those which are in my hands, and also doeth begin with the hystory

Despite these attempts, the episodic nature of romances, together with their narrative inconsistencies already posed serious problems to publishers and translators in the late 1580s and 1590s. They tried then to adjust the chivalry books they were dealing with to a conventional large-scale narrative continuity, so common in native English fiction. In Steve Mentz's view, it is the most distinguishing feature of late Elizabethan narratives, as they tend to present loose plots that are framed within a consistent, unified main plot.[47] Such sequential reading employed by the translators of Iberian chivalric romance in their paratexts may have been prompted by the readers' demand for narrative unity. Munday seems to be fully aware of that demand and partly adapts his translations, bearing it in mind. He often summarizes and omits large sections of his sources to make the main plots of his books easier to follow. As in the case of *Palmendos*, he tends to provide relative closures to his narratives while presenting them as separate items within a complex unified whole that can only reach completion once the cycle ends. By so doing, he manages to remain half-way between the very episodic, digressive medieval romance and the new modern type of fiction. Munday's plain speech and style had a similar aim, as he sided with the narrative trend that would prevail in the 1590s, no doubt influenced by Sir Philip Sidney, who had previously argued in favor of simplicity and against the rhetorical abuse of the euphuestic mode.[48]

Munday's Translations and the Boom of Prose Fiction in the 1590s

Munday had already translated and published the main books of the Iberian cycles by the turn of the century. His most prolific years as a translator of Spanish chivalric romance coincided with an extraordinary literary boom in England, a moment when literature and the arts surpassed such traditional subjects in the book market as history and politics.[49] Out

of Espladian, being the sonne of Amadis: intending by Gods grace *to proceed with the others in due order* as time doth permit. But as *concerning the other Bookes which rest in another mans right*, as they are not in my power, so can I make no promise when they shall be published." (A2^r) (The editor's emphasis)

[47] Mentz, *Romance for Sale in Early Modern England*, 11–14.

[48] *The Defence of Poesy*, 247. Munday's method and style are analyzed in depth in the second section of this introduction ("Translating Spanish Romances in Sixteenth-Century England: Munday's Method of Translation in *Palmendos*"), in which *Palmendos* is presented as a case study.

[49] See note 5.

of the 133 editions of prose narrative works that were produced, seventy-one were romances, thirty were novels,[50] twenty-four were short stories or short-story collections, and eight were autobiographical pamphlets.[51]

Romance was already a relevant genre in the English prose fiction market by the turn of the sixteenth century. Its popularity was probably due to the fact that the old traditional romance was branching out into various subgenres that could cater to various different tastes. Out of the aforementioned seventy-one editions, fourteen were Greek romances, eleven were pastoral or sentimental pieces, thirty-seven were chivalric books, and eight were hybrid forms that are difficult to assign to a particular subcategory.[52] Twenty-three out of those thirty-seven chivalric books were of Iberian origin. Eleven of them had been translated by Anthony Munday.

The competitive nature of the book trade required an increasing degree of specialization in authors, translators, and publishing agents, which in turn gave rise to a heterogeneous map of prose fiction and romance. Like most other contemporary authors, Munday tried to find his own niche in such complex literary and printing worlds, and, though

[50] The term "novel" as applied to early prose fiction has been highly contested and debated. Its meaning here is quite broad, mostly referring to lengthy prose stories. However, J. Paul Hunter's and Andy Kesson's views on the novel as being a work that remarks on the "daily, the trivial, the common, and immediate" (Hunter, *Before Novels*, 169–70) and offers "a very familiar form of domesticity and Englishness" (Kesson, *John Lyly and Early Modern Authorship*, 46) should also be considered. The works among these thirty editions include Lyly's *The Anatomy of Wyt* and *Euphues and His England*, Thomas Lodge's *Euphues Shadow*, Thomas Nashe's *Pierce Pennilesse* and *The Unfortunate Traveller*, Barnabe Riche's *Farewell to Militarie Profession*, Turner's *The Garland of a Green Wit* and *Doctor Faustus*, and David Rowland's translation of *The Pleasant Historie of Lazarillo de Tormes*, among others.

[51] The present figures do not completely match those proposed by Farmer and Lesser, as they have estimated 2.7% and 4.0% of the market share for prose romance and prose fiction and satire, respectively ("What Is Print Popularity?").

[52] These figures exceed the thirty editions of prose fiction narratives (sixteen of which were first published in this decade), while fourteen were reprints of previous works, such as the six editions of both parts of Lyly's *Euphues*. Short-stories and short-story volumes were still popular, though most of them (sixteen out of twenty-four) were reprints of old editions. Nine editions of Greene's pseudo-autobiographical narratives were issued in the decade—*Greenes Never Too Late* (1590, 1600), *Greenes Farewell to Folly* (1591), *Greenes Mourning* (1591), *Greenes Groatworth of Wit* (1592, 1596), *Greenes Vision* (1592), *The Repentance of Robert Greene* (1592), and *Greenes News from Heaven*, by Barnabe Rich (1593).

he kept exploring other genres,[53] he devoted himself mostly to two tasks; namely, his translation of the Palmerin and Amadis cycles—which he would finish in 1602, with the publication of the third part of *Palmerin of England*—and his work as a playwright and actor for the Admiral's Men.

At this time, Munday collaborated with his previous publishing agent Edward Allde,[54] but he also worked with other professionals who monopolized the production of chivalry books in England, such as Thomas Creede (active 1593–1617), Cuthbert Burby (active 1592–1607), and John Danter (active 1589–1599). Thomas Creede was the most prolific of them. He had been an apprentice to Thomas East in Cripplegate from 1578 to 1593, when he set up his own business, and so he might have been acquainted with Munday's agents in the 1580s. From the mid-1590s, Creede built up such an extensive network of printers and publishers that, in R. B. McKerrow's words, "much of the literature of the time passed through his press."[55] He soon made a clear bet on prose fiction, more specifically, on romance. From 1593 to 1603, he brought out thirteen editions, eight of which were chivalric books. In those same years he also acquired the rights to publish most of Anthony Munday's *Palmerin d'Oliua* and *Palmerin of England* books, which he would publish in 1597, 1609, 1615, and 1616. That such a prominent name in the

[53] For his political and sensational pamphlets, see *The Coppie of the Anti-Spaniard Made at Paris* (1590), *The Masque of the League and the Spanyard Discovered* (1592), *The Strangest Aduenture that euer happened: Containing a Discourse of the King of Portugall dom Sebastian* (1601), *News from Malta, Written by a Gentleman of that Island* (1603), and *A True and Admirable Historie, of a Mayden of Consolens* (1603, 1604). He also published a second edition of *The English Romayne Life* (1590). Munday translated classical and humanist treatises—i.e., *Axiochus* (1592), *Archaioplutos* (1592), Ortensio Landi's *Defence of Contraries* (1593, 1602), Alexander Sylvain's *The Orator* (1596), as well as medical and religious works such as Jacques Guillemeau's *The French Chirurgerye* (1598) and Antoine de la Faye's *A Breefe Treatise of the Vertue of the Crosse* (1599). Munday also contributed some verses to *Englands Helicon* (1600) and edited John Bodenham's *Bel-vedére or The Garden of the Muses* (1600). For more detailed information, see Hamilton's *Anthony Munday and the Catholics*, 199–204.

[54] He published Munday's *First Booke of Amadis of Gaule* (1590), which, according to R. U. Pane, he would reprint together with the second book in 1595 (listed in Pane, *English Translations from the Spanish*, no. 165). Allde would also reprint some works by Robert Greene such as *Philomela* (1592), *Greenes Vision* (1592), and *Penelopes Web* (1601).

[55] McKerrow, *A Dictionary of Printers and Booksellers*, 80–81. See also Straznicky, *Shakespeare's Stationers*, 243.

book trade should invest on Munday's works looks significant, as it suggests that Munday's reputation as a translator was already quite high or, at least, that Creede knew those titles would sell well. Creede also issued the first edition of *The Honour of Chivalrie* in 1598 and the eighth book of *The Myrrour of Knighthood* in 1599.[56]

Thomas Creede was, together with Cuthbert Burby, the main publisher of playbooks in the 1590s. Plays had become increasingly popular from 1594 and managed to secure a 4 percent share in the book trade.[57] Burby produced eleven chivalry book editions in this same period, though he was less prolific than Creede in other narrative genres. He showed a great interest in Munday's material in the early 1590s, for he published his *Gerileon of England* in 1592 (printed by Thomas Scarlet), the second book of *Amadis de Gaule* in 1595 (printed by Adam Islip), and the first and second books of *Primaleon of Greece*, both printed by John Danter and published in 1595 and 1596, respectively. The fact that Munday's main agents in the 1590s were also publishers of dramatic works cannot be coincidental, which points to the growing popularity of both genres in the market.[58]Anthony Munday, however, was not the only writer to become aware of the economic and literary potential of chivalric and dramatic literature. John Lyly, Thomas Lodge, George Gascoigne, and Robert Greene, among others, were at the same time playwrights and authors of romance or prose fiction and so their narrative and dramatic works constantly influenced each other, especially in terms of speech and plot.[59]

As mentioned above, Burby collaborated with John Danter (active 1589–1599) in the 1595 and 1596 editions of Munday's *Primaleon of Greece*.[60] Burby had already been in partnership with Henry Chettle

[56] Creede worked too with Greek and pastoral romance—i.e., his reprint of Greene's *Mamillia* (1593), William Burton's translation of Achilles Tatius's *Clitophon and Leucippe* (1597), and Robert Codrington's translation of Gil Polo's *The Troublesome and Hard Adventures in Love* (1594)—and other works of fiction, such as Deloney's *Haigh of Devonshire* (1600) and Kitowe's *Loves Load-Starre* (1600).

[57] Farmer and Lesser, "What Is Print Popularity?," 37, 40.

[58] The connection between these two genres is explored in more detail in Álvarez-Recio, "Translations of Spanish Chivalry Works in the Jacobean Book Trade."

[59] For a further comment on this reciprocal relationship, see Wilson, *Fictions of Authorship*, 1–3.

[60] Danter also achieved in 1596 the rights on *Palladine of England*, which he apparently never published (*SR*, III, 69).

(active 1584–1607), a close friend of Munday's who had also been apprentice to John Allde back in the 1580s. Chettle signs a letter addressed to "his good Friend M. Anthony Munday," in *The Second Booke of Primaleon of Greece* (A3^{r-v}), a work that Chettle admits "hath been longer looked for" and which he commends as he has not seen "a Historie more delectable continued, nor . . . anie thing by your selfe more pleasingly translated" (A3^{r}). Chettle signs this letter as "Printer" and includes a commendatory poem together with some other verses by Michael Drayton. Their presence in the paratextual material of Munday's translation illustrates the fact that many of those writers could simultaneously have a hand in poetry, drama, narrative fiction, and publishing. From 1597 to 1602, when he stopped writing for the theater, Munday collaborated with Drayton and/or Chettle in such plays as *Sir Thomas More* (1593?), *Mother Redcap* (1597), *Chance Medley* (1598), *The Funerall of Richard Coeur de Lion* (1598), *The Second Part of Sir John Oldcastle* (1599), *Owen Tudor* (1600), *Fair Constance of Rome* (First part, 1600), *The Death of Robert, Earl of Huntington* (1601), *The Downfall of Robert, Earle of Huntington* (1600), *The Rising of Cardinal Wolsey* (1601), *Jephthah* (1602), and *Caesar's Fall* (1602).[61] He also collaborated with other dramatists such as Thomas Dekker or John Webster, who wrote dedicatory poems included in the 1602 edition of *Palmerin of England.*

Munday's relationship with other fiction writers of the 1590s may be explored through the social network of contemporary printers. John Danter and Henry Chettle pose as possible links between Munday and Thomas Nashe, a key figure in the 1590s book trade. Nashe was then living, and probably working, with his publisher John Danter and Henry Chettle, Danter's professional partner at the time. That would have made it possible for Nashe and Munday to meet, given their common acquaintances. A considerable amount of Nashe's work went through Danter's press in 1591–1596, just when he was investing on Munday's chivalric cycles. Chettle himself was serving as an intermediary between Danter and his authors.[62] Besides, the first and third editions of Nashe's *Pierce Penniless* (1592, 1595) were printed by Charlewood and Thomas Creede, respectively, to be sold by Nicholas Ling (active [before] 1597–1607). The possibility of Charlewood and Creede's involvement in the publica-

[61] Hamilton, *Anthony Munday and the Catholics*, 201–4.

[62] Jowett, "Notes on Henry Chettle," 385–86; Nicholl, *A Cup of News*, 140–41.

tion of Munday's translations had already been considered, but it should be mentioned that Ling did also sell the 1582 and 1590 editions of Munday's *The English Romayne Life*, both printed by Charlewood. Nashe's *The Unfortunate Traveller* was first published in 1594 by Cuthbert Burby, practically coinciding with Burby's production of books one and two of Munday's *Primaleon of Greece*. Even if publishers were then specializing in specific fiction and romance genres,[63] the reciprocal connection of one and the other genre was unavoidable, as the great investment on both types of material by such central figures as Creede or Burby and, to a lesser degree, John Danter, seems to suggest.

The fact that Thomas Creede and other printers of Munday's works such as Richard Field (active 1589–1624), James Roberts (active 1564–1618), and Adam Islip (active 1585–1639) were hired by the Bishop of London to produce appellant documents against the Jesuits in the Archpriest controversy (1595–1602) strengthens the connection between the government and the printers of romance, prose fiction, and news-narratives also in the 1590s. Munday's ecumenic view of Christendom is complemented by his attacks on treason in his chivalric translations and his pamphlets siding with many of the arguments of the English appellants, who tried to be faithful Catholics while remaining loyal to the Queen. That Creede, Roberts, and Islip printed Munday's main chivalric translations at the time of the Archpriest controversy enhances Munday's and his agents' deep and long-lasting involvement in the religious controversies of the late Elizabethan period.[64]

Anthony Munday's successful first run of translations from the mid-late 1580s to 1602 prompted a second run of reprints in the years 1609 and 1615–1619. His success probably encouraged other translators and publishers to follow in his footsteps. That was the case of Thomas East,

[63] See, for instance, Abel Jeffes (active 1580–1599), who issued up to three different editions of fiction works and five romances—three of them following the Greek pattern but did not produce any single chivalric piece. Gabriel Cawood (active 1576–1602) produced six editions of prose fiction but no romance while Valentine Simmes (active 1585–1622) was a prolific printer of Greek romances who also produced prose fiction and short-story volumes but never issued a chivalric piece.

[64] The second and fifth books of *Amadis de Gaule* were printed by Islip in 1595 and 1598; Creede and Roberts printed the second part of *Palmerin d'Oliua* and the last part of *Palmerin of England* in 1597 and 1602, respectively. On Munday's and these printers' engagement in the Archpriest controversy, see Ferraro Parmelee, "Printers, Patrons, Readers, and Spies," 865–67.

who had published books 1 to 5 of *The Mirrour of Knighthood* in the early 1580s and after a break of twelve years re-issued them again in 1598 and 1599. Cuthbert Burby published the sixth, seventh, eighth, and ninth books in this series from 1598 to 1601, while Thomas Creede printed the English version of Gerónimo Fernández's *Don Bellianis* as *The Honour of Chivalrie* in 1598.[65] These same publishers also bet on works by such native English romance writers as Emanuel Forde, Richard Johnson, and Henry Roberts, who wrote their own chivalric pieces inspired by the vogue for Iberian romance well under way by the turn of the century. Thomas Creede published Emanuel Forde's *The Most Pleasant Historie of Ornatus and Artensia* (1599), *Parismus* (1598), and *Parismenos* (1599) as well as Henry Roberts's *Pheander: The Mayden Knight* (1595) and *Honours Conquest* (1598), whereas Cuthbert Burby published parts one and two of Johnson's *The Most Famous History of Johnson's Seven Champions of Christendom* (1596, 1597), printed by Edward Allde and John Danter, respectively.

These data confirm that the translation of Iberian chivalric books became a profitable genre in late Elizabethan England. Anthony Munday's engagement in the book trade very early in his career probably made him meet the market demands sooner, even if he was not the first author to translate Iberian chivalric romance into English. He seems to have been a prolific enterprising translator. The fact that he chose to translate the two main Spanish chivalric cycles reveals his ambitious design: he produced up to fourteen books before 1602, thirteen of them before 1597. By that time, his publishers were so interested in the Iberian series that they hired other translators to finish the *Mirrour* sequence and translate the *Bellianis*. By then, Munday was no longer that keen on chivalric literature; he stopped translating romances in 1602, when he took up work on civic pageantry and history. In the following decades, Iberian chivalric romances would still enjoy popularity, but publishers only issued reprints of late Elizabethan translations and stopped investing on new versions. Once again, Munday seemed to have been aware of the reading trend and knew when to stop.

As has been shown, Munday was deeply involved in the production of translations and prose fiction works from the 1570s to the turn of the century. His role in the development of early modern English fic-

65 For more precise information on these editions, see note 6.

tion deserves attention on the part of critics and literary historians. His possible influence on the English translation of Cervantes's *Don Quixote* has already been addressed by such scholars as Helen Moore.[66] Goran Stanivukovic has gone even further by pointing to the translations of Iberian romances—rather than to *Don Quixote*—as being responsible for a new mode in English fiction, a mode that contributed to bring about the modern English novel.[67] Thus, Munday's experimental approach to narrative, his prompt awareness of the possibilities of the narrative genre, and his pragmatic views on translation make him a key figure, worth taking into account when analyzing the birth and development of the English novel.

Translating Spanish Romances in Sixteenth-Century England: Munday's Method of Translation in Palmendos

The first section of this introduction has explored Munday's romance translations in relation to the development of English fiction in Elizabethan England. The map that has been drawn above cannot be complete, though, without a further reflection on the impact of translation in sixteenth-century literary culture. This section offers an overview of this phenomenon and approaches Munday's translating practice in the context of contemporary discourses on literary translation. Munday's method is explained, then, in detail taking *Palmendos* as a case study. His possible ideological interventions are considered as well.[68]

Although there had been English translations of Spanish romances from the 1540s, there was a significant increase after Prince Philip of Spain's marriage to Mary Tudor, when they became very popular in England, as the number of editions published in the sixteenth and early seventeenth centuries clearly attests.[69] The English rendering of Diego

[66] "'Heroick Madman': Speaking like Amadis in Seventeenth-Century English *Quixote* Translations." Unpublished. See also Álvarez-Recio, "Translations of Spanish Chivalry Works in the Jacobean Book Trade."

[67] See Stanivukovic, "Iberian Chivalric Romance and the Formation of Modern Fiction in Early Modern England."

[68] Most of the contents below have been previously published in Álvarez-Recio, "Spanish Chivalric Romances in English Translation."

[69] Cruz, *Material and Symbolic Circulation between Spain an England*, xvii–xix.

de San Pedro's *Arnalte y Lucenda* (first pub. 1491) appeared under the title *The Pretie Historie of Arnalt and Lucenda* in 1575. *Carcel de Amor* (first pub. 1492), by the same Spanish author, was translated as *The Castell of Love* and enjoyed three different editions in 1548, 1552, and 1555. *The Histoire of Aurelio and of Isabelle*, published in 1556 and 1608, had been translated into English from an Italian version of Juan de Flores's *Grisel y Mirabella* (first pub. 1495), while Thomas Paynell's *Treasurie of Amadis of Fraunce* (1572) was the English version of *Le tresor des Amadis* (1563), a French anthology of passages from the original Spanish series of *Amadís de Gaula*. It has already been mentioned how Margaret Tyler's *The Mirrour of Princely Deedes and Knighthood* (first pub. 1578), the first full translation of a Spanish chivalric book, became a commercial hit in late Elizabethan England with seven subsequent editions published between 1578 and 1601.[70]

As suggested elsewhere in this introduction, these data seem to confirm that English translators and printers decided to use Spanish chivalric material once interest in the English medieval romances declined in the late 1570s. English readers were already familiar with continental romances but were not yet familiar with the main chivalric cycles (Amadis and Palmerin) that had been so influential in Spain and France, despite their numerous detractors.[71] Their status as best sellers in Europe seemed to promise a similar success in England;[72] hence, by translating chivalric books, Anthony Munday got involved in two of the most profitable commercial literary ventures of his time—namely, translations, owing to their appeal to a wide range of the reading public interested in continen-

[70] Barker and Hosington, *Renaissance Cultural Crossroads*; Boro, "Reading Juan de Flores's *Grisel y Mirabella* in Early Modern England," 35–37; Moore, *Amadis de Gaule*, xv–xvi; Rothstein, *Reading in the Renaissance*, 32–38; Taylor, "Learning Style from the Spaniards in Sixteenth-Century England," 65–67.

[71] For contemporary criticism on chivalric romances in Spain and France, see Thomas, *Spanish and Portuguese Romances of Chivalry*, 155–78; and Wilson, "The Publication of Iberian Romance in Early Modern Europe," 203–5.

[72] For further information on the popularity of Spanish chivalric romances in Spain, France, and Italy, see Wilson, "The Publication of Iberian Romance in Early Modern Europe," 201–9; Bognolo, "Il Progetto Mambrino"; Eisenberg, *Castilian Romances of Chivalry in the Sixteenth Century*; Neri, "Cuadro de la diffusión europea del ciclo del Amadís de Gaula"; Pettegree, "Translation and the Migration of Texts"; and Thomas, *Spanish and Portuguese Romances*, 41–118, 147–55.

tal culture,[73] and chivalric books, because of their didactic but above all, entertaining function.[74]

In the title page of *Palmendos*, readers are told that the main source for this translation is a French edition. Given the privileged status of the French language in English literary translations, Munday's information about the French version implies that he regarded his source as an improvement over the original Spanish text.[75] Indeed, French translators felt quite free to tamper with their Spanish sources as, in Rothstein's view, "the greatest prestige resided in the target language."[76]

Munday must have consulted the Spanish original and, perhaps, Roseo's Italian version, as can be noticed in the variants from the French source that he includes in his own translation.[77] His use of a Spanish copy

[73] Indeed, the commercial, dynastic, and cultural ties among the different states of Atlantic Europe, mainly those of the Iberian Peninsula, western France, and the British Isles, had been extensive and regular since the thirteenth century and were only partially interrupted by the sixteenth-century religious controversies after the Protestant schism from Rome. See further information in Phillips, "The Frustrated Unity of Atlantic Europe."

[74] Romances were increasingly employed in Elizabethan England both as conduct books for young men—as they provided models of proper and successful male behavior—and as pedagogical tools in language training. On the didactic use of romances, see Boro, "Multilinguism, Romance, and Language Pedagogy"; Dolven, *Scenes of Instruction in Renaissance Romance*; Mack, *Elizabethan Rhetoric*, 76–101, 135–73; and Stanivukovic, "English Renaissance Romances as Conduct Books for Young Men."

[75] It is almost impossible to know whether this title page was composed by Munday or by his printer. However, if one pays attention to all first edition title pages of his romance translations, it can be noticed that the sentence "translated into English by A.M. one of the Messengers of her Maiesties Chamber" is repeated word for word in all of them. As those romances—*Palmerin d'Oliua* (1588), *Palladine of England* (1588), *Palmendos* (1589), *Gerileon of England* (1592), *Primaleon of Greece* (Part 2; 1596), and *Palmerin of England* (Part 3; 1602)—were printed by such different printers as Charlewood, Danter, Allde, and Roberts—it may be easily inferred that the information contained in this page may not be just the printer's but mainly the translator's decision.

[76] Rothstein, *Reading in the Renaissance*, 47.

[77] A 1559 edition of Roseo's *Primaleone* has been used for this collation. It is an extremely concise version in which large sections of the Spanish source have been either omitted or summarized, thus reducing the forty-five original chapters dealing with Palmendos to only twenty-one. When paraphrasing many dialogues Roseo does not keep the Spanish dynamic pace but does not add any embellished descriptions either, as Vernassal does. So, the former's translation is a poor version, probably issued for commercial reasons, as its publication in octavo attests. For the Spanish edition consulted, see

is evident when collating some instances in the original source with their counterparts in Vernassal's, Roseo's, and Munday's texts. For instance, in chapter 2 of the English edition, Belcar addresses Gracian, Alderina's page, by calling him "My Freend" (B3^{r}), as in the Spanish original—"Hay, amigo" (8). Vernassal and Roseo, however, had respectively translated such vocative as "mon frere" (A5^{r}) and "Frate" (6^{r}). Belcar's address to Gracian is repeated below in the same chapter with similar conclusions: Munday's "Ah my freend" (C4^{v}) follows the Spanish "Ay, amigo" (12) in contrast with the French "Helas mon frere" (B3^{v}) or the Italian interjection "Deh" (11^{r}), which is not followed by any noun. In addition, Munday seems to be partly following the Spanish source in his summary introducing chapter 22: "Howe Palmendos and Francelina going to the Queene of Thessalie, mette without the Castell dyuers Knights and Ladies of the Isle" (R3^{r}). The Spanish original refers to this moment in a different way in the chapter title introducing the same episode: "Cómo Polendos holgó mucho con Francelina y ella le pidió un don y él gelo otorgó y la sacó del castillo con mucha alegría" (65; Sp., About how Polendos and Francelina were together long, and she asked him a favor, which he granted, bringing her happily out of the castle), but agrees with Munday in its allusion to the castle. By contrast, in the summary introducing chapter 23 in his translation, Vernassal refers to the ladies and knights that Palmendos and Francelina meet "au sortir de la forteresse" (L5^{v}; Fr., on their going out of the fortress), while Roseo does not include any reference to a place in his summary (chapter 15). Another example appears in his account of Palmendos's adventures at the temple on the Isle of Delphos, in which Munday narrates how his hero despoils the idol of the temple of its "Crowne, Scepter and Booke" (H4^{r}). The Spanish original refers to the same items, which are arranged in the same order as those in Munday's: "corona, cetro y libro" (39). Vernassal alters this order "sceptre, liure, et couronne" (E3^{v}), while Roseo omits one of the elements: "la corona, e lo scettro" (28^{v}).[78]

From the examples above, it may be concluded that Munday must have used a Spanish copy, which would explain his deviations from his

Primaleón (Salamanca, 1512), edited by María del Carmen Marín Pina. For the French edition, see François de Vernassal, *L'Histoire de Primaleon de Grece*.

[78] A last example appears in Belcar's description, as he is supposed to be excellent in "feates of Armes" (B2^{v}) in the English version or "fecho de Armas" (7) in the Spanish original. Vernassal translates such phrase as "en l'exercise des armes" (A4^{v}), while Roseo simply refers to "ne le arme" (5^{v}).

main French source. He may or may not have employed an Italian edition, though, as only one deviation from his French and Spanish sources has been found to coincide with a similar instance in the Italian translation.[79] But this single case is not enough to make a hypothesis in this regard.

There is no evidence that Munday ever visited Spain or learned Spanish, but he had studied French and Italian with London Huguenot Claudius Hollyband and had traveled to France and Italy on his 1579 European trip.[80] So, if he was already familiar with both Italian and French, it would not have been difficult to approach Spanish.[81] Books written in Spain were sold in various European book fairs and were often printed abroad, mostly in France or Italy,[82] which means he may well have had access to a copy of the Spanish original in the course of his European tour.

Munday turned the original work into two different books. And so, if his sources had dealt with the adventures of Palmerin's two sons, he decided to publish two works, each one focusing on the deeds of one particular son—namely, Palmendos[83] and Primaleon.[84] That aim made him rearrange chapters, as he had to avoid any sort of discontinuity or lack of information as a result of his having made two books out of one. Thus, he

[79] In chapter 1, Munday narrates how Belcar leaves Palmerin's court in search of adventures and spends his first night "in the Castell of an olde curteous knight" (A2^{v}). This same sentence appears as "au chasteau d'un vieillard" in Vernassal (A2^{r}; Fr., in the castle of an old man), as "nel castello d'un cortese caualiero" in Roseo (2^{r}; It., in the castle of a courteous knight), and as "en un castillo de un cauallero muy bueno" in the Spanish original (4; Sp., in the castle of a very good knight). Though the four of them are different, Munday's sentence seems to be closer to the Italian version.

[80] Hamilton, *Anthony Munday and the Catholics*, xx.

[81] In some of his translations of other Iberian romances it is clearly specified that not only the French but also Italian and Spanish copies had been consulted. The title pages of *Palmerin d'Oliua* (1588) and *Palmerin of England* (Part 3; 1602) are quite illustrative in this regard. These references support the claim that he could at least read Spanish and, by extension, that he may have used a Spanish copy too when rendering *Palmendos* into English.

[82] The 1534 edition of the Spanish *Primaleón*, for instance, was published in Venice.

[83] The name Polendos (in the Spanish version) was turned into Palmendos in Jean Maugin's first edition of *Palmerin d'Olive* (Paris, 1546, Dd6^{v}) and in its subsequent reprints. Vernassal emulated Maugin and used the name Palmendos in his French translation of *Primaleón*. Anthony Munday named his hero as in his French source.

[84] On the segmentation of these contents, see the introduction's third section, "The Publication History of Anthony Munday's *Palmendos*."

translated the first thirty-two chapters of the French edition, which contained a total of fifty-six chapters.[85] He followed closely his French source in its first nineteen chapters, but then he discarded chapter 20, which he summarized briefly in one single paragraph at the end of chapter 19. He translated, however, all remaining chapters, which dwell on Palmendos's adventures.[86]

Munday's omission of chapter 20 was not naïve. This passage narrates how Rifarano, a Moorish hero, protects the Countess of Islande, a widow, from the attacks of her brother-in-law, who claims the lands she had inherited from her late husband. Rifarano, who eventually becomes her lover, lives with her for a long time before returning to the emperor's court. This knight, who constantly states his wish not to interfere in inheritance issues, claims to be simply trying to save a lady in distress, as the chivalric code demands. Munday, however, does not seem to have liked Rifarano's role, and so he decides to ignore the entire episode. The figure of the powerful widow administrating her husband's estate was already familiar to late Elizabethan readers, and so the translator may have decided that such a character would not have appeared unlikely to an English audience, even if the question of female inheritance might still have looked controversial in France or Spain.[87] On the other hand, the entire episode between the Countess of Islande and Rifarano may have been deemed inconvenient, due to their illicit relationship. The sexual experience of widows very likely endowed them with an advantageous position at the time, since they were no longer constrained by the social restrictions concerning their virginity. That is why the Countess of Islande feels free to enjoy her sexuality intensively with her lover, whose Moorish origins might have given free rein to all sorts of sexual fantasies among late sixteenth-century English readers.[88] Munday, perhaps aware of that possibility, offers a brief, more

[85] The French translator is mostly responsible for chapter reorganization, as he comprised the original 227 chapters into fifty-six. Munday would translate the last twenty-four chapters dealing with Primaleon's deeds in Vernassal's work as *The First Book of Primaleon of Greece*, published in 1595.

[86] For further information, see Álvarez-Recio, "Chapters Translated by Anthony Munday in *The History of Palmendos* (1589): A Long-Standing Error."

[87] On this topic, see Erickson, *Women and Property in Early Modern England*; Fink De Backer, *Widowhood in Early Modern Spain*; and Warner, "Widows, Widowers and the Problem of Second Marriage in Sixteenth-Century France."

[88] As Jack D'Amico explains, "In the Christian tradition the notion that Africans

politically correct summary, through which only the basic details of the love affair are actually told.

The last chapter in Munday's *Palmendos* is considerably shorter than that found in Vernassal's work. Indeed, the English translator only includes half of Vernassal's chapter 32. The French copy focuses mainly on two episodes: Palmendos's baptism and his betrothal to his beloved, and on the other hand, French prince Arnedes's melancholic state after his frustrated attempts at marrying the emperor's daughter, Alderine. The fact that Vernassal ends his chapter at this point makes sense, since the following chapter in his book begins when ambassadors from the King of France come to solicit the marriage of the prince to Alderine. Thus, Vernassal solves Arnedes's melancholy by marrying him to his beloved. Munday, however, postpones the translation of this episode, which would be included in chapter 1 of his following work on Primaleon's adventures. So, he shortens this last chapter in *Palmendos* in order to conclude with a conventional happy ending which presents the main hero's success: he is fully acknowledged by his father, gets engaged to his beloved lady, and becomes a Christian. If Arnedes's episode had been included at this stage, the conclusion would have looked anti-climatic and the sense of unity in the book would have been disrupted.

Hence, Munday seems to comply with two main translation principles that prevailed in late Elizabethan England—namely, imitation and accommodation.[89] His translation from the French edition of a Spanish

were descendants of Ham, the son of Noah cursed for looking on his father's nakedness, carried with it the punishment for breaking a taboo." By extension, moors were often represented as holding an extremely seductive and tempting power over Christians since the former's religion was believed to release the potent sexual forces that Christianity attempted to control (*The Moor in English Renaissance Drama*, 63–65). On the other hand, erotic interracial relationships recur in English Renaissance literature (mainly drama), which has been viewed by Lara Bovilsky as possibly satisfying "a deeper desire for and pleasure in the ostensibly disturbing representations of miscegenation themselves" (*Barbarous Play*, 44). Rifarano is indeed the result of an interracial relationship, he being the son of Trineus (Emperor of Allemaine) and Aurecinda (sister to the Soldan of Babylon), which may have appealed to the sexual fantasies of readers.

[89] Recent studies agree on the absence of any clear theory on early modern English translation, despite the contemporary active debate on this discipline. The only theory on translation by an English author seems to have been Laurence Humphrey's *Interpretatio linguarum*, written in Latin and published in Basel in 1559. Only Gabriel Harvey has been recorded to own an annotated copy, but there is no further evidence that it circulated widely in England (Braden and Gillespie, *The Oxford History of Literary Trans-*

original was part of a well-established tradition in which "the translator triangulates in sense and style from several secondary sources."[90] Given the troublesome Anglo-Spanish relations in the late 1580s, it would have been advisable to use an intermediary French source, since, as Andrew Pettegree has noted when writing about contemporary French translations of Spanish works, those texts "were carefully de-Hispanised."[91] Indeed, the English translator agrees with Vernassal in a good number of ideological interventions while he differs mostly in his aesthetic approach to the text. It is necessary then to focus on the variants introduced by Munday to determine to what extent he shares Vernassal's decisions and exactly where, and why, he deviates from his primary and intermediary copies.

The prestige of the French translations of the Amadis and Palmerin cycles lay on the French translators' great display of rhetorical elements. Mid-sixteenth-century debates on the status of French as a language paralleled nationalist discourses on the role of France in Europe. So, by expanding and embellishing their Spanish sources, French translators were not only improving their literary status but were indirectly trying to make up for Spain's cultural, and political hegemony, at least at a discursive level. Vernassal follows in his French colleagues' footsteps when translating *Primaleon*, thus showing a similar nationalist sentiment. His dedication to such a prominent figure as the Duque of Guise, and its publication in folio "auec priuilege du Roy" seem to match his especial care to improve his Spanish material.

Vernassal paraphrases and translates almost literally many sections of the Spanish original, but he also tends to enlarge his source by adding

lation in English, 89). Translators moved between literalism and freedom, and there were many other possibilities in between. Thus, the medieval approach, that implied a complete departure from the source text, coexisted with a more humanist perception that required only "a subtle manipulation of the rhetorical organization of the source text" (Morini, *Tudor Translation in Theory and Practice*, x). Verbatim translations were not disregarded, either, but, although literalism was considered a valid method of translation, it was superseded by the end of the century (Boro, "Reading Juan de Flores's *Grisel y Mirabella*," 23; and Rhodes, Kendall, and Wilson, *English Renaissance Translation Theory*, 38, 63). In Morini's words, those "rhetorical" translators did "not alter the invention and disposition of the sources but felt free to adapt elocution and style to their audience's taste" (*Tudor Translation*, 66). Thus, they could take verbal liberties as long as they stayed true to the *sensus*.

90 Braden and Gillespie, *The Oxford History of Literary Translation in English*, 97.

91 Pettegree, "Translation and the Migration of Texts," 120.

new elements. For instance, he inserts three letters—the first one is not even mentioned in the Spanish work, the second one is just alluded to, while the third one is summarized in four lines in the original—whose contents he expands largely (C4^{r-v}, E6^{r}, K6^{r-v}). Munday, who at this stage follows Vernassal closely, includes the three letters in his narrative, although he tends to be less descriptive and shortens their contents (E4^{r-v}, I3^{r-v}, Q1^{v}–Q2^{r}). Vernassal also adds two love poems and two epitaphs, mainly aimed at laying emphasis on the poetic skills of various characters, presented in the narrative as models of courtly attitudes. None of those poetic pieces come from the Spanish text, but Munday inserts them, even if he just paraphrases their contents and alters both the number of lines and their rhyme pattern. Thus, the French version boasts of a greater variety of literary genres. Those extra pieces also contribute to the psychological development of characters, who can by those means express their most distressing inner feelings. The Spanish source's main concern, however, seems to have been to make a consistent plot through which the characters' feelings may indirectly be revealed. Munday, following in the footsteps of Vernassal's version, reproduces all those additional pieces, though he normally shortens them and often feels free to re-elaborate them, thus sticking to a middle position between original and intermediary sources.

Vernassal also enlarges most descriptive passages. Despair, anger, desire, melancholy, or love feelings are highlighted by the French translator, and so, very basic references in the Spanish original become long, hyperbolic, detailed descriptions that often interfere in the narrative pace. Munday seems to have been aware of such setback, and so he limits those emotional outbursts. That is why he resorts to paraphrase, literal or quasi-literal translation, and omission, perhaps because he tries to preserve a certain sense of decorum. He certainly shows interest in the psychological presentation of characters without overdoing it.

Vernassal's constant use of figurative speech and classical references, normally missing in the Spanish original, would have been certainly welcome by his learned French readers, but would not have pleased Munday's middling-class public. The English translator is quite restrictive with regards to figurative speech (Vernassal, L4^{r-v}; Munday, R1^{v}), but he still adjusts to his French source by retaining many classical references and most love and courtly speeches, which may have posed a serious challenge to his less educated readers, even if they still enjoyed an elaborate style traditionally restricted to the scholarly elite.

The Spanish original offers a series of detailed violent scenes which Vernassal reproduces almost literally, but Munday tends to leave out by summing them up (Munday, K2^{r-v}; S3^{v}–T1^{v}; Y1^{v}). Munday's lack of interest in violence may derive from his commitment to teaching courtly manners and virtues to his readers; he does not disregard violence altogether, but just seems to avoid all sorts of excessive, irrational behavior; hence, by sticking to the basic tenets of the chivalric code, he rewrites various comments in the Spanish and French editions, simply for his young audience's sake.[92] For instance, when referring to Recinde, a knight from Palmerin's court, and his thirst for adventure, the Spanish text states that he "ganoso era de ganar honra, provándose con los buenos cavalleros" (77; Sp., he was

[92] Munday was very likely aware of contemporary criticism against such displays of violence in chivalric romances, hence his attempts to modulate them. He was also catering for a wide audience that included young men, who needed proper models of conduct, and women, who would probably grow weary of such lengthy violent episodes. By summing them up, Munday was killing several birds with just one stone. On the one hand, he satisfied the taste of female readers who would have felt more at ease with courtly scenes. On the other, Munday's treatment of violence may have sided with early modern notions of combat in relation to the "humanist subject." In Jennifer Feather's words, "two different perspectives on combat—one that sees combat as granting the victor agency and glory at the expense of turning the victim into an inert object and the other that views it as a mutual relation between equals—run through early modern and especially sixteenth-century literature, structuring compelling notions of self and nation" (*Writing Combat and the Self in Early Modern English Literature*, 3). Though these English renderings of Iberian romances were still deeply influenced by the medieval tradition, their depiction of violence was highly mechanical and mostly focused on the hero vanquishing his opponent. It was the individuality of the hero that prevailed and so, these scenes may not have been that lengthy since they ultimately served one purpose, to provide evidence of the hero's individual worth and justify his project. Since violence was essential to understand aristocratic identity in the late sixteenth century, those violent outbursts with a clear focus on the heroic self must have appealed to those gentle readers to whom Munday addressed most of his chivalric translations. However, as Goran Stanivukovic remarks, they could also attract young men of the rising middle class since romances promoted what he calls "a narrative of success" that presented progress, "romantic and territorial conquest," "travel and adventure" as cultural goals for these young males to accomplish in their maturity process, especially at a time of nationalist fervor ("English Renaissance Romances as Conduct Books for Young Men," 63–65). On romances' traditional appeal for young people, see also Eisenberg, *Castilian Romances of Chivalry*, 89–90, 93–97; Goodman and Robin, *Chivalry and Exploration, 1298–1630*, 7–9, 34–37; and Hardman, "Popular Romances and Young Readers." On women as readers of romance, see Hackett, *Women and Romance Fiction in the English Renaissance*; and Lucas, *Writing for Women*.

willing to win honor by challenging good knights) which is paraphrased by Vernassal as "qui auoit grande volunté d'acqueir honneur par tout" (N3^{r}; Fr., he was quite willing to acquire honor anywhere). In the French and Spanish versions, the character seems to yearn for personal honor, while in the English work he strictly obeys the code of chivalry: "Recinde [was] desirous to win honor by succoring the distressed, and hoping he might find the knight he sought for at Macedon" (T2^{v}). As a good knight errant, he must help the helpless; as a faithful servant, he must prove his loyalty to his master by obeying his commands and seeking Palmendos.

Although the French version is longer than the Spanish original, Vernassal has shortened, for instance, certain direct speeches and dialogues, which become mere paraphrases. That is why the French translation is more narrative and descriptive, which means that it lacks the dramatic appeal of the Spanish version. Vernassal dispenses with many dialogues, thus enhancing the role of the narrator over the personages. Munday sometimes imitates Vernassal, and so he turns many conversational exchanges into narrative, although he usually summarizes those narrative parts (Vernassal, M6^{r}–N1^{v}, P5^{r-v}; Munday, S4^{r}–T1^{v}, Aa3^{r-v}). Some other times, however, Munday combines both the Spanish and French approaches, as he translates some dialogues quite faithfully from the Spanish original, while he omits others and summarizes the narrative parts that had been expanded by Vernassal (Vernassal, P2^{r-v}; Munday, Y3^{v}–Y4^{r}; Marín Pina, 88–89). By doing so, Munday provides his text with some of the dramatic nature of the Spanish source while still retaining some of the French embellished descriptions.

Vernassal also disposes of a series of items from the Spanish original that may have been deemed contrary to the decorum expected by his readers. For instance, when the lovers express sexual desire for one another in the Spanish text, the French translator, while enhancing those exchanges, only offers some veiled, rather vague allusions to their sexual encounters or simply ignores them. In fact, many references to physical contact, such as Palmendos's kisses to Francelina or the sexual games they play (Marín Pina, 66–67) are missing in the French version (Vernassal, L4^{v}–L5^{r}). Vernassal also censors other allusions to indecorous behavior, even when they do not involve any kind of physical contact. For instance, in chapter 30 he tells the story of Marencida, the Great Turk's daughter, taken by Palmendos to his father's court. Her sexual appeal attracts Ozalio's attention.[93] The Spanish edition reads "Y como ella iva desnuda y con el gran pesar que llevava no se sabía encobrir víonle todos su gran fermosura, ansí de su cuerpo como de su cara. Ozalias, que bien la miró, fue muy pagado d'ella y començola de amar muy afincadamente" (91; Sp., And as she was naked and so sorrowful, she could hardly cover herself; thus, everyone could see her wonderful beauty, both of body and face. Ozalias, who stared at her intently, felt strongly attracted to her and began to love her passionately). Vernassal softens this depiction and avoids any direct reference to Ozalio's gaze, thus silencing any allusion to his voyeuristic desire:

> Et pource qu'elle n'auoit rien sur soy qu'vne chemise de toile bien desliée, tous virent facilement l'excellente beauté don't Nature doua tant la superficie de son corps bien composé, que le visage mieux acomply en ses requisitions: si que tel chef d'oeuure penetra tant dedans l'esprit d'Ozalie (plus que de touts les autres) que des l'heure il commença à l'aimer d'vne sort excessiue ardeur. (P4^v)

> [And because she had nothing upon her but a loose blouse of fine linen, everyone could easily behold the excellent beauty Nature had conferred upon the surface of her well-formed body and face in the best accomplished graces, and that sight penetrated Ozalio's soul (more than any others') and so from that very moment he started to love her most ardently.]

Munday shares Vernassal's views on decorum and suppresses all overtly sexual allusions in his narrative. Both the French and English translations are rather careful about describing sex before marriage and refer to Francelina's virginity in somewhat vague, periphrastic ways. Such strict sense of self-censorship is of course alien to the Spanish original (69), which is still influenced by the medieval courtly love tradition, since it was published in the early sixteenth century.[94]

93 Palmendos's best friend and companion.

94 "Y Francelina mostrava todo el amor qu'ella podía y porque jamás se apartava de la Reina no podían ellos estar a su voluntad, y amava tanto a Polendos [Palmendos] que todo cuanto él quisiera fiziera ella" (69; Sp., And Francelina showed all her love, but since she was never away from the queen, they [Francelina and Polendos] could not act freely, and she loved Polendos so much that she would do anything he wanted her to). Vernassal rewrites this part: ". . . la belle Franceline, qui par signes & oeillades monstroit à son amant toute la ſaueur dont son esprit s'auisoit. Pource que ne s'essoignant iamais d'auec sa mere, ilz ne pouoyent donner tel contentement à leurs cueurs comme ils eussent bien desiré en deuis & propos amoureux seulement: *consideré qu'autre plus pri-*

In addition, while the Spanish work presents a less biased view of the main villains, both French and English translators erase any positive traits in them, and so they clearly divide characters into two clear-cut groups, good and bad. This is quite evident in some pagan and female figures. For instance, the Spanish author casts a positive light on Marencida (the Great Turk's daughter) and her role at Palmerin's court. Since she has been kidnapped and brought to the court by Palmendos, she refuses to speak or submit to the emperor, thus showing her contempt for her captor: "Mas ella no se quiso omillar ante él ni responderle a cosa que le dixesse, y todos se maravillaron de su gran coraçón" (96; Sp., But she refused to abase herself before him or to answer any of his questions, and everyone was amazed at her good heart). In both the French and English editions, however, she is neither courageous nor dignified, and her attitude is shown to be improper and unnatural: "mais elle ne se voulut incliner onc deuant luy, ny respondre à la moindre parole qu'il luy dist, don't fut toute la flote and des Barons and du peuple qui la regardoit moult esbahie: de sorte que l'apellant femme de viril and robuste courage, disoyent Nature auoit failly

uée habitude que de baiser n'estoit encore interuenue parmy leurs ieux, ny n'auint iusques au iour des noces, que Palmendos luy rompit le Seston, autrement dit la ceinture impollue, qu'elle auoit tousiours portée iusques à ce iour là". (M2[r]) (The editor's emphasis). [Fr., . . . beautiful Francelina, who through signs and gazes showed her lover the favor her soul devised. Because she never went away from her mother, they could not content their hearts with amorous designs and words, as they would have desired, for no other private signs but kisses had been practiced in their games, none until the day of the wedding, when Palmendos undid the certainly unpolluted girdle that she had always worn up to that day.]

Munday does not mention the lovers' desire to be together in private and just says that Francelina wants her beloved to go and save her father the King of Thessaly, so that when he comes back both lovers may "knit up all their ioyes with the Presence of the King her Father" (R4[v]). Thus, he pays less attention to the couple's sexual desire and focuses on what he considers most important: their marriage and Palmendos's inheritance of the kingdom of Thessaly. Munday finds no problem to speak openly about sexual consummation once the wedding has taken place. For instance, after Ditreus and Esquivela's wedding party, the Spanish author says "Y el Emperador fue con el novio y luego todos se fueron a sus posadas" (47; Sp., And the Emperor went away with the bridegroom, and then they all went to their own lodgings), which is translated literally by Vernassal: "l'Empereur y fit compagnie à Ditreus, puis chacun se retira en son logis" (H2[r]; Fr., the Emperor accompanied Ditreus and then they all retired to their lodgings). Munday, however, expands it—"the Bridegroome who was soone after *honourably* conducted thether by the Emperour, and *so committed to enioy her* whom he had so long desired" (M4[v]) (the editor's emphasis). Sex after marriage is then dutifully accomplished.

ne la faisant homme" (Vernassal, Q3^{v}); "but shee would not once bowe herselfe or make any aunswer, whereat the standers by very much wondred, tearming her a Woman of rough and vnseemely behauiour, saying nature might much better haue made her a man" (Munday, Bb2^{v}).

Munday is more explicit than Vernassal in his defense of contemporary social codes as can be inferred from his harsh censure of some of his characters' actions. For instance, there are some implicit comments on the Duke of Pera and his beloved's decision to escape and marry without her father's consent: "Mandóle venir [the lady] muy encubiertamente y qu'ella se iría con él" (Marín Pina, 19; Sp., She [the lady] made him come to her secretly and told him she would elope with him); "luy promit que si son maistre la vouloit venir enleuer secretement d'aupres de son pere, elle s'en iroit voluntiers quant & luy" (Vernassal, C5^{v}; Fr., she promised him that if her lord wanted to take her secretly away from her father's, she would willingly go with him); "if his maister could cunningly steale her from her Father, she would goe with him whether he pleased" (Munday, F2^{r}). While in the Spanish and French versions, both lovers are given equal agency and are blamed for their secret actions, Munday replaces such secrecy with a more negative expression ("cunningly steale") that shows his negative opinion about this kind of behavior. The use of the Duke of Pera as the syntactic subject of this verb provides him with more agency and responsibility than in the other editions. In the three versions Pera is killed by some enchanted dogs sent by his beloved's father. She commits suicide after learning about his death. Both lovers are buried in a tomb which is later found by Palmendos, who does not hesitate to take up the sword used by the lady to kill herself. The Spanish and French versions emphasize Palmendos's eagerness and extreme desire to seize this sword (Marín Pina, 28; Vernassal, E1^{v}), which he finally does, even though this act could be viewed as an affront to the dead. Munday reinterprets this action by turning it into a commemorative act, a lesson to learn: "he tooke the sworde in his hand, and in remembrance of the accident, as also of the beautie thereof, hee hunge it at his side" (H1^{v}). His euphemistic description of a such tragic scene as an "accident" shows his lack of empathy with either of the lovers.

Ozalio and Marencida's love relationship, quite obvious and innocent in the Spanish version, seems to have puzzled both translators, and so they introduce certain changes which influence Palmendos's characterization too. The Spanish author narrates how Marencida, at first moved by Ozalio's constant and gentle care, ends up by falling in love with him (93), and so, when Palmendos decides to have them married, that decision seems to be quite natural. Vernassal and Munday do not refer to Marencida's love for Ozalio, as they try to prevent readers from sympathizing with her, and so they present Ozalio's marriage to this lady as being despotically imposed by Palmendos. Vernassal then introduces certain vague allusions to Ozalio and Marencida's growing mutual love in chapter 32, but Munday omits any references to those lovers in this chapter (which is the last one in his version) and simply focuses his narrative on the main hero's wedding and promising future.

It may be stated that all three versions present Palmendos's decision to kidnap Marencida with a certain uneasiness, but the Spanish version at least provides some reasons for it: his taking Marencida to Emperor Palmerin's court is a direct affront to the Great Turk (90), and Palmendos's comforting words to this lady sound false once the hero's real intentions are known. That may be the reason why Palmendos's intentions are omitted in Vernassal and Munday's narratives. But even if neither of the two translators mentions them, they cannot prevent some disappointment over Palmendos's behavior. Such motives may not have been well accepted by readers, but by developing the aforementioned love relationship, the Spanish author succeeds in softening a possible negative view of the hero. In the French and English editions, however, the presentation of this episode is not satisfactory, since the reader is not provided with the basic information needed to understand Palmendos's motives, and thus the hero's attitude may be regarded as capricious or despotic.

Another example is given in the Spanish original when Palmendos, after defeating and imprisoning Ocurites the Turk, visits him in prison; they talk to each other and the hero gets to understand and pity his enemy (38–39). Such view of the hero as compassionate and kind to his adversaries is absent in both the French and English texts, which fail to insert this passage. Munday's view of pagans is generally harsher, less tolerant than that of both the Spanish and French editions.[95] His Palmendos feels no remorse for his unfair and dishonest attitude to infidels for he may feel

[95] Some of his omissions are rather significant. For instance, in the episode about Palmendos's defeat of Giant Baledon in the Spanish and French sources, Baledon's wife and son are made prisoners and are sent to Constantinople. Once there, Baledon's son is given a second opportunity and becomes a good knight (Marín Pina, 25; Vernassal, D4v). Munday replaces this character by a female one, who eventually marries a good knight. Munday's changes reveal his unwillingness to reward the son of a pagan enemy with a promising chivalric future.

that the ends justify the means.[96] This is quite obvious when he seduces Iffida, the Captain of Albayzo Castle's daughter, so that he may gain free access to the castle and release the King of Thessaly who has been kept imprisoned within its walls. The hero succeeds only after deceiving and killing everyone, which results in Iffida and her page committing suicide. Both the Spanish and French texts point to Palmendos's disturbing feelings of remorse when observing the outcome of his courtship of Iffida. His treacherous deceit is not presented in a completely negative light, since Palmendos had promised to make the lady Queen of Tharsus, and he had made her understand (without ever committing himself) that he was going to marry her (Marín Pina, 84; Vernassal, $O4^{r}$). He was in fact thinking of marrying her to Ozalio and so, his promise is partly true, as Palmendos can only be accused of equivocation or mental reservation, but not of being a liar.

Munday's approach is radically different. Palmendos states his alleged willingness to marry her ($X3^{r}$) but does not consider the possibility of marrying her to his friend. Munday's character does not use mental reservation and it is only later, when the truth is found out, that he offers Iffida the possibility of marrying Ozalio, which she obviously rejects ($Y2^{r}$). Palmendos does not like seeing her suffer but does not feel guilty about it either. The text seems to imply that it is not worth having any remorse over immoral deeds done to infidels. Moreover, Munday prefers his hero not to employ equivocation or mental reservation, two attitudes which the English often associated with the Jesuit Society since the 1580s. Given Munday's problems with the Jesuits, one may presume that he decided not to include those references, which he omitted at the expense of presenting a more negative view of his protagonist than that of his sources.

The way Palmendos was begotten may have seemed embarrassing to the translators too. The Spanish version makes it clear that it was an act of Providence (98), but both Vernassal and Munday present it as the result of a magic spell, thus leaving God out of it (Vernassal, $Q6^{v}$; Munday, $Cc1^{v}$). Vernassal suggests rather vaguely that God may have permitted such a magic conception ($R1^{r}$), while Munday ignores it ($Cc1^{v}$). Indeed, Vernassal tends to do away with most of the references to God or to the Virgin Mary from the Spanish original, especially those mentioned by pagan characters. Munday goes even further and also omits other reli-

96 On the view of the enemy as a means to reinforce the hero's individuality, see note 92.

gious allusions that had been kept in Vernassal's translation. There are, for instance, fewer allusions to God in Munday's speeches than in those of his sources. He does not mention Saint Mary as he translates the passages that recount Palmendos's decision to have a church and a monastery built on Baledon's island after his death (F2^{v}), but both the Spanish and French editions allude to a statue of the Virgin Mary that should be kept in a shrine in that church. Munday, it may be assumed, was always careful when it came to image worship.[97]

He of course omits all references to the Catholic mass throughout his narrative and does not even reproduce the expression "Catholic" which in pre-Reformation days might have simply been synonymous with "Christian," but that as from the 1550s was normally associated with the Roman Church.[98] Munday was probably aware of contemporary attacks on chivalric works, which were often regarded as tools for Catholic instruction.[99] That is why he, very likely guided by his pragmatic view, tries to avoid any controversial issues and appeals to an ideal pre-Reformation Christian world.

His commercial interest is also evident throughout this work, as his numerous marketing strategies in the paratext and text of his translation attest.[100] Munday advertises the books that he has already translated and are still available—namely, *Palmerin d'Oliua* (A2^{r}, M3^{r}, S2^{v}, Cc3^{v})—as well as those he plans to publish soon after *Palmendos*—*Primaleon*, *Palmerin of England*, and *Amadis of Fraunce* (Cc3^{v}).[101] Since those intertextual ref-

[97] For instance, the Duke of Pera's beloved dies in a temple with an idol described by Vernassal as having a "diuine splendeur" (E1^{v}). Such comment on the image's divine nature is omitted by Munday, who only points to its "surpassing excellencie" (H1^{v}).

[98] The first entry in the *OED* dates back to 1554.

[99] For further information on contemporary attacks on chivalric books in England, see Álvarez-Recio, *Iberian Chivalric Romance*, 3–6; Davis, *Chivalry and Romance in the English Renaissance*, 6–18; and Werth, *The Fabulous Dark Cloister*, 7–14. However, as Melissa Furrow claims, attacks against the genre were not originally Protestant but Catholic. The Catholic world was indeed as worried as the Protestant about the affective impact of romance reading (*Expectations of Romance*).

[100] For Munday's appropriation of French paratextual conventions, see Krause, "Serializing the French Amadis in the 1540s" and Wilson, "The Publication of Iberian Romance," 209–11.

[101] *The First Booke of Primaleon of Greece* was first published in 1595 though it had been licensed in 1589. *Palmerin of England* was licensed as early as 1581 but did not appear in print up to 1596. Munday also refers to his *First Book of Amadis of Gaul*, pub-

erences also appear in the French and Spanish copies, Munday was only imitating certain successful practices. However, these allusions are more numerous and explicit in the English text, in which a larger number of direct addresses to the reader are inserted as well. Throughout his narrative, Munday molds his relation to his audience and depicts himself as a professional author who tries to ensure a positive reception of his work.

Munday's personal, quite distinct approach to translation catered for a wide, heterogeneous audience. He appealed to the more sophisticated readers by retaining the multiple classical and historical references, as well as the generic variety of his French source, though he adapted them to the taste of a late Elizabethan audience who loved a plain style. In doing so, he would also appeal to his middling-class readers, who would have the opportunity of enjoying and learning about a style that had so far been restricted to the aristocratic elite. Munday, like various other contemporary authors, argued in favor of romances as instruments of instruction, presenting clear, heroic, and courtly attitudes as models for young Englishmen. His choice of a vaguely pre-Reformation atmosphere may point to his own views on the virtues of a united Christendom, as his disregard for heathenish characters seems to indicate. However, his censorship of explicit references to Catholic rituals and beliefs reveals not only an irenic approach to his sources but his resolution to avoid any items that might interfere in his career as a professional author. His numerous intertextual references and addresses to the reader attest to his own, or his and his publishing agents', commercial aims, but also show his debt to common printing practices on the continent, mostly in France.

Such practices can be better understood once the publication history of Munday's *Palmendos* is considered. This is fully detailed in the last section of this introduction, which also explores the circulation and reception of this book up to the early eighteenth century.

lished in 1590—the first four books of this cycle had entered the Stationers' Register in 1589 (Thomas, *Spanish and Portuguese Romances of Chivalry*, 250, 253; Scanlon, "A Checklist of Prose Romances in English," 146–47).

The Publication History of Anthony Munday's Palmendos[102]

The Honourable, Pleasant and Rare Conceited Historie of Palmendos (1589) is based on the Spanish book *Primaleón de Grecia* I, first published in Salamanca on July 3, 1512. This romance was in its turn a sequel to *Palmerín de Olivia*, also printed in Salamanca one year before. The work soon became a bestseller in Spain, as there were eight editions between 1512 and 1588 and numerous translations into diverse continental languages. An Italian version by Mambrino Roseo appeared in 1548,[103] while a French translation by François de Vernassal was published in 1550, with ten subsequent reprints issued in Paris, Antwerp, and Lyons.[104] Henry Thomas also mentions a Dutch translation by Felix Van Sambix issued in Rotterdam in 1619.[105]

Towards the end of 1588, Anthony Munday translated Vernassal's French version and issued his English *Palmendos*, which entered the Stationers' Register on January 9, 1589.[106] Munday advertises his translation as an entertaining piece to be read in the spare time, which associates this type of work with the nobility or with middling-class readers, more concerned with money but equally keen on leisure books. His aim at making his works accessible to middling-class readers would account not only for the textual segmentation but also for the quarto editions and the use of black letter—a format he would repeatedly employ in his translations of Iberian chivalric romances. According to Sánchez-Martí, "publishing books in quarto reduced production costs, thus allowing a wider distribution among the middling classes, the cornerstone of the romance book trade in early modern England."[107] The black letter also reveals his interest in reaching a wider reading public, as it was the main font employed in romance and other popular genres.[108]

[102] The contents of this section were first published in Álvarez-Recio, "Anthony Munday's *Palmendos* (1589) in the Early Modern English Book Trade: Print and Reception."

[103] This version is not included in EDIT16. See Neri, "El *Progetto Mambrino*. Estado de la cuestión," 581.

[104] More detailed information on these editions appears in the USTC.

[105] Thomas, *The Palmerin Romances*, 141.

[106] *SR*, II, 513.

[107] "The Publication History of *Palmerin d'Oliva*," 195.

[108] Sánchez-Martí, "The Publication History of *Palmerin d'Oliva*," 195; Bennett,

Munday's *Palmendos* was printed by John Charlewood, who had actively complained against the patent system imposed by the Stationers, as it highly limited the options of finding non-patented material to publish.[109] Thus, his collaboration with Munday points to Charlewood's instinct to identify profitable literary modes and to his special ability to engage a faithful audience. Munday's letter to the reader in his first edition of *Palmendos* is quite revealing, as it corroborates the close relationship he tries to establish with his reading public and the links between this book and those that came immediately before and after in the series:

> Hauing finished this History of Palmendos, I commit the same to thy fauourable censure . . . hope I thou wilt accept it friendly, as thou hast done heretofore my works of the like matter. To make any commendation therof to thee, I will not, first reade thy fill thereon, and after iudge as thou findest occasion: yet with thy wonted fauour, to encourage me in proceeding in translation of Primaleon, which by the next Tearme I hope will be accomplished.[110]

His allusions to money, serial reading, and time production in the aforementioned letter to the reader must be viewed not just as Munday's attempt to present his work as a simple commodity but as his means to

English Books and Readers, 253; Wilson, "Writing Romance Readers in Early Modern Paratexts," 120. The fact that he addresses his introductory letter to "the courteous Reader" (sig. π4v) may also be significant. Phillips is certainly right when considering such references as being the means to engage middling-class readers ("Chronicles of Wasted Time"). However, Munday's possible appeal to a noble audience, given the Elizabethan courtly taste for chivalric culture, and the dedications of his early translations to the seventeenth Earl of Oxford (*Palmerin d'Oliua*) and Sir Francis Drake (*Palmendos*) should be taken into account as well. By the late 1580s, Drake had already become a national hero in England due to his travels to the New World and, above all, because of his multiple raids against the Spanish navy and Spain's possessions in America. Knighted by Queen Elizabeth in 1581, he had become the Vice-admiral of the English navy that would defeat the Spanish Armada in 1588. In dedicating his *Palmendos* to Drake, Munday was partly acknowledging the interplay between chivalric romance and Elizabethan colonial or imperial discourse, thus allowing for different readings of his translation. The fact that colonial enterprises involved people from all social ranks may also attest to the ability of Munday's translation to reach a wider audience. On Munday's dedication to Drake, see Álvarez-Recio, "Sir Francis Drake," 52–58.

109 Phillips, *English Fictions of Communal Identity*, 129.

110 Munday had also announced the publication of *Palmendos* and *Primaleon* at the end of *Palmerin d'Oliua* and *Palladine of England*, both published in 1588.

negotiate the status of his book with his publishing agents and readers. In fact, his concern with the accuracy of his text points to his professional interest in selling a high-quality work. The series of stop-press corrections that can be found in the different copies suggests that Munday revised his first edition of *Palmendos* before publication in order to suppress all possible mistakes. That first edition could then be regarded as a point of convergence in which the literary, commercial, entertaining, and didactic interests of author, publisher, and readers are all satisfied alike.

At John Charlewood's death in 1593, his widow married printer and bookseller James Roberts, who took over Charlewood's shop and stock of books up to 1606, when he sold them to William Jaggard (active 1591–1623) before retiring.[111] Joseph Ames's transcription of a manuscript note listing all volumes in Roberts's stock shows that, at some stage between 1593 and 1606, there were still seven copies of "The History of Palmendos and Primaleon" available.[112] That might explain why *Palmendos* was not reprinted, as was the case of most of Munday's chivalric translations, in a second run expanding from 1595 to 1619.

Interestingly enough, a different English version of the French *Primaleon* was issued by William Barley in 1596 under the misleading title *The Delightful History of Celestina the Faire*. Despite its title, Barley's work was in fact a different translation of the chapters dealing with Palmendos's adventures in François de Vernassal's French version. Barley was apparently trying to disguise his work, and so he changed title and character names and started translating at the second (and not at the first) paragraph of his French source. However, he did not plagiarize, but simply adopted a different translation method.[113] Barley had been fined before and after 1596 for publishing without a license,[114] and his printer Abel Jeffes had been imprisoned for disorderly printing; so their decision to issue this translation suggests their desperate need to make money.[115]

There was apparently no new edition of Munday's *Palmendos* up to 1653 and, as Thomas Hayes states, such absence is quite puzzling, since

[111] Kathman, "Roberts, James (b. in or before 1540, d. 1618?)."

[112] Ames, *Typographical Antiquities*, 342.

[113] For a comparative analysis of Munday's and Barley's translations, see Álvarez Recio, "Palmendos."

[114] *SR*, I, 555; II, 823.

[115] Brault, "English Translations of the *Celestina* in the Sixteenth Century," 304–5.

the book must have been quite popular.[116] The fact that the Epistle to the Readers in the 1653 and 1663 editions is signed "A. M." (Munday's initials) reinforces Hayes's argument that there must have been another, now lost edition, issued before Munday's death in 1633. Helen Moore, however, disagrees with Hayes and insists that, for its "style and sentiments" the epistle must have been written in the 1650s "in order to present *Palmendos* in terms similar to those used in the translations of French heroic romance popular at the time." Moore adds that the terminology employed by the author of the epistle ("gracefulness of discourse," "sublimity of conceits," or "fecundity of language" (Munday 1653, sig. A3^{r-v}) "is that of the mid- rather than early seventeenth century" and that the writer's description of his romance as "the very Quintaessence of Romancy" (Munday 1653, sig. A4^{r}) seems to date the composition of this epistle to the 1650s, when this term became fashionable owing to its relationship with the French romances mentioned above.[117]

The solution to the enigma does not seem to be easy. On the one hand, if Moore's views are accepted, the "A. M." signature in the epistle may be considered a mere marketing device employed by the 1653 and 1663 publishers, who would then be suggesting that their editions had been penned by Munday himself. If, as Hayes suspects, this letter could have been part of a lost edition issued before Munday's death, then it may be dated after 1625, when Charles married the French Princess Henrietta Maria and French influence was stronger in England. The fact that the first entry of the word "romancy" registered in the *OED* dates from 1621 (Mary Wroth's *Urania*, 504), with the same meaning as that used by the writer in this epistle, would also support Haye's hypothesis and so, it would point to Munday's romance as a predecessor of those that became popular in the 1650s and 1660s.[118] Munday and his agents' decision to publish this edition in the late 1620s could be explained because Barley had issued his

[116] Hayes, "Anthony Munday's Romances of Chivalry," 71. Francis Meres's inclusion of *Palmendos* in his *Palladis Tamia* (1598, 268^{r-v}) together with other romances to "be censured of" such as *Amadis de Gaule*, *Palmerin d'Oliva*, *Primaleon of Greece*, *Palladine*, and *The Mirror of Knighthood* confirms its popularity among contemporary readers.

[117] Moore, "Ancient and Modern Romance," 339.

[118] The similarity of the title of the 1653 and 1663 editions (*The Famous History of Palmendos Son to the Most Renowned Palmerin D'Oliva*) to that of the 1619 edition of *Primaleon* (*The Famous and Renowned Historie of Primaleon of Greece*) can also support the existence of an early seventeenth-century edition.

Celestina the Faire in 1596, thus discouraging any other works on the same story for a length of time.

The 1653 edition of *Palmendos* was printed by Elizabeth Alsop (active 1647–1664) to be sold at her own house in Grub Street. Elizabeth was the widow of Bernard Alsop, an important printer and bookseller active from 1602 to 1653, when he died. In 1616 Alsop had been in partnership with Thomas Creede, whom he succeeded in 1617 after inheriting the latter's printing materials.[119] As mentioned above, Alsop and Creede had published the fourth editions of *Palmerin d'Oliua* (1615) and *Palmerin of England* (1616). The issue by Alsop's widow of *Palmendos* in 1653 once again reinforces the thesis of a lost edition, presumably published by Creede and Alsop, or only by Alsop, late in this second run, even if there is no reference in the Stationers' Registers to any transfer of rights from Charlewood or Waterson (active 1583–1635) to any of the aforementioned printers.

As no copy of the supposedly lost edition has been preserved, it is not possible to evaluate whether the 1653 work is a new edition or a mere reprint. However, when compared with the 1589 version, some important conclusions may be drawn: first, there is a significant number of alterations, which underlines the corrector's intention to intervene in the original text;[120] second, the corrector seems to have made an attempt at "improving" the 1589 text, as the new edition is advertised as "Newly Corrected and Amended" on its title page, and a considerable number of changes in spelling, punctuation, and syntax are introduced with this intention; and third, the omissions, paraphrases, and summaries suggest that the corrector was also interested in making certain parts clearer and more attractive to contemporary readers, thus adapting the text to their taste.[121] His/her tendency to modernize certain archaic words also reveals

[119] Plomer, *Dictionary of the Booksellers and Printers*, 3–4.

[120] As employees at printing shops, correctors were responsible for reading proofs and marking corrections before the manuscript copy was passed on to the compositors. They sometimes inserted aids to readers such as tables of contents, indexes, and chapter titles. They basically shaped "the impression that a book would make on its readers" (Grafton, *The Culture of Correction in Renaissance Europe*, 13–16).

[121] For instance, highly descriptive passages are often simplified by means of summaries. This technique is especially employed in chapter 21, which includes no narrative, but only the first encounter between the hero and the heroine, and the dialogue that follows. In the 1589 edition, this chapter is highly descriptive and lyrical, as it focuses on the emotions and intimate relationship of both characters; it also recreates the setting (the castle where Francelina has been imprisoned for many years) as a *locus*

this same purpose. However, the fact that most changes do not seem to follow a regular pattern and that opposing types of alterations may occur simultaneously in the text point to the main problem this edition presents—namely, a lack of consistency.

The 1663 edition was reprinted ten years later with very slight changes, basically consisting in correcting a few errata and reducing the physical space of the text. Its publisher, Thomas Fawcett (active 1621–1655), was probably a son of Bernard Alsop's partner,[122] from whom he must have obtained the text. This reprint was to be sold by Francis Coles (active 1624–1680), quite celebrated at the time for publishing ballads, another extraordinarily popular genre when in print. This work is even shorter than its predecessor, for the 1589 book consisted of 199 leaves, whereas those of the 1653 and 1663 editions had 192 and 176 leaves, respectively. The editors' intention to make the text shorter and cheaper is especially clear in this last version, for its chapter titles are compressed, and there is very little space left between chapters, while the poems and letters that appear throughout this version are hardly separated from the rest of the text. Although its quality seems to be poorer than that of the 1653 version, it includes two beautiful engravings, each featuring a chivalric knight on a horse, bearing the inscriptions "BELLCAR"[123] and "PALMENDOS," respectively.[124] No engravings of this kind have been found in the other two versions. However, the fact that neither of these two editions contains a dedication or postscript and that both are much shorter and less ornamented than the 1589 version indicates that they were very likely cheap editions issued basically for commercial reasons. The very existence of the 1663 edition attests to the popularity of its nearest predecessor, as no reprint would have been made if there had been sufficient copies of the 1653 work in stock.

The publication of these seventeenth-century editions of *Palmendos* suggests that the text enjoyed some popularity in the second half of the

amoenus. On the contrary, the printers of the seventeenth-century editions seemed more interested in the narrative action, which they seem to regard as the main source of entertainment. So, they omit or shorten long passages that may be deemed distracting, or merely boring literary discourses dwelling in Petrarchan and Neoplatonic conventions, which may be already outdated by the mid-seventeenth century.

[122] Hayes, "Anthony Munday's Romances of Chivalry," 71.

[123] Bellcar is the name of the second main hero in the book.

[124] At the end of the book there is also a list of thirty-six "Histories" (both prose fiction and drama, in quarto and octavo) that could be bought at Coles's shop "at the Lamb in the Old Baily."

century, as was the case too of other chivalric translations. A copy of the 1653 edition has been located in Sir William Clarke's (1623/4–1666) library, in a bound volume containing also a 1650 version of *The Honour of Chivalry* (*Don Bellianis*) and a copy of the 1661 edition of *Parismus.*[125] Clarke, a prominent administrator during the civil war and secretary-at-war in the Restoration,[126] held an important collection of pamphlets and books, among which there were numerous works of prose fiction. For Guyda Amstrong, the presence of these works illustrates "the ownership of such books by a highly literate, but non-literary-specialist audience."[127] The presence of another copy of the 1653 edition of *Palmendos* in the catalog of the Earl of Bridgewater's library[128] also supports Amstrong's thesis. John Egerton, the First Earl of Bridgewater (1579–1649), who began this important collection in the early seventeenth century, had died in 1649, so the *Palmendos* volume mentioned above would most likely have been acquired by his son, John Egerton, Second Earl of Bridgewater (1623–1686), a politician and a "patron of works of learning" who devoted himself to augmenting his father's collection.[129] The presence of these copies of the 1653 edition of *Palmendos* in the libraries of such reputed figures demonstrates that the consumption of popular chivalric literature also expanded to the social and cultural elite.

However, despite the vogue for chivalric works in the second half of the seventeenth century and except for the examples above, it has not been easy to find records of contemporary English libraries having some *Palmendos* volumes among their holdings.[130] The only evidence for

[125] This volume would later be gifted to Worcester College with the whole of Clarke's collection by his son George Clarke (1661–1737) on his death in 1736 (Armstrong, "Print, Paratext, and a Seventeenth-Century Sammelband," 96–97).

[126] Henderson, "Clarke, Sir William (1623/4–1666)."

[127] Armstrong, "Print, Paratext, and a Seventeenth-Century Sammelband," 95.

[128] Collier, *Catalogue, Bibliographical and Critical, of Early English Literature*, Preface, 204–5.

[129] Despite his royalist sympathies, Egerton held important local offices in the 1650s. In the Restoration, he improved his political position both in Parliament and the Privy Council. Fiercely anti-Catholic and sympathetic to Puritan dissenters, he sided with the Whig party during the Exclusion crisis and afterwards (Espinasse, "Egerton, John, Second Earl of Bridgewater [1623–1686]").

[130] A total of 123 catalogs, included in the *List of Catalogues of English Book Sales* and in the EEBO, have been consulted, in an attempt at locating a copy of *Palmen-*

the existence of a copy of the 1589 edition of *Palmendos* has so far been found in a manuscript catalog of Dr. John Webster's (1611–1682) books in the archives of Chetham's Library in Manchester (MS.A.6.47).[131] In his thorough introduction to Webster's library, Peter Elmer states that this manuscript is "almost certainly a copy of an original draft, composed by Webster himself, probably for the purpose of evaluating his estate."[132] His collection consisted mostly of works on medicine, theology, and history,

dos. However, no entry to any *Palmendos* edition has been found in any of them. No reference has been identified either in any of the eight volumes edited by Fehrenbach and Leedham-Greene in their *Private Libraries in Renaissance England*, containing 162 book lists from the inventories of books donated to Oxford University between 1507 and 1653. Few English translations of Spanish romances are found in those catalogs and they are basically mid- and late seventeenth-century editions. A 1664, a 1679, and two 1673 volumes of *Don Bellianis of Greece* have been located, as well as a 1640 edition of *Amadis de Gaule*, a copy of the 1637 edition of *Palmerin d'Oliva*, and two volumes of the 1664 and 1610 editions of *Palmerin of England*. Five undated books of *Bellianis*, *Palladine of England*, *Palmerin d'Oliva*, *Palmerin of England*, and *Primaleon of Greece* feature in three of the catalogs. For the undated *History of Palmerin d'Oliva*, *The Famous History of Primaleon of Greece* and *Prince Palmerin of England, 3 Parts*, the 1640 volume of *Amadis* and the 1679 copy of *Bellianis*, see *Catalogus librorum*, fol. K1^{r-v}. For the undated *Palladine of England*, see *Bibliotheca curiosa*, Miscellaneous books in quarto no. 176; for the 1664, 1673, and 1692 copies of *Don Bellianis*, see Shelton, *Catalogue of Greek, Latine and English Books*, 27; Millington, *Appendix to Mr. Charles Mearne's Catalogue of English Books*, 56; Kidner, *Catalogus variorum & insignium librorum*, 17; and *Catalogue of Vendible and Useful English and Latin Books*, fol. 46A. For the 1637 volume of *Palmerin d'Oliva*, see *A Catalogue of Choice English Books*, 14. For the 1610 and 1664 volumes of *Palmerin of England*, see Greville, *Catalogus librorum*, 61 and *A Catalogue Containing Variety of English Books*, 19, respectively.

[131] A schoolmaster and polemicist, he was born at Thornton on the Hill in Yorkshire. He worked as a chemist, a doctor, and a teacher. In 1632, he was ordained minister and sent to the parish of Kildwick (Yorkshire), being deprived of his living in 1637 probably for his radical sympathies. He became well-known during the Commonwealth for his attacks against the established church, the clergy, and the universities. By the late 1650s he felt deeply disappointed by the English revolution and so he declared his loyalty to the new monarch after the Restoration. By the 1670s he had clearly abandoned his previous religious radicalism. Webster's learning and scientific interests are attested by his own works on multiple disciplines, such as religious controversy, witchcraft, chemistry, or mineralogy (Clericuzio, "Webster, John [1611–1682])."

[132] Elmer, "The Library of Dr. John Webster," 15. The fact that this catalog was originally written for private use and never reached a wider public through print might explain why Webster included *Palmendos* and other chivalric works, in contrast with the scarcity of references to this kind of literature in printed seventeenth-century book-sale lists.

but it also included 148 ancient and modern literature volumes, among which forty-one were prose romances and fiction in different languages (English, French, Spanish, and Italian), many of them published in the 1640s and 1650s.

Webster's catalog is relevant in this study since it includes a first edition of *Palmendos*, with an estimated value of one shilling and eight pence.[133] In a 1950 article, Francis R. Johnson concludes that book prices remained fairly constant from 1560 to 1635 within the range of 0.40 to 0.55 pence per sheet with a growing tendency to move to 0.55 pence by the end of that period. After the sudden rise in book prices by 1635, such average jumped to 0.70 and 0.75 pence per sheet at the end of the decade.[134] The price paid for the 1589 edition of *Palmendos* according to Webster's catalog would suggest its purchase in the 1640s as its cost per sheet is significantly higher (0.80 pence) than those paid per sheet for printed books in earlier years.[135] The volume must have been new, first hand,[136] and most probably unbound, as no information about binding, which would have increased its price, is given in the catalog.[137]

One can only speculate on Webster's reasons for holding an important section of prose fiction in his library given his professional activity as a doctor, his puritan background, and the overwhelming presence of works on natural philosophy (647 volumes) and theology (397 volumes) among his holdings. His learning and love for reading seem to suggest that his interests went beyond the mere preservation of books, and that most of those volumes were actually read and enjoyed by their owner.[138] Their presence in his library confirms the recreational use of this literature in

[133] Elmer, "The Library of Dr. John Webster," 150; entry no. 957.

[134] Johnson, "Notes on English Retail Book-Prices, 1550–1640," 89–90.

[135] The first edition of *Palmendos* contained ninety-nine leaves in twenty-five sheets. The estimated price in Webster's catalog is one shilling and eight pence (twenty pence) for the volume, which amounts to 0.80 pence per sheet.

[136] Johnson only considers the prices of new books. He does not work with second-hand volumes.

[137] This amount contrasts with that of a first edition of *Palmerin d'Oliva* (Elmer, "The Library of Dr. John Webster," 149; entry no. 953; 4s). Though the volume was considerably larger than that of *Palmendos* with 176 leaves in forty-four sheets, the average price paid per sheet (around one shilling) differs from that paid for *Palmendos*.

[138] Elmer, "The Library of Dr. John Webster," 37. This hypothesis also applies to the aforementioned book collectors, Clarke and Bridgewater.

the mid- and late seventeenth century. Besides, the prices paid for the volumes reveal their progressive commodification in the circuits outside the London book trade too. Unfortunately, it seems that none of the copies included in Webster's catalog has survived, which renders the analysis of the aforementioned *Palmendos* volume utterly impossible.

Some further information about the circulation of this first edition of *Palmendos* in the seventeenth century can also be provided by a manuscript inscription found in one of the surviving copies of *Palmendos* (1589), now in the Bodleian Library (Vet. A1. e.110). The earliest inscription is situated at the top-left corner of the first flyleaf added at the back of the book (verso). Written in black ink, it reads "returne nine shillings | Rob J Pollard." The price and reference to the bookseller help locate this copy as early as the mid- to late seventeenth century. Robert Pollard was in fact a London bookseller working in the period 1655–1658.[139] The purchaser must have noted the price, which differs considerably from the amount paid for the aforementioned volume at John Webster's library, which cost one shilling and eight pence.

Margaret Willes, who has analyzed Lord Herbert's notes on his purchase of books in the early seventeenth century, concludes that quarto format volumes cost between two and ten shillings bound, "with the number of pages and the presence of pictures as determining factors."[140] These data agree with the prices paid for some works of prose fiction in those years according to Francis R. Johnson's article.[141] Then, in the late 1650s, twenty-five years after the rise of book prices in 1635, selling this copy of *Palmendos* for nine shillings would be quite plausible, particularly

[139] Plomer, *Dictionary of the Booksellers and Printers*, 148.

[140] Willes, *The Making of the English Gardener*, 115.

[141] Johnson mentions, for instance, two bound copies of a 1619 English translation of Cervantes's *Persiles and Sigismunda* (399 leaves) for which two shillings and eight pence and two shillings and ten pence were paid respectively. He also refers to two editions from 1580 and 1585 of *The Mirror of Knighthood* (179 leaves and 258 leaves), an English translation of Ortuñez de Calahorra's chivalric romance, for which four shillings were paid unbound ("Notes on English Retail Book-Prices," 99, 107, entries 110 and 366). Henry Plomer refers to a "Palmeryn, 2 parts," sold for two shillings and four pence sometime before 1585 ("Some Elizabethan Book Sales," 328). According to Ronald Crane, this reference must be to *Palmerin of England*, since the first edition of *Palmerin d'Oliva* was published in 1588 (*The Vogue of Medieval Chivalric Romance during the English Renaissance*, 39).

since it was bound.[142] The production of two further, cheaper editions of *Palmendos* in 1653 and 1663 corroborates the contemporary interest in the story and the economic revaluation of the first edition, seventy years after its publication.

Despite their lasting popularity, contemporary criticism of chivalric romances had increased since the early seventeenth century when the chivalric mode became a clear object of parody and satire by authors such as Ben Jonson, Francis Beaumont, William Vaugham, or Thomas Shelton. Despite the subsequent boom of chivalric literature in the 1650s–1670s, such prejudices did not disappear but sometimes became even more virulent. Thus, in *The Essex Champion* (1690?, 1699), a mock chivalric romance in the mode of *Don Quixote*, William Winstanley recreated a scene not unlike that of chapter 6 in Cervantes's work:

> Next (said the curate) here is Palmerin D'Oliva in three parts, Primaleon of Greece in three parts, Palmerin of England in three Parts and Palmendos in one . . . By my say, said Thomassio, these Palmerins and Amadisses were notably cutting and slashing blades, which made a great disturbance in the world, but we shall reconcile them all in one fire together, notwithstanding they were such big fellows in their time. (1699, 61).

In the original *Don Quijote* and also in the 1612 and 1620 English versions by Thomas Shelton, the only book from the *Palmerin* and *Amadis* series which is cast in the fire is *Palmerin d'Oliva*. *Primaleon* or *Palmendos* are not even mentioned, while *Amadis de Gaule* and *Palmerin of England* are praised, and so they avoid burning. In Winstanley's text, the complete destruction of the volumes in both cycles and the detailed allusion to the different parts each book consisted of reveal a more prejudiced view than that of their sixteenth- and early seventeenth-century detractors.[143] So, the

[142] The book cover is made of blind tooled original calf leather. The front and rear covers are framed in blind by triple fillets. There are five raised bands across the spine with no decoration or title inscription. Fore-edges are stained in red color. Front and rear paste-downs are made of plain cream paper and remain now in very poor condition. The binding of the volume is quite simple and must not have been very expensive originally, although it would have contributed to increase its value in the late 1650s.

[143] However, it should be borne in mind that Winstanley also gives a fascinating account of the role of popular fiction in Restoration England, mentioning numerous chivalric books both of English and Iberian origin. See Álvarez-Recio, "La ficción inglesa en prosa a finales del siglo XVII."

few references to such chivalric volumes in contemporary sale catalogs are not surprising. *Palmendos*, like many other English translations of Spanish books of chivalry, was still far from being given a proper literary status.

The publication history of *Palmendos* covers a span of seventy-four years. Although, apparently, there were only three editions of the book, published in 1589, 1653, and 1663, it has been proved here that the printing history of this work must have been much more complex. According to Sánchez-Martí, 48 percent of the prose fiction works published from 1559 to 1591 was reprinted within twenty years[144] and that was the case too of all of Munday's chivalric translations, except for *Palmendos*. William Barley's decision to publish a different version of the same chapters in 1596 should explain why *Palmendos* was not reprinted in the second run of Munday's chivalric translations (1595–1619). The Stationers had limited the number of copies per edition to 1250–1500,[145] so an average of 2500–3000 copies on the history of Palmendos (Munday's and Barley's) were accessible to English readers by the late 1590s, and that would not have recommended any further publication of the same story. The fact that only three copies of *Palmendos* and four copies of *Celestina the Faire* have survived may indicate that both works were heavily read. Moreover, if the hypothesis of the existence of another edition of *Palmendos* issued in the 1620s is accepted, such numbers would increase.

That the book must have been popular through the seventeenth century is also attested by the publication of the 1653 and 1663 editions, by the presence of *Palmendos* volumes in a number of reputable libraries of the period, and by references to this work by other contemporary authors. The history of the book, however, ends at this point. No further edition or reprint appeared after 1663. By the turn of the century, remaining copies of the 1589, 1653, and 1663 versions entered the circuits of the leading antiquarians and book collectors. *Palmendos* also featured in the catalogs of the main book sales all through the eighteenth and, mostly, nineteenth centuries, which points to the interest this story still raised among literary scholars and to its progressive commodification as rare material.[146]

[144] Sánchez-Martí, "The Publication History of *Palmerin d'Oliva*," 206.

[145] *SR*, II, 43.

[146] For further information on the subject see Álvarez-Recio, "Provenance and Reception of Iberian Chivalric Books in English from the Seventeenth to the Twentieth Century."

Anthony Munday's

The Honorable, Pleasant and Rare Conceited History of Palmendos

[π1r] The Honorable, pleasant and rare conceited Historie of Palmendos. *Sonne to the famous and fortunate Prince Palmerin d' Oliua, Emperour of Constantinople and the Queene of Tharsus.* Translated out of French by *A. M.* one of the Messengers of her Maiesties Chamber. *Patere aut abstine.*[a1] AT LONDON Printed by I. C. for Simon Watersonne, & are to be sold in Church- yarde at the signe of the Crowne. *Anno. Domini. 1589.*

[π1v]

[π2r] Fortissimo, et militae naualis Peritissimo viro,
Domino Francisco Draco Equiti Aurato.[2]

Desinat Herculeas iam Grecia vana columnas[3]
Mirari, aut Minyas,[4] *Dulichiumue*[5] *ducem.*[6]
Amphitryoniadem[7] *superas fortissime Drace,*
Iasonaque,[8] *et comites, Penelopesque virum.*[9]
Neptunusque suum credit tibi iure tridentem,
Cedit Sceptra libens, imperiumque maris.
Palmendos *tanto laetus, tutusque Patrono*
Audet in innumeras peruolitare manus.[10]
Zoilus[11] *inuideat rumpantur et ilia Codro,*[12]
Palmendos *Draco vindice tutus erit.*
It, volat, et gaudet, spernitque minacia verba,
Nempe soles tumidas spernere Drace minas.

Antonius Mondaius.[13]

[a] The Honorable . . . Patere aut abstine] The famous History of PALMENDOS Son to the most Renowned Palmerin D' Oliva, EMPEROUR of CONSTANTINOPLE, And the Heroick Queen of THARSUS. Wherein is likewise A most pleasant Discourse of Prince *Rifarano*, the Son of *Trineus* Emperour of *Almain*, and *Aurecinda*, Sister to the Soldane of *Persia*. With their Knightly Deeds, and Acts of Chivalry; Their Famous Adventures, and most Worthy Resolutions. Newly Corrected and Amended, and most Profitable and Delightfull for all sorts of People. P2, P3

[π2v] To the courteous Reader.

Hauing finished this History of *Palmendos,* I commit the same to thy fauourable censure. And though it bee not floorished foorth with borrowed phrases of eloquence,[14] yet hope I thou wilt accept it freendly, as thou hast done heertofore my works of the like matter.[15] To make any commendation therof to thee, I will not, first reade thy fill thereon, and after iudge as thou findest occasion: yet with thy wonted fauour, to encourage me in proceeding in translation of *Primaleon,*[16] which by the next Tearme I hope will be accomplished. From my house at Cripple gate[17] the fifth of Februarie. 1589.[18]

Thine in all courtesie.
Anthony Monday.

[A1r] The history of *Palmendos,* sonne to the famous Palmerin d' Oliua,[19] Emperour of Constantinople, and the Queene of Tharsus.[20]

Discoursing likewise of the Prince Rifarano, Sonne To Tryneus[21] Emperour of Allemaigne, & Aurecinda,[22] Sister to the Soldane of Persia: theyr Knightly deedes Of Chiualrie, famous aduentures, and woorthy resolutions.

CHAPTER I.

Howe Belcar *and* Tyrendos *beeing in the Courte of the Emperor* Palmerin, *receiued theyr order of knighthoode, and how* Belcar *departed secretly from Constantinople: and of the Combat hee fought in the Realme of Macedon,*[23] *against the three Sonnes of a Knight that lodged him.*

Not long[a] after the destruction of the magnificent and proud[b] Monarchie of the *Romaines*, was erected[c] a new Empire in *Greece*,[24] which the incomprehensible bountie diuine, fauoured with continual happines, placing the good Prince *Palmerin*[d] *d'Oliua*, in the Crowne and lawfull gouernment therof: as wel in respect of his great prowesse, high and knightlie paradoxes,[25] which with vigilant care he vsed for the defence of such an estate, the onely renowne whereof brake the desseignes of manie, that by hostilitie sought to disquiet him: as also in regarde of the notable linage and posteritie discending from him, of whose vertues and heroycall perfections, this[e] present **[A1v]** Historie of *Palmendos* his Sonne is contriued, and therefore to be placed at the ende of his Fathers trauels. In which discourse alreadie extant,[26] (gentle Readers) you haue vnderstood, howe the Emperour *Palmerin* so looued and honored Knights errant, that from the furthest parts of the world they came to his Courte, because yeerelie hee continued a sumptuous spectacle in forme of a Tourney, for the exercise of knightly and millitarie discipline: and with such religious zeale was this worthy practice followed, as[f] the Court might well be called the Schoole of Armes, and Nursse of ciuilitie.[27] For this cause, many Kinges, Princes, and great Lordes, sent their Sonnes to bee there educated,[28] among whom, the good Knight *Frysoll*[29] King of *Hungaria*[30] sent one of his, named *Belcar*, and the Duke *Eustace* of *Mecaena*[31] another, called *Tirendos*:[32] that they might deserue their knighthoode at the hand of the Emperor, the true mirrour and Idea

[a] Not long] Shortly P3

[b] and proud] *om.* P2, P3

[c] erected] directed P3

[d] Palmerin] Prince P3

[e] this] *om.* P3

[f] as] that P2, P3

of manhoode, and so consequentlie they to participate some part of his bountie and prowesse.[33]

The time then beeing come, that *Belcar* Son to King *Frysoll*, shoulde receiue his order of knighthood, he humbly intreated the Emperour, that he might enioy it at his hand, and *Tirendos* Sonne to Duke *Eustace* of *Mecaena*, desirous of the selfe same honour, made like[a] request vnto his Maiestie, whereto the good Emperour (who looued them both with singuler affection, knowing how well Chiualrie woulde bee imployed by them) right willinglie condiscended.[34]

Heereupon, after they had performed the accustomed vigill,[35] he knighted these two Princes with great royaltie, desiring God to bestow such fauour on them, as at no time they might degenerate from their famous predecessours. And to *Belcar*, embracing him in his armes,[36] he sayd. My good Nephewe, heauen accomplish in you such perfections of manhoode, as each one may knowe you to be the Sonne [A2r] of the worthy Knight Sir *Frysoll*, a Prince so hardie and valiant, as anie that euer followed Armes. The ceremonies beeing ended, they all returned to the Pallace, where the newe Knights beeing vnarmed, rich Robes and Mantles were brought them, for greater[b] honour of the feaste, which in the Courte at this time exceeded. But *Belcar* tooke little pleasure, in beholding the diuers occurrences at this assembly, because his minde was more busied with expectation of future glorie, which made him thus to commune with himselfe. *Belcar*, thou hast now no longer time to rest, seeing thou hast receiued the honorable order of knighthood, and that at the hande[c] of the Emperour thyne Unckle, whom the diuine prouidence hath endued with so manie laudable vertues: nor dooth any thing want in the King thy Father, that is required in a man at Armes. If then hetherto thou hast liued in pleasure and delights, hencefoorth thou must bequeath thy selfe to trauaile, to shewe that thou doost resemble and imitate[d] in some things thine Auncestors, who with great labour and industrie[e] haue attained such fame and renowne, as the memory therof shal remaine immortall.[37]

[a] like] the like P2, P3

[b] greater] the greater P2, P3

[c] hande] hands P2, P3

[d] and imitate] *om.* P2, P3

[e] and industrie] *om.* P2, P3

And if thou wilt not darcken this honour, then must thou hasten thy departure from the Court, and follow the search of strange aduentures, as they dyd in their daies for thine example.[38]

After many and sundry thoughts, that fought together within his spirit, he concluded to depart accompanied but with one Squire, and that so secretly as could be deuised. Thence would he trauaile directly towards *Macedon*, to make the first proofe of his valour in the aduenture of *Francelina*, who was enchaunted in the Isle of *Carderia*,[39] as was declared in the History of *Palmerin d' Oliua*.[40] And at thys time was little talke of any other thing, then of the number of Knights that daily sought to winne her in marriage, and with her the Kingdome of *Thessalie*:[41] for such was the promised guerdon and recompence, to him that coulde deliuer her out of the enchaunted Castell,[42] but hetherto all **[A2v]** the Knights lost their labour, for no one[a] was able to finish the aduenture. *Belcar* beeing earnestly prouoked with the fame of this occasion, which was generally reputed strange and full of daunger, resolued to frame his iourney thether, because hee earnestly desired to bring the enchauntment to ende: his reason heerein not to be disallowed, for beyond the atchiuement of great honour and praise, hee shoulde be endowed[b] with so faire a Princesse, as coulde not be iudged inferior to anie. In this surpassing desire, concealed from anie one but himselfe, in regard of his perfect hope to compasse the same: three daies he honored the feaste with his presence, and the fourth day early in the morning, putting on a costlie[c] Greene Armour, which for this purpose he had secretly prouided, carying likewise in his Sheelde for hys deuise, a Castell Guelles in a Fielde argent, vnseene of any he left the Cittie, ryding on towarde the Realme of *Macedon*.

The Emperour soone after vnderstanding heerof, was not a little glad of his woorthy enterprise, which hee witnessed in the presence of al his Lords and Barons, saying. So helpe me God, as my opinion and hope is perswaded, that *Belcar* will so honourablie followe Armes, as each of you will reioyce to heare the discourse of his fortunes: heauen fauour and further[d] his attempts, directing all his actions in such sort, as no tongue may controll his noble forwardnes.[43] *Belcars* departure was liked of euery

[a] no one] none P2, P3

[b] endowed] endued P2, P3

[c] costlie] rusty P2, P3

[d] fauour and further] further and favour P2, P3

one,[44] except *Tirendos*, who was therat meruailously offended, because he had not acquainted him with his intent, for gladly wold he haue borne him companie, and therfore he determined neuer to giue ouer trauaile tyll he found him, as it came to passe verie soone after. In meane while, *Belcar* made such speede in his iourney, as without meeting any aduenture to hinder him, in short time hee attayned the limits and confines of the Empire: and entering the Frontiers of *Macedon*, that night he was lodged in the Castell of an olde curteous Knight, who sitting at his Gate, and seeing *Belcar* **[A3r]** passe by in the euening somewhat late, intreated him for that night to let him be his Hoste, which he not willing to refuse, was wel content to accept his offer. After that *Belcar* was vnarmed, the olde Knight so well liked his braue constitution of bodie, his affable qualities and modest speeches,[45] as he had great pleasure to sitte and talke with him:[46] and falling from one circumstance to another, the good olde Knight perceiued in the ende, that his guest was one in great fauour with the Emperour *Palmerin*.

Now must I let you vnderstand,[47] that this curteous old Knight had three Sonnes, by nature proude and euill dysposed, enuying the liberall hospitalitie which their father vsed to trauailing passengers: wherfore the good old man, too well acquainted with their mallicious behauiour, tooke them aside to admonish them, that they should vse no frowning or discourtesie to his guest. Know my Sonnes (quoth he) that this night we haue in our house one of the Emperours Knights, whose countenance doth witnes that hee is of high discent: I pray you therefore doo him all the honour you may, entertayning him with cheerefull and hartie good will, not vsing any speeches but such as are modest and meete for Gentlemen. They answered that they woulde fulfill his commaundement, yet their Father was no sooner gone, but they concluded altogether, on the morrow to assayle *Belcar* at the entraunce of a Forrest, which was not farre distant from the Castell, to try if he were such a man as their Father commended him to bee: and beeing thus resolued, they would not be seene at Supper, but earlie in the morning clasping on their Armour, they rode to the place of their appointment. The reuerend Father, seeing the ingratitude and disobedience of his Sonnes, did all the honor hee possibly coulde to *Belcar*, who requiting hys gentlenes with many thanks, in the morning set forward on his iourney: and scantly[a] had hee ridden two leagues, but

[a] scantly] scarcely P2, P3

he met the three brethren vnder a wood side, when the eldest of them came to him with these speeches. Sir Knight, **[A3v]** you must of necessitie Ioust with mee, otherwise your passage may not be permitted, for now am I[a] desirous to make proofe, if thou be so valiant as men doo esteeme thee. *Belcar*, who stood in doubt of a greater ambushe, tooke his Launce from his Squire, and in very courteous manner thus replyed. You may bee ashamed Sir Knight, to assaile any Gentleman belonging to the Emperour in this sorte, and happily you may deale with such a one, who shall giue you but little time to sitte downe and repent ye. Trouble not your minde with such imaginations, quoth another of the Brethren, but prepare your selfe to try the euent. At which words they fetched theyr carire, and encountred together with such vigour, as their Launces flew in shyuers vp into the ayre, *Belcar* beeing not mooued in his saddle, where contrariewise, he gaue his enemie such a puissaunt stroke with the counterbuffe of his staffe, as it was too late for him to call for a Chirurgion.[48] When the other two Brethren saw this spectacle, and beeing perswaded that theyr elder Brother was wounded to the death: prouoked with extreame rage and indignation, they came to *Belcar* with these wordes.

In an euill howre (Knight) didst thou giue that blow, because thy death shall recompence the same. So ran they[b] both together fiercely against him, the one fayling in the meeting, and the others happe so good,[49] as hee gaue *Belcar* a small wounde on the arme: yet beeing of resolute courage he buckled with them so close, as one of them he sent to keepe company with his eldest brother, and the other he brought into such extremitie, that he fell from his Horse depriued of his sences. The Squire that came with these three brethren, seeing the bad fortune of his Maisters Sons, rode presently backe to the Castel, and finding the aged Knight in his Chamber, thus began.

Alas my Lorde, in an vnhappy howre did you entertaine the Knight that lodged heere the last night, who (as it seemeth) came onely to kill your Sonnes. So deliuered **[A4r]** he the whole discourse of the fight, which prouoked the sad Father to shedde forth aboundaunce of teares: yet did hee especiallie condemne his Sonnes, whose pryde and arrogancie had thus caused their owne death.[50] His Seruaunts vnderstanding the cause of his laments, went presentlie to the place where the Bretheren were discom-

[a] am I] I am P2, P3

[b] ran they] they ran P2, P3

fited, and there they founde two of them depriued of life, the thirde likewise in very great daunger, vnlesse speedy prouision were made to preuent it. So causing him to be layed in a Litter, and the other two on a knightly Beere, they thus brought them to their Fathers Castel, where their Ladie mother met them with wonderful effuse of teares and lamentations, as one wold haue iudged her altogether voide of sence and discretion, then any way pertaker of humaine wit or reason.[51] Like sorowe was made by one of her daughters, who loued her brethren very deerely, and after shee had somwhat pacified herselfe, she made a solemne vow to her mother, neuer to take rest in her mind and thoughts, vntil she were thorowly reuenged on the murtherer.[52] Wherfore when her two dead brethren were buried, she departed against her Fathers will, accompanied onely wyth two Squires to seeke *Belcar*, intending to be auenged[a] on hym by one meane or other.

[A4v] CHAPTER II.

How Belcar *came vnknowne into Macedon, where he bare away the pryze of the Tourney, which King* Florendos *had appointed, to honour the marriage of the Princesse* Denisa*: and howe hee discouered himselfe to* Alderina, *Daughter to the Duke of Pontus and Durace.*

B*elcar* ryding in great haste towarde *Carderia*, finding the heate of the day very troublesome, he alighted at a faire Fountaine to refresh himselfe a while, where long he had not stayed, but in a pathe leading directly to the same place, hee behelde a company of Knights and Ladies comming, attended on with a very sufficient trayne. It was the Duke of *Pontus* and *Durace*, who rode to *Macedon*, to the mariage which the King *Florendos*[53] had made, betweene his Daughter *Denisa*[54] and the King of *Thrace*,[55] Nephew to the Wife of *Caniano*.[56] This Duke had his espoused Lady *Laurana* with him, as also one of his fayre Daughters named *Alderina*, who rode formost in the troupe, beguiling the time in talk with her Ladies: yet intending to stay tyll the heate was past, and in the meane while to sollace herselfe at the Fountayne.[57] There shee arryued before *Belcar* had put on his Helmet, so that she beholding[58] his amiable countenaunce, his rich Armor, and yet hauing no company but one Squire: as a Ladye wyse and well gouerned she saluted him very graciouslie, wherat

[a] auenged] revenged P2, P3

Belcar was somwhat amazed, doubting she knew of whence and what hee was. But soone did hee alter that opinion, and rather thinking this kindnes to proceede of **[B1r]** debonaire curtisie, imagined her of high calling, for which cause he made her humble reuerence, and seeing how manie followed this Lady, among whom he might peraduenture be knowne, he called for his Horse, minding to ryde a contrarie waie. *Alderina* heerat somwhat mooued, because shee desired to knowe of whence hee was, thus spake.[59] Sir Knight, abide heere hardlie at your ease, and for our comming doo not forsake a place so sweete and delectable: you see the heate of the daie is such, as scantlie will permit yee to trauaile. If you goe to aduenture your fortune in the Tourney at *Macedon*, you may ride with the Duke my Father, who will be verie glad of your companie: and much more my selfe, because my good hap was first to finde you heere.

Belcar, humblie thanking her for this courtesie, made an excuse that he could not goe to *Macedon*, because he had vrgent affaires els where, and whether he must trauel with all speede: wherefore taking his leaue againe of her, hee rode which waie him liked best, onely to escape vnknown of this companie. And meeting a Squire, that came after the traine with the cariage, he demaunded if he knew the Lord that rode by so well accompanied, to whom the Squire aunswered, that it was the Duke of *Pontus*, who rode to *Macedon*, to the feaste of the King *Florendos*, for the mariage of his Daughter *Denisa*, and that the Duke had his fayre Daughter *Alderina* with him, to see the Iousts and Turnament which was nowe prepared.[60] So soone as *Belcar* heard these words, he presentlie coniectured, that the Lady which came first to the Fountain was the Dukes daughter, of whom report had made great commendation. Heeruppon he[a] determined to goe see this assemblie, in the most secrete manner he could deuise: for he had time enough to accomplish his voiage. So forsooke hee the way to the Isle of *Carderia*, framing his iourney toward *Macedon*, and comming neere the Cittie, he ouertooke two Knights that rode to the Tryumphe: they hauing riciprocallie saluted eache **[B1v]** other, the two Knights demaunded of *Belcar* if he came to Iouste? I come (quoth he) to see[b] what men at Armes wil enter the Fielde at this time of braue exercise. Then let vs ride together if you please, (said they) for wee left our Countries for the selfe same cause. Thus rode they on freendlie together,[61] and arriuing at *Macedon*, they

[a] he] *om.* P3

[b] (quoth he) to see] to see (quoth he) P2, P3

founde the Fielde all couered with Tents, which belonged to the Noble personages that were come to the feaste. For this cause, the two Knights gaue in charge to their Squires, to prouide their Pauillion, which was purposelie brought with them, intreating *Belcar* likewise to keepe them companie: whereto (because hee woulde not enter the Cittie) he gladlie consented, thinking hee shoulde hardlie finde a more conuenient[a] lodging.

On the morrow there arriued the Duke of *Pontus*, before whom rode the King *Florendos*, as one willing to welcome his newe kinred: but *Alderina* shewed such maiesty in countenance, as euerie eye wondred at her rare perfections, notwithstanding, she was somewhat sad and pensiue, the cause proceeding from her desire, to know the Knight she saw at the Fountaine, whom yet she could not by anie meanes forgette. When *Belcar* behelde her arme in arme with the King of *Thrace*, and in what costlie garments she was attired: hee imagined her more faire then when hee sawe her at the Fountaine, so that he resolutlie intended, if hee coulde not finish the aduenture of *Francelina*, to giue himselfe to trauaile, and to enterprise such attempts, as might be thought worthie the loue of this Ladie.[62] All thys while the Queene *Griana*, wife to the King *Florendos*, verie honourablie entertained the Duchesse *Laurana*, and the young Princesse *Denisa* accompanying *Alderina*, woulde not forsake her till the marriage night.[63]

On the morrow following, the King, the Queene and the newe maried couple, came into the Field to behold the Turney, where they were no sooner mounted on the Scaffoldes, which were sumptuously adorned as beseemed so **[B2r]** great personages: but bothe on the one side and the other, they might behold great store of armed Knights, cheefelie they that came from the Court of the Emperour, who because he could not be present at his Sisters mariage, sent manie of his bolde Barons to honour the assemblie. The braue exploits in feates of Armes there performed, surpassed them of greatest reputation, and among other, the Dukes of *Anemon* and *Mensa* so well behaued themselues, as they had well neere gained the honour of the first assaulte,[64] if *Belcar* had not suddainlie arriued, who staied a while to behold the order of the Ioustes, intending to helpe the weaker part, when at length he saide to his companions: follow me my Freendes to assist the vanquished. So giuing his Horse the spurres, he ranne fiercelie with his Sworde drawne, against *Bellequin* the Sonne of *Mosso*, who dyd the greatest harme to the other side: and with him he

[a] a more conuenient] *om.* P3

met so brauelie in his carire, as Horse and man went bothe to the grounde. Afterward, he delt so roughlie with all them that durst meete him in the face, as in short time courage began to reuiue in those Knights, who (in the iudgment of all the beholders) were before esteemed vanquished.

Which the Duke of *Anemon* perceiuing, and his companie to grow into such disgrace, he was therat exceedinglie offended, and thrusting himselfe among the thickest, gaue *Belcar* a very great stroke with his Sworde on the Helmet: for which he receiued speedie repayment, for *Belcar*, raysing himselfe in his stirrops, returned the Duke such a cruel blow through the sight of his Helmet, as he fel to the ground astonied betweene his Horse legs. Then breaking in amidst the preasse, he gaue such sharpe entertainement to all that met him, as the King *Florendos*, and the other great estates that accompanied him, were driuen thereby into great admiration: nor was he knowne to anie[65] there but the Princesse *Alderina*, who being seated on the right hand of the Queene *Denisa*, could not smoother her thoughts, but thus spake. What thinke you (Madame) of the Knight **[B2v]** in Greene Armour? What doo I thinke? aunswered the Queene, certes[a] neuer did I see the man, who might equal or paragon himselfe with him, for that he alone hath doone more in this Tourney then all the other: and greatly wold it content me, to know if he be discended of noble bloode, as hee deliuers good testimonie of his knowledge in feates of Armes.

Madame, (quoth *Alderina*) I cannot thinke him lesse then you doubt of, in respect he concealeth himselfe so closelie,[b] and would not willinglie be knowne of anie. Heerwith she recounted how she founde him at the Fountaine, bare headed without his Helmet: and this I can assure you, quoth she, that as you confesse him valiant at Armes, so canne I witnes him of such braue feature and complexion, as there is no one absolute point wanting in him. Your speeches said the Queene, makes me much more desirous to knowe him, wherefore I will sende one to him for the same purpose. Then I beseeche your Maiestie, answered *Alderina*, to sende one of my Pages, who shall attend for him til the ende of the Tourney, and then coniure him in your name, that he send you worde of whence and what hee is: and if he stand lothe to be known, to resolue him from your Maiestie and me, that no liuing creature shal bewraie him by our meanes. Your counsell I verie well allowe, saide the newe maried Queene,

[a] certes] truly P2, P3

[b] closelie] P2; close lie P1

but I woulde that this Embassage should rather goe from you, because hee remembring what knowledge you had of him at the Fountaine, will happilie manifest himselfe vnto you rather then anie other. Heereuppon *Alderina* called one of her Pages named *Gracian*, artificiallie instructing him in his errande to the Greene Knight: that vsing instant intreatie, accompanied with a singuler desire, he should gaine the meane to returne with his name and parentage.

All this while *Belcar* shewed such rare deedes of Chiualrie, as hauing well laboured the aduersarie, and none left that woulde confront him: hee went as Conquerour **[B3r]** forth of the Lystes, where he mette the two Knights that came with him thither, who staied more desirous to note his behauiour in the fight, then to intrude themselues in place of such daunger, and beeing not a little gladde of the honour he had doone them, in that their companion bare awaie the palme of victorie, they rode on eache side of him towardes their Tent, beeing followed all the way by the Princesse Page, who awayting due time to deliuer his message, tooke *Belcars* Horse by the bridle, and vsing such meanes of secrete conference, as *Belcar* stouped to heare him, hee softlie thus whispered with him. Sir Knight, I wold it might like you to ride aside a little, that I may deliuer a matter of secrete[a] to you. He who was so courteous and affable as anie man coulde be, presentlie left his two companions, when *Gracian* thus began his message. My Lord, *Alderina* Daughter to the Duke of *Pontus* and *Durace*, hath at this time sent me to ye, to let you vnderstand, that she hath receiued iust cause of offence towards you, in that shee comming to see this Tourney, you disdained to make offer of your companie. Notwithstanding, if you wil graunt one request that she makes by me, forgetting al passed vngentlenes, shee will gladlie leaue further to misdeeme of you. My Freend answered *Belcar*, the thing must bee very difficult or impossible, that I woulde not enterprise, to obtaine the gracious pardon of so choise a Ladie as is thy Mistresse: it may bee, that I haue trespassed in duetie towards her excellencie, but in sooth meere ignorance of her estate was the onelie cause. And when I left her at the Fountaine, farre was my intent from comming to this Tourney, in so much as I was thereto (in a manner) constrayned, notwithstanding excuses of as great importance as those I vsed to thy gentle Ladie.

[a] secrete] secresie P2, P3

It resteth nowe (quoth the Page) that you graunt my Mistresse her earnest desire, which is, to knowe what you are, and why you conceale your selfe in such sorte: for beholding your noble and valiant behauiour, shee sets you **[B3ᵛ]** beyond all other in her conceit, and promiseth withall, vnder the word of so great a person as shee is, not to reueale it to anie, if you be willing it should[a] be so. Highlie may I commend my fortune, said Belcar, that a Princesse so gentle and perfect, would daine to enquire after my poore deserts: and though I had vowed to conceale my selfe from the whole world, yet would I straine courtesie wyth that vowe for her sake. Saie to her therfore, courteous Page, that my name is *Belcar*, Nephewe to the Emperor of *Constantinople*, and the cause why I woulde not willinglie be knowne to anie, is the[b] small portion of time since I receiued my Knighthoode: and hauing not yet doone any thing worthie my name, or to be accounted among the actions of honor, I determined not to publish the same, vntil[c] I might doo it with good testimony. Thou maist also assure her from me, that henceforth I shall serue as her deuoted Knight: hoping vnder fauour of her name to gaine such account, as[d] I and mine shall remaine perpetually bound to her excellencie. And when I haue accomplished anie thing, that may be reputed worthy honourable commendation, I wil come my selfe, and offer therwithall to her my hart, which hath receiued such an impression of obeysaunce to her,[66] as hencefoorth it will attempt nothing but in her sweete regarde.[67] Proofe may she make heereof in commaunding me, for such is my desire to be imployed in her seruice, as were I assured my death consisted in the attempt, yet coulde not anie feare thereof with-holde me. Let me further intreate her, not to disclose my name to anie one, because at this time I will not visite the King *Florendos* and the Queene, albeit[e] I am so neere allied vnto them. With this aunswere returned *Gracian* to his Ladie, who attended his comming in great deuotion, that[f] he was no sooner entred the Chamber, but she demaunded the successe of his message. All wel Madame, answered the Page, but you must keepe it very secret, because the Knight himselfe

[a] should] could P3

[b] the] this P3

[c] vntil] til P2, P3

[d] as] as both P2, P3

[e] albeit] notwithstanding P2, P3

[f] that] so that P2, P3

hath so desired. Which after she had faithfullie promised to doo, hee tolde her that [B4r] the Knight was *Belcar*, Son to the King of *Hungaria*. May it be so? quoth the Queene *Denisa*, then is he[a] my Nephew, and thinkes hee scorne to be knowne to vs? right gladlie would I haue seene him, for from our infancie wee were nourished together: and well may you assure your selfe Madame *Alderina*, that he hath beene euermore benigne and courteous, which makes me not reioyce a little, that his fortune in Armes is equall with his other vertue, yet seeing he desires to passe vnknowne, let vs keepe the same so secret as we may. It were needles to demaund if *Alderina* were pleased, when she heard that *Belcar* was issued of so great and illustrious blood, offering himselfe withall so religiously[68] her Knight: wherefore she now beganne extreamelie to affect him, and imprinted the remembraunce of him so liuelie in her spirit,[69] as nothing might deface it againe.[70] Thus hourely raunged loues passions in her harte, wherein they tooke immediate ambush, so soone as she beheld him at the Fountaine.

[B4r]CHAPTER III.

Howe Belcar *fearing to be knowne, departed secretlie from* Macedon, *and by the way met with a Knight whom he vanquished: and how he fought a cruell combat with him that defended the bridge, where the faire* Francelina *was enchaunted.*

So soone as *Belcar* hadde ended with *Alderinaes* Squire, hee minded to departe presentlie, fearing least the King *Florendos* would sende for him, as indeede he did soone after: for hee greatlye desired to knowe the Knight, that bare away the honour of the Tourney. But hys [B4v] expectation was greatlie deceiued, in that *Belcar* was alreadie departed: whereof the King coulde not be perswaded, but that he missed his presence in the Tryumphe following, which hee compared with[b] the pastime of little Children, in respect of the former day, when the vnknown Knight performed matters[c] of incredible valour. And albeit the Queene *Denisa* and the Princesse *Alderina*, hearde euery iudgment passing on the Knight, yet woulde they yeelde no other aunswer, but that hee seemed to bee one

[a] is he] is P3

[b] with] to P2, P3

[c] matters] matter P2, P3

of the best esteemed Knights in the Emperours Court. *Belcar* then hauing graciously thanked his two companions, for the courtesie and humanitie they had vsed towardes him: tooke his freendlie farewell of them, fayning an earnest constraint, which commaunded his presence in matters of importaunce. The Knightes lothe to loose so good a Freende, made offer to accompany[a] him in his trauaile: but hee excused their requeste with a necessarye denyall, wherewith they were pleased, and hee had libertie to depart.

And ryding along the way where hee met *Alderina*,[71] he happened into a faire greene Meddow, where (because no lodging was neere at hand) he determined to make his hostage that night: but as hee thought to enter[b] a sounde sleepe, a suddaine imagination caught hold on his sences, presenting them with the rare beautie of *Alderina*, during which passion, he was constrained thus to parle with himselfe. In sooth *Belcar*, right well maist thou bee charged with discourtesie and ingratitude, hauing made so slender shewe of ciuilitie to so faire a Princesse as is[c] the Dukes Daughter of *Pontus*: full well may it beseeme thee to amend this fault, and by the dutifull repentaunce fitting a Knight, recouer the note of thy former blemishe.[72] After many amorous discourses, he concluded (if hee could finish the aduenture of *Francelina*) to make choyse of thys Ladie onelie as his Wife.[73] And in these imaginations a sweete slumber ouertooke him, wherin he continued till the next **[C1^r]** morning, when mounting on horsebacke, and ryding not past the space of two miles, hee mette with a Knight at Armes: who demaunded if hee came from *Macedon*, and if the nuptials of the Kings daughter were finished: *Belcar* answered, that they were now in performing, and if it liked him to trauaile thether, he should there finde matter enough to be imployed in. The Knight left Belcar to his iourney, and so without anie further speeches they departed.

But if you be desirous to know the man, it was *Cardino*,[74] who departed from *Constantinople* with *Colmelio*, in search of the Damosell that brought such a suddaine message to the Emperour *Palmerin*, as you may reade in the last Chapter of his Historie.[75] And albeit they had trauailed manie Countries to finde her, yet coulde they not heare anie tydings of her: because she presentlie returned to the Castell of *Carderia*,

[a] accompany] go with P2, P3

[b] enter] enter into P2, P3

[c] is] *om.* P2, P3

from whence the Fayries[76] sent her to the Court on that occasion, the intent thereof beeing no other, but onelie to extol and commend the future prowesse of *Palmendos*, Sonne to the Queene of *Tharsus* and the Emperour *Palmerin*, and that the Knight who should come to finish the enchauntment of *Francelina*, might be receiued with greater honour and magnificence.[77] *Cardino* had tried his fortune in this aduenture, but hee could speede no better then others had doone before him, wherefore hearing of the Feaste and open Court held at *Macedon*, he went as one doubtfull to come short to the Tryumphes, till *Belcar* had thereof certainlie resolued him. These Knightes were not parted the space of a mile, but *Cardino* met the Damosell, who was Sister to the two Bretheren slayne by *Belcar* in the Woode,[78] shee hauing followed him to the Court of the King *Florendos*, was aduertised by a Squire of his successe in the Tourney, and howe he rode the common high waie leading to *Carderia*, whereupon shee made good haste after him, and mette with *Cardino* soone after[a] their departure, to whom she began in this manner. **[C1v]**

I beseech ye Gentleman to resolue me certainlie, if ye met a Knight in Greene Armour or no, the most trayterous and disloyall man that this daie liueth: for my Father hauing doone him al the honour he could deuise, while one night he came and lodged at his Castell, and on the morrow morning (the more to content him) commaunded my three Bretheren to accompanie him somewhat on the waie: but he, a most inhumaine and vnthankfull wretch, without anie occasion slewe two of them, and put the thyrde in great daunger of life.[b] And in this iust cause I pursue the vyllaine, in hope to meete with some worthie man, who detesting such notorious and horrible ingratitude, will (in taking compassion on my greefe) reuenge this iniurie.[79] So well could the traytresse couller her speeches, and set such a smoothe foyle[c] on her cautelous prosopopey:[80] as shee imprinted in the hart of *Cardino*, a dutiful regard to reuenge such wrong,[81] wherefore he thus answered.

Damosell, if it be so as you say, the Knight cannot excuse himselfe, but that he is bothe a Traytor and a fellon, nor will the God of Heauen suffer him to escape vnpunished in this world. The Damosell with terrible othes protested what shee had saide, desiring him to giue her ayde, if no

[a] after] P2; after ter P1

[b] life.] his life. P2, P3

[c] such a smoothe foyle] so fair a glosse P2, P3

other occasions might hinder her sute. Right gladlie (quoth *Cardino*) will I performe my duetie heerein, for that I am a professed enemie to such offenders, and shal cause him to paie deerelie for his trecherie.[82] So rode he with the Damosell after *Belcar*, but all that daie they coulde not ouertake him. On the morrowe they gotte sight of him on the edge of a Mountaine, whereat the Damosell not a little contented, desired *Cardino* now to rouse his forces, against the Tyrant that had so dishonoured her. *Cardino* promising to accomplish her desire, gaue the spurres to his horse and galloped after *Belcar*, and in a great brauado thus cried to him. Stay Traytour, vnworthy the name of a Knight, and receiue thy guerdon at my hand, for slaughtering them that entertained thee with all humanitie. *Belcar* hearing **[C2^r]** himselfe thus iniuried, was immediatlie prouoked into choller,[83] and turning towardes him that touched him with disloyaltie, hee thus sternelie aunswered. But[a] little to thy profite will it bee, to pursue mee with such false and lying accusations.[84] So clasping his Helmet, he ran furiously against *Cardino*, who mette him with no lesse courage and viuacitie, and breaking his Launce brauely, somwhat scared the skinne of his enemie: but *Belcar* welcommed him with so sound a salutation, as he fell downe with the saddle betweene his legges, so sore astonied wyth hys fall as he was not able to stirre hand nor foote, which *Belcar* perceiuing, rode on and there left him. The Damosell, seeing *Cardino* in such woful plight, alighted from her Palfray,[85] and with the helpe of his Squire binding vppe hys wounds, determined to bring him to some place for helpe, vsing the greatest shewes of lamentation that coulde bee. Ah heauen[86] (quoth shee) why giue[b] yee strength to wicked men against the good and vertuous? suffer not that[c] disloiall villaine to doo anie further daunger, but rather giue some miserable ende to his vnworthie life. By this tyme the Squire[87] had mounted *Cardino* on his Horse, and so they returned the same way they came, happening to the place where *Belcar* had broken his faste the morning before.

There they vnderstoode by the[d] Hoste, that he was gone to proue the aduenture of *Francelina*, whether the Damosell would gladlie haue followed him: yet was she lothe to leaue *Cardino* in such daunger, and therefore abode there with him three daies, vsing all the meanes shee coulde to

[a] But] *om.* P3

[b] giue] have P3

[c] that] this P2, P3

[d] the] their P2, P3

heale him, because[a] for her sake he was so wounded: where we will leaue them, and returne to the onely thred of our Historie.

So long rode *Belcar*, that hee arriued within halfe a daies iourney of the Castell where *Francelina* was, thys Fortresse appertained to a Ladie that was a widdowe, who had two fayre Daughters, and a Sonne already knighted, of no lesse valour in feates of Armes, then learned and wel [C2v] seene in diuers other discipines. In this place was hee meruailous well entertained, the Lady of the Castell beeing a Woman of great honour, and her Daughters of verie Courtlie and ciuill[b] behauiour. After Supper, *Belcar* entred into conference with them, and among manie other thinges, enquired the cause that mooued so many Knights to attempt the aduenture of that Isle, when the Ladies Sonne, who was named *Lypes*, answered him in this sort. Beleeue me Sir, I haue euermore[c] accounted the man but badlie councelled, that takes such paines to trauell hether, seeing it is so long time since any Knight arriued here, who returned not without dishonour: because the action and exploit of this enchauntment (so wonderfully compacted by the three Fairies) is of such efficacie, as it behoueth hym that shall finish the same, to bee of most rare and exquisite perfection.[88]

But tell mee then (quoth *Belcar*) the state of this aduenture, and wherein consisteth the greatest perill thereof: for as yet haue I not met with anie one that could tell me the trueth, to satisfie my long and earnest desire. Better then any other, aunswered Lypes, can I dyscourse the same vnto you, because I haue often accompanied Knightes trauailing thether as you nowe doo, and seene many Combat with him that defendes the entraunce on the Bridge, albeit to their great disaduantage. Know then gentle Sir, that the Isle of *Carderia* stretcheth in diameter very far, beeing on the one side enclosed with the Sea, and on the other are most wholesome Bathes and Ryuers, which hinder the salte waters from comming neere the Castell: at the foote whereof is builded a meruailous artificial bridge,[89] heeretofore accessable for all Knights errant, but since the time that *Francelina* was enclosed within the great Dungion, there might not enter anie straunger, those of the Isle onelie come and goe, but others not. Vpon this Bridge are erected three Turrets, one of them beeing in

[a] because] because that P2, P3

[b] ciuill] evil P3

[c] euermore] euer P2, P3

the middest, and the other two at eyther ende. In the first is a Knight, [C3r] surpassing the common stature and proportion of men, so fierce, hardie and couragious, as since the time of this enchauntment, hee hath not beene dealt withall by any one, that coulde in ought disable his prowesse: onely the Lorde of the Isle of *Lique* excepted, Son to him whome the Emperour *Palmerin* vanquished, when in the Tourney hee conquered the Sagittarie.[90] He,[a] beeing named *Lynedes*, was so resolute and magnanimious, as hee fought against the Knight of the Bridge from morning til night, and though the Combat was fierce and cruell, yet coulde no want of courage be discerned in him: which fel not out so with the gardant of the Bridge, because the losse of his bloode so weakened him, as his hart began vtterly to dismay. But a huge[b] ill fauoured Dwarffe, who neuer styrres from the Beacon of the first Turret, to discouer such Knightes as come along the Fielde, by winding[91] an enchaunted Horne that hunge about his neck, therwith so reuiued the Knights strength again, as though[c] he had but euen then entred the Combat.

In thys sorte the fight continued till Sunne setting, when *Lynedes* perceiuing his enemie to were feeble againe, and that the Dwarffe as yet blew not his Horne: brought the Knight of the Bridge into such extreamitie, as[d] hee fell vppon his hands to the ground. Then running nimbly[e] ouer the Brydge, he came to the Turret in the midst thereof, the Gates whereof beeing open before: clapt together at his arriuall wyth such a fearefull trembling of the whole buylding, as *Lynedes* fell to the earth in a swoune. In this traunce hee remayned a great whyle, that[f] hys Squires fearing he was dead indeede, bemoned their Maister with[g] very greeuous lamentations: but when hee came to his former feeling, they sawe he was so cruelly wounded, as they caryed him into[h] his Tent, where three daies he remained to reobtaine his health, and on the fourth, feeling himselfe able to sit on horseback, and not willing to make any further proofe of thys aduenture,

[a] He] *om.* P3

[b] huge] *om.* P2, P3

[c] though] if P2, P3

[d] as] that P2, P3

[e] nimbly] swiftly P2, P3

[f] that] so that P2, P3

[g] with] P2; with with P1

[h] into] to P2, P3

hee departed thence [C3v] sorrowing for his bad fortune. And this I tell ye Sir for a certaintie, that when the Dwarffe sits as Sentinel in the Lanthorne of the first Tower, perceiuing the Knight of the Bridge to haue the worst of the Combat: with[a] the sound of his Horne he[b] renues his strength, which is the cause that no man is able to deale with him. Seeing then thys enterpryse bryngeth such daunger, and oftentimes death withall: I could wysh that heereafter no man would attempt his owne ruine.

You tell me matter of meruaile, answered *Belcar*, and ryght skylfull were the Fayries in framing thys enchantment, so it shoulde seeme, that they haue not enclosed the Lady there without great occasion, beeing assured that some Knight shal end the aduenture: to which each one trauaileth with this couragious hope, that hee is the man for whome it is reserued. Nor can I bee disswaded from it, if manie heeretofore haue fallen in that errour, therefore no doubt of what shall happen can[c] hinder my determination. If I happen in my tryall to be ouercome, I shall but encrease the number of them, that could not attaine the height of their enterprise, and no other dishonour can I receiue. *Lypes* earnestly intreated him to forbeare the voyage, and so did his Sisters likewise, into whose grace he was greatlie entred, especially the yongest, fayre and debonayre beyonde the other: but all their perswasiue reasons could not chaunge him, for *Belcar* hauing trauailed so farre for that purpose, might not by any occasion whatsoeuer bee wythdrawne from making proofe of his fortune. When *Lypes* saw him so obstinatlie inclined,[92] he made offer to beare him company, if it were but onely to shew him the way, which freendly courtesie *Belcar* accepted, so one the morow they mounted on horsebacke, and came to the Isle about mid-day. There was set vppe a riche Tent for thys young Prince, which the Sisters to[d] *Lypes* hadde sent thether by three Squires, with all necessary prouision for his attempt, and in the euening *Belcar* went to view the Isle, regarding [C4r] the Towre wherein *Francelina* was imprysoned: inuocating on God in his spirite, to endue him with such abilitie, as he might deliuer her, and beare away the honour of the aduenture. These imaginations so busied his thoughts as all that night hee coulde entertaine no other, but oftentimes thus talked with himselfe.

[a] with] he with P2, P3

[b] he] *om.* P2, P3

[c] can] shall P3

[d] to] of P2, P3

Ah *Belcar*,[93] why shouldest thou thus delay time, and not[a] rather couragiously attempt the execution of thys enterprise: admit thou want answerable force[b] to a matter of such dignitie: yet should the renowne and generositie of thine auncestours[c] stimulate thee heereto, beeing Sonne to one of the best Knights that lyueth thys day under the Zodiack, and Nephew to the great Emperour, with whom none may bee equalled.[94] In these conceits[d] hee consumed the night, and in the morning (hauing Armed himselfe) came to the Brydge, where in a conuenient place neere the first Towre, he espied the Knight that defended the passage: whose huge stature somewhat amazed *Belcar*, and as he offered to steppe on the Brydge, the Knight very proudely thus spake.[95]

Withdraw thy selfe Knight, vnlesse thou wilt enter fight with mee, for I am heereto denie passage to any. For no other cause come I, answered Belcar, but to try thy manhoode, and passe the Bridge if possibly I may. With these wordes he gaue the Knight such a sound stroke on the Helmet, as[e] he thought the fire flewe foorth[f] of hys eyes, and so they beganne a long and daungerous Combat, the Knight gyuing *Belcar* many cruell blowes with hys yron Mace, and he defending them so well as hee coulde: tyll hauing somewhat wearyed his enemie, and thinking to doo as he heard of *Lynedes*, but the Knight gaue him such a forcible stroke on the shoulder, as he was constrayned to sette one knee to the grounde to escape the fal. Herwith the Dwarffe blewe his Horne, which reioyced them within the Castel: albeit the Prince was astonied thereat,[g] yet he dyssembled the same from beeing espyed. The Knight hauing recouered his former strength, assayled *Belcar* with meruailous **[C4ᵛ]** furie, who notwithstanding helde out couragiouslye: and one thing comforted him aboue all other, which was, that none of his aduersaries blowes gaue him any bleeding wounde, but brused his fleshe a little vnder his Armour, whereby he fought at his owne pleasure. Three times the Dwarffe blew to animate his Champion,

[a] and not] *om.* P3

[b] answerable force] force answerable P2, P3

[c] auncestours] P2; anncestours P1

[d] conceits] and such like conceits P2, P3

[e] as] that P2, P3

[f] flewe foorth] flashed out P2, P3

[g] thereat] hereat P2, P3

by which meanes *Belcar* was ouer much laboured,[a] because hee could finde no opportunitie to rest himselfe: but considering if hee shewed lesse valoure then hee had doone, in vaine he might account his trauayling thether, and greatly would it redound to his shame, if the Emperour should be aduertised thereof. In the end, he had brought his enemy into such a state, as he got on the Brydge without any more resistance, and came to the Towre that stoode in the middest thereof, but the Gates closed together so furiously, as[b] hee was smitten to the earth depryued of his sences. *Lypes* being glad that he had recouered the Brydge, came to him, and wyth the helpe of the Squires caryed him into the Tent, where suddainly vnarming him, they applyed such remedyes as brought him to his former sences. He had no sooner feeling of himselfe, but he entred into many rufull lamentations, as well for his misfortune and dysgrace, as also wyth the payne hee felt of his aduersaries strokes, whereof his Armour beeing battered to peeces was a sufficient wytnesse.[96] Comfort your selfe my Lorde (quoth *Lypes*) and let your wonted courage exile this anguish, remembring that these eyght yeeres no Knight came to the Isle, onely *Lynedes* excepted, that wunne like honor as you haue doone at this instant: greater reason haue yee then to cherish your fortune, then thus to condemne it with acclamations.[c] Ah my freend, answered *Belcar*, little pleasure take I in this successe, for that my intent proceeded further, but seeing there is no remedy, I must with patience beare my shame. For of matters so deuillishly enchaunted, can seldom arise greater good: but cursed be the Fairies and their hellish charmes that deale so discourteously with poore trauailing Knights.

[a] ouer much laboured] much overlaboured P2, P3

[b] as] that P2, P3

[c] acclamations.] exclamations. P2, P3

[D1r] CHAPTER IIII.

Howe Belcar *concluded to combat with all such as came to prooue the aduenture of* Francelina*: and howe (among other) he fought with the Marquesse of Trosse, whom he vanquished, and afterward with* Tirendos*, to whom he made himselfe knowne.*

Belcar beeing indifferently calmed by the courteous behauiour of *Lypes*, determined to recouer his passed[a] foyle by actions of Chiualrie, and therefore resolued to continue in that place, to combat with al such as came to trie the aduenture:[97] but to his intent hee added this principally, that what deeds of Armes be there performed, or in anie other place where he might be imployed, all should be for the loue of *Alderina*, Daughter to the Duke of *Pontus*, whom aboue all other he meant most constantly to loue. And if his fortune were to be vanquished by anie Knight, he woulde then forthwith returne to the Court of the King *Florendos*. This disseigne he discouered to *Lypes*, who was not a little glad therof, saying, that he should apprehend great matters by his enterprise,[98] because continually many good Knights resorted thither. And because (quoth hee) you are so resolutlie minded, nothing shal make mee to forsake your company: but to behold the knightly Chiualrie, which I am out of doubt to see executed by you. I offer my selfe to accompanie you in al loyall seruice. Nowe the better to furnish their wants, hee sent to his Mothers house for all kind of prouision, that might agree with the time of their abode there. By this time [D1v] *Belcar* founde himselfe able to beare Armes, and therfore went to take his place of charge, at what time the Marquesse of *Trosse*[99] came to hazarde his fortune. This Marquesse was a braue and hardie man at Armes, and although he came from his Countrey wel accompanied with Knights, Squires and Pages: yet caused hee them to stay a pretie distaunce from this[b] place, and came thether but wyth one Squire that caried his Launce. When *Belcar* sawe him make so couragiouslie toward the Bridge, he mounted on horsebacke, and comming to him, thus spake.

[a] passed] forepassed P3

[b] this] that P2, P3

Gentleman, you may not passe heere, except you first trie the Iouste with mee, because I haue established heere such a Lawe, as[a] no Knight shall haue battaile with him that kept the Bridge, vntil hee haue first dismounted me: for hauing receiued some foyle in this place, not manie daies since, I wil not suffer anie one to preuaile in this aduenture, vnlesse hee bring me first into subiection. Great boldnes is this in you (aunswered the Marquesse) that you will take in hande to beare a burthen of such waight: but I thinke you doo it to this ende, that you would depart hence with greater shame and confusion, then euer you sustained heeretofore. That quarrell (quoth Belcar) shall our Swordes soone discide, and so without any more speeches they fell to the Combat, wherein the Marquesse shewed verie knightlie and gallant behauiour,[100] albeit *Belcar* cast him from his Saddle, and afterwarde fought with him on foote a long while: but in the end the Marquesse was vanquished, and vnderstanding the name of his Conquerour,[101] returned to the place where hee left his companie, and after he had recouered better health, he rode[b] straite to *Macedon*, where he recounted his ouerthrowe by *Belcar*.[102] Of these[c] newes the King *Florendos* and the Queene were verie ioyfull, saying they had a Nephew that was so named, wherefore they desired to knowe what Armes hee wore? when the Marquesse tolde them hee was in Greene Armour. Without question[103] (quoth the King) it was the same **[D2r]** Knight that wunne the honour of the Tourney, and went hence secretlie least he shoulde bee knowne,[104] wherewith I cannot be iustlie offended, because bothe in this enterprise and knightlie valour, he resembleth his woorthy[105] Father King *Frysoll*.

Eache one in Court was well pleased with these tydings, but aboue all other the Princesse *Alderina*, because she had bequeathed his remembraunce to the secrete closet of her hart,[106] and as the daies, so her louelie affections to him increased, in respect of the great praises was euerie where bruted of him, which made manie woorthy Knights to aduenture their fortune with him, with whose conquest hee still gaue grace to his owne report. But let vs now return to the Damosell that followed *Belcar*, to bee reuenged for her Bretherens death, shee seeing *Cardino* was indifferentlie recouered, tooke her leaue of him,[107] because shee intended to prosecute her enemie. It so fell out, that *Tirendos*, Sonne to the Duke *Eustace*, who

[a] as] as that P2, P3

[b] rode] then rode P3

[c] these] this P2, P3

trauailed to finde his companion *Belcar*, arriued at the same lodging where the Damosell was, and noting her complaints, which shee could deliuer verie artificiallie: he tooke compassion on her, promising to assist her in what he could. Demaunding the cause of her sorrowfull lamentations, she tolde him, howe she had two Bretheren trayterously slayne, by a disloyall Knight whom her Father entertained into his Castell, and she pursuing the murtherer, met a courteous Knight that vndertooke to reuenge her cause: yet his misfortune was such, as hee was likewise daungerously wounded, which made her greefes the more impatient.[108] These flattering gloses[a] so beguiled *Tirendos*, as hee againe made her promise of his ayde, enquiring of her where the wounded Knight was?[109]

My Lord (quoth she) he is heere in his Chamber, meetelie well recouered by my pains and dilligence. No sooner was Tirendos entred the Chamber, but hee immediatlie knew Cardino, for whose hurt he was a great deale more **[D2ᵛ]** sorrowfull: and therefore vowed to him and the Damosell, if euer he met the Knight to bee reuenged on him.[110] After many courteous embracings and kind speeches, he told *Cardino*, how *Belcar* and hee were bothe Knighted in one daie, by the Emperour of *Constantinople*, from whence hee very suddainlie and secretlie departed:[111] and euer since haue I followed in searche of him, yet in no place can I heare anie tydings of him. What Armes dooth hee beare? saide *Cardino*. White, as I take it, aunswered *Tirendos*, and such as are bothe rich and costlie.[112] No such Knight haue I seene, (quoth *Cardino*) happilie he may be now at *Macedon*, at the magnificent nuptialles of the Princesse *Denisa*.

Thether would I goe, sayd *Tirendos*, had I not past my promise to this Damosell: nor can my minde enioye anie quiet, vntill I haue found the Knight that so wronged her and you. All this night they were merie[b] together, especiallie the Damosell for *Tirendos* his promise, because hee seemed a man of sufficient valour to accomplish her desire. On the morrow they tooke their leaue of *Cardino*, and iournied toward the Isle of *Carderia*, where they arriued as *Belcar* was managing his great Horse: and no sooner had the Damosell espied him, but she presentlie knew him by his Armour, wherefore dissembling pittifull lookes, shee thus spake to *Tirendos*. Beholde Sir the Traytour that did[c] my Bretheren to death, I

[a] gloses] griefs P2, P3

[b] merie] very merry P2, P3

[c] did] did put P2, P3

thinke the heauens[113] stayed him in this place, that vengeaunce might be taken on him for the shame he hath doone me.[a] *Tirendos* was not a little glad heereof, because he should nowe make the first tryall of his Chiualrie. But *Belcar* (who knewe him by his Armour, beeing the same wherein he receiued his order) was scant well pleased with his presence, because hee doubted that he was sent to finde him: notwithstanding, he would make a little proofe of him in the Ioust, and therefore hee came to him with these words. You may passe no further this way Sir Knight, because I stand here to make denial **[D3r]** thereof. Little count shall I make aunswered *Tirendos* of such as thou art, that trayterously murderest Gentlemen, who gaue thee welcome beyond thy deserte, which I wyll cause thee buy full deerelie. That would I faine see, sayde *Belcar*, if it be in thee to make mee confesse that which I neuer thought, much lesse committed. Thou liest as a homicide, answered *Tirendos*, I wil make good what I haue sayd, therefore get ye to your tooles. Heerewith they gaue the spurres to their Horsses, and met very valiantly together, so that with breaking their Launces, they gaue each other a little wounde, *Belcar* loosing his stirrops, and *Tirendos* cast foorth of his saddle to the ground: but recouering himselfe presentlie, he came against his enemie with his Sword drawne, saying. Alight Sir you were best, or I shall slay your Horse.

That will I gladlie doo (quoth *Belcar*) but it shall bee to embrace ye, for I haue no will to enter Combatte wyth ye. Alas Sir, said *Tirendos*, it is no time now to scoffe, albeit I am from my Horse, I am not vanquished. Great pleasure tooke *Belcar* to reason with his singuler good freend, and alighting from his Horse, thus replied. I speake for your good (Sir) if you can see it: but seeing reason wil not rule you, I am content to deale with you a little. *Tirendos* somewhat offended at his fall, beganne to strike at *Belcar* very roughlie: but he who was lothe to wrong his freend, threw his Sword and Shield to the grounde, and with open Armes came to embrace him, saying. My perfect freend *Tirendos*, I haue heeretofore had experience of thy valiant behauiour, wherefore forgiue thy Brother *Belcar*, for not acquainting thee with my departure from *Constantinople*, yet was I assured that thou wouldest follow in searche of me.[114]

Howe nowe? Quoth *Tirendos*, are you then my Lord and louing Freende[115] *Belcar*? in sooth the errour committed, was only ignoraunce of you: put off your Helmet that I may be resolued, for your disguised

[a] me.] *om.* P3

Armour made mee **[D3v]** mistake ye.[116] So casting downe their Helmets, they embraced eache other verie courteously, when *Tirendos* thus spake to *Belcar*. Hardlie can I be perswaded my Lorde, that you would consent to such treason as this Damosell hath enformed me withal. Declare I pray you (quoth *Belcar*) whence aryseth this slander, for an other Knight (who I thinke I haue slayne or sore wounded) pursued mee wyth the like quarrell: doubtlesse this Damosell is some badde Woman, to accuse me with anie such disloyaltie. She told me, sayde *Tirendos*, that you beeing honourably entertayned at her Fathers Castell, where one night you were verie freendlie lodged: on the morrow her three Bretheren bare you company on the waie, and two of them without any cause you murdered,[a] leauing the thirde in verie great daunger.

Ah trayterous Damosell, aunswered *Belcar*, what an euident slaunder hath she raysed on me? and herewith hee rehearsed the whole discourse, according as you haue read it in the first Chapter of this Booke.[117] Shee seeing the two Knights agree thus freendlie, with the teares in her eyes gaue forth these speeches. Miserable and vnfortunate that I am, what a subtill collusion doo I heare? this Knight is as false and disloyall to me in not reuenging my shame, as the murderer that hath so highly wronged me: but seeing I am thus circumuented, and hee a periured wretche by breache of his promise, vnlesse I speedily die, I will cause him to repent it, and bee sufficiently reuenged on them bothe.

So galloped she the same waie shee came, and *Belcar* with *Tirendos* went into the Tent, where they discoursed together on many matters: *Tirendos* declaring howe *Cardino* was the other Knight that fought in the Damosels cause, for which the Prince was greatly offended with himselfe,[118] and to weare away that conceit, acquainted *Tirendos* with his fortune at the Castell, and of the taske he had taken in hande, which he liked so well, as he concluded **[D4r]** likewise to beare him companie. Thus *Lypes* and they two remained there together, oftentimes resorting to visite his mother and Sisters, who would not suffer them to want any thing: and such was the fame of *Belcars* victories, as the whole Realme of *Macedon* and the Emperors Court of *Greece*, was cloyed with the dailie reports thereof. But heere will we leaue these Champions awhile, and speake of the good Knight *Palmendos*, Sonne to the Emperour *Palmerin*, and the Queene of *Tharsus*.

[a] murdered] did murther P2, P3

[D4r] CHAPTER V.

How Palmendos *vnderstanding that he was Sonne to the Emperour* Palmerin, *caused himselfe to be armed Knight. And how he intreated licence of the Queene his Mother to goe see* Constantinople, *which at length verie hardlie he obtayned and what happened thereon.*

Carefully did the Queene of *Tharsus*[119] nourish her younge Sonne *Palmendos,* whom shee had by the Emperour *Palmerin,* when he folowed the exercise of Armes and was entertained by the Admiral *Alfarano*[120] in the Realme of *Pasmeria,*[121] as you may reade in his worthy[122] History.[123] This Childe, as he grewe in yeeres, so did he increase in all vertuous behauiour, beeing vnable to shadowe his royall discent: yet to hinder his desyre from searche after his Father, (the Queene and all the Nobilitie[124] so intirely affecting him) no knowledge might bee giuen him thereof, least by that meane he should become a Christian. And that he might be instructed in those heroycall quallities, which beseeme a Prince of so high calling, [D4v] the Queene committed him to the charge of the Brother to the deceased King her husband: a Knight of great wisdome and valour, by whom hee was so worthilie educated, as he wunne the loue of euery one in generall.[a][125] Rigour he would requite with mercie and clemencie, and charitie he preferred in[b] all his actions: notwithstanding, as he shewed courteous and benigne countenaunce towards the good, so did he sternelie and seuerelie oppose himselfe against the badde, so that by his exquisite prudence and choyse care in honourable causes, in his youth hee woulde learne to manage the affayres of the Realme, wherein he shewed himselfe so quick of spirite and susceptible, as he wered to bee such a pollitique oeconomie, that the Queene intended to put the royall Gouernment into his handes. If hee were thus enriched with all perfect vertues, nothing wanting in him for braue constitution of bodie, whereof he made no shewe of pryde or presumption: but became so famous through all the neyghbour Marches and limitrophes of *Tharsus,* as the very best woulde come to offer him theyr seruice.[126]

The Courte was filled with resort of Nobles and others, for beside the royall nature hee brought from his Mothers wombe, according to

[a] in generall.] P2; ingenerall. P1

[b] preferred in] P2; preferred P1; preferred to P3

the Idea and celestial influence of his constellation, hee was borne and naturally inclined to Armes, which made him euermore conuersse with the most skilfull that way addicted.[a][127] But one day before he was armed Knight, a very aged, decrepite and ouer-spent woman, came and sate down on a steppe in the Porche of the Pallace, attyred in such poore Garments, as her naked fleshe was seene in manie places: and there sate she trembling in such sorte, as though her soule were ready to forsake her bodie. Such as passed in and out the Court, were greatly amazed heereat, and mooued to pittie her case very much, so that *Palmendos* came himselfe to behold her: and seeing she would vse no speeches to him, went in againe and sate downe to Dinner. Afterwarde, comming foorth to walke **[E1ʳ]** abrode for his delight, he found her sitting there stil in the same place, wherefore hee called his Cozin *Ozalio* to him, who was Sonne to his Vnckle and Tutour, saying. Can we not vnderstand what this poore olde Woman woulde have? *Ozalio* as desirous as the Prince, came to the olde Woman, demaunding of whence she was, and if she stood in neede of anie thing? but shee without aunswering one worde, gaue him a verie frowning countenaunce, and afterward scornefullie turned her back towards him, wherewith *Ozalio* somewhat offended, gaue[b] her such a spurne with his foote, as she tombled quite beside her seate, wherat *Palmendos* and his Lordes merilie laughed:[128] but theyr pastime was soone[c] altered into admiration, for after the Woman arose againe, shee seemed of such huge deformed stature, as eache one was amazed that had beheld her before, and turning her selfe angerlie towardes the Prince, vsed[d] these speeches.

Ah *Palmendos*, little regardest thou to resemble the Emperour of *Constantinople* thy Father, whose gentlenes and sweetnes stretcheth as wel to the meanest persons, as them that are Lordes and of great account. What gainest thou in reioycing at the iniurie doone mee by thy Knight? I pray that the great imperious[129] Monarch *Cupid*, (quoth shee with lifting her eyes and handes to heauen)[130] may so cruellie wound thy hart with the looue of faire *Francelina*, and cause thee to conceiue such gracious thoughtes of her: as thou maist leaue this idle and delicious life thou leadest, to winne the honour that is got with paine and trauaile.[131] So did

[a] that way addicted.] in that science. P2, P3

[b] gaue] did give P2, P3

[c] soone] quickly P2, P3

[d] vsed] she used P2, P3

thy Father heeretofore for the Princesse *Polynarda*,[132] whom he loued so religiously, as with the dexteritie and strength of his bodie, he assaied to gaine the reward which Fortune prouideth for her cheefest fauourites:[133] whereon imperially he is now amounted, accompanied with the greatest felicitie, that can happen to anie one vnder this Hemisphere. Leaue then these wanton and Courtlie surfettings, wherein thy Mother laboureth to containe thee, and **[E1ᵛ]** nowe beginne to manage Armes, which may make thy name perpetuall, and yeelde the rewarde of immortal glorie: for it will redound to thy great shame, beeing Sonne to so rare and inuincible a Knight, not this way to imitate his laborious deedes.[134] And when I shall see thee thorowlie wrapped in the passions of loue, I will thinke myselfe satisfied with reuenge of the dishonour, which thou hast suffered to be donne to me in thy presence.

The olde Woman so breaking off,[135] immediatly vanished away, to the great terrour of all the beholders, especiallie of the young Prince *Palmendos*, whose sences were for a while estraunged, and walking vppe and downe musing on the olde Womans wordes, his hart was so enflamed with the loue of her he knew not, as he was enforced thus to commune with himselfe. What may the Ladie be, with whom (at the report of this Woman) I find my selfe so distraughted?[136] Doubtles if her words be no Fables, but that I am Sonne to the Emperour of *Constantinople*, it behooueth me to enterprise such actions, as I may be iudged somewhat to resemble him. While his spirit was thus busied with diuersitie of these thoughts, and no one daring to interrupt him: *Ozalio* went into the Queenes Chamber, and telling what had happened, she was therewith greatlie displeased.

Immediatlie she came downe into the great Hall, and finding her Sonne thus perplexed, tooke him by the hand, causing him to sitte downe by her, and then began to him in this manner. I knowe not my Sonne what follies (it should seeme) the olde Hagge hath troubled your minde withall: but refraine from giuing credite to them, and I shall tell yee the verie trueth of all. Madame aunswered *Palmendos*, I am certaine you will not dallie with mee, notwithstanding, I cannot but meruaile, that you woulde all this while conceale the originall of my byrthe: for the Emperour *Palmerin* beeing such a woorthy accomplyshed Knight, as he is esteemed of euerie one, little occasion haue **[E2ʳ]** I of disdaine to be his Sonne, and you much lesse to keepe it from me. Wherfore I humblie intreate your Maiestie, to resolue me faithfullie of this present doubt, to the end, if it be so: I may shewe my selfe forwarde in duetie, in causing the bud to floorish, that came from such a noble and vertuous stalke. And feare not that for his sake[137] I will abandon you: because it is impossible for me to leaue the Law wherin I haue hetherto liued, for a strange opinion which I am ignoraunt in.[138]

Ah my Sonne (quoth the Queene) the Gods so inspire and direct your desseignes, that you may perfectlie accomplish what you haue promised: for the onely feare to loose your companie, hath caused me conceale the thing you are so desirous to know. But seeing you haue hearde what I can no longer dissemble: assure your selfe my Sonne, that the olde Woman hath tolde nothing but trueth. Heereupon she recounted the whole Historie, howe to haue issue by such a peerelesse Prince (imitating *Thalestria*, Queene of the *Amazons*, who for like[a] cause acquainted her selfe with the valiant King *Alexander*)[139] she by the counsell of a wise Magitian, amourously beguiled the Emperour *Palmerin*. Lastlie, shee intreated him not to forsake her while she liued, because her life was onelie prolonged by his presence.

Great matters haue you tolde me, answered the young Prince: the Emperour then knowes not that hee hath anie Childe by you? No verilie, replied the Queene, nor would I he should know[b] for the whole world. Nor can hee (I thinke) vnderstand it by anie, said the Prince, yet (in mine opinion) I count it necessarie, that one day I should goe see my Father: but trust me Madame, it shall not bee without speedie returne, because I am determined not to leaue you, or giue ouer (with my will) the Countrey and Kingdome which the heauens[140] haue appointed me to rule and gouerne. Thus reasoned the Mother and her Sonne on diuers matters, and hencefoorth the Prince shewed **[E2v]** himselfe more cheerefullie disposed, intending very shortlie to be armed Knight, and to be called the Knight of *Cupid*, bearing for his deuise an hart wounded with an Arrowe.[141] For himselfe hee prouided an Armour as redde as bloode, and for *Ozalio*, whom hee loued as his Brother, a faire white Armour, and were bothe knighted by Ozalio his Father, who was one of the best Knights in all those parts.

Hauing thus receiued their order, a very sollemne feast was made in honour thereof, during which time, *Palmendos* gaue away sundry sumptuous gifts: yet coulde he not be vnmindfull of *Francelina*, or forget one iote of the olde Womans words, because he had lodged them so neere his hart, as they were a martirdome (in manner)[c] to him. For ease whereof

[a] like] the like P2, P3

[b] know] know it P2, P3

[c] a martirdome (in manner)] (in manner) a martyrdom P2, P3

he minded[a] to goe see[b] *Greece*, as also to visite the Emperour his Father, and learne some tydings of his vnknowne Ladie: for he perswaded himselfe, that the old Womans speeches grew vpon no small occasion. And finding the Queene his Mother one afternoone at good leysure, among diuers other proceedings betweene them, *Palmendos* earnestlie entreated her to graunt him one request: which the Queene (who looued him as her proper life, and not thinking he wold haue desired any such thing) agreed vnto verie willinglie. Then woulde I good Madame (quoth he) not haue you conceiue[c] anie displeasure, if I make a breefe voyage to *Constantinople*, to see the Emperour my Father, and the good Knights in his Courte: for since the time you assured mee that I was his Sonne, my desires haue beene vnmeasurable to trauaile this iourney. Yet I sweare, by the sincere and inuiolable faith, which the Child aboue all other oweth to his Mother, to returne againe with all possible speede. Alas my Sonne (quoth the Queene) giuing a bitter sighe, your words haue so sharplie pierced my hart, as me thinkes I feele my very thred of life cut in sunder, the feare of this present extreamitie, with-held me from vttering mine owne ruine: but seeing **[E3r]** I cannot hinder what I haue willingly[d] consented to, with what patience I can I will beare my misfortune. One thing yet woulde I commend to thee, if zeale and looue to thy Mother may sollicite anie compassion: that thou wouldest return to the place of thy birth so[e] soone as thou canst, that mine eyes beholding thee once more before I die, my soule may passe with greater comfort into another world. So helpe me God, answered *Palmendos*, as I intende not to breake the least of your commaundements, nor will I deceiue you in my short and speedie returne. Sith then my Sonne, quoth the Queene, you will needes vndertake this voyage, I would aduise ye to haue good store of hardie Knights with you, that your entertainment by the Emperour may be the more honourable. Madame, (quoth he) I am certaine my Lorde will not esteeme any thing the more of me for my companie, because it shall suffise that I am King of *Tharsus*,

[a] minded] determined P2, P3

[b] to goe see] to see P2, P3

[c] not haue you conceiue] not conceive P3

[d] willingly] *om.* P3

[e] so] as P2, P3

wherein consisteth the poynt of my renowne: as for any[a] paine of[b] trauaile, some report of good successe in Chiualrie shal wipe that away. For (as you are not ignorant therof) his Maiestie trauailed alone through the world, opposing his vnconquerable mind against al aduentures whatsoeuer:[142] yet did the diuine bountie euermore sheeld him from perill and death, and as he, so manie other famous Kings and Potentates.[143] What emprise[c] was more dangerous then that of *Iason*, when he won the Golden fleece in the Isle of *Cholcos*?[144] or that of the gentle Champion *Theseus*, when he conquered the Minotaure in the inextricable Labirinth of *Creete*?[145] yet the Gods defended them in all their attempts. In my time (Mother) I haue seene, that poore and simple Ships haue sailed in the Sea, with great fortune in tempests and outrage, and at length haue returned home richlie furnished: on the contrary I haue noted, that sundry gallant vessels, haue cut with full sayle through calme and quiet Seas, fauoured both with winde and wether, and at the verie entraunce of the Hauens mouth, haue splyt on some Rocke, or sustayned other mischaunce.[146] **[E3v]** Needles then were my feare of the Sea or Fortune, because (where ere I goe) Death tracks mee, as my shadowe, and dare not strike till he be commaunded:[147] therfore I am thus determined, to haue none with me but *Ozalio* and two Squires, because we wil trauaile as meane Gentlemen, and try our manhoode with the Knights of *Europe*, before the Emperour shall haue anie knowledge of me.

The Queene would no more contrarie his intent, but referred all things to his owne disposing, wherefore *Palmendos* hauing sent for the cheefe Lordes of the Realme, declared to them openlie his minde: giuing them this expresse charge, to obey the Queene his Mother, and his Unckle, whom he left as Lieutenaunt generall of the Prouince in his absence. They all sorie that hee woulde so soone depart, knewe not howe to hinder it hee beeing so resolute: notwithstanding, they promised to fulfill his commaunde, wyshing him a tranquile and prosperous nauigation. Soone after the Queene went into her Cabinet, where her hand discharging[d] the office of the[e] tongue, shee wrote a freendlie Letter to the Emperour, which shee

[a] any] my P2, P3

[b] of] in P2, P3

[c] emprise] enterprise P2, P3

[d] discharging] supplying P2, P3

[e] the] her P2, P3

accompanied wyth a Ring, like to that she gaue him at his departure: to the ende that by this Iewell, *Palmendos* might be the sooner known of him.

Shippe and all thinges readie for this voyage, hee tooke his leaue of his Lordes and Subiects, and afterward of the Queene his Mother: who byting in her greefe so well as she could, deliuered him the Ring and the Letter, the contents whereof thus followeth.[148]

[E4r] *The Letter of the Queene of Tharsus, to the Emperour Palmerin*

To the most illustrious and famous *Palmerin d'Oliua*, Emperour of Constantinople, the most loyall of Louers, most accomplished of Knights, and aboue all the Princes that inhabit the center of the earth: the Queene of Tharsus his intire and perpetuall freend, sendeth health, humblie kissing the hand of his Maiestie.

If the Heauens had so bountifully bestowed those perfections on mee in my cradle, which the most accomplished Ladies make their vaunt of, as Fortune was afterward fauourable and courteous vnto me, in adorning my head with the royall Diademe of *Tharsus*: needeles had my recourse beene to Charmes or Magick (O fauoured and fortunate Prince) when I sought your acquaintance in the Realme of *Pasmeria*. But sith by that small talent wherewith nature endowed me, the Destinies graunted mee the sweete aspect of your loue, after I behelde you with our Admirall *Alfarano*: my pristinate[a] vertue could not preuaile against vnquenchable desire, because the fame of your renowne was so caractred in my spirit, as my former chaste and bashfull continencie, was in the ende irrecuperably contaminate. Yet can I not repute this chaunce as matter of misfortune, seeing the heauenly powers were so benigne, as from that acte proceeded *Palmendos* our onelie Sonne:[149] from whom I still hidde that you were his Father, albeit by straunge meanes he was not long since aduertised therof, from which time hee hath so preuailed by intreaties, as he hath constrained me (not without great greefe, and doubtfull feare neuer to see him againe) to suffer him come see **[E4v]** his noble Father. And hardlie could I yeelde thereto, but that my confidence in you is such: as you will quickly returne him againe, so soone as you haue seene and knowne him for your Sonne.

[a] pristinate] pristine P2, P3

At this accident I hope you will not be offended, when you consider the world enioyes a young Prince: whose vertuous quallities and good cariage of himselfe, presage his future commendable fortune. In this sort haue I sent him, accompanied onelie with his Cozin, because hee thus perswaded me: that when you trauailed the worlde, it was commonly alone, and as a simple Knight errant. And least you should be scrupulous in acknowledging him your Sonne, beside the coniectures of his phisnomie, proportion of bodie, and other your perfect resemblaunces: I haue by him sent you a Ring, like that which I gaue you when you parted from mee, which Ringes if you compare together, you will remember the wordes I spake wanted no relation.[150] Once more I coniure ye, by the honour and reuerence of the firme looue,[151] you alwaies bare so religiously to the onely Mistresse of your hart: that you will quicklie returne our Sonne againe, that hee may yet be some comfort to my following date of time, while I enioy my beeing in this nether Region.[152]

The most humble of your freendes,
the Queene of *Tharsus.*

[F1r] CHAPTER VI.

Howe Palmendos *by meanes of a tempest on the sea, was brought to the Isle of* Delphos, *where after hee vnderstood the aduenture of the Temple, he went on shore. And howe he afterward*[a] *conquered the Sonne to the Gyant Baledon, who helde the Islande in forcible subiection.*

Palmendos with *Ozalio* and their Squires embarqued, the Marriners hoysed saile and sette awaie merilie, the Prince commaunding the Pilotte to make towards *Thrace,* because he hoped to heare some tidings there[b] of *Francelina,* whom he had made cheefe Mistresse of his affections. But after they had sayled halfe a daie, a violent contrarie winde arose, which droue them three daies and three nights so furiously,[c] as the Marriners coulde scant tell in what part they were. At length this rough

[a] he afterward] after he P2, P3

[b] there] *om.* P2, P3

[c] so furiously] *om.* P2, P3

and boysterous tempest ceased, when *Palmendos* beeing[a] desirous to know in what Country they were: was aunswered by the Maister that they were in *Europe* and[b] the *Mediterranian* Sea, verie neere to the Isle of *Delphos*,[153] where after so long and vncomfortable wether, *Palmendos* wold goe on land to refresh himselfe. In this Isle the Pagans were often wont in ancient time, to come and visite the temple of *Apollo*, as[c] also to consult with his Oracle,[154] and at this time was Lord therof a Gyant named *Baledon*, the most fierce and cruell Tirant, that liued[d] in all those three parts of the world.[155] This Gyant had a Son no lesse valiant then himselfe, and after hee had by force **[F1ᵛ]** gotten this Island,[156] hee builded a strong[e] Castell on a little Promontorie: discending so artificiallie into the Sea, as hauing a huge Rocke on either side thereof,[f] it was wel defended from the extremitie of the water. No other Porte for landing woulde he permitte in all the Island, then this onelie, hemde in with the two Rocks, betweene which hee had fastened a great chaine of yron, which commonlie laye somewhat shallowe in the water. But when anie Vessell came to anker in that Porte, certaine villaines[157] which hee kept in Towres for the purpose, woulde hoyse them vppe with the chaine in such sort, that they could depart no more thence except the Gyant pleased: and thus woulde he rob and spoile all that landed there, that al those parts lamented to heare of his villanie.[158] If happilie hee mette with any Knights who resisted his will, then woulde he outrage them by force of Armes, and afterward put them into an infectious stincking Pryson. The Merchaunts and others that vsed traffique, from them would he take all they had, and afterward deliuer them ouer to[g] a most cruell death, so that all such as had notice of his tyrannie, fled that place as the daungerous Gulfe of *Caribdis*.[159]

Yet not withstanding, there was in this Island a great aduenture, for in the time of the Gentiles, there inhabited a welthy Prieste, a Magitian and wonderfull inuestigatour of hidden thinges, hee was high Priest of the Sanctuarie in the Temple, as also he had the generall administration

[a] beeing] *om.* P2, P3
[b] and] in P2, P3
[c] as] and P3
[d] that liued] *om.* P2, P3
[e] strong] *om.* P3
[f] thereof] *om.* P2, P3
[g] ouer to] unto P2, P3

through the whole Prouince:[160] he hauing a comlie beautiful Daughter, endued with al vertues requisite in a Virgin, and her he gaue to the seruice of the Oracle. It so fell out, that the Duke of *Feria*, a very gentle and gracious youth, became enamoured of her onely by report, for oftentimes he had hearde her commended, to exceede in beautie the choyset Dames of that Countrey: wherfore he made sundrie requests to enioy her as his Wife, but all his labour was to no purpose, because her father would not part with her.[161] And as it often happeneth, that the Messenger **[F2ʳ]** who is twyse or thryse sent to one place, to obtaine a matter earnestlie desired, will deuise what meanes hee can for the behoofe of his Maister, more to escape the shame of refusall, then for anie great good will (happilie) to the partie: euen so fell it out with the minister of this sute, for seeing hee went and returned so often without auaile, hee gotte one daie to speake with the Maiden herselfe, whome he laboured with so manie perswasions, and whetted on to ioyne[h] in a secrete marriage: as shee became rauished with the loue of the Duke, and promised if his Maister coulde cunningly steale her from her Father, she would[b] goe with him whether he pleased.[162]

The Duke not a little glad of this aunswer, presentlie iournied to the Island, where beeing arriued, hee aduertised the Damosell: that he would stay for her in a conuenient place neere her fathers Pallace, whether she should[c] not fayle to come, so soone as the silent night had brought euery one asleepe. But the Prieste, who by meanes of his Magick foresaw all these practices, and knowing the place where the Duke of *Feria* staied for his Daughter: caused two fierce enchaunted Lions[163] to discend from the Mountaines, which ranne[d] with rauenous mouthes on the vnprouided Duke, and he no way able to defende himselfe, they rent and tore him cruellie in peeces. Which pittifull spectacle when his Squire that came with him behelde, he gaue such a lamentable shrike, as the Damosell (whose eyes and eares were carefullie waking) easilie hearde it. In like sorte did diuers others of the house, who came foorth with lighted Torches to vnderstand the cause: but the Mayden hearing too soone in what case they founde the Duke, came running from the Castel as a mad Woman[164] to accomplish the Sacrifice. Such was her greefe to beholde her vowed Husband[165] thus

[h] ioyne] it P3

[b] would] should P2, P3

[c] should] would P3

[d] ranne] came P2, P3

cruellie massacred, as she taking his Rapier, sette the pommell thereof to the grounde, and placing the point opposite to her hart: with meruailous violence threwe herselfe thereon, as one disdaining to liue, beeing **[F2ᵛ]** robbed of her loue.[166] Neuerthelesse, she was heerein deceiued, for the Sword passing through her right side, shee fell vpon the dead corpes, and so lay awhile aliue, breathing foorth many greeuous sighes and lamentations. And finding in her bosome a sheete of paper, with her owne bloode shee wrote twelue mornefull verses in forme of an Epytaph:[167] then seeing her latest howre to hasten on, with rufull mones she deliuered these speeches. Seeing it is so, my sweete choyse and paragon of courtesie, that for my sake thou hast endured this martyrdome:[168] it will remaine as a gall in my conscience, that I did not ende thy funeralles according to thy desert. And that my Father may knowe what wrong he hath doone vs, I will leaue some occasion for his too late repentaunce: yet I desire no other recompence, but causing our bodies to bee[a] buried in one Coffin,[169] he will suffer (for a perpetuall remembrance of this stratageme) this Epitaphe to be engrauen thereon.

Forbeare mine eyes more to bemone thy freend,
Whose peereles vertues time nor death can staine:
Despise the man that thus procurde his ende,
And hath (withall) his onely daughter slaine.
Ah angrie fate, and planet most unkinde,
What more inhumaine act could ye deuise:
Then step betweene the hart, the eye and minde,
And pierce that vaine which could them all suffise?
But sith in life our fortune was so bad,
To misse of that which we desired most:
Yet nowe in death the same is freelie had,
Wherefore of loue in death we make our boast.[170]

This Epitaphe ended, shee yeelded the humaine tribute to nature, for afterward her bodie made no motion of vitall mouing: and it cannot be esteemed as fabulous that loue should cause the death of anie one, because in auncient Histories, we may finde innumerable of recent and moderne **[F3ʳ]** examples thereof.[171] But returne we to the Priest, who vnderstanding

[a] bee] *om.* P3

that his Daughter ranne foorth with such a clamour, followed her immediatlie, fearing she woulde offer some violence on herselfe, and finding her deade, holding the Epitaphe in her hand, he was in great daunger to make a third in this wofull tragedie.[172] Ah miserable and desolate wretch (quoth hee) if thy knowledge had efficacie in working the Duke of *Ferias* death, why was it not sufficient to preuent thy Daughters mishappe? Vnhappy was the houre when first I practised this deuillish sorcerie.

Many other sorrowful lamentations he made ouer the dead bodies, whom we may aptlie compare to the loyall Louers *Piramus* and *Thisbie*:[173] but afterward hee erected a costlie Sepulchre of Brasse, and hauing embalmed them according to the auncient ceremonies of funerall pompe, hee imtombed them in the Temple bothe together, and caused the Epytaphe to be cunningly grauen thereon. Not long after, considering himselfe depriued of his lawfull heyre, and howe greatly he had peruerted the course of nature, very extreame greefe ended his daies: but ere he died, hee enclosed the[a] Treasure of the Temple with such enchauntments, and with so strong and fearefull a guard, that from the time of his death, it was very dangerous to come neere the place. And tell the time of *Palmendos* arriuall there, there durst not anie one make tryall thereof, albeit before *Baledon* abused the Islande, Knights of diuers Regions came to prooue theyr fortune: and the Giant himselfe came thether for the same occasion, but seeing hee coulde not approche the Temple, perceiuing the Island to be faire and delectable: he got it by force of Armes, the people thereof beeing vnable[b] to resist his hostilitie.

Let vs nowe remember where we left before, the arriuall of *Palmendos* in this Islande of *Delphos*, to whome one of the Marriners told all these thinges, as also the horrible villanies[c] of the Gyant: wherefore he intreated him not to anker in that Porte, because (quoth he) we shal all **[F3v]** bee either slayne or taken prysoners. Why? sayd *Palmendos*, is no man able to punish his pryde and tyrannie? seeing Fortune hath conducted me hether, and will permitte me but[d] to haue a sight of him:[174] I will not departe without some proofe of my selfe. For if I bee Sonne to the Emperour *Palmerin*, I must not bee frighted with the name of Gyants, who rather

[a] the] *om.* P3

[b] vnable] unable any way P3

[c] villanies] villainy P2, P3

[d] but] *om.* P2, P3

resemble huge *Colosses* without anie soules,[175] then humaine creatures: much lesse strange aduentures, howe harde and daungerous soeuer they seeme. If I woulde acquire prayse and honour immortall, long time must I followe millitarie exercise, as my Father did in his yonger dayes, preuailing against diuers such Monsters, and bringing innumerable enterprises to happy ende:[176] turne prowe then towarde shore, and bodlie let vs enter the Porte, without anie feare[a] of this difformed *Golias*.[177] With much a doo they sette into the Porte, where they were no sooner entred, but they sawe themselues enclosed with the chayne, which sight dismayed bothe the Maister and Marriners: but *Palmendos* and *Ozalio* presently put on theyr Helmets and[b] Gauntlets, standing ready for defence of all the rest.

The Gyant beeing aduertised that a rich Ship was gotte within the chaine, commaunded his Sonne presentlie to take Armes, and with sufficient assistaunts to goe take[c] all the Strangers prysoners: wherto the young Tyrant was very readie, and entring with three Knights into a boate, came[d] directly to the Shippe, where *Palmendos* standing formost, the Gyants Sonne thus spake to him.[178] Howe darest thou Knight be so bold, as to enter our Porte without licence? I dare doo more then that, answered Palmendos, in despight of such disloyall villaines as you are, who by trecherous meanes intrap the innocent, and afterward exercise what crueltie you please vppon them: but nowe is the time come, I hope, that shal guerdon you with recompence aunswerable to such brutish behauiour. The Gyants Sonne dyspleased with these wordes, sought with **[F4[r]]** his Knights to enter violently the Ship: but *Palmendos* and *Ozalio* beeing to high aboue them, gaue them so many sharpe repulses, as[e] young *Baledon* receiued his deathes wounde at the Princes hande, and *Ozalio* sent one[f] of the Knights to beare him companie. With this foyle the boate speedilie returned, and they aduertised *Baledon* what[g] had happened, bringing his Sonne slaine vp into his Chamber, wherwith he was so wonderfully enraged: as[h] he vowed

[a] feare] *om.* P3

[b] and] and their P3

[c] goe take] go and take P2, P3

[d] came] he came P2, P3

[e] as] that P2, P3

[f] one] another P3

[g] what] of what P2, P3

[h] as] that P2, P3

to buy[a] his bloode with the death of all the strangers. In bitter anguish of hart, he called for his Armour, preparing himselfe to the dismall attempt: in meane while[b] the two Knights that escaped backe aliue, stoode on the shore reuiling the Prince, wylling[c] him to prepare, for his death was comming.

If your Maister (quoth *Palmendos*) bee so valiant as you reporte, let him deale alone with mee in single fyght, and if I chaunce to vanquishe him, let him accomplishe what I shall sette downe, and I will graunt him life. On the contrary, if hee conquer mee,[179] let him doo with mee and mine as him pleaseth:[d] tell him,[e] these[f] brauadoes and proude speeches cannot daunt resolute mindes, and if hee dare[g] graunt me safe conducte, with good assuraunce not to offer mee anie wrong,[h] I will presentlie come[i] on shore and try my fortune with him.[j]

[F4v] CHAPTER VII.

Howe Palmendos *came on lande to combat with the Gyant* Baledon, *whom he vanquished, and afterwarde deliuered many Knights out of his prysons, among whom were two young Princes, beeing Moores: who in trauailing to the Emperours Courte, were by a tempest cast on this Islande.*

Right[k] soone went the Knightes to the Gyant with *Palmendos* challenge, who beeing very[l] wel pleased therewith, came downe proudelie to the Port with these speeches. Which is the wretched

[a] buy] revenge P2, P3
[b] meane while] the mean time P2, P3
[c] Prince, wylling] Prince, with dreadfull and opprobious words, willing P3
[d] pleaseth:] best pleaseth. P3
[e] tell him] And tell him (from me) P3
[f] these] *om.* P2, P3
[g] dare] will dare P3
[h] to offer mee anie wrong,] to offer or doe me anie wrong by treachery, P3
[i] come] come to him P3
[j] with him.] with him in combate. P3
[k] Right] Very P3
[l] very] right P3

Knight, that dare so peremptorilie venture on shore, to receiue the death he hath iustly deserued? I am the man, aunswered *Palmendos*, and I will be so good as my worde, if thou wilt faithfully promise mee safetie from thy people. By the hallowed fayth, sayde *Baledon* that I owe to our Gods, thou shalt be as secure as thou canst require, albeit I die vnder thy Sworde in Combat. The Prince lothe to waste the time in wordes,[180] called for a Skiffe to carrie him on shore, which the Marriners vnwillinglie consented to, beeing loth to loose a Knight so valiant. In breefe, he came on lande, and no one with him but his Cozin *Ozalio*, who woulde not at anie time forsake his companie. *Baledon* praunceth vppe to the plaine before his Castell, commanding his attendants on paine of their liues, not any waie to trouble or molest his enemie. Now are the Champions couered with their Swords and Sheeldes, and with such furie doo the weapons clasche[a] vpon the Armour, as though **[G1r]** *Vulcan* and his *Cyclops* were at worke with their hammers.[181] You must thinke that the Gyant, beeing a man of monstrous stature, dealing with a young Prince, but a grystle (in a manner) in comparison of him, did often bring his life to very perrillous exigents: notwithstanding, so did the heauens fauour *Palmendos*, and despise the manifold tyrannies of the Gyant, as after a long, cruell and bloodie fight, *Baledon* had receiued so many woundes, as hee was constrained to fall at the Princes mercie:[182] for which *Palmendos* humblie thanking heauen,[183] boldlie sette hys foote vpon the Gyant, saying, Confesse thy selfe (*Baledon*) vanquished by me, and let mee enioy the prysoners which thou uniustlie detainest in thy Castell, for the remainder of thy life hangeth on the poynt of my Sword.

When the Gyant behelde his great pompe so ouerthrowne, and hee had no meane nowe left wherewith to defende himselfe: he breathed forth these sorrowfull speeches. Ah angry Gods, howe strange and diuers are your iudgments, in suffering bothe mee and my Sonne to bee foyled by one Knight?[184] Now see I well, that myne infinite and wicked offences, committed against men without desert, hath throwne this wreakefull sentence on me.[185] Then calling his Seruaunts, hee commaunded them to conduct the Prince into the Castell, and to[b] deliuer all his prysoners to him, with any thing els hee shoulde commaunde them.

[a] clasche] P2; clanche P1

[b] to] *om.* P2, P3

So went the Prince with his Cozin *Ozalio* and two of the Gyants Seruaunts to the Castell, the rest remayned to bring theyr Maisters deade bodie, and when they were entred[a] the base Courte, they met the Gyantesse heauilie lamenting, and curssing the Knight who was cause thereof. But *Palmendos* made no account of her wordes, commaunding all the prysoners to bee presently brought before him, which in sooth[b] were very many, both Knights, Merchaunts and other trauayling Strangers, who had long time beene kept there in captiuitie: and nowe seeing **[G1ᵛ]** they were so generallie called, they verilie thought to die, or endure some cruell torment, but finding the contrarie, I leaue their ioy to the Readers iudgment.[186] Then *Palmendos* called for the Knights Armour, that eache one knowing his owne Armour might bee armed therewith: for this their happie deliueraunce, they all fell downe at the Princes feete, desiring God to reward his honourable paynes.

But among the prisoners, there were two young Knights of comelie stature, beeing both Moores, who had not long time beene held in that seruitude, and witnessing by their countenaunces that they were discended of royal parentage. The one of them was *Rifarano*, Son to *Trineus* Emperor of *Allemaigne*, and *Aurecinda* the Soldans Sister, as you may reade in the History of *Palmerin d'Oliua*:[187] the other was named *Lecefin*, Son to the Soldane of *Persia*: beeing the youngest of three which he had by the Princess *Zephira*.[188] These two young Lords were nourished together by the Soldane, because hee behelde the towarde[c] inclination of *Rifarano*, whom hee euer imagined would prooue a worthie Knight: and for[d] he was Sonne to his Sister and the Emperour *Trineus* his great freende, he looued him as *Lecefin* his owne Childe. *Rifarano* comming to the age of tenne or twelue yeres, wered very forward in all commendable exercises, and one day reasoning with his Mother: desired her to tell him the cause, why she went so continually clad in mourning, the truth wherof she discoursed to him, and how his Father was the Emperour *Trineus* of *Allemaigne*. When *Rifarano* vnderstoode, that he was Sonne to one of the cheefest Princes in Christendome, hee made greater account of himselfe then he did before, and dysposed himselfe to matters of higher quallitie, so that beeing of

[a] entred] entred into P2, P3

[b] in sooth] indeed P2, P3

[c] towarde] towardly P2, P3

[d] for] because P2, P3

yeeres to receiue his Knighthoode,[189] he requested the Soldane to honour him therwith: which he with right good will performed, causing Ioustes and Tournaments to sollemnize that time withall, wherin **[G2r]** *Rifarano* still bare awaie the pryze. Following Armes and Chiualrie he still continued, and with good successe wunne such fame through all *Persia*, as the Soldane thought to ioyne him in marriage with the King *Maulerinos*[190] eldest Daughter.[191] But he would neuer harken to such matters, for that hee had secretlie vowed, first[a] to see the Emperour his Father, whereto his Mother (whose dayes long sicknes had new shortened) euermore prouoked him: that *Trineus* beholding the fruite of her loue, might thinke the better of his acquaintaunce with her.

After the obsequies and royall funerall, as wel beseemed a Princesse of so great regarde, and *Rifarano* lothe to stay, his Mother beeing dead: hee desired the Soldane that he might trauaile to *Constantinople*, to see the Courte of the Emperour *Palmerin*, and thence he woulde goe to his Father in *Allemaigne*. Albeit very vnwilling, yet the Soldane condiscended, whereat the young Prince *Lecefin*, who loued *Rifarano* as himselfe, beganne to conceiue great sorrowe: wherefore he intreated his Father that hee might trauaile with him in companie, perswading him that it would be a cause of his Cozins more speedie returne. The Soldane liked heereof very well, and although he was yet verie young, he gaue him his knighthoode: and so with diuers presents from his Father and *Zephira*, as also Letters to both the Emperours, accompanied with thirtie hardie Knights they tooke shypping,[192] and by meanes of an exceeding rough tempest on the Sea, they were driuen perforce into this Isle of *Delphos*, where beeing hemde in with the chayne, and flattered by the Gyant to come on the[b] shore, without suspecting anie treason they went to his Castell, and finding outward freendlie entertainement, they were fetched foorth of their beddes and thrust into pryson, and twentie of the Knights that came with them cruelly murthered, the rest were brought into the Dungion to their Maisters, and afterward the Gyant tooke the spoyle of the Ship at his pleasure.[193] **[G2v]**

But to come to our purpose, *Rifarano* and *Lecefin* seeing themselues deliuered from this dollorous life, much worse then that of the slaues in[c] the Gallies, they spake to *Palmendos* in this maner. Tel vs in courtesie,

[a] first] *om.* P2, P3

[b] the] *om.* P2, P3

[c] in] of P2, P3

good Knight, by what meanes haue you[a] obtained our libertie? for wee meruaile that[b] we see not the Gyant, who brought vs hether by villanie and treason. Gentlemen, (quoth the Prince) I am a Knight borne farre hence, and beeing by the angrie Seas cast vpon this Island, I determined to come on shore, where beeing no waie able to escape the death present before mine eyes, I was constrained to Combat with the Gyant you talke of, who to allure me the sooner to the battaile, promised me securitie from any saue himself. But heauen giuing me strength, to erect a mortall Trophe of his slaughtered bodie, hath thereby giuen you all freedome againe.

Might we not, said *Rifarano*, knowe your name, to whom wee are so much indebted for our deliueraunce? as for vs, it is necessarie you should knowe of whence and what we are, that if we should growe heereafter[c] ingratefull for this kindnes, the meanest in the worlde might iustlie condemne vs. This young Prince, (quoth hee) is named *Lecefin*, Sonne to the noble Soldane of *Persia*, and I his unworthie Nephew, issued from *Trineus* Emperour of *Allemaigne*, brother by mariage to the incomparable Prince *Palmerin d'Oliua*: heereto hee added the whole discourse of their trouble, which you haue heard alreadie.[194] In happie time came I hether, aunswered *Palmendos*, to succour so good and noble Knights as you are, cheefelie for your neere alliaunce to the Emperour *Palmerin*, whom I continuallie desire to serue, and shortly shall present myself vnto him: but first (by the fauour of Fortune,)[195] I woulde haue his eares so acquainted with some actions of account, as might mooue his spirite with the more affection to see me.[196] And seeing you goe so soone to his Courte, let me intreate this fauour at your handes, as to conducte this company **[G3r]** with you which I haue deliuered from prison, and present his Maiestie with them from me, as also the wife and daughter of *Baledon* the Gyant:[197] for it is both iust and reasonable, to dispossesse this Island of such bad people, as haue wyth such horrible tirannies so long time abused the same.[198] For I dare say, the people that inhabite this Isle, will more gladly submit themselues to the Emperours regiment, then be held in slauerie by such helhoundes.[199] In meane while, wee wyll leaue some good Knight of this soyle as gouernour thereof in his highnes name, vntil he haue disposed thereof as shal seeme best in his wisedom. Willingly wold I make proofe before your departure,

[a] haue you] you have P2, P3

[b] that] *om.* P2, P3

[c] growe heereafter] hereafter grow P2, P3

of a strange aduenture couched in the Temple: that if I die in the attempt, you may reuenge my death, and happily liue to finish the same. *Rifarano* and *Lecefin* made answere, that they would fulfil any thing he pleased to commaunde them, for which *Palmendos* requited them with many thanks.

[G3r] CHAPTER VIII.

How Palmendos *placed in the gouernment of the Isle of* Delphos, *an auncient wyse Knight named* Guillador, *by whom he vnderstood the daunger and*[a] *difficultie of the aduenture in the Temple, whether (notwithstanding) he afterward trauailed: and how he fortunatly ended the same.*

After all the Knights and Gentlemen had armed[b] themselues,[200] *Palmendos* caused the Gyantesse and her daughter,[201] to be fastened with a strong chaine to a piller, least they shoulde offer some violence on themselues,[202] and the chayne in the Port he commanded to be taken away, with all [G3v] other daungers that might hurt trauaillers: then sommoning the people of the Island, he thus beganne to conferre with them.

My Bretheren and Freendes, I cannot thinke but you all reioyce, to see your selues deliuered from the miserable seruitude, wherein the Tyrant *Baledon* hath long time held you, henceforth therefore I intend, that you shal acknowledge for your liege Lord and Soueraigne, the famous and vertuous Emperour *Palmerin d'Oliua*, to whome I will make present[c] of this Island, which the God of heauen hath suffered me to conquere:[203] for you knowe that[d] the Gyant is slaine, his Wife and Daughter[204] likewise remain my prisoners, and to his Maiesty wil I shortly send them. Let me therfore intreate ye, to continue his true and loyall Subiects, and I shall so behaue my selfe with his highnes, as he shall henceforth defend this Island and you: for the gouernment whereof in meane while, I will leaue one that shall bee chosen among you, who shall sweare to resigne his office, to him whom the Emperour shal please to send hether.

[a] and] and the P2, P3

[b] armed] P2; Armed P1

[c] present] President P3

[d] that] *om.* P2, P3

The Knights and Gentlemen of the Island were greatlie contented, hearing[a] *Palmendos* vse such gratious speeches,[205] acknowledging themselues happy to remaine the Emperours vassailes: whereupon they swore fidelity to him, and elected a reuerende Knight of the Island named *Guillador*, to whom the authoritie of Deputie was committed, and then they caused the Gyants bodie to bee burned, for the horrible villanies he had doone in his life time, to which execution all the people of the Island resorted, not so much for the sight thereof, as to honour the Patrone of their deliueraunce. Euery thing thus wisely and discreetlie pacified, he determined to try the aduenture of the Temple, whereupon the newe Gouernour desired him, not to hazard himselfe in a matter so perrillous, for that manie Knights had lost their liues in the attempt: which made *Palmendos* far more desirous, to know wherin the greatest **[G4ʳ]** danger thereof consisted, at whose request, *Guillador* thus beganne the discourse. Know my Lorde, that the Temple wherein our Priestes great Treasure is hidde, is a place now ouergrowne as a thicket of young Trees, by reason of the long time since anie one durst approche the same, and in that Woode is a sauage wilde Bore, of more cruell nature certaine, then that which *Hercules* slewe on the Mountaine *Erymanthus* in *Arcadia*.[206] And when anie one dooth offer to enter the Temple, he commeth forth of his denne, and makes him sure for euer returning againe.[207] In sooth, quoth the Prince, these newes are very terrible in hearing, yet neuer was there any aduenture in the world so difficult, but one or other hath accomplisht it, and I trusting onelie in the helpe of God, will try if this enchauntment were ordayned perpetuall, not fearing all the Bores or deuils in the world.

I am sure my Lorde, quoth *Rifarano*, that if you finish not this enchauntment, it will neuer be accomplished by anie other: therefore boldly sette vpon it, for gladly would I endure part of the paine, and by the faith of a true Knight, I shall assist ye with my vttermost endeuour. No other helpe doo I desire, answered *Palmendos*, then the fauour of the Gods onelie, and I hope they will not be farre from me, if so I stand in need thereof: notwithstanding, I humblie thanke yee for your good will, and if I happen to fayle in mine enterprise, you shall make no better witnesse of your wordes, then courteously to hazard the aduenture, to recouer the honour lost by me: for which cause, as also to beguile the tediousnes of trauaile, you shal accompany me to the Temple. So wylling the Merchaunts

[a] hearing] when they heard P2, P3

and other prisoners to stay in the Castell, *Palmendos, Ozalio, Rifarano, Lecefin*[208] and the rest of the Knights, beeing all wel armed, sette toward the Temple, many of the Islande trauailing with them, to guide them the way and doo other needefull seruices. Now had *Palmendos* caused to be made by meruailous subtill cunning, a coate of Armes, composed of **[G4v]** waxe and other like clammie myxtures, wherewith he couered all his Armour, that the sharpe brystles and tuskes of the Bore might haue no power to hurt him: and in this sorte they rode on together. Beeing at length come to a conuenient place, which was within sight of the Temple, he beheld the brushie thornie plaine, which made him doubt how he should gette thether with his Horse. Yet resolute for all chaunces,[209] he takes an yron Mace, that he hath[a] brought from the Gyants Castell, and forward goes to the Temple: desiring all his companions, that not one of them shoulde follow him: wherewith *Ozalio* and *Rifarano* were somewhat offended, yet lothe[b] to breake his commaundement, they stayed, vsing hartie and zealous inuocations for hys good successe.

Palmendos making way with his Mace through the enchaunted bryers, espied a Knight before him, who presently winded a mightie Horne, at the sounde whereof the ouglie and monstrous Bore came forth of his Denne, and ranne before the Temple Gate: there staying for *Palmendos* with such horrible grynning of his tuskes, as the very sight thereof was sufficient to fray a manne of good courage. By this time the Prince gained a conuenient place by the Temple side, when beholding the cruel beast come running fiercely towardes him, he commended himselfe to the heauens, and fell to his worke.[210] So thicke as hayle flewe the enchaunted bristles from the Bore at the Prince, but the coate of waxe so confounded their strength, as they could not pierce his Armour, which onely had been the death of many Knights before: But the Prince gaue the Beaste such a sounde stroke with his[c] Mace on the head, as he staggered to and fro vnable to sustaine himselfe, and following this good aduantage, thrust his Sword so deepe downe his throate, as casting forth a great deale of bloode vpon the Prince, at length he tombled downe on his side, when halfe a dozen good strokes with the Mace, made him safe for stirring any more. And although thys was a **[H1r]** naturall Bore, yet had he beene deuilish-

[a] hath] *om.* P3

[b] lothe] being loth P2, P3

[c] his] the P2, P3

lie enchaunted, and brought into that place by the Priestes Magique, as the Lyons were that kild the Duke of *Feria*, this Bore was appointed by him to guarde his Treasure in the Temple, which (as you heare) was slaine by the hande of *Palmendos*. And euen as the Bore of *Calydonia*, that was sent to torment the whole Countrey, died by the valour of *Meleager*, who afterward[a] made a present of his head to the fayre *Atalanta*,[211] as a notable experience of his magnanimitie, in like sort did the Prince of *Tharsus*, as a remembraunce to all that should come thether, cut of the Bores head, and as a signe of his spoyle and Trophe,[b] set it on a Pyller in the same place where he got the victorie.[c] He had no sooner put off his coate of waxe, which was well loden with the Bores brystles:[212] but he sawe the Knight of the Horne come towards him with a huge Mace in his hand, saying, Vnhappie was thy (Knight) into this Desert, when thou must buy thy boldnes with thy deerest bloode. Heerewith he gaue the Prince such a cruell blowe, as made him sette one knee to the ground, and so long endured the sharp fight betweene them: as they bothe beeing farre spent and ouerlaboured, fell downe to the ground not able to styrre themselues.

Palmendos in short time recouering strength arose, and seeing his enemie was not to be founde: boldly went to enter the Temple, the Gates whereof stoode now wide open,[d] which greatlie augmented his desire to enter. Being come within the Porche, two Images of Brasse stoode on eyther side, who with monstrous Trompets blewe such forcible wind on him,[213] as hee was three or foure times carried forth againe therewith:[214] but pressing on still with all the strength hee had, he gotte such sure footing within the Temple, as he felt no more of that violent winde. Passing forward in the bodie of the Church, he came to the magnificent Sepulchre, wherein the Duke of *Feria* and the high Preestes Daughter were interred, which was so riche, **[H1v]** sumptuous and rarelie inuented, as he had neuer seene the like before. Hauing read the Epitaph,[215] he espied the Sword, wherewith the most perfect Damosell in looue slewe[e] herselfe,[216] then mounting on the bars that inuironed the Tombe, he tooke the Sworde in his hand, and in remembraunce of the accident,[217] as also for the beau-

[a] afterward] after P2, P3

[b] signe of his spoyle and Trophe] trophie of his victory P2, P3

[c] got the victorie.] obtained it. P2, P3

[d] open,] P2; ~. P1

[e] slewe] had slain P2, P3

tie thereof, hee hunge it[a] at his girdle, determining to take it with him, and so walked higher[b] to find out the Treasure. At length he came to the Sanctuarie, where stoode the auncient costlie Altare for the Sacrifice, hauing thereon an Idoll of massie Gold, vppon the head whereof was a rich[c] imperiall Crowne, and in his right hand a Scepter so curiously framed, as[d] it was impossible to see Iewels of greater price. In the Idolles other hand was a Booke, fast sealed with foure great buckles of Gold, and in such a meruailously costly Chaire was the Image sette: as nature her selfe woulde haue beene driuen into admiration, to behold a matter of such surpassing excellencie. All about the Altare stoode many Basons of Golde, and before it hung diuers Images of siluer with lighted Lampes, from whence came such a sweete smell of Mirrhe and other Aromatique drugges, and the light caused the precious stones in the Idoll so to glister, as it wold haue rauished anie eye to note the Maiestie thereof.[218] *Palmendos* carried away with contemplating this sight, and not able to withdrawe his eyes from gazing thereon: at length beheld the darke night to draw on, the Lampes in this holie conclaue hauing so beguiled him, wherefore hee concluded not to depart thence till the morning, that hee might behold the other[e] singularities of the place.

[H2r] CHAPTER IX.[f]

What illusions appeared to Palmendos *in the Temple, one whereof resembled the beautie of* Francelina, *wherewith he had a great deale of talke: and how* Ozalio *with the other Knights came and found him.*

P*almendos* sate downe on a curious piller, intending to repose himselfe till the next morning: but immediatlie he hearde such a bruite and rumour, as though the whole worlde had beene in one moment assembled. Heereupon he arose, and couragiously drawing his Sworde (because hee doubted some ambushe or newe charge) went directly to

[a] it] the same P2, P3

[b] higher] thither P3

[c] a rich] a most rich P2, P3

[d] as] that P2, P3

[e] other] *om.* P3

[f] IX.] P2; ~, P1

the Sepulchre of the Duke, where hee behelde a Damosell with her hayre about her eares, and all her garments soyled with blood,[219] which verie sight greeued him to the hart.[220] This was the shaddow and representation of the Priestes Daughter, who after shee had deliuered manie bitter sighes, with a voice hollow and trembling thus spake.

Am I not more wretched and vnfortunate, then anie other vnder the Globe of heauen? yes questionlesse, seeing the fatall Destinies hath appointed me, to endure perpetuall, cruell and rigorous martirdomes, for thy sake noble Duke of *Feria*, the onely recorde of mine afflicted soule, for whom loue tooke such priuiledge on me, as I feared not to offend my selfe with mine owne hande. But who hath robbed me of the Sworde, that so suddainly made the sad execution of my life? Ah *Palmendos*, thinke not to carry it away so lightlie, for that Sworde is yet more necessary for **[H2v]** me. With these wordes she ranne violentlie vppon him, and shooke him as if she would haue torne him in peeces:[221] at which instant there arose such a thunder and trembling of the earth, as hee thought verilie the Temple woulde haue suncke, and the foure elements resolue and turne in their former state of *Chaos*.[222] By reason heereof,[a] the Prince coulde not continue his magnanimious and wonted vigour, but fell downe depryued of his vnderstanding, as though pale death had taken possession of him. During this traunce, a faire Virgin richlie accoustred, (whom the olde Woman that told him of so manie thinges at *Tharsus*,[223] had sent thether by her poste) came and tooke him by the hand, saying.[224]

Arise *Palmendos*, my noble Lorde, and come to her, who seeing the fearefull state wherein you are, onely by fantasies represented to your eyes: doo intreate you not to disable your heroycall and noble courage, at the sight of vaine and fantasticall visions, for it beseemeth not so good and accomplished Knights, as you are, in such sort to passe thorow strange aduentures. Be of good cheere then, and repute this houre of your renowne, to surpasse all the brauest men in the worlde: because since the essence of thys enchauntment, no Knight coulde enter this Temple but you alone. Wherefore by good reason ought the treasure to be yours, which hath so long time beene concealed here: take hence then the Golden Idoll on the Altare, with all the other rich and precious Iewels, and send them to the vertuous Emperour your Father. And for your sake shall this Temple heerafter be frequent and accessable for any, which you shal consecrate to the

[a] heereof] whereof P2, P3

name of Christ, and of the Treasure you shall yet finde, you shall erect a Monasterie of Virgins, in honor of that incontaminate mayden, that brought the Sauiour of all man kind into the worlde, who hath giuen you strength to runne thorowe these actions: that this place may bee reuerently and devoutly vsed, which heertofore hath been blasphemed with Idolatrie, contrarie [H3r] to the bountie inexpuisable, making to sinful men vowes, offerings and sacrifices. And albeit you are not as yet a Christian, yet for my sake enter that vnspotted faith, for the time will come, when[a] you shall sundry times say, happie was that howre wherein you found me.[225] Hauing taken good order for all that I haue said, contayne your selfe no longer in these Countries, because in other clymats is reserued a tryumphall Scepter for you, enriched with honor and eternall praises.[226]

In vaine it were to aske, if *Palmendos* was filled with great meruaile, hearing the Damosels voyce, who came to comfort him in this austere calamitie, and could so well discipher his affayres, for the extasie and rauishment of hys spirite, which euidently appeared in his countenaunce, deliuered ample testimonie thereof. Nor were these words anie thing els, but fuell to encrease loues fire already burning:[227] neuertheles, seeing himselfe in a place so commodious, where freelie hee might holde chat with this Damosell, he called vp his spirits, and bodly made this answer. Madame, for the reuerend honour you beare to your God, conceale not who you are that knowe mee so well, intreating ye to pardon my presumptuous request, because your rare and perfect beautie, which is the onely spurre to my demaund, hath confounded mee with greater admiration, then all the strange sightes I haue yet beheld: all which, (in respect of your excellence) I holde as diabolicall and friuolous, for you seeme celestiall, and sent by the Gods into these nether Regions, where hauing discouered the future euent of my Destinies, my hart hath thereby receiued incredible ioy and contentment.[228] Bee not abashed courteous Knight, quoth she, at any thing I haue said, for it is long since I knewe what I haue vttered, and in regard of your worthy valour, I loue and esteeme yee aboue all other in the world,[229] so that I haue left the Countries of my originall, onely to see and tell yee what I haue doone: desiring you to excuse me in the rest, as concealing of whence and [H3v] what I am, because at this time you cannot be satisfied therewith, yet ere it be long we will meete againe, and then shall you vnderstande more of mee, by one request I must make to

[a] when] wherein P2, P3

ye, which as yet may not bee manifested.[230] Wonderful will that consolation be (quoth the Prince),[a] to me, that you will commaunde anie thing wherein I may expresse my forces, and in that deuotion I have vowed, euermore faithfully to continue your freende: offering in witnes of this obeysaunce, to serue hencefoorth as your Knight, with promise not to preiudice the least of your commaundements, so long as my starres giue mee leaue to breathe.[231] Nor will I further presse ye to tell me what yee are, seeing your will standeth not thereto: but till the[b] gracious howre of commaundement come, I will accomplyshe your appointment, erecting heere a Monasterie of vyrgins for the seruice of your God, and your words haue made me thirst with vnquenchable desire, till I bee resolued as concerning that fayth. While she returned him many thanks for his freendly offers, the old woman arriued, who made him enamoured with the loue of *Francelina* in his Realm: she taking the Damosell by the hand, said. Goe wyth mee faire Daughter, and leaue this most discourteous Knight, who suffered me to be misused before him in *Tharsus*:[232] wherof I hope to take sufficient reuenge, by the extreame passions his hart shall endure heereafter.

No sooner had she ended these wordes, but immediatlie they bothe vanished away, wherewith the Prince greatly admiring: was driuen into such a profounde conceit of her rare beautie, as he thought euen there to yeelde vppe his ghost, because hee imagined neuer to haue seene her like. Heerein his iudgement was no whit beguiled, for he did as many young Louers doo, shewe themselues fauourable Iudges in their own causes.[233] Now enters he into conceit, because the olde woman had taken her away, that this Damosell was *Francelina*, she whom he had so liuelie imprinted in his hart,[234] as for her loue he had left his natiue **[H4r]** Countrey. Thus compassed with greefe on euery side, hee entred into these termes. Alas olde Woman, I know not what thou maist be, yet very true doo I find thy wordes: but small to my auaile did *Ozalio* smite thee in my presence, that I must requite with so long, yrkesome and lingering penaunce. Ah cruell enemie, why didst thou robbe mine eyes so soone of their unspeakeable content? thou sufferedst me to see, that my loue might growe the more immesurable: but thy wordes were such daggers to my hart, as neuer can I taste a sharper corasiue.[235] And if this were the obiect of *Francelina*, (for fayrer creature did the Sunne neuer shine vpon) at no time shall my soule

[a] Prince)] P2; Prince, ^ P1

[b] the] that P2

enioy rest, till once more I haue seene her againe. Thus entercoursing a thousand opinions, he stoode a long time as driuen to the *Antipodes*,[236] accusing himselfe with base pusillanimitie, and blaming the olde woman, who had so robbed him of his forces, as he could not stay the Lady with him, by whose presence and gracious speeches he supposed himselfe in an eternall beatitude.

But now is the clowdie night chased toward the Occident, when hee determined to effect what the Damosell had commaunded him, and going to the Altare, hee tooke the golden Basons and the other sumptuous thinges, making them readie to be caryed thence, dispoyling likewise the Idoll of the Crowne, Scepter and Booke.[237] But as hee would haue lifted the Image foorth of the Chayre, he found it so heauie as he was not able to stirre it: wherewith he beeing offended, said. And I shall doo thee more honor then thou hast yet receiued of me: so lifting vppe his Mace, he made it fall in peeces to the grounde. From out the bodie of the Image, flewe a very strange Byrde all blacke, gyuing such fearefull shrykes and cryes, as the Prince was thereat amazed: and following her out of the Temple, he beheld a great many more such like Birds with her, they flying altogether with that noyse, the same way where *Ozalio* and the[a] Knights attended, whereat they likewyse **[H4v]** meruailing, were certified by the men of the Islande, that this prodigie signified *Palmendos* entrance into the Temple: for they had heard before, by sundry learned Nigromancers, that these were certaine infernall spirits, which should be chased forth of the Countrey, when the aduenture of the Temple was finished. *Rifarano*, *Ozalio*, and all the Knights glad of these newes, went where they beheld the monstrous wilde Bore, and thence to the Temple, where *Ozalio* first found the Prince opening a great chest, which contained the Priestes principall Treasure, consisting of such rare and inestimable Iewelles, as (it was thought) the like was neuer seene before. *Palmendos* beholding his freend *Ozalio*, ranne and embraced him meruailous kindlie, the like did hee to *Rifarano*, *Lecefin* and the rest, all of them extolling the happy starre[238] that guided the Prince: and he acquainted them with all things since his departure from them, sauing his conference with the Damosel, because none of them shoulde suspect his looue.[239] Then intreated he *Guillador* to send for some skilful man, who might vndertake to deuise and build the Monastery: in short time the greater part of the Clergie was sent for, and among them to

[a] the] his P2, P3

a vertuous man of special knowledge, he gaue the charge and superintendaunce of the worke, as also bountifull store of Gold and Siluer, which was taken out of the Priestes welthy Chest. All things hee committed to the trust of *Guillador*, that the Temple, Monasterie and waies thereto, shoulde be doone in decent order: but he whose hart was onelie dedicated to the Ladies beautie, which appeared vnto him vnder forme of a bodilie illusion, tooke small delight in any thing els, but in her gracious and diuine remembraunce. Now did he hasten the daie of his departure, desiring *Rifarano* and *Lecefin* to make speede to the Emperour, and present the Gyantesse, her Daughter and the other prysoners to him, as also all the Treasure was found in the Temple, from a strange Gentleman religiously vowed to his seruice: who in respect of **[I1[r]]** great affaires that called him els where, coulde not come to kisse his Maiesties hand, which he wil doo with all speed possible. *Rifarano* and *Lecefin* were lothe to leaue *Palmendos*, but seeing it must needes bee so, they soone after conuaied the Gyantesse and her Daughter on shipboord, they making great mone to bee carried from the Island. In the same Shippe was the Crowne, Scepter, Image, Basons and all the other Treasure carryed, and in an other Ship, the prisoners found in the Castell on the promontorie, with all things els expedient for the voyage: then *Rifarano* and *Lecefin* taking their leaue of *Palmendos* and *Ozalio*, went on boord where the Gyantesse and the Treasure was, commaunding their Ankers to be weyed and theyr sailes hoysed, the winde then seruing fitte and fauourable, and so are they sailing toward *Constantinople*.[240] As yet abode *Palmendos* in the Isle of *Delphos*, to see what *Guilladors* workmen would compasse, in so great a worke as he had giuen them charge of.

CHAPTER X.

How Rifarano *and* Lecefin *with*[a] *all theyr trayne arriued in* Constantinople, *where they were honourablie receiued by the Emperour and them of the Court, greatly meruayling at the newes hee hearde of* Palmendos, *and what afterward followed.*

At what time *Rifarano* and *Lecefin* should arriue at *Constantinople*, there were assembled manie great Lordes and Barons, in honour of a sollemne Feaste, which the Emperour made for the marriage of

[a] *with*] ED; (~ P1

the *Hungarian* Prince, *Ditreus* sonne to King *Frysoll*, and twinne Brother to [I1v] *Belcar*.[241] *Dytreus* so soone as he was armed Knight, went to the Emperours Court where hee was woorthilie welcommed, and albeit he was his Maiesties Nephew, yet he looued him with a particuler affection, his courteous and ciuill maners, ioyned with his forwardnes in Armes, gaue hope that he would prooue a valiant Knight heerafter.[242] Hee had not beene long in the Emperours Court and thorowlie acquainted with euery one, but hee grewe enamoured with the beautie of *Esquiuela*,[243] Daughter to the Soldane of *Babilon* and *Alchidiana*[244] so that beeing one day in the Chamber of his Cozin *Philocrista*, eldest Daughter to the Emperour, deuising with her and her Sister *Melicia*:[245] hee got such apt time and occasion, as hee made his intent knowne to *Esquiuela*, she modestlie answering him,[a] that if he faithfully meant to make her his wife, shee woulde settle her choyse vpon him onelie. *Dytreus* who was thereon resolued, desired the Emperour and Empresse to graunt that marriage, they beeing willing to gratifie theyr Nephewe, as also to preferre the young Princesse: with the consent of King *Frysoll*, affianced them together, and *Dytreus* fearing the mariage would be deferred too long, sollicited the Emperour in such sort, as hee sent with all speede to make the same known to the Soldane. In meane while, his Maiestie summoned the cheefest Lords of the Empire, to prepare a Tryumphe in honour of this Feaste, for the accomplishment whereof nothing wanted, saue onely the Embassadours returne that went to the Soldane.

But nowe are *Rifarano* and *Lecefin* entred the Hauen of *Constantinople*, intending to lande before the Emperour should knowe any thing of them, because they came not in such equipage as happilie he woulde expect. Beeing then all Armed, except with their Helmets, they rode through the Cittie but with two Squires onelie that bare[b] theyr Launces and Helmets, they beeing wonderfullie noted of euerie one, and reputed for some strange Lordes of great birth, and in this sort they came to the Pallace, wher very [I2r] boldlie, they woulde haue entred: but the Guarde stayed them, to vnderstand the cause of their comming. We are, quoth they, two Knights of Countreyes far hence distant, and hether wee come to see and serue the Emperour *Palmerin*. You must then leaue these offensiue Armes, aunswered the Guard, if you meane to goe where his highnes

[a] him] *om.* P2, P3

[b] bare] brought P2, P3

is: or els declare your proper names to vs, that wee may goe see if it be his pleasure you shall come in this sorte before him. Our Armes we will not leaue, said *Rifarano*, because it ill beseemes an honest Knight to doo so:[246] but you may goe certifie his Maiestie, that heere is *Lecefin* Sonne to the Soldane of *Persia* and the Princesse *Zephira*, in whose companie is *Rifarano*, Sonne to the Emperour *Trineus* of *Allemaigne*, who humblie desire to kisse his highnes hand. His Maiestie had no sooner notice of their names, but (in exceeding contentation) he sent his Sonne *Primaleon*[247] with diuers other Knights, to entertaine them as beseemed: and the Moore Princes seeing euery one giue place to him that came formost, immediatlie they reputed him to be the Emperours Sonne, whereupon they allighted, when *Primaleon* courteously embracing them, said.

My Lordes, you are more then welcome to my Fathers Court, his Maiestie beeing not a little glad of your arriuall: so taking each of them by the hand, he conducted them into the great Hall, where the Emperour sat in hys Chaire attending their comming, and they[a] approching the state, made offer to kisse his highnes hande, but hee tooke them in his armes and would not suffer them, saying, Know my good Cozins, that I account my selfe greatly indebted to you, in that you woulde forsake your owne Countreyes to visite me so farre off, and that I may not faile in the vse of your names, let me vnderstand who[b] of you is *Rifarano*, albeit you bothe stande equall in my grace and fauour: yet beeing singularlie desirous to continue my loue to the Princesse *Zephira*, I must consequently esteeme and affecte all that come from her.[248] On the other side, as well for the **[I2ʳ]** indissoluble amitie, intirelie grounded in our young yeres betweene the Emperour *Trineus* and me, as also in regard of the alliaunce vnited betweene vs: I am constrained to loue his linage and posteritie, and thus I woulde haue you bothe perswaded, that greater good coulde not happen to me, then the sight of them I[c] esteeme so deerelie. Heauen so prosper and fauour you in all things, as they haue thorowlie comforted my spirits, by the very hearing of my good Freendes and confederates the Soldane and *Zephira*, whose health I pray ye resolue me of, for it is long since I hearde any thing from them.[249]

[a] they] then P2, P3

[b] who] which P2, P3

[c] I] they P2, P3

My Lord, answered *Rifarano*, at what time we departed *Persia*, we left their personnes in most safe disposition, and they by vs (humbly kissing your Maiesties hand) haue sent this Letter in signe of the reuerence and looue they beare yee: now for they could not themselues come so far, they haue sent this Prince their Sonne, named *Lecefin*, in their stedde to doo anie seruiceable duetie in your royall Court. As for my selfe, I am *Rifarano*, Sonne to *Aurecinda*, expresly leauing my Countrey to haue knowledge of your excellencie, and with my vttermost endeuours to follow your seruice: crauing this licence, that I may goe see the Emperour *Tryneus* my Father, whose Sonne I account my selfe not onelie happie to be, but greatlie accuse my selfe of ingratitude, that I haue so long time deferred this voyage.[250] *Lecefin* kissing the Letter, vpon his knee deliuered it to the Emperour: which he commaunding to be opened, tooke and read as followeth.[251]

[13r] *The Letter of* Zephira, *wife to the Soldane of* Persia, *to the Emperour* Palmerin.

To the right happy and most fortunate Prince, Palmerin d'Oliua, *mirrour of courtesie, and surpassing all good Knights:* Zephira *wife to the Soldane of* Persia, *perpetuall vowed freende*[252] *to your imperiall Maiestie, kisseth your highnes hand, wyshing your increase in all felicitie.*[253]

Knowe (most noble Emperour) that the long and vehement affection of my Sonne *Lecefin* to see *Constantinople*, onely to offer you his seruice, and beholde the magnificence of your Court: hath caused the Soldane my husband and me, nowe to sende him in company of *Rifarano*, Sonne to the Emperour *Trineus*, to satisfie the desire they had, in visiting you on our behalfe. And albeit they deserued greater royaltie for such a voyage, yet woulde they[a] no other companie then thirtie Knights; knowing that ostentation in shewe, woulde not purchase them the more estimation at your handes, and therfore they come no otherwise accoustred.[254] Not withstanding, if the sincere amitie you euermore shewed mee, hath acquainted you with the inwarde integritie of my harte, whereby you haue deigned me place among your most affectionate Freendes:[255] I desire

[a] woulde they] would they have P2, P3

you in regard of that zeale, to entertaine these two, and accept of this present, as comming from the hand of her, who hath not her equall in good [I3v] will to your excellencie. And to witnes my bounden duetie in acceptation heereof, I vowe both me and mine euermore to your obeysaunce:[256] perswading my selfe, that your woonted debonaire courtesie, will not suffer me disdained in the offer I make.

The most obedient of your freendes,
Zephira, *Soldanesse of* Persia.[257]

For this gentle Letter from the Soldane and *Zephira*, the Emperour gaue *Lecefin* their Son manie thanks, againe and againe welcomming him to the Courte, then turning to *Rifarano*, he said. I well perceiue my Lord *Rifarano*, that you are the vndoubted Sonne of the Emperor *Trineus*, because you so liuelie resemble him in face,[258] well haue yee doone to come see so good a Father, and the more doo I thank God for your arriual heere, at this time when we intend to holde open Court, to honour the approching mariage of our beloued Cozin: and so please ye to stay the intended Tryumphes, heere shall yee see good[a] store of worthie Knightes, that meane to tempt Fortune for the Garland of honour.

These[b] newes dread Lorde, aunswered *Rifarano*, are not a little welcome to vs, in respect that next the principall point of our voyage, which was to kisse your Maiesties hande: wee were desirous to beholde the valour of your Knights, for their renowne is spredde thorowe the whole worlde, and now we shall wel witnes the same, comming at a time so apt for the purpose. Nor can we forget a worthie Knight whom we met in our iourney, beeing named *Palmendos*, without his seconde or match in martiall affaires, and I thinke there is no one manne liuing, except your highnes, the mirrour and Paragon of Chiualrie,[259] that worthilie may be equalled with him:[260] right sorrie are we, because wee can deliuer no better knowledge of the man, [I4r] by reason of his desire to passe vnknowne, and therefore concealeth himselfe in al places where he trauaileth. This famous man (right noble Lord) humbly kisseth your highnes hand, hauing sent yee such rare and inestimable riches, as when you haue seene them, you will iudge that the like present was neuer giuen to anie King or Emperour, as we are to present you withal from this vnknown Knight. The

[a] good] *om.* P3

[b] These] This P2, P3

charge of this message we vndertooke, in that our selues with diuers other Knights, were deliuered from the cruell bondage of *Baledon*, the Gyant in the Isle of *Delphos*, where we endured miseries not fit to be recounted in this gracious assemblie. Yet the heauens[261] gaue *Palmendos* power to kill this Tirant, after which victorie hee hath seazed the Island subiect to your Maiestie, vntill you sende some such Gouernour or Lieutenaunt as best liketh you: wherwithall, as testimonie of his honourable victorie, hee hath sent ye the Wife and Daughter[262] to the Gyant, to dispose of them as shall seeme best in your wisedome: heereto he added the whole discourse of the Temple, and howe *Palmendos* had ended the enchaunted aduenture therof. Without doubt,[263] (quoth the Emperour, beeing driuen into great meruaile[a]) I cannot imagine who this worthy Knight shoulde be, for if he haue ended such a waightie enterprise, it must needes follow that he is peerelesse in Chiualrie: and if it be his fortune to see our Court, I shall requite him withall the honour I can: but tell me, is he a Moore or a Christian?

A Moore borne as I thinke, aunswered *Rifarano*, notwithstanding he well vnderstandeth this language: and such is his braue constitution of bodie, as I thinke a more gallant Gentleman was neuer seene.[264] But may it please your Maiestie to sende for the Wife of *Baledon* and her Daughter, as also the rich present abyding in your Porte? The Emperour requiting them with manie thankes, sent for the prisoners to be brought on land, commaunding the two Princes to bee vnarmed, and sent them two costlie **[I4ᵛ]** Turkish Robes,[265] which his Sonne *Primaleon* and *Dytreus* sawe effectually executed, with all things els necessarie for men of such calling, in meane while he sent for the Empresse and his Daughters, to behold the rare and precious Treasures sent by *Palmendos*.

When the Empresse and her Daughters were come into the Hall, they entertained the strange Knights exceeding courteously, but *Lecefin* regarding the beautie of *Phylocrista*, grew into such conceite of her singuler feature, as she stoode in his thoughts beyond all compare.[266] Shee wyth her Sisters *Flerida*, *Bazilia* and *Melicia*,[267] for so were the Emperours Daughters named, gaue them a Maydens welcome to the Court, such as beseemed them towardes Knights errant, as also because they were Princes of so honourable birth.[b] After that the Gyantesse, her daughter, and the rest of the prysoners, through a mightie throng of people were brought to

[a] meruaile] admiration P2, P3

[b] birth.] abirth. P3

the Pallace, one of the Knights in behalfe of all the rest, kneeling before the Emperor, thus spake.

Mightie and inuincible Monarche, the hardye Champion and flowre of Knights named *Palmendos*, who deliuered vs from cruell *Baledon* in the Isle of *Delphos*, hath sent vs (with this inestimable Treasure) vnto your Maiestie, as to the onelie Lorde and Prince of the worlde, of whom he caryeth most humble and religious opinion, that you should take compassion on our miseries, and graunt vs accesse to our owne houses. Good freendes, said the Emperor, your honest report of this Knight, to whome I am so much beholding,[268] doth make mee more earnestlie long to see him in our Court, whether you all (for his sake) are so hartily welcome, as ye shall well perceiue the same before yee depart, afterward (in Gods name) goe when ye please. And these were not wordes alone, but deedes did confirme the same, the Emperor rewarding each one of them with such liberall gifts, as they esteemed his largesse and munificence, equall with that of *Xerxes, Iulius Caesar*, or *Alexander* **[K1^r]** the great.[269] Afterwarde hee sent for the Gyantesse and her daughter, and to them offered very honourable kindnes: but their harts were so swollen and confounded with greefe, as they would make no aunswer at all, whereupon he appointed them a conuenient place in the Cittie, with prouision of all thinges for their necessarie vses: but the Gyantesse falling into an extreame lunacie, dyed soone after thereof, yet her Daughter became a Christian, and lyued long time in the Emperours fauour.[270] Now are all the sumptuous vtensilles brought before his Maiestie, the Idolles Chaire, the[a] Crowne, the Scepter, Booke and the rest, which beeing well and aduisedly regarded, were iudged the like to be neuer seene before: whereupon his Maiestie tooke the Booke, labouring with al his strength and cunning to open the same, and after deliuered it to his Barons to trie what they could doo, but all their labour beeing lost, he said.

I thinke this Booke can bee opened by none other, then him onelie that conquered it, let it therefore bee carefullie kept till his comming.[271] Nowe call I to minde the Damosels wordes, that departed so suddainlie without aunswer: and verilie I am perswaded this Knight is the man shee spake of, who hath sent vs this Treasure from the Isle of *Delphos*.[272] With these speeches of the Emperour, diuers of his Knights grew somewhat offended, to heare such commendation passe on him who was vnknowne:

[a] the] his P2, P3

wherefore they intended if euer he came thether, to make such proofe of his valour and prowesse, as the Emperour shoulde perceiue he spake but by affection. Not long after, his Maiesty sent one of his cheefe Knights to *Delphos*, and with him such a trayne as beseemed the expedition, there to see all thinges ordered to his highnes vse, and to preuent insurrections if anie were like to grow, giuing the Knight charge if he found *Palmendos* there, to request him with al speede to visite the Emperour. But the Knight came to[a] short of **[K1ᵛ]** his intent, for he had sette saile towarde *Constantinople*, according as you shall heare heereafter: notwithstanding, the Knight was very graciously welcommed thether, and the possession of the whole Island surrendred to him, which in the end was transferred to one of *Palmendos* Sonnes,[273] beeing a pleasant, fayre and opulent Countrey, nauigable for all passengers whatsoeuer.

CHAPTER XI.

Howe Palmendos *sayling in the Aegean Sea, recouered the Soldanes Sonne of Babylon*[b] *from* Ocurites *King of* Culaquin,[274] *who rode along that coast of Greece: and howe after he had ouercome his strength, hee tooke him prysoner and sent him to the Emperour* Palmerin, *with dyuers Christians which he delyuered from his captiuitie.*

Rifarano and *Lecefin* beeing no sooner set from *Delphos*, but *Palmendos* followed the speedy building of the Monasterie, causing religious obseruations to bee vsed in the Temple:[275] for the people of the Island were good Christians, although the Gyant *Baledon* was a Pagan. The Monasterie being stored with faire Virgins, he would haue them called the Sisters of *Francelina*, and manie Ladies of great byrthe resorted thither, to liue religiously in seruice of the worldes Creator: *Palmendos* much delighting[c] to behold the Christians Religion, meaning when time and place serued, to be further instructed therein.

Hauing ordered euerie thing to his own contentment, **[K2ʳ]** and placed *Guillador* in Iustice till the Emperour sent some other: hee with *Ozalio* tooke shipping, sayling sixe daies with prosperous windes towards

[a] to] *om.* P2, P3

[b] the Soldanes Sonne of Babylon] the Soldan of Babilons Son P2, P3

[c] delighting] delighted P2, P3

Constantinople, yet first he determined to lande in *Thrace*, because hee woulde heare some newes of the Emperours Courte, and of *Francelina* if possiblie he could. Ryding thus with the fauour of *Aeolus*[276] and *Neptune*, he came within sight of the two destroyed Townes *Sestus* and *Abydos*,[277] when one of the Pylots certified him, that he sawe diuers Ships and Foystes eagerlie fighting together, which made *Palmendos* to come vp on the decke, to see if he coulde discerne what they were. Hearing the great tumult and cry made in the vesselles, especiallie in two that seemed better prouided for warre then the other: hee was desirous to goe more neere them, wherefore he commaunded the Maister so to doo, that they might helpe them which too much were oppressed. Nowe to acquaint ye with the cause heerof, it is so, that when the Soldane of *Babylon* and *Alchidiana* vnderstoode the mariage intended by the Emperour, betweene their daughter and *Dytreus* Prince of *Hungaria*:[278] they were very ioyfull of so great alliance, and therefore would sende them great store of ryches by their youngest Sonne, who had not yet receiued his order of knighthood. This young Prince was named *Abenunco*, a gentle youth and very well gyuen, who earnestly intreated his Mother, to obtaine so much of the Soldane his Father, that after his Sisters mariage, he might stay a while at *Constantinople*, which sute at her request the Soldane graunted, and therefore sent him by Sea well accompanied with Knights. *Abenunco* sayling along the cost of *Thrace*, mette with *Ocurites* King of *Culaquin*, who was Sonne in law to the great Turke, and reputed the hardiest Knight among al the Turkish Nobilitie: his Maiestie hauing giuen his Daughter in mariage to this *Barbarian*, shee beeing one of the most accomplished Ladies in all Heathenesse. *Ocurites* knowing the inueterate mallice betweene the Emperour and his Father in **[K2v]** Lawe, (the more to please him) prouided himselfe of good strength by Sea, and dailie came vppon the Coastes of *Greece*, sending vauntcourriers with strong Brigandines before him, to discouer what Christians stirred abroade, and sundry times tooke many of them captiues, as nowe he intended to doo by the Soldans Sonne. When *Ocurites*[279] by the streamers[280] and banderolles heard of the *Babilonian* Prince, and knewe (withall) that his father was a cheefe Freende to the Emperour: in great furie with his Ships he sette vpon him, *Abenunco* with his Knights defended themselues so well as they coulde. During this conflicte *Palmendos* approched very neere them, and of a Galley filled with Christian slaues, he demaunded the cause of this fierce encounter.

Sir, answered one of the slaues, he to whom this great traine of shypping appertaineth, is *Ocurites* King of *Culaquin*, and Sonne to the great Turke, that with diuers of his league and faction dailie coastes on *Greece*, to endamage the Emperour *Palmerin*, enemie to his Father, and those he had nowe mette withal, belong[a] to the Soldane of *Babilon*, they sayling (as we vnderstand) toward *Constantinople*. When the Prince heard what the Christian had said, he brauelie encouraged his Cozin *Ozalio*, in assisting the wel-willers to the noble Emperour: so comming to the Kings Ship, he thus spake.

Nor shalt thou *Ocurites* offend so good a Prince, as is the Emperour of *Constantinople*, heerewith he beganne to lay about him valiantlie, and *Ozalio* not one inche behind him, made the enemie well vnderstand his inuincible courage. *Palmendos* knowing the King by his rich Armour,[281] gaue him such a peazaunt stroke with the hilttes of his Sword on the Helmet, as made him stagger, and at length fall downe, when offering to rise againe, *Palmendos* caught him so strongly by the Helmet, as he pulde it violently from of his head:[282] keeping him stil vnder his Sword in such subiection, as at length he was caryed prisoner into the Princes **[K3ʳ]** Cabin, and there committed him to the charge of foure trustie Knights. In meane while *Ozalio* fought with the Kings Brother, who vnderstanding that *Ocurites* was taken prysoner, did what he coulde to recouer him againe: but *Ozalio* stept betweene him and his purpose, still labouring him with so manie hardie strokes, as at length he smote his head from his shoulders.[283] The rest beholding theyr King taken and his Brother slayne, beside the great massacre made among them, and that they were no way[b] able to withstand theyr fortune; a number fel hedlong into the Sea, rather then they wold die vnder the enemies sword. *Palmendos* seeing no further resistaunce, but that the Turks were vtterly discomfited: he[c] caused such prisoners as were taken to be made sure, the Ships likewise to bee seazed on as his owne: then comming to *Ozalio*, whose forwardnes he commended, he willed him to see all things disposed as beseemed such a victory, afterward he embraced the Soldans Sonne, and diuers courteous ceremonies passing between them, the one for his happy deliueraunce, the

[a] belong] belonging P3

[b] no way] not P2, P3

[c] he] she P3

other reporting[a] what he had doone was for the Emperours sake, at length *Palmendos* vsed these speeches.

My Lorde, willingly woulde I beare yee companie to *Constantinople*, but that a voyage of great importance dooth vrgentlie call me to an other place, yet seeing you are deliuered from the Tyrant *Ocurites*,[284] and all your Knights in sufficient safety, let me obtaine this fauour at your hands, to take the King with ye to *Constantinople*, and all the Christian prisoners deliuered from captiuitie. Them shall yee present on my behalfe to the Emperour *Palmerin*, requesting that this auncient Christian enemie may be safelie kept,[285] vntill I come to see his Maiestie, which shall bee with all the expedition I can. Woorthy Sir, aunswered *Abenunco*, it greeues me that your iourney lyes not presentlie to *Constantinople*, because I shoulde thinke my selfe happie in hauing your companie, beeing the man to whom I am continuallie bounde for my life and libertie: and **[K3ᵛ]** heereof I am assured, that ouer and aboue your gracious welcome, you shall winne the honour of the famous Tryumphe, ordained by the Emperour at the marriage of my Sister with the Prince of *Hungaria*.

And hartilie sorrie am I,[b] aunswered *Palmendos*, that I cannot be present in so woorthy an assemblie: whereof at this time you may well excuse mee, not doubting but I shall come with some sufficient amends for my stay. These speeches he vttered, his thoughts beeing farre otherwise, for so soone as he heard of the Ioustes at *Constantinople*, he determined to goe thether secretlie, without making himselfe known to anie, but as a strange Knight to aduenture his fortune among other:[c][286] wherefore he departed from *Abenunco*, who offered him manie riche presents for hys great kindnes, yet woulde not hee accept of anie.[287] *Abenunco* returned him manie thankes, cheefelie for hys promise, that hee woulde in shorte time visite the Emperour in personne: so after many courteous speeches, and sundry familliar farewelles, *Palmendos* commaunded his Pilot to launche into the high Seas, for that he intended an other kind of course.

[a] reporting] reported P2, P3

[b] am I] I am P2, P3

[c] other] other P3

CHAPTER XII.

Howe Abenunco *arriued at Constantinople, whose comming greatly reioiced the Emperour, but much more his Sister* Esquiuela. *And howe* Lynedes *Lorde of the Isle of Lique, and the Countie of Pelada his Cozin, came to Ioust against the Knights of the Courte, attending the Tourney for the mariage of* Ditreus.

Greatly did *Abenunco* commende his fortune, in finding so good succour at a time of such necessitie, and all the Knights in hys companie held opinion, that *Palmendos* was the only flowre of Chiualrie: but aboue all other the Christian slaues, accounting their deliuerance for a miracle imagined the Author thereof was some great Freende to the Emperour. In this ioy they sayled till they came to *Constantinople*, where his Maiestie beeing aduertised that the Soldans Sonne was arriued, commaunded *Primaleon*, *Ditreus*, and many of hys best Barons to goe conduct[a] him to the Court. In meane[b] while, *Abenunco* clothing himselfe most sumptuously, caused the King *Ocurites* and the Christian prysoners to be carryed on shore, that hee might not fayle in the charge giuen him by *Palmendos*: so the *Babilonian* Prince riding to the Courte, with all the prisoners going orderlie before him, he gave charge to one of his cheefest Knights, that hee should present them to his Maiestie, and beeing come into the Emperours presence, the Knight deliuered these speeches.

High and mightie Monarche of the world, behold heere **[K4v]** the King of *Culaquin*, Sonne to the great Turke, who keeping the Seas with a stronge[c] power to endaunger[d] your Empire, our Maister the Prince *Abenunco* and wee, fell into his daunger: from which a woorthy Knight named *Palmendos*, by deedes of rare and hautie Chiualrie, deliuered vs in a time most needefull, and therefore hath sent bothe vs and him to your excellencie, desiring that *Ocurites* should be safely kept till he come himselfe. These sundry good turnes receiued from a Knight vnknowne, droue the Emperour into wonderfull admiration, and for hee could not imagine whence they should proceede, therefore he was the more desirous to

[a] conduct] and conduct P2, P3

[b] meane] the mean P2, P3

[c] stronge] great P2, P3

[d] endaunger] endamage P2, P3

beholde the Knight: whereuppon hee committed the King into[a] a strong Towre, commaunding hee shoulde haue all thinges necessary for hys health, and a Page to attende on him least he shoulde offend himselfe.[288]

But nowe is *Abenunco* by *Primaleon* and the other Princes brought to the Emperour, who embracing him very honourably in his armes, gaue him such entertainement as beseemed his estate, and for[b] hee was not yet knighted, he willed[c] he should be bedfellow to his Sonne *Primaleon*, which vnited a faithfull league of amitie betweene them, hoping one day to trauell as companions in Armes together.[289] *Abenunco* hauing likewise tolde the Emperour of his good successe, and wonderfull deliueraunce by the meanes of *Palmendos*: gaue no little contentment to *Rifarano* and *Lecefin*, who imagined themselues as much beholding to the Prince as anie. Afterward he was conducted to the Empresse Chamber, where she and her Ladies graciously welcommed him: but especially the Princesse *Esquiuela* his Sister, because hee came to confirme what she most desired. My Lord and Brother, quoth she, nothing coulde happen to my greater contentment, then to haue your presence in the honour prepared for me, whereto seeing our gracious parents coulde not come, they haue for my sake sent you in their place: and doubt not but your **[L1ʳ]** entertainment shall be such, as shall agree with theyr expectation and your owne woorthines. Faire Sister, aunswered *Abenunco*, the Soldane our Father hearing what[d] honour the Emperour intended, by giuing you in mariage to the Prince *Ditreus* his Nephew, hath sent me to thank the Emperour on his behalfe, offering for this contract to articulate with his Maiestie, in all such thinges as with honour hee shall demaunde. As for our gracious Mother *Alchidiana*, she hath sent ye by me Iewels and Treasure beseeming your degree, that on your mariage day yee may witnes the royall race from whence you are discended, not doubting but before you depart this Courte, to make the magnificence of the *Babilonian* Prince so famous, as the most opulent Lorde of *Asia* shall not compare therewith. Diuers other speeches passed betweene the Brother and the Sister, till the Coffers of Treasure were brought and deliuered to the Princesse, which when *Ditreus* behelde, hee iudged them to exceede the limits of all frugalitie,

[a] into] to P2, P3

[b] for] because P2, P3

[c] willed] willed that P2

[d] what] of the P2, P3

and might full well beseeme the greatest state in Christendome.[290] Now did the Emperor cause the Tourney to be openly proclaimed, and the fift day[291] following the mariage was solemnized, great store of worthy Knights resorting day by day to the Court, that all the field appointed for Tryumphes was couered ouer with Tents.

Among other came thether *Lynedes* the Lorde of *Lique*, he that hazarded himselfe so farre in the aduenture of *Francelina*, beeing (in sooth) reputed one of the most valiant men at Armes in all *Greece*,[292] and the renowne of thys mariage drew him from his Castell, accompanied onelie with the Countie of *Pelada* his Cozin, who albeit hee was younger then *Lynedes*, yet was he thought little inferiour to him in Chiualrie. This Countie had espoused a Ladie of great parentage, and loued her with such singuler affection, as hee brought her in company to see the Ioustes at *Constantinople*. Beeing there arriued, they woulde not enter the Cittie, but sette vppe their Tent far distant from **[L1v]** all the rest, and afterward sent a Squire to the Courte, to publish that whosoeuer would hazard himselfe in the Tourney: shoulde finde two Knights there ready in the fielde, that woulde Ioust with anie one[a] durst enter the Lystes, such therefore as were minded to make proofe of their valour, might be entertained for three or foure courses. These speeches beeing heard by the Duke of *Pera*,[293] he stept to the Squire, and thus answered.

You may my Freende returne to your Maisters, and say that such as are minded to Ioust, will not stay long ere they enter the Fielde: then turning to the Knights of the Court, he proceeded in this manner. Doubtlesse these Knights are valiant and hardie, that are lothe to shewe themselues slothfull in any vertuous exercise. With this aunswer the Squire went[b] backe to the Tent, and the two Cozins beeing satisfied therewith, prepared strong Launces at the entraunce of their Pauilion, for all such as shold come to Ioust against them: but the Countie intreted *Linedes*, to suffer him make[c] the first triall of his fortune, which he did in regarde of his loue to his Ladie, who had caused the Tent to be so commodiously placed, as shee might at pleasure beholde all the pastimes, decking herselfe in most gorgious attire, and brauelie attended on by her waighting woman, to out countenance such as came against her Lorde and Husband.

[a] one] one that P2, P3

[b] went] returned P2, P3

[c] make] to make P2, P3

The Emperour vnderstanding what message the Squire had brought, imagined that these two Knights were *Palmendos* and his Cozin *Ozalio*: for when one thing continuallie beateth on a mans conceit, hee imagineth euerye thing conformable to the same.[294] Wherefore hee tolde his opinion to the Prince *Rifarano*, who could not think them to be the Lordes of *Tharsus*, yet to satisfie the Emperours minde, he mounted on horsebacke, and accompanied[a] with other Knights of the Court, rode to the Tent where the two Cozins remained. Saluting the Squires, hee entred finding *Lynedes* vnarmed, but his Cozin was prouided at **[L2r]** all points except his Helmet: whereuppon he demaunded if they were the Knightes that sent the challenge to the Court? to whom the Lord of *Lique* aunswered, that they were, then *Rifarano* proceeded thus. Gentlemen, ye haue attempted a thing (in mine opinion) but little for your ease: but I thinke you did it to this ende, that you might meete with some one to abate your pride and presumption.

When that comes to passe, aunswered *Lynedes*, wee shall but accompanie manie other,[b] who vnable to effect their hautie enterprises, haue remained frustrate in theyr disseignes: in vaine therfore shal ye take any further care for our affaires, but if you wil goe Arme your selfe, return and prooue what this Knight can doo, who is more desirous to fight with his Sworde then[c] his tongue,[295] otherwise you offer iniurie to the order, which euery noble minde preferreth as his proper life.[296] *Rifarano* somewhat mooued wyth these words, tooke his leaue and returned to the Emperor assuring him that these Knights were not *Palmendos* and *Ozalio*, notwithstanding they seemed good and hardie Champions, discended of some great birthe, in that they were so woorthilie accompanied, with women of choyse and[d] singuler beautie, as also Gentlemen[e] of ciuill behauiour.[297] Heereupon many Knights Iousted with the Countie, who styll bare away the honour of the fielde, *Lynedes* all this while not arming himselfe, for the woorthy successe of his Cozin deserued high commendation, wherof his Lady was not a little proude, to see her husbande performe such Chiualrie. *Rifarano* and *Lecefin* enuying the Counties glory, intended to see how they

[a] accompanied] being accompanied P2, P3

[b] other] others P2, P3

[c] then] then with P2, P3

[d] and] of P3

[e] Gentlemen] of Gentlemen P3

shoulde speed in the Ioust, yet they desired to defer it til the last day, when they vanquishing the Countie and *Lynedes* his Cozin, might beare away the whole praise of the Tryumph: but others came in meane while[a] and altered their intent, as you at large shall perceiue heereafter.[298]

[L2ᵛ] CHAPTER XIII.

Howe Arnedes *Sonne to the King of Fraunce, and* Recinde *his Cozin, Sonne to the King of Castile, came to Constantinople, where* Arnedes *vanquished* Lynedes *and his Cozin in the Ioust, by which occasion they were greatly honoured of the Emperour.*

The King of *Fraunce*, Father to *Lewes* Duke of *Burgundie*, beeing at the extreame poynt of his life, among other things remembred, that when the peace was concluded betweene the Emperour *Palmerin* and him, they determined vpon an alliaunce by marriage, if God graunted them issue wherby to doo it: to the end that in the heroycall house of *Fraunce*, Sonnes and daughters might be nourished, proceeding from such worthie auncesters, as the like might not be found thorow the whole worlde.[299]

For this cause, when the time likewise shoulde conueniently agree therewith, he commaunded his Sonne to remember the Emperour of his promise: which Prince *Lewes* promising his dying Father to performe, with exceeding sorrow accomplished his funeralles, and making choyse afterward for his owne fancie, in hope to fulfill his Fathers desire in his issue,[300] hee maried with the daughter to the King of *Castile*, by whom hee had three Sonnes and two Daughters that were borne at a byrth.[301] His eldest Sonne was named *Arnedes*, whose minde was euermore giuen to Armes and Millitarie discipline, wherein time [L3ʳ] and vse made him so expert, as he was esteemed the onelie Champion of *Fraunce*. It came so[b] to passe, as the King of *Fraunce*, marryed one of his Daughters with the Kyng of Scicilie, at whose marriage *Arnedes* wunne such fame by his Chiualrie, as the report of him was blazed thorowe manie prouinces. To this marriage likewise came one of his Cozins, Sonne to the King of *Castile*, and named *Recinde*,[302] who conceiued so good liking of *Arnedes* behauiour, that they swore an inuio-

[a] meane while] the mean time P2, P3

[b] so] *om.* P3

lable league of amitie betweene them twain, neuer to forsake eche others companie in matters of Armes:[303] wherewith the Queene was highly contented, because shee looued her Cozin *Recinde* with intire affection.

King *Lewes* seeing his Sonne *Arnedes* of yeeres to haue a Wife, and fearing he should els where dispose hys lyking, one day called him into his Chamber, and thus conferred with him. My Sonne, such is the naturall inclination of my looue towards thee, as I would not wyshe anie thing to thee, but to haue thee as well contented therwith as my selfe: to this end[a] I vse these speeches, for that our late kinglie Father of famous memorie, at the verie shutting vppe of his latest dayes, gaue me charge to ioyne thee in marriage with the Emperours Daughter of *Constantinople*, that such issue (as no doubt) shall proceede from you bothe, may some what resemble their famous auncesters. Wherefore I am determined, right soone to send an Embassage to him, to sollicite this mariage which I hope he will like well of: and this I can assure thee, if Fame tell no leasings, that the Princesse *Philocrista* nowe aged sixteene yeeres,[304] is a Ladie of such rare and singuler beautie, as Nature hath not framed the[b] like vnder the moouing of these eyght Spheres.[305]

When the Prince *Arnedes* saw that his Father talked so courteously with him about these affayres, he humblye intreated him not to trauaile any further in the matter, for there was time enough heereafter to deale in such occasions: [L3v] wherwith the King pacified him, because he saw his Sonne so colde (as he thought) in matter of marriage, nor would he trouble him any more therewith afterward. But the young Prince, wise and aduised in concealing his owne desires,[306] hauing long before heard faire *Philocrista*[c] commended beyond compare, as also the deedes of the Knights in the Emperour *Palmerins* Court, he had no leysure now to forbid them his remembraunce, so that fayne would hee compasse a secrete iourney to *Constantinople*, intending if the Princesse pleased, to demaunde her of the Emperour in marriage, and if his Maiestie would not consent thereto, hee intended to doo such exployts in *Greece*, as the honourable prayse of them should compasse his loue.[307] Thys was the proiect of *Arnedes* resolution, which in secrete he imparted to his Cozin *Recinde*,[d308] who with mighty

[a] selfe: to this end] P1H-P1Bod: selfeto this: end P1BL

[b] the] her P2, P3

[c] Philocrista] P2; Pilocrista P1

[d] Recinde] P2; Recind P1

perswations annimated him heerein: vowing that till death they would loyallie continue freendly companions, and so well gouerne themselues by disguising[a] theyr persons, and contrarying their languages in these affayres, as the moste skilfull head shoulde not searche the depth of their intent. When the two Cozins were thus determined, *Arnedes* imagining it no wisedome to iugle with his Father,[309] went and requested a fauour at his highnes hande, the effecte whereof was thus.[b]

Gracious Lorde and Father, quoth hee, my desire is (without your displeasure) that I may goe see the Princesse *Philocrista*, as well to like as loue before any motion of marriage: and for[c] my Cozin *Recinde* will beare me company, I wold haue your Maiestie so perswaded, and[d] in secret disguising[e] we will passe vnknowne of anie, much lesse giue occasion of suspect what we are, not doubting but by our vertuous behauiour, to yeelde you content by our voyage, and our selues good report.[310] Beside, the worlde is well acquainted therwith, that this Emperour of *Constantinople* had not wunne such fame and renowne, but onely by the innumerable Trophes, erected in diuers Regions of hys **[L4r]** youthfull trauailes, which are examples sufficient for Knights of high desire, not to desist from worthy enterpryses for the obiect of death, who without regarde of time or place, pursueth in ambush the steppes of the woorthiest.[311] Nor let doubt of our stay in *Greece* hinder vs, good father: for as we goe not to build any dwelling there, so is the hope of our returne to be expected more speedie. It greatlie dyspleaseth mee, answered the King, that I haue promised to myne owne dyscontentment, and which much more wyll redownde to your disaduantage:[312] but seeing I haue past my worde, and in thys sorte you meane personally to vysite *Greece*, goe in Gods name, who guyde and sende you safely home agayne, els will your stay more hurt mee then you can imagine.

Humbly taking his leaue of the King, because he wold not haue his departure knowne, hee secretly gotte him to *Marseilles*,[313] accompanied with none but his Cozin *Recinde*, his Dwarffe and three[314] other,[315] where finding a Ship readie, they hoysed sayle and away, landing at the first Porte

[a] disguising] P2; disgusing P1

[b] thus.] this. P3

[c] for] because P2, P3

[d] and] that P2, P3

[e] disguising] distinguishing P3

they came to in *Greece*, and commaunding the Shyppe to stay for them at *Constantinople*. One day *Arnedes* and *Recinde*[a] rested themselues where they landed, and the next day rode forward on theyr iourney, vnderstanding by the way what[b] braue Tryumphes were ordayned at the Courte,[316] which pleasing them not a little, they made such dilligent speede, as they arriued there three dayes before the sports were ended:[317] euen at the very instant, when the Countie[318] had vanquished an other Knight in the Ioust. *Arnedes* beholding the braue behauiour of the Conquerer, and that the Knights made daintie who shold try his fortune next, noting beside the honourable assemblie there present with the Emperour (who meruailed what these two newe come Knights should be, vntill hee had aduisedlie marked theyr Armes, when immediatly hee iudged them to bee *Frenchmen*:)[319] gaue the spurres to hys Horse and ranne against the Countye,[c] eache of them breaking theyr staues **[L4ᵛ]** gallantly without any further daunger.[320] At the seconde course the Countie was vnhorssed by *Arnedes*, whereat the Emperour and his Lordes very much reioyced, highly commending the behauiour of the *French* Knight. Needes must we thinke that *Lynedes* was offended, seeing his Cozin throwne so furiously to the ground, wherefore Arming himselfe speedily and mounting on horse backe, with a very strong Launce he angerly encountred *Arnedes*, who gaue his enemie as good as hee brought. *Lynedes* was very chollericke[321] that he had spedde not better, whereuppon at the seconde race, *Arnedes* met him so full in the carrire, as he cast him out of his saddle ouer the crupper of his Horse: he thinking to recouer himselfe, and lothe to forsake the raynes of hys brydle, caused his horse to fall bacwarde vppon him, that hee was the worse for this fall[d] long time after.[322] But *Arnedes* he remayned fresh and frollick, as though he had yet doone nothing at all,[323] wherefore hee came to hys companion, saying.

Nowe let vs goe kisse my Lord the Emperors hand, seeing there is no more to be done here: and so in the troupe they withdrew themselues, each[e] one meruailing at thys *Frenchmans* valour, because they knew *Lynedes* was accounted one of the hardiest Knights in *Greece*. When the

[a] Recinde] P2; Recind P1

[b] what] *om.* P2, P3

[c] Countye] ED; Conntye

[d] fall] *om.* P2, P3

[e] each] early P2; every P3

Emperour saw them comming toward him, hee auaunced himselfe to entertaine them, and embracing them graciously in his armes,[324] sayd. Right welcome are yee Gentlemen into thys Countrey, where you haue exceedingly contented mee by your fortunate successe: let mee therefore know of whence and what ye are, that I may loue and esteeme ye accordingly. It is the wonted grace and vertue of your Maiestie, answered *Arnedes*, that makes ye[a] euermore regard poore trauailing Knights, although theyr deserts be nothing equiualent: the renowne whereof spreading thorow al Regions, caused vs forsake[b] *Fraunce*[325] to come[c] offer ye[d] our seruice. Wee are, my Lorde, Knights attending on the King of *Fraunce*, where hearing the daily report, **[M1r]** what magnificent Chiualrie was heere continuallie exercised: we came (so please it your Maiestie) to liue in your Court, as men willing to learne the rules of Martiall discipline, not doubting but to gaine such grace, as shall satis-fie the desire that mooued vs heereto. I thanke you, quoth[e] the Emperor,[f] for the paine you haue endured in this iourney, which amplie declares the generositie of your braue mindes, because such principles cannot proceede but from[g] hautie and resolute courage: with these wordes (for thys daie) he returned to the Pallace, commaunding *Arnedes* to goe on his right hand, and *Recinde* on his[h] left, they both meruailing to see the goodlie traine of Knights that attended on the Emperour.

All the way his Maiestie eyed *Arnedes* verie much, imagining he saw the liuelie countenance of *Lewes* Duke of *Burgundie*: and therefore desired to know his name and parentage, telling him whom he resembled in many points. In trueth my Lord, answered the *French* Prince, it not beseemes[i] me to dallie with your Maiestie, I am King *Lewes* his eldest Sonne,[j][326] therfore I am the more like to him.[327] And for his sake, said the Emperour, must I

[a] ye] you P2, P3

[b] caused vs forsake] caused us to forsake P2, P3

[c] come] come and P2, P3

[d] come offer ye] come and offer you P2, P3

[e] quoth] answered P2, P3

[f] Emperor,] ED; Emperor ^ P1

[g] from] from a P2, P3

[h] his] the P3

[i] not beseemes] doth not beseem P2, P3

[j] Sonne,] P2; ~. P1

needes loue yee[a] the more, because heeretofore I receiued by him and his Brother very[b] great honour:[328] yet for his highnes[c] perceiued that *Arnedes* was willing to be vnknown,[d] he cut off these speeches, and being come to the Pallace, after the Princes were bothe vnarmed, hee welcommed them as beseemed theyr estates.

Primaleon dailie accompanied *Arnedes* and *Recinde*, because his Father had so commaunded him, yet could not the *French* Prince but meruaile, that all this while hee might not see *Philocrista*, the cause whereof was, the Ladies were lothe to be seene till *Dytreus* wedding day, when each one would then[e] surpasse in brauerie, till which time he was glad and faine to holde himselfe contented. Nowe had *Bruquell* his Dwarffe leysure to gette acquaintaunce with *Risdeno Primaleons* Dwarffe, for they were bothe **[M1v]** of like[f] stature and qualitie, and therfore their familiaritie was not long in breeding. *Lynedes* and the Countie displeased with their hard fortune, yet they were in hope to recouer their foile at the mariage Tourney, which made their greefes the better pacified: nowe leaue we them a while, to speake somewhat of the Princes of *Tharsus*.

CHAPTER XIIII.

Howe Palmendos *and* Ozalio *landed foure dayes iourney from Constantinople, from whence they parted after they had changed theyr Armour: and howe by the way they lodged in the house of an auncient Knight, of whom Palmendos heard the dyscourse of the aduenture of* Francelina, *and what they did afterward.*

Our gentle Knight *Palmendos*, merilie sayled on, hoping in short time to content his earnest desires, and hauing left *Abenunco* by *Sestus* and *Abydos*, hee commanded his Pilot to strike to the nerest Porte for *Constantinople*, so with fauourable wind and weather they

[a] yee] you P2, P3

[b] very] *om.* P2, P3

[c] for his highnes] because he P2, P3

[d] willing to be vnknown] unwilling to be known P2, P3

[e] then] *om.* P2, P3

[f] like] the like P3

came to Saint *Lordin*, which is a marine[a] Cittie, foure daies iourney from *Constantinople*. There hee and *Ozalio* went on shore, onelie to chaunge their Armour and Sheelds, because they would gladlie escape vnknown:[329] and hauing made a quicke dispatch, they rode till they came to the house of an auncient Knight,[330] poore in goods, but noble of harte and person, who inuited them freendly to be his guestes:[331] and there were they right courteously entertained, though not with daintie and delicate viands, yet with indifferent **[M2r]** good cheere and kind humanitie, which speciallie proceeded from the Knights Wife and her faire Daughter, who dilligentlie noted the behauiour of these Knightes. Such was the countenaunce of the young Damosell, as by the continual office of her eyes, her hart began to be somwhat touched, and faine woulde shee participate of the pleasure her minde conceiued: whereto *Palmendos* likewise was somewhat prouoked, seeing his eyes ouerbusied with bathing in the floode of delight, which the presence of thys Damosell onelie procured.[332]

All Supper time these queint glaunces endured, when among other talke they had together, the olde Knight demaunded of his guestes, if they trauailed to the Tourney at *Constantinople*: for yesterday, quoth hee, came I thence, not a little meruailing, to see the number of Knights come thether from all Countreyes: herewith he discoursed the successe of *Arnedes* against the Countie of *Pelada* and hys Cozin, likewise[b] howe the two *Frenchmen* continued Maysters of the fielde. But canne none in all[c] the Emperours Courte, quoth *Palmendos*, where are such store of valiant Gentlemen, out goe those *French* Cozins in deeds of Armes? Truelie Sir, answered the old Knight, it is a matter much to be meruailed, neuerthelesse, I thinke if *Belcar* Sonne to the King of *Hungaria* and Brother to the Bridegroome that shall be, coulde come thether, he would dispossesse the *Frenchmen* of the victorie, which[d] they haue gotten of the[e] Countie and *Lynedes*, considering what fame is dailie bruited abroade of him, for his rare prowesse in garding the aduenture of *Francelina*. And since the time of his famous attempt, no Knight hath arriued there[f] in hope to ende

[a] marine] maritine P2, P3

[b] likewise] and P2, P3

[c] all] *om.* P2, P3

[d] which] *om.* P2, P3

[e] the] *om.* P2, P3

[f] arriued there] there arrived P2, P3

the enchantment, but *Belcar* euermore had beene his Conquerour, yet *Francelina* continueth in the Castell of the Fayries styll, and shall till some Knight (more fortunate then *Belcar*) can gette her foorth, notwithstanding, hee hath vowed no one shall doo it, seeing himselfe hath fayled in the tryall, except he first surpasse him in valour and prowesse.[333] **[M2v]** *Palmendos* hearing the name of *Francelina*, was assayled with such a suddaine and vehement passion, proceeding from the vnquenchable flame, wherein his hart lay burning for her loue: as his countenaunce altered, and his very soule was touched with the word *Francelina*.[334] Wherefore most instantlie hee desired the Knight his Hoste, to tell him of what race the Ladie was discended, and (withall) to proceede in discourse of the aduenture, which so manie woorthy Knights had lost their labours about: likewise to tell him in what Country the Castel was, where the Fairies had appointed this enchauntment, because he had sundrie times heard speeches therof, yet could not meete with anie one to resolue him of the trueth.

Knowe then good Sir, answered the old Knight, that this Ladie is one of the fairest and moste gracious Princesses, that this earthlie habitation enioyes betweene the two Tropiques of heauen,[335] Daughter to the King of *Thessalie*, nowe prisoner to the great Turke, shee beeing taken foorth of her Cradle, and enclosed in the Castell of *Carderia*, by the three enchaunting Sisters of the Island, because they foresaw by theyr Magicall arte, that her Father (who was theyr noble Freende) neuer could be deliuered from the captiuitie of the Infidels, but by the meanes of some perfect accomplished Knight.[336] Thus did they directe thys enchauntment, that the renowne[a] of *Francelinaes* beautie, might be blazed by them through all Regions, and desire to gaine the kingdome of *Thessalie*[b] (for hee that shall deliuer the Ladie, must enioy her as his Wife, next heire after the death of the captiue King)[337] might encourage Knights to come prooue this aduenture: whether many haue gone in hope of happy conquest, as the afore named Prince *Belcar* did, but he wants strength as sundry other haue doone, yet will he make the accesse to this[c] Fortresse more diffycult, vntill he for whom the Princesse is destinied, arriue there with such puissaunce and magnanimite, as shall enforce him to forsake the place. Manie

[a] renowne] readinesse P2, P3

[b] *Thessalie*] P2; ~, P1

[c] this] the P2, P3

other thinges as [M3r] concerning the Historie of *Francelina* (alreadie set downe in the Booke of *Palmerin d'Oliua*,)[338] did the olde Knight recount to the Prince *Palmendos*, who hauing with greate attention noted all, was strooken mute and much amazed: for so was his spirit caryed awaie with newe and dyuers thoughts, that he could hardlie[a] tel what to doo or say. Now he remembers the olde Womans wordes, and sawe there was some likelihoode of trueth in them, thinking because shee had spoken so much of *Francelina*,[339] that shee was one of the Fayries which framed this enchauntment: the ende and abolishing whereof hee thought was reserued for him onelie, comparing all passed coniectures together, which made his hart conceiue incredible ioy, and thus often to parle with himselfe.

Alas *Palmendos*, well mightest thou account thy selfe fauoured of thy[b] starres and Fortune, if thou couldest conquer a Ladie of so faire[c] and perfect beautie, and therby attaine the Kingdome of *Thessalie*, adioyning to the confines of thy Lord and Fathers Empire. Such was his inwarde ioy conceiued by these newes, in hearing her spoken of whom his hart most of all honoured, as he said to the olde Knight. When you vnderstand, gentle Sir, that *Palmendos* is come to the Emperours Court, let me intreate yee to trauaile thether, and there shall I cause him to requite the courtesie, which we beeing strangers haue heere receiued. Then commaunded he one of his Squires to bring a great bagge of Gold and Iewels, which hee powred foorth vppon the Table, giuing the olde Knight and his Daughter the most part thereof: to the end hee should see her honourablie married, and furnish her with all things beseeming such a beautifull Bride.[340] The Knight and his daughter seeing so much Treasure, fell downe on their knees and would haue kissed his hande: but he very kindly tooke them vppe in his armes,[341] saying this was nothing in respect of that he would doo for them heereafter. For his minde beeing euer giuen to liberalitie, receiued such contentment [M3v] by the speeches of his Hoste: as rare and precious thinges seemed of no account, for her sweete sake who was the Goddesse and Mistres of his hart. All this night hee passed in premeditating what hee ought to doo in the present occasion, at length he resolued to goe[d] see the Tourney, without making himselfe knowne to anie one,[342]

[a] hardlie] not P2, P3

[b] thy] the P2, P3

[c] faire] rare P2, P3

[d] goe] *om.* P3

because soone after he would iourney to the Isle of *Carderia*, heerupon he sent a Squire in the morning to S. *Lordin*, to leaue order that the Shyp should meete him at *Macedon*. Then courteously taking their leaue, *Ozalio* and he rode towarde *Constantinople*, whether the old Knight wold haue borne them companie, but *Palmendos* perswaded him to the contrarie, and so sette away in great haste, arriuing in the euening within two miles of *Constantinople*, from whence he sent a Squire to the Cittie, to vnderstand what was doone at the Court, and when the cheefest day for[a] the Tourney shoulde be. The Squire well discharged his Maisters commaund, and returned with full satisfying him in euery point, wherefore *Palmendos* and *Ozalio* determined betweene themselues, not to ryde together in companie, but eche one alone with his Squire, and to returne thence very secretly againe: nor woulde they stay there but the two cheefest dayes, least happilie they might be discouered, and so slack their iourney to the Isle of *Carderia*.

[M4r] CHAPTER XV.

Howe Palmendos *came to Constantinople, where he wunne the honour and pryze of the first Tourney: and how he intended to depart thence on the morrowe, least he should be sought for on that occasion, and what els happened.*

When the long expected daie of mariage was come, the Emperour with all his Knights were very richlie clothed, but especially *Arnedes*, Son to the King of *Fraunce*, hee was exceeding braue bothe in attire and countenaunce, for the hope he had to see faire *Philocrista*, to whom he hadde religiously dedicated his hart.[343]

Nowe set they forwarde in order to the Temple, the Empresse with *Phylocrista* and her other Daughters accompanied the Bryde, with al the Ladies of blood royal in the Courte: so that if one shoulde sitte downe to decipher their sumptuous attire, or els in speeches to commend theyr surpassing[b] beautie, it would ouer-trauaile the eloquence of *Demosthenes* or *Cicero*. But *Philocrista* was the fayrest starre among them all, which drewe the Prince *Arnedes* minde into such admiration, as hadde not his eyes beene witnesses of the same, hardlie coulde report haue induced him to

[a] for] of P2, P3

[b] surpassing] *om.* P2, P3

beleeue it. For euen as the Sunne, the most excellent of all the Planettes,[344] shewing it selfe in the Horyzon, dooth confounde the brightenes of all the starres together, and dazels theyr eyes which long gaze theron: euen so resembled **[M4v]** the Princesse *Philocrista*, whose celestiall portrature disgraced all the other Ladies, and altred the iudgement of *Arnedes* in such sort,[345] as he reputed her far beyond the Goddesse, that appeared to the Sheephearde *Paris*[346] on the Mountaine of *Ida*, when of him she was iudged to bee fayrest of the three.[347]

The Empresse and her Ladies all mounted on theyr Palfrayes, with such pompe and state as was neuer seene the like: *Primaleon* on a lustie Courser of *Barbarie*,[348] wyth rich caparisons[349] after the Turkishe manner, conducted the Bryde, and *Abenunco* her Brother rode with the Princesse *Philocrista*. *Lecefin* who looued her more aduisedlie, rode on her otherside for companies sake, but *Arnedes* whom loue[350] impatiently ouermaistred, vsed such meanes by managing his Horse, as he gotte the Prince of *Babilon* out of his place, mooued thereto by earnest desire, that he might contemplate her beautie more easilie:[351] whereat *Lecefin* was meruailously offended, conceiuing a mortall hatred against him, perceiuing he had a ryuall in his loue. *Recinde*[a] accompanied the Princesse *Melicia*, who in his eye seemed bothe fayre and modest, *Rifarano* telling her by the way, that this Knight came with him which[b] conquered the Countie, and for his laudable vertues deserued estimation: whereupon she began to conferre with *Recinde*, which she coulde doo with singuler regarde, in respecte of the rare gyfts bestowed on her by nature. In breefe,[352] thys royall trayne is come to the Temple, and there is the marriage sollemnlie effected, returning to the Pallace with selfesame[c] maiestie they went thether. What should we waste time in speaking of the Feaste, when there is none so simple but considereth, that the Feastes of Emperours exceede common repetition: then may wee repute this solemnitie aunswerable to that of the Gods, made at the nuptialles of *Peleus* with the Goddesse *Thetis*.[353] After Dinner the Lordes and Ladies fell to dauncing, a fitte occasion for Louers to commune with their Ladies, yet dyssembled **[N1r]** with such cunning modestie, as the eye and action were cheefe messengers of the hart,[354] eche Ladie

[a] *Recinde*] P2; *Recind* P1

[b] which] that P2, P3

[c] selfesame] the self-same P2, P3

holding such opinion of her beloued, as their seuerall hope[a] was for the honour of the Tourney.

The time beeing so passed ouer, as the newe married couple must to the place of amourous contentation, the Empresse with her Daughters brought *Esquiuela* into the bride Chamber, leauing her in bedde attending for the comming of the Bridegroome, who was soone after honourably conducted thether by the Emperour, and so committed to enioy her whom he had so long desire.[355] Now are the Knights close in their Chambers, when *Arnedes* thus communed with *Recinde*. What thinke yee Cozin of the beautie of Madame *Philocrista*? did you euer see a more rare and perfect creature? right soone must I giue end[b] to these vrgent affaires, and ease the burthen of mine ouer-charged spirit: therefore will I presentlie dispatch a Courrier to the King my Father, that he may with speede send honourable Embassadors to the Emperour, whereby this desired mariage may be concluded. Meane while I wil sound the bottome of this amorous floode, and trie if the iudgement of fayre *Philocrista*,[356] bee aunswerable to her excelling[c] beautie, and if the inward vertue agree with the outward singuler perfections,[357] I may repute my selfe the happiest Knight in the world, in compassing the looue of so inestimable a Iewell. In sooth my Lord, aunswered Recinde, great cause haue ye[d] to commend the Lady, and I desire that the like fortunate successe may befall mee, as I doubt not but will speedilie happen to you: for on mine owne behalfe, the grace and courtesie of *Melicia* hath giuen me a fauourable entrance, which if it proceed not to my harts desire, much better had it beene that I neuer had seene her. With these wordes *Arnedes* embraced his Cozin, saying. Howe sweetlie doo these speeches sound in mine eares, seeing thereby thou art my trustie companion in all thinges: lette this hope perswade thee, that he on whom all actions doo depende, wyll **[N1v]** by his[e] diuine bountie so direct our course, as we shall enioy a succesfull ende. If I speede according to my hartes content,[f] in thy cause will I endeuour my selfe to the vttermost: therefore let vs continue our resolute courage, and make the *Grecians*

[a] hopes] P2; hope P1

[b] end] ease P2, P3

[c] excelling] P2; exeelling P1

[d] ye] you P2, P3

[e] his] this P3

[f] content] intent P2, P3

vnderstand, that *Fraunce* yeelds as good Knights as anie Countrey els, and thus concluding, they slept for that night.

On the morrowe, the Emperour, the Empresse, the Bride and the young Princesses,[358] went to the Scaffoldes richlie prepared for the sight of the Tourney, where no voyde place was left, but euery where filled with Lords, Ladies and Gentlewomen. Wonderfull was the resort of Knights and hardie Champions, eche one in Armour verie costlie and curious, hauing their fethers, pendents and fauours, deckt with the deuises and coullers of theyr Ladies, as it was a most beautifull spectacle to beholde them, yet heereon consists not the substance of our Historie. Nowe stryue *Lynedes* and the Countie his Cozin like two furious Lyons, to recouer the foyle they sustained by *Arnedes*: who perceiuing this was the time to winne[a] him honour, when the Goddesse of his thoughts[359] sate to beholde him, welcommed the challengers as hee had doone before. In like sort did *Rifarano* behaue himselfe, for he vnhorsed euerie Knight that ranne against him. But by this time is *Ozalio* got in through the thronge, and he begins to deale with the Courtiers very roughlie, which made the Lordes and Ladies wonder what hee was. And then *Palmendos* seeing his Freende well wearied, comes brauely prauncing into the fielde, so disguised as[b] *Abenunco* and *Rifarano* could not knowe him.[360] A while hee stoode regarding the Emperour his Father, so honourably placed with his noble Lordes and Barons on the Scaffoldes: then viewing the Empresse with her gracious traine of Ladies, he wondred at such pompe and magnificence, thus speaking to himselfe.

Soueraigne Creator[361] and director of all thinges, how **[N2r]** am I bounde in duetie to thy Maiestie, hauing made me the Sonne of such a Father: as not onelie is reputed the best Knight vnder heauen, but also is[c] the mightiest Prince on the face of the earth. Seeing then thou hast bestowed on me such grace and fauour, as[d] I shoulde issue from such an excellent personage, I must endeuour my selfe to resemble him, and by some thing declare that I am his Sonne: for though[e] nowe[f] I goe against

[a] to winne] P2; towinne P1

[b] as] that P2, P3

[c] also is] is also P2, P3

[d] as] as that P2, P3

[e] though] although P2, P3

[f] nowe] *om.* P3

the Knightes of his Court, I hope hee shall[a] haue small cause to mislike of mee, when he knowes my forwardnes in other matters on his Maiesties behalfe.

Then beholding a Knight readie to encounter him, he brake off his musings, and gaue him so braue[b] a welcome, as he tombled hedlong downe to the ground. Like successe had diuers other Knights of the Courte, which *Arnedes* angerlie seeking[c] to reuenge, accompanied the other in misfortune, and after him *Pernedin*, Sonne to the Duke of *Pera*, one of the best esteemed Knights in *Greece*. *Rifarano* next ranne against *Palmendos*, and three courses they past brauelie with the breake of the Launce, but at the fourth *Rifarano* was dismounted: whereupon *Recinde* came to reuenge his Cozin *Arnedes* foyle, whose fortune was as bad as any of the other, and *Lecefin* had his disgrace likewise for companie.

The Emperour mooued to admire this Chiualrie, ignoraunt who this gallant should be, affirmed that hee neuer sawe his equall in prowesse: the like did *Primaleon*, being very desirous to know his name, to whom *Abenunco* aunswered, that he imagined him to be *Palmendos*, because hee much resembled him in braue constitution of bodie. At these speeches the Emperor was exceeding ioyful, requesting *Abenunco* to goe vnderstand the trueth thereof: but *Palmendos* had so[d] thrust himselfe in the thickest of the crowde, which now went foorth[e] of the Lystes, because the sports were ended for that day, as[f] *Abenunco* could by no meanes come neere him, and therefore was fayne to **[N2ᵛ]** return vnresolued. So went *Palmendos* closely to his lodging againe, where beeing vnarmed, he found[g] he had receiued three woundes that day in the Ioust, the greatest wherof he took by *Recinde* the Prince of *Spayne*, but when hee sawe *Ozalio* in good disposition, he was right ioyfull, commending him for his woorthy behauiour. And for[h] hee was wounded, he stayed there two dayes without returning to *Constantinople*, least if he went againe, his intent might be preuented:

[a] shall] will P3

[b] so braue] such a brave P2, P3

[c] angerlie seeking] seeking angerly P2, P3

[d] so] *om.* P2, P3

[e] foorth] out P2, P3

[f] as] so that P2, P3

[g] found] found that P2, P3

[h] for] for that P2, P3

afterwarde he rode to the Realme of *Macedon*, in the selfe[a] same Armes he wore at the Tourney, continually hauing *Francelina* in his minde.[362]

CHAPTER XVI.

What conference Arnedes *had with the Princesse* Philocrista *after Supper, whereupon he sent a messenger to the King his Father: and howe after* Recinde, Rifarano *and other,*[b] *had wonne the pryze of the seconde Tourney, they intended to follow in searche of the Prince* Palmendos.

Verye much ashamed were the vanquished Knights, of the harde entertainment they had receiued by *Palmendos* and moste of all the Prince *Arnedes*, because hee was vnhorssed before hys Mistresse *Philocrista*, wherfore he vowed to be reuenged, or hee woulde die the death, and so diuers other Knightes that murmured against the Conquerer, did the like.[363] But the Emperour perceiuing this discontentment, came to *Arnedes*, *Recinde*, and *Rifarano*, and to put them from these melancholie [N3r] conceits, hee shewed them verie pleasaunt countenaunce: saying they ought not to mislike with what had happened, in that themselues shewed very sufficient Chiualrie,[364] and desired them at the next Tourney to compasse the knowledge of the strange Knight. If hee come againe, aunswered *Arnedes*, it may bee happily[c] to his disaduauntage: for he hauing alreadie disgraced so manie, the sporte will hardlie ende without his foyle.[365] By this time was *Abenunco* come backe to the Emperour, declaring howe hee could not speede of[d] his intent, wherwith his Maiesty somwhat offended, said.

Nor will anie quiet sleepe enter my head, vntill I know the name of that worthy Knight: and were it not I shold be esteemed ouer fonde, I woulde my selfe trauaile tyll I founde him. All the Knights meruailing at these speeches, concluded when the Tryumphes were ended, if so bee the strange Knight returned not againe, to aduenture themselues in the searche of him: and they who were most forward heereto, were *Arnedes*, *Recinde*, *Rifarano*, *Lecefin*, and *Pernedin*, Sonne to the Duke of *Pera*, these

[a] selfe] very P2, P3

[b] other] others P2, P3

[c] happily] happily be P2

[d] of] in P2, P3

gallants without any further conference together, constantly vowed to die, or bring backe the Knight again to the Emperor, if they might meete with him in anie place.[366] Supper being ended, *Primaleon* and *Ditreus* tooke *Arnedes* and *Recinde* with them, going to sitte and deuise with the Ladies, when *Arnedes* got the meane to courte *Philocrista*, and *Recinde* his chosen Mistresse *Melicia*: what contentment they receiued by this good opportunitie, I referre to such as are desirous to breake the Ise of their amorous passions, to them that hold them in so seuere seruitude.[367] Diuers familiare speeches tossed vp and downe, as of the Tourney and their vnhappy disgrace: *Philocrista* pittying that *Arnedes* should take it so discontentedly, thus spake. Me thinks (Sir) you shoulde not be offended at so small a matter, for oftentimes the best Knights haue no better successe: and we haue so well beheld your valiancie, that the Conquerers **[N3v]** haue cause to complaine of your comming, as the vanquished haue of the Knight departed, who as yet is vnknown to any in this Court. *Arnedes* hearing the gentle speeches of *Philocrista*, bashfull modestie with-helde him a while from making anie aunswere,[368] yet at length looue vnlocked his lips in this manner.

Madame, quoth he, the rare ornaments wherwith nature hath accompanied your diuine perfection,[369] causeth you to speake so fauourablie on my behalfe, although no desert in me can apprehende the least part of this kindnesse: but were I possessed with anie such abilitie, the very glaunce of her eye, who hath power to commaunde me, would increase my strength and make me inuincible, wherfore my desires cannot be satisfied, till[a] I recouer my libertie[370] lost in this Tourney, the conceite whereof is more intollerable to me, then the labor to *Sisiphus* in rolling the restlesse stone.[371] The heauens[372] will further your attempt heerein, answered *Philocrista*, and I hartilie desire it may so come to passe, because it were against reason, that you comming so farre to see my Lorde the Emperour, should receiue so vnkind a rewarde for your labour. This sweete reply redoubled the *French* Princes ioy, for which he humbly thanked *Philocrista*, with so manie courtesies and amorous shewes, as[b] she well perceiued the effect of his greefe, proceeded from the passions of a louers spirit.

[a] till] untill P2, P3

[b] as] that P2, P3

Recinde (on the otherside) had so communed with *Melicia*, as[a] she perceiuing howe manie offers he made to bee her Knight, fauourably gaue him entertainment: and more then any thing els, it pleased him to note her beautie, wisdome and good grace, which sette his eyes and all his sences to worke. And if they that are in such delight wyth their Ladies, giue some refrigeration to their harts enflamed with the fire of loue: how could *Lecefin* but be in extreame iealouzie,[373] seeing his ryuall thus to parle with *Philocrista*? gladlie could he haue wished him without raunsome in the strongest prysonne of *Persia*. But nowe is the **[N4ʳ]** howre of rest come, when the Emperour withdrewe himselfe to his Chamber, and al the Knights likewise to their lodgings, where *Arnedes* still meditating on the words of his beloued, immediatly wrote to the King his father, that hee shoulde sende Embassadours to the Emperour for conclusion of the marriage: and til they came he would there stay at the Court, without any further speeches of the matter till their arriuall, so sealing his pacquet as it shold bee deliuered to his Fathers hands, he sent one of his Squires the next morning away therewith in poste, who made no lesse speede then the Prince had commaunded him. Afterward he called *Bruquell* his Dwarffe aside, commaunding him not to stirre out of *Constantinople*, because hee was to depart about some matters of importance, and if the Emperour in[b] meane while asked for him, to make him that aunswer, or anie other that enquired after him. Moreouer, that he should from time to time conferre with the Princesse *Philocrista*, assuring her of his zealous affection to her seruice, which that he might the better execute, he was rydden[c] abroade to take the ayre of the fields: the Dwarff very willinglie performed euery thing hee had in charge, not daringe to breake the least article hee was commaunded.

The time beeing come of the Tourney, rare Chiualrie was there deliuered on all sides, but *Arnedes*, *Recinde* and *Rifarano* had the cheefest honour, attending when the strange Knight should shewe himselfe againe: and when they sawe he came not, they immediatlie determined the execution of their enterpryse, without returning into the Cittie, or knowing which way each other rode, but euen tooke theyr chaunce as Fortune directed them. The Emperour was glad that his Knights had wunne the day, yet

[a] as] that P2, P3

[b] in] in the P2, P3

[c] rydden] riding P3

could hee not but meruaile that the stranger was seene no more: then comming to the Pallace, and seeing none of these[a] fiue which were departed in the search of *Palmendos*, hee coulde not tell what to imagine. Of euery one he desired to **[N4v]** be resolued, yet coulde he not be aunswered to his content, wherefore *Bruquell* made aunswer for his Maister as hee was commaunded: which made his Maiestie then to conceiue the trueth indeede, whereof he was not a little glad, hoping nowe to heare more of the strange Knight. When the solemne Feast for the marriage was ended, the Knights returned to their owne Countreyes, so did *Ditreus* and *Esquiuela* towarde *Hungarie*, with an honourable trayne sent by the Emperor. *Philocrista* was sorie for the departure of *Esquiuela*, whom she loued as[b] she had beene her sister, because from their young yeres they were educated together: nor could *Abenunco* her Brother goe with them so farre as happilie hee woulde, because the league of amitie betweene him and *Primaleon* enforced him to stay.[374] King *Frysoll* receiued his Sonne *Ditreus* and his faire Daughter *Esquiuela* with incredible ioy, humbly (by Letters) thanking the Emperor for the honor he had doone him, returning his Knights with rich and precious gifts.[375] But come we now to the fiue Knights, that were departed in searche after *Palmendos*.

CHAPTER XVII.

How Arnedes *met with* Palmendos, *who left him halfe dead, and had afterward beene slayne by* Lecefin *if* Pernedin *had not happily arriued: and what folowed.*

Alreadie you haue hearde, howe *Arnedes* secretly departed[c] from *Constantinople*, in searche of the Knight that foyled him in the Tourney, demaunding of euerie one hee mette by the way, if they saw not a Knight in redde Armour, hauing a little Siluer Flower for his deuise in his **[O1r]** Sheeld:[376] but no one could aunswere him to his expectation,[377] whereupon, the night beeing harde at hand, he came to an Hermitage at the foote of a Mountaine,[378] where with the olde Father he lodged that night, contented with his poore and homelie refection.[379] On

[a] these] those P2, P3

[b] as] as if P2, P3

[c] secretly departed] departed secretly P2, P3

the morrow, bidding his Hoste courteously[a] farewell,[380] hee had not ridden[b] an arrowe shotte from the Hermitage, but hee espied two Knights come ryding together, and staying to see what they were, at length he knew the one to be *Palmendos*, which good happe pleasing him not a little, hee intended by faire meanes or force to cause him returne again, wherfore he came to him with these words.

Sir Knight, I think my selfe fauoured of Fortune by meeting you heere, in that I left the Emperours Court for nothing els but to seeke you, because his Maiestie desireth to see and know you, in respect of your braue behauiour at the Tourney: therefore I entreate ye for the loue ye beare his highnes, to return back with me, that I may discharge my promise heerein to his Maiestie.[381] You did not wel Sir, aunswered *Palmendos*, to promise anie thing depending on an other mans wil, and for[c] at this time I haue vrgent occasions els where, I cannot satisfie his highnes desire, albeit I am readie in anie thing els to doo him seruice, and so I beseeche you aunswer on my behalfe. Knight, quoth *Arnedes*, I pray you consider heereon a little better, and thinke that such speeches cannot discharge mee of my duetie: therefore determine right soone to goe with mee wyllinglie, otherwise I must compell yee to returne perforce. Perforce? no, said *Palmendos*,[d] well may I goe with my wil if so be I please. I wish it[e] for your good aunswered *Arnedes*, and the remembraunce of your valour in the Tourney, causeth mee to beare with you very much: but seeing you will not willinglie yeelde heereto, prouide for the Combat, and thinke not that your brauerie at the Tryumphe, shall anie thing auaile yee[f] now in this place. If yee[g] will needes enforce me to it, quoth *Palmendos*, let yours then[h] **[O1^v]** be the shame: as for my selfe, in respect of my looue to the Emperour, I woulde be lothe to Combat with yee.[382] Heereupon they so furiously encountred together, that bothe of them were sent to the ground, and afterward they fought a cruell Combat at the Sword, till *Arnedes* with the great expence of his

[a] courteously] heartily P2, P3

[b] ridden] rode P2, P3

[c] for] for that P2, P3

[d] Palmendos] P2; Palmendo P1

[e] wish it] wished P3

[f] yee] you P2, P3

[g] yee] you P2, P3

[h] then] *om.* P2, P3

bloode, hauing receiued many a greeuous wounde, fell downe at the Prince of *Tharsus* feet, who hauing made cleene his Sworde that was very bloodie, and put it into the sheath, said.

I thinke yee will not seeke heereafter[a] to enforce anie Knight, remembring how deerelie you haue paide for this boldnes: so mounting on horsebacke, (albeit hee was likewise wounded) hee rode on his iourney with *Ozalio*. The Hermit where[b] *Arnedes* lodged all night, hauing behelde this Combat, mooued with charitie and compassion came downe the Mountaine,[383] to succor *Arnedes* who lay bleeding in the grasse, and vnclasping his Helmet to giue him ayre, in short time he recouered his sences againe: when seeing none but the Hermitte, and that the Knight was gone, he reputed it for an act of great humanitie, in not kylling him out-right, his life standing at his mercie,[384] afterwarde, he thus spake to himselfe. What shall I now doo, if not complaine on[c] the instabilitie of Fortune? was not my comming into these Countryes vnhappie, where I thought to winne honour and renowne, when all things turne to my shame and reproofe? sith my strength is not correspondent to the valoure of my minde, I must giue ouer the exercise of Armes, which Fortune (I see) enuies I should follow. Longer would he haue continued in these pensiue mones, but the Hermit interrupted him in this manner.

My Sonne, giue thankes to him[385] that deliuered thee out of the Knights hands, and hath not suffered both bodie and soule to perrish: let idle and vndecent thoughtes[386] bee nowe abandoned, and lift[d] thy minde to the place of eternall comfort. With these wordes he bound vp his wounds so well as he could, minding to lead him to his Hermitage, **[O2r]** but as one mischaunce happeneth not alone, so fell it out at this instant, for hee was no sooner gotten on foote, but *Lecefin* his mortall enemie arriued, and knowing him to be his riual in loue, drawing his Sword, thus spake. Now shall I teache thee my capitall enemie, what it is to looue her whom thou art not woorthy to serue, and that shall I make thee presently confesse, or buy thy boldnes with the price of thy bloode: for a Ladie of so rare perfections, standeth too farre[e] out of a *Frenchmans* reache. Heerwith

[a] seeke heereafter] hereafter seek P2, P3

[b] where] with whom P2, P3

[c] on] of P2, P3

[d] lift] lift up P3

[e] farre] high P2, P3

he violentlie strooke at *Arnedes*, whom the good olde Hermit seeing in such dangerous case, tooke[a] him in his Armes, desiring *Lecefin* not to seeke his death, that had of late escaped it so neere. But *Lecefin* beeing a Moore, and therefore the more inexorable,[387] wold giue no eare to his words, but cruelly gaue the olde man such a stroke on the head, as[b] therewith he fell downe dead to the grounde. Ah dogged and disloyall Traytour,[388] said *Arnedes*, when he beheld this tragicall act, why hast thou slayne this religious Father that neuer offended thee? the heauens I hope will not let thee passe vnpunished, but plague thee as such a damnable deede requireth.

So taking his Sword, as well as he might, by reason of his former hurtes, he seekes[c] to defende himselfe and reuenge the Hermits death: but all was in vaine, (for with out a meruailous chaunce) *Arnedes* death was nowe ordayned. In a happy howre arriued there *Pernedin*,[389] sonne to the Duke of *Pera*, one of them that departed in the search of *Palmendos*, who knowing both the Combatants, stepped betweene them, saying. Why how now Gentlemen?[390] are courtly[d] freendes become enemies in Field? *Arnedes* who was no longer able to holde out, falling downe to the earth, sayd.

Ah *Pernedin*, reuenge my wrong on this inhumaine wretche, who seeing mee cruellie wounded before, by the Knight that bare away the honour of the Tourney, without any cause sette violently vpon me: and this villainous **[O2ᵛ]** Moore, not content to wronge mee alone, hath slayne this holie Hermit, because he disswaded him from dealing with me, that had beene so hardlie intreated before. What tyrannie is this in a Knight? aunswered *Pernedin*, by my Sworde, did not my looue to *Rifarano* ouerrule mee, the gentle Prince that brought thee to the Court, heere I wold make thee to breathe thy last: but I shall declare this treason before the Emperor and his Barons,[391] what manhood thou hath vsed to a wounded man, whom ye[e] durst not deale with had he beene in health: wherefore gette thee gone I aduise thee, or I shall sende thine accursed soule to hel. At these words, *Lecefin* was so ashamed of himselfe, as mounting presentlie on *Arnedes* Horse, he rode away not speaking to eyther of them, know-

[a] tooke] did take P2, P3

[b] as] as that P2, P3

[c] seekes] sought P2, P3

[d] courtly] your courtly P3

[e] ye] thou P2, P3

ing hee had notoriously blemished his honour: wherefore he went[a] to a Monasterie of Nunnes neere at hande, to haue his woundes bounde vp that he had receiued by *Arnedes*.[392]

When the Sisters knewe that hee was of the Emperours Court, they entertayned him very courteously, and one of them beeing a cunning Chirurgion, vndertooke in shorte[b] time to heale his woundes. Nowe was *Pernedin* both offended and greeued, to see the olde Hermitte slaine and *Arnedes* in such daunger, wherefore calling the Nouice that alwaies attended on the olde Father,[393] they leade[c] the wounded Prince into the Hermitage, and afterwarde fetching the dead bodie, buryed it as they coulde conuenientlie, applying soueraigne salues (whereof the good olde man was neuer vnprouided) to *Arnedes* woundes. But *Pernedin* seeing there was no more helpe, and they likewise ignorant in those kind of vnguents, thought it more meete they should goe straite to the Cittie of *Constantinople*.[394]

There may ye, quoth he, sooner recouer your health, because men of skill and knowledge shall take special care of you: and for my parte I will willinglie accompany you thether, albeit I haue not sped in the cause of my departure. **[O3r]** It will be to my shame, answered *Arnedes*, that the Emperour should see me in this daungerous plight: notwithstanding, I will at this present be councelled by you, beeing neuer able to recompence thys honourable kindnes.

CHAPTER XVIII.

How Pernedin *brought* Arnedes *to Constantinople, where the Emperour, the Empresse, with theyr Daughters* Philocrista *and* Melicia *came to uisite him: and what talke the two Dwarffes had together.*

Presently after that *Arnedes* was brought (by the meanes of *Pernedin*) to *Constantinople* in a Litter, because he could not endure to sit on horsebacke: newes of this mischance was brought to the Emperour, who growing into extreme anger against the Moore, said. Well may *Lecefin* resemble the Soldane his Father, a man full of trecherous and ignoble

[a] went] sent P3

[b] shorte] a short P2, P3

[c] leade] led P2, P3

practises,[395] but he must not thus thinke to wrong a Prince of *Fraunce*: So stepping frowninglie from his Chayre, hee went to the Princes Chamber to see him, charging his Phisitions and Chirurgions to tende him so[a] well, as if they had his owne person in cure.

Then *Arnedes* reuealed the whole discourse of that which happened between *Palmendos* and him, at the end whereof the Emperour thus aunswered. I wonder that the Knight should be so desirous to doo me seruice, and yet dooth flye in this sort from mee, doubtlesse hee is gone to prooue the aduenture of *Francelina*, if hee rode that way **[O3v]** you say he did, and it may be his fortune to ende it I hope, except our[b] Nephewe *Belcar* exceede him in valour, and that I can hardlie beleeue he will.[396] When the Emperor departed, hee commaunded that the Empresse and her Daughters should goe visite the Prince, which she accordinglie did, taking *Philocrista* and *Melicia* with her, shee beeing greatly offended at the iniurie doone to *Arnedes*. And[c] *Philocrista* very much bemoned his mishappe, yet wiselie and discreetlie as became a sober virgin, for the looue she bare him was deriued from gentlenes and vertue, which shee noted him to preferre in all his actions, and nothing hadde she in more especiall account, then to conserue her chastitie pure and vnspotted.[397] *Arnedes* was ioyfull to see her beeloued so deerelie, how she sorowed his hard fortune, and blamed *Lecefin* as a disloyall Traytor: which gentle speeches did more comfort his hart, then all the phisick or cunning in the world could doo.

While the Empresse and her Daughters beguiled the time with him, *Amenada* a woman Dwarffe that attended on *Philocrista*, and *Risdeno* her Nephewe, came to *Bruquell Arnedes* Dwarffe, who vsed sundry lamentations, for the great mishappe had befallen his Maister.[398] *Ameneda* comforted him in the best sort she coulde, saying, that in respect his woundes were not mortal, there was no doubt but he would soone recouer them, and the rather, because the Emperour had giuen such charge of him, as his owne person could not be better attended. Ah, quoth *Bruquell*, would God it were no worse: then breaking forth a renting sigth, he proceeded in this manner.

Ah my noble Lorde *Arnedes*, how deere doth her beautie cost thee, for whom thou left'st thy Countrey? Where the onelie reputation of thine

[a] so] as P2, P3

[b] our] your P3

[c] And] *om.* P2, P3

estate, being extracted from such an high and illustrious linage, was sufficient to haue obtayned her, without hazarding thy life in so manie perrils and daungers. *Amenada* meruailing at these words, was immediatlie wrapt with a curious desire, to knowe [O4r] which was the Knight he named, and therefore she labored *Bruquell* with intreaties:[399] for her Ladie *Philocrista*[a] knew his Maister to be a Knight of *Fraunce*, yet none but the Emperour could tell that he was the Kings Sonne. All things that I can possible (quoth the Dwarffe) will I doo for ye,[b] this onely excepted, which without his commaund I dare not attempt, because my libertie stretcheth not so far, yet will I promise yee[c] to aske him the question, and if hee bee pleased I will satisfie your desire.

Melicia, who was earnest in affection to knowe more as concerning her[d] louer *Recinde*, seeing these *Myrmedons* thus conferring together, and ouer-hearing some of theyr speeches: after they were departed to their Chambers, she demanded of *Amenada*, what talk she had with *Arnedes* Dwarffe? whereupon she repeated the whole dyscourse, to the no little content of *Philocrista*, because thys way she might attayne to more knowledge of the *French* Prince. And as she heard her say that he left his Country for the loue of a Ladie, shee presumed immediatly her selfe to be the same, for commonly it falles out, that Louers wil fauour themselues in semblable iudgments and coniectures: wherefore she commanded *Amenada*, to awaite *Bruquel* for performaunce of his promise. The Dwarffe when hee sawe conuenient time to talke with his Maister, hee gaue him to vnderstand what had past between him and *Amenada*, which pleased him so well as nothing could doo more, and commended to him the pursute of this practise. On the morrow, the Emperour and *Primaleon* dyned together, wherefore *Amenada* went to finde out *Bruquell* at hys lodging, and he meeting her by the way, first of all tolde her, that he would performe the promise he made the daie before: but (quoth he) before I satisfie you herein, I must request one thing of you.

Demaunde hardlie what thou wilt, quoth *Amenada*, for thy sute beeing honest, thou canst not be denyed. You must promise me then, sayde *Bruquell*, that to no lyuing [O4v] creature except Madame *Philocrista*, you

[a] *Philocrista*] P2; *Philocista* P1

[b] ye] you P2, P3

[c] yee] you P2, P3

[d] her] his P3

disclose what I shall reueale vnto[a] you. So is it *Amenada*, that for the loue of her onely, *Arnedes* my honourable Lord and Mayster, eldest Sonne to the King of *Fraunce*, hath forsaken his natyue Countrey, in that the renowne of her excellent beautie, spredde by Fame thorow all those partes, caused him to cutte through the daungerous Seas, to credite with his eyes what his eares were cloyed withall. And hauing at full contemplated her sweete face, he findes, that Nature willing industriouslye to embellishe this[b] cheefe peece of worke, hath taken all abilitie from humane report, howe curious or eloquent so euer it be, thorowly to accomplyshe the prayse of her merite: wherefore hee hath sent a Courrier to the King his Father, that his Maiestie should send Embassadours hether, to conferre with the Emperour on a marriage betweene my Mayster and your Ladie, and til they come to dispatche this occasion, he will not be known heereof to anie one, except it be to her gracious selfe onelie. Humbly then desire her, with some benigne clemencie to intreate the hart, which her diuine figure hath secretlie rauished and made her thrall, so shall she gyue cure to hys woundes, and make him the most fortunate Champion that euer entred the fielde for his Ladie:[400] otherwise he can not long enioy his vitall motion, and by his death shall occasion diuers other beside, especially his Cozin *Recinde*, Sonne to the King of *Castile*, who looueth him as his proper life, and as hee bare him company in thys voyage, so wyll he take part of the hardest fortune, for the looue and neere alliaunce that is betweene them.

So well could this tall *Pigmey*[401] vse his language, to gain successe for his Maisters intent, as he made no more difference betweene the two Princes, in respect of their loyall[c] vnanimitie together: then was betweene the two *Pithagorick* companions,[402] *Orestes* and *Pyllades*,[403] or *Nisus* and *Eurialus*,[404] that woulde one dye for an other. Greatlie did *Amenada* meruaile, hearing that a Prince of so high and **[P1r]** great birth, would aduenture thorow such dangerous trauailes, onelie for the accomplishment of a marriage, and might haue gained it with much lesse labour, wherefore she thus answered.

In sooth, if I had not promised to acquaint my Ladie heerewith, I durst not for my life discouer such waightie matters, because I cannot tell

[a] vnto] to P2, P3

[b] this] the P2, P3

[c] loyall] royal P3

her the whole discourse, in that her Sister *Melicia* is neuer from her, and then shall she know as much as my Mistresse. That hurteth not, replied *Bruquell*, neuer conceale it through feare of her presence, for shee is such a wise and well gouerned Princesse, as she will rather modestly hide it, then anie way seeke to spread it abroade, and will (beside) nothing at all mislike thereof. This he spake, for that she had her part in the play, namely by her looue to the Prince *Recinde*, and if perhaps *Philocrista* should be slow or opinitiue in her loue, *Melicia* happily woulde councell her not to refuse so good an offer: in breefe, that they might reciprocally aduise one another, as sicke folkes who had surfeited bothe of one disease, and so oftentimes it comes to passe, that two thoughts afflicted with one kind of martirdome, receiue together more consolation, then they coulde by anie other that feele not the like torment.[405]

Bruquell hauing doone his endeuour, for the conciliation of *Philocrista* with his Maister, returned immediatlie to him, whom he found attending in silent deuotion, to vnderstand the issue of this amorous stratageme, and after that the Dwarffe hadde worde by worde recounted all his negotiation, *Arnedes* was rapt into[a] such vnspeakable ioy, as hee imagined the howre happy when he mette with such an ingenious Trucheman. *Amenada* on the other side, when she espied time for the purpose, interpreted so well and faithfullie the intent of the Prince to her Mistresse *Philocrista*, as she therewith was carried into a thousande imaginations. And albeit the Knight dispayred not in his sute, but rather imagined so sweet a countenance **[P1ᵛ]** would be inclined to mercie: yet she had so lost her libertie in this cause, by seeing her beloued so daungerously wounded, as now she feared to send him anie seuere or rigorous aunswer, wherefore she thus spake to her Dwarffe. I am offended that thou didst promise *Bruquell* to acquaint mee with these[b] newes, but seeing what hath happened cannot be preuented: thou shalt then goe to *Arnedes*, and tell him from me, that I meruaile he would thrust himselfe into so manie perrils, for which I account my selfe beholding to him, and promise[c] in requitall of his hard sufferings, to accept of him as my loyall Husband,[406] if my gracious parents will so permit it: with this condition, that hee aduenture not the least speeches hereof to me, but hold himselfe suffised by knowing

[a] into] in P2, P3

[b] these] this P2, P3

[c] promise] promise him P2, P3

my will heerein. And that I may bee assured of the vehement affection he beareth me, desire him to feede on this aunswere, as on the most souer-aigne Balme of perfect Cataplasme, that may soonest of all consolidate his woundes: so hastening his cure and conualescence, that (if it may be) he honour me with his presence to morowe.

After *Philocrista* had instructed *Amenada* in her Embassade, she tooke *Melicia* aside, to whom (because they loued eche other with sin-cere affection) *Philocrista* discouered this amorous intent, and *Verbatim* reported what the Dwarffe had tolde to her: which discourse well con-tented *Melicia*, cheefely when she heard that her Knight *Recinde* was of the royall blood of *Castile*. By this[a] time is *Amenada* come to the *French* Prince, and hath deliuered the message from *Philocrista*, wherwith he was so cheerefully animated, as soone after he determined to forsake his bed, but before the Dwarffe returned againe he desired her to conuay a *French* dittie[407] to her Mistresse, which for her sake he deuised that morning, and withal to intreate the Maister of the Emperours Chappell, to order it in partes after the arte of Musique: the dittie was thus. **[P2r]**

The finest Gold is by the touch discernd,
The Adamant the sturdie yron drawes:
The proofe heereof in loue may well be learnd,
For by these twaine I shape a louers cause.
You Madame framed of the finest Golde,
Vpon the touchstone of my hart is tryde:
And I composed of the yron molde,
Followe the vertues that in you abide.
Then sith the touch telles if the Gold be pure,
And rugged yron shewes the vertuous stone:
Take touch and yron both into your cure,
For (Madame) they belong to you alone.[408]

After that *Amenada* had receiued this Dittie, she saide to the Prince, that shee coulde not tell howe her Mistresse would like of her, bringing her such a presumptuous message: yet if she were displeased therewith, she woulde disguise euery thing so well, as eache of them in the ende should receiue contentment. So returning to the Princesse *Philocrista*,

[a] this] *om.* P3

she tolde in what extreamitie the Prince was for her loue, and to mittigate his passions, had framed that dittie: which when she had read and well noted, shee accounted her conquest greater, then if she were possessed of all *Asia*. Sundry times[409] did the Empresse and her Daughters visite the *French* Prince, to the vnspeakable contentment of the secrete Louers, who awaited nothing but the comming of the *French* Embassadours, for the confirmation of their long desired hope: but let vs leaue them a while, and come to *Rifarano*, who is all this while in the searche of *Palmendos*.

[P2v] CHAPTER XIX.

How Rifarano *beeing in the search of* Palmendos, *mette wyth a Dwarffe trauailing toward the Emperour, to complayne on the*[a] *wrong a Knight had doone him, and howe to reuenge the Dwarffe, and gratifye the Emperor heerein, Rifarano went to combat with the Knight before hys Castell.*

Sixe dayes together rode *Rifarano*, after his departure from *Constantinople*, without hearing anie tydings of the Knight he sought for, and nowe in the euening,[410] hee mette a Dwarffe on horsebacke,[411] accompanied wyth foure Squires, of whom hee enquired likewise as concerning the Knight.[412] In sooth, quoth the Dwarffe I saw not any such, but tell me I pray yee from whence you nowe come. From the Court of the Emperor *Palmerin*, aunswered *Rifarano*. Howe happy then am I, sayd the Dwarffe, to meete you here, because I haue euermore heard, that thence commeth manie good and vertuous Knightes: wherefore I shall pray[413] (in respecte of the good I wishe to so benigne a Prince) that you may soone finde the man you looke for, and likewise that his Maiestie may pittie my cause, in reuenging mee on a Knight that hath shamefullie out-raged mee, I giuing him no cause of offence in the world. With these words he gaue a meruailous sigth: whereuppon *Rifarano* desiring to vnderstande the cause, the Dwarffe thus began. Knowe gentle Knight, that albeit God hath fashioned me as ye[b] see, yet did hee bestow [P3r] on me riches and possessions, and among other thinges, I haue a strong Castell not farre hence, there fel I in loue with a beautifull Damosell, Daughter to a Gentleman my neere neighbour, with whome I dealt in such sorte,

[a] the] a P2, P3

[b] ye] you P2, P3

as soone after I enioyed her in mariage. Liuing afterwarde in all prosperous felicitie, wee walked abroade to recreate our selues, in a pleasant field neer adioyning to my house, where this proud and discourteous Knight, (who long laboured to haue my Wife in mariage, and by reason of his euill conditions could not obtayne her) came accompanied with two of his Kinsemen, (as badde disposed men as him selfe) and there tooke my Wife perforce from me, carying her to a Castell of his two dayes iourney hence,[a] where he keepeth her vnder strong guarde,[414] and hath sent me worde by one of his[b] Squires, that if I complayne heereof to anie liuing creature, he will come kill[c] me with his owne hande in my Castell.[415] Yet being vnable to endure this villainous oppression, I am going to tell my cause to the Emperour *Palmerin*, who I hope will speedilie doo me iustice herein, beeing a Prince thereto greatlie addicted as I haue heard report.

Rifarano, meruailing at this horrible iniurie, sayde to the Dwarffe. Shewe me the Castell where the Knight abideth, for I doubt not but to do so much in the right of thy cause, as he shall yeelde recompence for this faulte, and feare heereafter to offer any one the like,[d] without any further troubling the Emperour heerein. The Dwarffe accepting this freendlie offer, that night lodged *Rifarano* at hys Castell, where hee was exceeding well entertained,[416] and on the morrow, taking sixe Squires with them, rode to the Knights Castell, where espying one vpon the walles, *Rifarano* demaunded if his Lorde were within. Mary is he, answered the Squire on the walles, hee is nowe sporting himselfe with that tall fellowes loue:[417] but I am sorie that[e] you would be so badlie councelled, quoth he to *Rifarano*, as to come ende[f] your life in this place.[g] Be not thou so careful **[P3v]** for me, aunswered *Rifarano*, but goe lette[h] thy Maister vnderstand that I woulde speake two or three wordes[418] wyth him, on matters[i] that greatlie[j] con-

[a] hence] from hence P2, P3

[b] his] my P3

[c] come kill] come and kill P2, P3

[d] any one the like] the like to any one P2, P3

[e] that] *om.* P3

[f] come ende] come to end P2, P3

[g] place.] peace. P2

[h] goe lette] go, and let P2, P3

[i] on matters] on certain matters P2, P3

[j] greatlie] very nearly P2, P3

cerne his honour. The Squire went presentlie to his Maister, who hearing that the Dwarffe had brought a Knight with him, tooke the Gentlewoman by the hande, and brought her with him to a windowe, where opening the casements[a] that they might see her, said.

Knight that didst call me hether, say boldly what thou canst, for I wel perceiue thou commest to seeke thine own ruine. And there didst thou finde thy dishonor, aunswered *Rifarano*, when by force and treason thou abusedst[b] thys Gentleman, who neuer gaue thee any cause of offence: wherefore restore[c] his Wife whome thou vniustlie detaynest, or if reason may not thereto perswade thee, come downe and enter the Combat with me, and I shall let thee know the price of thy villainie. I had not thought, replyed the Knight of the Castell, that thy indiscretion had beene so great, as to thinke I would win a thing so hardlie, and deliuer it from me so lightlie,[419] nor shall the paragon of my hart, bee[d] in the custodie againe[e] of so base an excrement of nature: then spake he[f] to the Dwarffe in this manner.

Thou wretched and ridiculous creature, commest thou likewise to make one in the Tragedie? begin with thyne owne hand thou wert best, or I shall plague thee with extreame torments. So tooke he the Gentlewoman[g] in hys armes, and oftentimes laciuiously kissed her, shee stryuing in teares to hinder his embracings,[420] wherefore hee sayde. Good Madame, seeke no occasion whereby to offende yourselfe, for yee shall see me plucke downe the brauery of this Knight, and make the Monster your husbande safe from troubling you anie more. Tush, these are but wordes, quoth *Rifarano*, let me see thee come Armed into the fielde, then shall I liue in hope of some deeds. And if you[h] wilt haue me imagine thee couragious, bring down the Ladie with thee, that the Conquerer may carrie her whether him pleaseth. **[P4r]** I am content, answered the Knight, because thou shalt see howe little I esteeme thy threatning, and soone shall all controuersies be

[a] casements] P2; Casements P1; casement P3

[b] abusedst] didst abuse P2, P3

[c] restore] restore restore P3

[d] bee] be again P2, P3

[e] againe] *om.* P2, P3

[f] spake he] he spake P2, P3

[g] Gentlewoman] Gentlewomen P3

[h] you] thou P2, P3

ended betweene thee and me,[a] that heereafter may arise on this occasion. Quickly had he Armed himselfe and came foorth leading the Lady in his hande: which when the Dwarffe saw, he durst not tary, but gotte him a bowe shoote further off. So fell the Knight and *Rifarano* to the Combat, which continued long time doubtfull on eyther side, but at length *Rifarano* had the vpper-hand of his enemie, because he had[b] giuen him many cruell woundes on his bodie. When the Squires of the Castell sawe their Maister ouercome, they woulde forcibly haue caryed the Ladie into the Castell again: but *Rifarano* aduertised thereof by her cry, made them forsake her and runne hastilie into the Castell. Then[c] taking her by the hand, sayd. Come with me Ladie, and I shall deliuer ye to your Husbande that loues yee loyallie, as you may be perswaded by this I haue doone at his earnest intreatie. Many humble thankes she requited him withal, seeing her selfe free from her[d] iniurious enemie, and the Dwarffe seeing this fortunate successe, came and humbled himselfe at the Conquerers feete, embracing his Wife in[e] aboundaunce of ioy, being neither of them able to expresse theyr contentation, for that teares and inward motions of comfort had depriued them of speech. Afterward the Knight had recouered himselfe againe, and came stealing on *Rifarano* thinking to murder him, but the Dwarffe espying him, cryed out,[421] whereupon the Prince returned, and getting him once more[f] into subiection, with his Sworde smote hys heade from his Shoulders.[422] The Dwarffe not a little ioyfull for this victorie, desired the Prince that he would accompany him to his Castell, because that trayterous Knight had a Brother and two Cozins, who hearing of his death, wold presently pursue them. Whereto *Rifarano* courteously condiscended, and mounting the Gentlewoman[g] behind her Husbande, they iourneyed thence with all speede possible. **[P4^v]** But ere they could recouer the place where they wold be, they were pursued by the Knights Brother and his two Cozins. When the Dwarffe and his Wife nowe verilie thought to die: notwithstanding, such was the braue behauiour of *Rifarano*, that one after

[a] thee and me] me and thee P2, P3

[b] because he had] having P2, P3

[c] Castell.Then] P2; ~ , then P1.

[d] her] this P2, P3

[e] in] with P2, P3

[f] getting him once more] once more getting him P2, P3

[g] Gentlewoman] Gentlewomen P3

another they spedde as[a] the Knight of the Castell had doone, and so without any more interruption they gotte home to their Castel, where they feasted the Prince very sumptuously. On the morow he departed thence, continuing his trauayle after *Palmendos*, and by the way he succoured a distressed Countesse, against a Cruell Brother in Lawe of hers, named *Diole*, who sought forcibly to depryue her of her possessions: but by the rare Chiualrie of *Rifarano*, hee lost his life in that bad attempt.[423] And here wyth the Countesse we will leaue *Rifarano*, because wee haue[b] too long forgotten our cheefe Knight *Palmendos*.[424]

CHAPTER XX.

Howe Palmendos *arriued in the Isle of Carderia, where first he vanquished*[c] Tyrendos *in the Ioust, and next the Knight that guarded the passage of the Bridge, and also dyuers other that assayled him at the thyrde Tower, and howe he came to the Gardengate where* Francelina *was.*

Not long since you vnderstoode, how after *Palmendos* had vanquished *Arnedes*,[425] hee followed his way with long desire to see *Carderia*, wherfore omitting all occasions that might hinder his voyage, he determined to make no stay till he came[d] to the Isle: and very soone after it was his [Q1r] chaunce to arriue there,[426] when he implored the helpe of heauen in fynishing this aduenture, and as a sacrifice after victorie, he promised to offer his soule to the holy caracter of Christianitie, and to be baptized so[e] soone as he could.[427] At this time *Belcar* kept not the passage of the Bridge,[428] because he was departed certaine daies before, to visite the King and Queene at[f] *Macedon*: for they hearing of his wonderfull deedes of Armes, in defending that Bridge, sent for him to the Courte by an expresse messenger. And truelie he woulde not haue gone (so resolute was he in his enterprise) but that the Princesse *Alderina* secreatly

[a] as] all P3

[b] because wee haue] having P2, P3

[c] vanquished] was vanquished P3

[d] came] come P2, P3

[e] so] as P3

[f] at] of P2, P3

commaunded him, by a Letter written with her owne hande: she[a] hauing discouered the trueth of all to the Queene *Griana*, intreating her by some meanes to continue the Duke her Father there, till time that[b] *Belcar* came from the Isle of *Carderia*.

The Queene liked heereof exceeding well, and knowing her Nephewe could not ioyne in more honourable mariage, then with the chaste and vertuous Ladie[c] *Alderina*: she conferred with the Duke and Duchesse of *Pontus*, who likewise were glad of so noble alliaunce. For this cause the Queene sent one of her Gentlemen to *Belcar*, accompanied with *Alderinaes* Page, who closely deliuered the Prince the Letter, the substance whereof followeth thus.[429]

[Q1v] *The Letter sent by the Princesse of Durace, to* Belcar *Sonne to the King of Hungarie.*

To the right valiant and renowned Prince Belcar, *Sonne to the King of* Hungarie*: a Maiden very easie to be deceiued, sendeth health condigne to his deserts.*

Excuse mee, Lord *Belcar*, if I write to you what the aboundaunce of my spirite enforceth, because if it were of anie thing els, I feare I could not ende, without confused wandring in this discourse: so extraordinarily are my sences heerein perplexed, as they can enioy no little breathing time of rest or quiet. And if you woulde exactlie consider, from whence this molestation proceedeth, you should finde the grounde thereof to be violent and excessiue loue, which on my behalfe was faithfully entertained, and dedicated to none but onely you:[430] a reason to procure this Letter the more fauourable entertainment, and to bee reade with as good will as it was written. Knowe then, that I doo not without greate occasion silently complaine of you, because me thinkes you seeme a promise breaker, or rather a preuaricatour in looue towardes mee:[431] as the reading of thys Letter will cause yee[d] to confesse, if that reason bee not

[a] she] the P3

[b] till time that] till that time P2, P3

[c] Ladie] *om.* P2, P3

[d] yee] you P2, P3

alienated from your iudgement, which ought to directe your compasse in all affayres.

What thinke yee will nowe[a] be the vulgare opinion of your attempt? nothing but that you desire to haue the name of *Francelinaes* true Champion, considering the meruailous exploits in Armes, which dailie you perfourme in her defence: making heereby the renowne of her excellencie more memorable, and all Gentlemen more desirous to visite that **[Q2r]** Isle. Wherefore I nowe perceiue you are not my Knight, but rather that your seruice is onelie for the faire Princesse *Francelina*, which induceth mee to beleeue, that the speeches vsed on your behalfe, when you departed from the Tourney at *Macedon*, were meere forgerie and dissimulation: an acte sufficient wheron to rayse condemnation (vnlesse I speedilie perceiue the contrarie) and to repute you the most disloyall Prince, that euer made profession of manhoode. But to preuent this perswasion, (whereto common speeche by your absence hasteneth me) and that it may not bee resolutlie sette downe in my minde: I pray you come hether with what speede you canne, before my departure hence to *Durace*, that I may apply some remedie to the[b] continuall martirdome, which in looues unquenchable fyre my hart suffereth by your occasion.[432] Els sende mee worde suddainly what is your intent, as concerning the principal poynts dilated, and by no other Messenger then this bearer, whom I charge with some speeches by word of mouth: him[c] you may boldly trust and acquaint with your secrets, as the most faithfull messenger I could deuise to sende.

The Lady knowne to you, whose death is neere at hand:
If pittie cause ye[d] *not to come, the perrill to withstand.*[433]

This Letter and other matters of credence, wherewith *Alderina* right well instructed *Gracian*, were the only meanes that the Prince *Belcar* came to *Macedon*, who left *Tirendos* (in meane while) defender of the Bridge at *Carderia*, hoping to returne thether againe very shortlie: but other mat-

[a] yee will nowe] you now will P2, P3

[b] the] my P2, P3

[c] him] in whom P3

[d] ye] you P2, P3

ters happened vnto[a] him which excused that labour, according as you shall reade heereafter.[434]

Nowe come we to the Prince of *Tharsus*, whom *Tirendos* perceiuing to approche the Brydge, came and denied him passage according to the order: wherupon they fel to the Ioust, *Tirendos* fortune proouing so badde, as hee was sent to measure his length on the ground, wherat the [Q2v] beholders were greatly amazed, for that since the departure of *Belcar*, he had preuailed against many a Knight. Among the rest, the Queene of *Thessalie* Mother to *Francelina*, who was come thether fiue or sixe dayes before, because the last of the three Fayries that caused the enchauntment in the Fortresse, foreseeing shee coulde not liue long, hastened the comming of *Palmendos*, as you haue hearde before,[435] and afterward sent word to the Queene, that soone after her death she should see her desires accomplished.

The death of the Enchauntresse was no sooner known to the good Queene, (who had an extreame affection to see her Daughter free from the Magicall coniurations, that thereby the King her Husbande might be deliuered, from cruell seruitude among the Heathen) but she departed from *Thessalie*, and came to the Isle of *Carderia*, where shee, nor any of hers could passe further then the Bridge: wherfore they erected Tents and Pauillions in the Fielde, attending there the end of the aduenture, when she seeing that *Tyrendos* was vanquished, wished such successe to the newe come Knight, as[b] hee might happilie finish the enchauntment.

Palmendos perceiuing how his first aduersarie would trouble him no further, approched to the Gates of the first Tower, wher he behelde the great Knight ready to offer him battaile, wherefore hee alighted from his Horse, and drawing his Sworde, saide. If the prouidence of the heauens haue destenied me to conquer this enterprise, far bee all pusillanimitie and cowardise from me, till I haue deliuered the gentle Princesse heere enclosed: forbeare then mine eyes as yet to couet the sight of *Francelina*, albeit yee burne in desire[c] to beholde her, and I will keepe promise with yee[d] so soone as Fortune pleaseth.

[a] vnto] to P2, P3

[b] as] as that P2, P3

[c] yee burne in desire] you desire P2, P3

[d] yee] you P2, P3

After these words, hee closely buckled with the Knight of the Bridge, continuing a long, dangerous and doubtfull combatte with him, the Dwarffe in the Lanthorne sundry times with his Horne renewing his Champions [Q3r] forces: yet by the man of inuincible courage, who was ordained to be his Conquerer, hee was confounded mauger all his deuillish helps. So forwarde hee marched to the seconde Tower, and as the Gates were clapping together, according as they did to the Prince *Belcar*, hee thruste hys Sworde betweene the Gates, when immediatly the thunder ceased, and[a] they fell backe wide open as they were before.

At this good happe the beholders greatly reioyced,[b] especially the Queene of *Thessalie*, who followed on styll accompanied with *Ozalio*, and to him she highly commended the worthy behauiour of this Knight: *Ozalio* answering her, that she had good cause to applaude her stars, hauing sent thether[c] a Knight of such royal discent, as his like was not to bee founde thorowe all[d] Christian kingdomes. *Tirendos* in this while was caryed into his Tent by hys Squires, where he so greeued for his disgrace, as hee was readie to die in despight thereof. Now is *Palmendos* come to the last Tower, which was defended by three Knights armed *cap a pe*, and they with three sharpe Launces stood readie to receiue him at the poynt, wherewith hee beeing somwhat amazed, said to himselfe. Wheron thinkest thou *Palmendos*? What? beginnest thou now to dismay? tushe man be of good cheere, thou labourest for her, with whose beautie none in the worlde may compare: if by comming so farre thou hast doone more, then anie Knight before thee could performe, commit thy selfe to God and Fortune for the rest, and followe thine intent though thou die therein.[436] Nowe begins he couragiously to aduenture on them, who ioyning altogether against him, ouerthrewe him that hee could hardly arise againe, notwithstanding recouering his feete, hee pursued with such vnconquerable hope, as at length he droue them before him ouer the Bridge, when bothe they and the first Knight of the Tower vanished away together, and in like manner did the Dwarffe that sate in the Lanthorne, with a horrible shaking of the earth [Q3v] and the whole Fortresse. The Queene, *Ozalio* and the rest, fell downe and honoured heauen for this victorie, perswading themselues

[a] and] *om.* P3

[b] greatly reioyced] were greatly amazed P2, P3

[c] thether] hither P2, P3

[d] all] all the P2, P3

that the worst of the aduenture was past: as for the Prince himselfe, hee followed the matter with such alacritie, considering faire *Francelina* was the reward of his trauaile, as nothing seemed to him nowe[a] impossible. So passing on, he found the posterne that guided the waie to the Garden, which was garded by two furious enchaunted dogges, there through the wickette he beheld a Fountaine, with sundry goodly[b] Damoselles about it, and in the middest, in a curious Chayre of clothe of Golde, sate *Francelina* the sweete Goddesse of beautie, so wonderfull gorgiouslie[c] decked in rich ornaments, as it would haue made any hart enamoured to beholde her. *Palmendos* rauished with the sight of her, stept in at the doore not dreading any perrill, when presentlie the enchaunted dogs ranne vpon him, as though they woulde haue rent[d] him in peeces, and long time very dangerously they did assayle him, tearing his Armour cruelly in peeces, that he was now dryuen to dispaire of his life: yet in the ende with much a doo he preuailed against them, albeit they brought him into exceeding great perplexitie, as hee neuer felt the like in all his life before.

[Q4r] CHAPTER XXI.

What gentle speeches and gracious deuises, Palmendos *had with faire* Francelina *in the Garden, wher they supped together: and howe after hee had tolde her what*[437] *he was, he gaue her the Ring, which he receiued of the Queene his mother at his departure from* Tharsus.

Francelina alreadie had felte the flames of looue, in as vehement manner as the Prince *Palmendos*, because the Fairies (knowing the end of the enchauntment was at hand) told her that ere long shee should be conquered, and deliuered from that Castel by one of the best Knights in the world, shee beeing at her byrth appointed his Wife, in recompence of his aduenturous trauayles.[438]

And this discourse shee sealed with so many rare commendations of the Knight, as her hart was[e] surprised with loue in such sort, that shee

[a] nowe] *om.* P2, P3

[b] goodly] good P3

[c] wonderfull gorgiouslie] wonderfully P2, P3

[d] rent] torn P2, P3

[e] was] were P3

longed euery howre to see the man appointed for her Husbande. And as the Pilot long perplexed with outragious tempests, mounts to the toppe to see if any Hauen for[a] reskewe is at hande: so this Lady tossed to and fro in the roughe billowes of looue,[439] oftentimes left her Dungion and came vpon the walles, expecting the comming of this promised Knight. By good hap she espyed when *Palmendos* came to the Bridge, beside, the trembling of the Castell at the departure of the Knights, touched her hart with a signe of present comfort, whereupon in this brauery shee went with her Damoselles into the Garden, expecting the issue of the Knights fortune that **[Q4v]** presaged so much before hand. In breefe,[440] he beeing entred the Garden, as you haue heard already,[441] she beeing directed by the Fairies what she shoulde doo, when shee perceiued the dogges ouercome: arose with her Damoselles and went towards the Knight, shewing many gracious countenaunces for his welcome, but *Palmendos* seeing her approche so neere him, fel on his knee offering to kisse her hand, wherat *Francelina* bashfullie blushing, offered him the like, saying.

It is my duetie, Sir Knight, to vse such humilitie, albeit your courtesie hath preuented me, for this wondefull aduenture finished by you, declares your rare perfection in Chiualrie,[b] beeing second to none that at this day beareth Armes.[442] Yet ere you take me hence, I woulde request one fauour at your handes, not any thing to make you doubt the losse of her, who freely giueth herselfe as your owne, but for[c] you haue deliuered me from the enchauntment, my request graunted, you may dispose of me as your loyall spouse and Wife. Madame, answered *Palmendos*,[d] I now thinke my selfe no lesse belooued of heauen, then fauoured by Fortune, hearing you say that I am yours, and you are mine, which makes mee thinke all my labours nothing in respect of you: therefore demaunde what you please, for I beeing your professed seruaunt, must with all reuerence obey your commaunde. A thousande thankes good Knight, quoth shee, albeit such speeches agree not with your calling, I beeing onely in your subiection, and ready to attend as your hand-mayden: but me thinkes it were necessarie you should take a little rest, beeing good to regard the ende and periode of all thinges, let me therfore humbly intreate yee, to come refreshe

[a] for] or P3

[b] Chiualrie] perfect Chivalry P3

[c] for] for that P2, P3

[d] Madame, answered *Palmendos*] ED; Madame ˆ answered, *Palmendos* P1

your selfe for the better conseruation of your health. So went they both together to the Fountaine, where *Palmendos* was vnarmed by the Princesse *Francelina* and her Damoselles, and a costly Mantle was brought to wrap about him, then sate he down by hys Ladie, in another Chayre couered all ouer with Gold, and **[R1r]** as if *Herebus* had sent his Daughter to hide the day light, spreading darke night all ouer the Hemisphere, so were great store of Torches and Tapers alighted.[a][443] There was felt the odorifferous smell of Roses, Violets,[b] and al the sweet flowers of the Garden,[c] beside the incomparable beauty of *Francelina*,[d] her[e] Maydens beguiled the time with sundrye sorts[f] of Instrumentes, and thereto sung many dainty canzonets, as if *Apollo*, *Orpheus*, *Arion*,[444] and all the other fathers of heauenly Musique had beene present, which so attracted the sences of the Prince, as his memory began to were drowsie and forgetful, imagining himselfe in a very beatitude, where he seemed to see, not only the perfect beautie of a Goddesse, but a diuine shadow, which caried awaie both his hart and eyes in contemplation.[445]

Of like[g] opinion was the young Princesse, meruailing at the braue constitution of her Knight, and esteeming her selfe beyond all other in happines, that Fortune[446] had sorted her out such a Husbande: and in sooth these Louers were the fayrest couple that euer were ioyned in mariage together, not vnfitly compared to *Leander* and *Hero*,[447] the two goodliest starres that were in their times. In this surpassing contentation they continued, till a Damosell (vnderstanding that supper was prepared) there set before them a Table readie couered, the wood whereof was very precious, deliuering a sauour much like to the[h] Balme, and theron was sette all sorts of costly viands: hard by stood a Cupboorde richlie adorned with Basons and Cups of Golde, which were embellished with such precious stones, as the value of them was reputed inestimable. But these louers[448] coulde

[a] and as if Herebus . . . alighted.] *om.* P2, P3

[b] There was felt the odorifferous smell of Roses, Violets] There was Lillies, Roses, Violets P2, P3

[c] of the Garden] that the earth afforded P2, P3

[d] beside the incomparable beauty of Francelina] and of incomparable beauty P2, P3

[e] her] the P2, P3

[f] sorts] sounds P2, P3

[g] like] the like P2, P3

[h] the] *om.* P2, P3

eate verie little, because they had worke enough to regard eche other: for there is nothing in the worlde more agreeable to one enamoured, then to contemplate the obiect of his thoughts, because loue making a breach into the bodie, and planting his siege against the very soule, hinders the passage of nourishing meates, and makes them feed on his louely deuises,[449] which are such, as euery one of you that **[R1v]** haue tasted thereof, can distinguish whether they be bitter or sweet:[a] Hence proceedeth the pleasure conceiued by beholding,[b] when the eye takes his course to the hart, carrying with it the liuelie draught and effigies of the thing seene, making so sound impression therof in the spirit, as nothing els may be represented therto: in the end, this Idea passing through the penetrailes and secret rayons of the stomack, engraues[c] on the hart the perfect portrait of the thing beloued.[450] And what morsel more delicious, what wine more plesant, or licquor more ambrosius can one find, wherwith to satisfie the soule esprised with the brandon of *Venus*,[451] then the exact contemplation and secret discourse, which the spirit maketh to his onlie choise, when he beholdeth himselfe riciprocally beloued of her whom hee loueth? doubtles none at al: happily some other might be spoken of, which seeme to yeeld more content, but then they are transitory and of no continuance. In this sort supped *Palmendos* and *Francelina*, when the Damosels withdrawing the Table, went to take their own refection, leauing these twaine to deuise together: then approching[d] the Knight to the Mistres of hys hart, said.[e452] Madame, how happy may I name the howre of my natiuity, seeing the celestiall bodies appointed me such a planet, as made me gaine the honor of your loue: now find I that for truth which you told me in the Temple at *Delphos*,[453] and[f] in short time I should see you at mine own pleasure. Commaund then I beseech you what you would haue mee doo, and shew me the way to gather some fruit, by the perpetual seruice I haue vowed

[a] distinguish whether they be bitter or sweet:] best apprehend the pleasure and sweetnesse thereof. P2, P3

[b] the pleasure conceiued by beholding] delightfull dreams and fancies of the mind P2, P3

[c] when the eye . . . engraues] when the eye taketh a full view, and the lively drought of the object beloved through the penetrails and rayons of the stomack, which graves P2, P3

[d] approching] approached P2, P3

[e] said.] and said. P2, P3

[f] and] that P2, P3

to your diuine beauty, that I may giue some cooling to the vnquenchable flame, wherin my hart is more and more tormented. And if the artificiall fire which we receiue from between two stones for our vse, is lesse then nothing in respecte of the naturall, as namelie the most noble of the foure elements lodged neere the celestial region:[454] I dare, and by experience can affirme, that the violence of the diuine, surpasseth the action of the other two, because if they light on any body, they may quickly be extinguished: **[R2^r^]** but much more contrary is the other, the vehemence wherof euery way increaseth paine, without lymitting the life of the sufferer, as the very least of the other doth.[a] My Lord, answered *Francelina*, in regarde of the fire which happily you now feele, esteeme the same to proceede from the spark, that equally hath taken hold on me, wherof I make no such admiration (considering the disposition of the destenies) as to heare you say that you haue seene mee in an other place:[b] in sooth at the age of three yeeres I was fatally enclosed in this Castell,[455] where neuer since entred Knight or anie other straunger, but onely you. As for my request whereto you haue promised, thus[c] it is, that you attempt not against my chastitie, vntill our mariage be solemnly performed, which may not be, til you first haue rescued the King of *Thessalie* my father, from the long imprysonment wherein the Turke hath kept him.[456] This aduenture you must needes vndertake, which doubtles yee shal worthilie effect, and so be Lorde of me and the[d] Realme of *Thessalie*, wherto I am lawful heire after my Fathers decease: for performaunce whereof, I commit my selfe into your custody, prouided you keepe your former promise. *Palmendos* attentiuely noted her words, and afterwarde remained a while silent, imagining whether he should sende or accompanie his Ladie to the Emperor, or in meane space keepe himselfe vnkowne to anie, till he had ended the aduenture in *Turkie*, bringing at his returne the King of *Thessalie* with him, if the heauens fauoured him in his deliueraunce, at length breaking off this silent determination, he answered in this sort. Madame, so feruent and inexpuisable is the loue I beare ye, as to gaine the Monarchie of the whole world, I woulde not offende the very least of your vertuous thoughtes: and albeit I had

[a] And if the artificiall . . . of the other doth.] *om.* P2, P3

[b] My Lord . . . in an other place] The Princess replied. My Lord, I cannot but admire to hear you say that you have seen me in another place P2, P3

[c] thus] this P2, P3

[d] the] of the P2, P3

not promised what you required, mine[a] own regard shoulde haue taught me better gouernment. For I account my selfe the happiest Knight vnder heauen, not by anie honour or prayse gotten in this aduenture, but onelie to see my selfe subiect **[R2v]** to such incomparable beautie, which henceforth shal make me so forward in Chiualrie, as the race from whence I am discended, shall thereby atchiue eternall commendation.[b] And heerof Madame resolue your selfe, that paine or trauaile shall not with-hold mee, from restoring the King your Father to his pristinate libertie, if my wonted fortunate starre shine on me in the action.[c] In meane whyle[d] I will leaue you to the Emperours charge, the Prince whom I loue and desire to serue, bearing patiently the burden of my greefe in your absence, till time allow vs a gracious meeting. Be heereof assured[e] my noble Lorde, quoth she, that neuer shall I loue anie but you, to whom the fatall destenies haue onely appointed me, and no lesse wyll my torments be in your absence, then yours, beeing nowe depriued of my former libertie, and the same transferred to your disposing.[457]

Spending the time thus in amorous conference, at length he told her al that happened to him in the Temple at *Delphos*, where if he sawe her not in person, yet did hee[f] beholde her liuely representation, and had a great deale of talke with her: whereat *Francelina* coulde not but meruaile, yet commending the wisedom of the Fayries in appointing her so noble a husband. Now she desires to vnderstand his name and birth, wherewith at large hee truelie acquainted her, yet willing her she should not reueale it to anie, till he returned with the King of *Thessalie* her father. Then did he giue her the Ring, which hee receiued of the Queene his Mother when he came from[g] *Tharsus*,[458] requesting her to keepe it carefully, because hee

[a] mine] my P2, P3

[b] which henceforth . . . commendation.] and one so nobly descended. P2, P3

[c] And heerof Madame . . . in the action.] And now Madam as I shall not account any pains or travel too much for you, thinking my self sufficiently happy, that the stars did so fortunately shine upon me in this action. P2, P3

[d] In meane whyle] I shal intreat you not to return to your fathers house, but P2, P3

[e] heereof assured] assured hereof P2, P3

[f] did hee] he did P2, P3

[g] from] to P3

must shewe it to the Emperour his Father, as the token whereby he[a] shold discerne him to be his Sonne.

[R3r] CHAPTER XXII.

Howe Palmendos *and* Francelina *going to the Queene of Thessalie, mette without the Castell dyuers Knights and Ladies of the Isle, which*[459] *attended theyr comming: what reuerence the Lord of the Isle did him, and how he brought the Queene to see the Castell.*

Highlie pleased was the Princesse *Francelina*, when she knewe her spouse to bee Sonne to the Emperor *Palmerin*, and al this night they beguiled the time with sundrye discourses pleasing to them both.[460] The next morning, the Princesse brought her looue to beholde her stately lodging, where shee caused him to put on a costly blacke Armour, left there by the Fairies purposelie for him, as also a goodly Sword, by vertue whereof hee might bring such as him pleased into a sound sleepe, so causing two Damosels to beare his Helmet and Launce, they intended to walke foorth of the Castell. Nowe shined faire *Francelina* brighter then the morning starre, her heade attire adorned all ouer with Carbuncles, Diamondes, Rubies, Emeraldes and Orientall Saphires, and her vpper garment beeing a long Robe of cloth of Golde, curiouslie figured with pearles and precious stones, as the valewe thereof was imagined inestimable.[461] In this, and far greater pompe then I can sette downe, they left the Castell,[462] meeting by the way sundry Knights and Ladies of the Isle, and among them all was an auncient graue Gentleman, Father to the three Fairies,[463] whom they inuested in the gouernment of this Isle after their death, he falling on his [R3v] knee before *Palmendos* and *Francelina*, deliuered these speeches. Aduenturous and most fortunate Knight, happie was the Planet that ruled at thy birth, seeing that by thy vertue and wonderful prowesse, thou hast made this place accessable, which so long time hath continued full of trouble. Reuerend Sir, answered *Palmendos*, the soueraigne bountie hath made mee the instrument of your good, and therfore I reioyce a great deale the more: if you be either Father, Vncle, or allied to those noble Dames,[464] that by their knowledge haue doone so much for me, I giue yee all the right heere to bee had by the conquest of *Francelina*. I humbly thank ye

[a] he] she P3

Sir, answered the Knight of the Isle, for offering me such a courteous gift, whereof I am altogether vnwoorthie, albeit my Daughters by their secrete Philosophie, in this action still directed your course: but leaue we these speeches till better opportunitie, and goe we to comfort the Queene of *Thessalie*, who on the Bridge attendeth your comming,[465] for till you haue brought her Daughter ouer the Bridge, the enchauntments are not ended, and then shall the Castell be in the former state, as it was when *Francelina* came first hither.[466] And is my gracious Queene and Mother heere? said the Princesse, then I see my ioyes will meete altogether. So walked they louinglie[a] ouer the Bridge,[467] attended on by manie Lordes, Barons and Ladies, when the Queene seeing her Daughter come towardes her, hardly could she refraine from swouning in the armes of *Ozalio*, who was likewise readie to doo as much at the ioyfull sight of his Freende *Palmendos*, yet at length shee embraced her Daughter, saying.[468]

What aboundaunce of teares haue issued from myne eyes, since the time I sawe my beloued Daughter? Howe many bitter anguishes of hart haue I endured, and breathed innumerable sighes and clamours into the ayre, for the absence of thee and the King thy Father, euery houre expecting the release of you both from imprisonment? how yrksome is the remembraunce (O perfect substaunce of **[R4ʳ]** mine entrayles) that I was a Mother so cruel and seuere to banish thee so long time from me? but heerein I consented to the perswasion of the Fairies, who promised that by thine imprysonment, I shoulde recouer the King my Husband out of thraldome, it now remaineth whether theyr words will sort to effect or no.[469] Wherfore sir Knight, seeing you haue exalted the soule that lay dispayring in the floods of extreamitie, by deliuering my daughter from these Magicall charmes: let me intreate thee to follow thy fortune, and accomplishe all my ioyes together, in restoring him for whom this sorcerie was inuented, that the remainder of our life may be more happy, then it hath beene since the time we met first[b] together. *Palmendos* sorrowing to see the Queene thus lament, encouraged her in this sorte.[c] Good Madame torment not your selfe with any further greefe, seeing I haue determined to loose my life, or els to bring with me the King of *Thessalie*, in meane[d] space

[a] louingly] willingly P2, P3

[b] met first] first met P2, P3

[c] sorte] *om.* P3

[d] in meane] in the mean P2, P3

asswage your sorowes by the presence of your daughter, whom the heauens haue allotted to be my Wife, and thereby confirmed you my gracious Mother.[470] By this time the Knight of the Isle had made such prouision in the Castell, as they might there[a] lodge according to their content, because more conuenient place there was not neere at hande, and there three daies they sported themselues in pleasure, meruailing at the ingenious deuises there framed by the Fayries, so that the Castell seemed as a terrestriall Paradise. Which *Palmendos* perceiuing, and that it was seated in a sweet and fertile clymat, hee intended to sende for people of his owne natiue Countrey, whereby it might be the[b] better inhabited,[471] and because some memory of him and *Francelina*, might be reserued to following posterities.

The Knight of the Isle feasted them very royallie, and nothing was wanting that any way might[c] delight them, when *Palmendos* falling in[d] conference with the Queene, desired that she would accompany her Daughter to *Constantinople*, there to stay with her in the Emperors Courte **[R4v]** as sent from him: and that she should[e] moreouer assure his Maiestie, that hee hauing finished his voyage into *Turkie*, would no longer conceale himselfe as he had doone. My noble Sonne, quoth the Queene, I shall wyllingly performe what ye haue appointed, but I would know if you meane to take any strength with you against the Turke, because I would sende for ayde to *Thessalie*, and beside craue assystaunce of the Emperour, who I am sure will succour mee with all his legions. Gracious Madame and mother,[472] answered *Palmendos*, I wil take no other company with mee then I brought hether, for such busines must be doone rather by aduenturous hazarde, then by bringing forces into the fielde:[473] so that were yours and all the Emperors vnited together, yet shoulde wee neuer compasse our intent that way. But you shall vnderstande that I beeing on[f] the Sea not long since, met with the King of *Culaquin*, Sonne in lawe to the great Turke, as hee coasted along *Thrace* with his Rouers and Pirats, onely to endomage the Empire so farre as he might: yet by good happe I tooke him prisoner, and sent him to his Maiestie at *Constantinople*.[474]

[a] there] *om.* P3

[b] the] *om.* P2, P3

[c] any way might] might any way P2, P3

[d] in] into P2, P3

[e] should] would P3

[f] on] upon P2, P3

If happilie by secrete subtiltie I cannot preuaile, I shall mooue an exchaunge of these two Kings, cullouring the matter with manie plausible reasons: in breefe, I wyll doo as the occurences shall best aduise me, wherein I hope the diuine bountie will direct mee the best course, that I may compasse the issue of mine affectionate desire. The Queene reioyced verie much, when she heard that the King of *Culaquin* was likewise prisoner, and hoping to haue her Husband in exchaunge for him, she more dilligentlie hastened the departure of *Palmendos*, the like (though lothe to leaue his companie so soone) did faire *Francelina*, not doubting but her Lord and Husband woulde soone returne, and knit vp all their ioyes with the presence of the King her Father.[475]

[S1r] CHAPTER XXIII.

Howe the Queene of Thessalie and Francelina *her Daughter, departing from the Isle of Carderia, were accompanied on the way by* Palmendos *and* Ozalio, *when taking theyr leaue each of other, the Queene and her Daughter rode to the Emperours Court, where they were very graciously entertained.*

Lothe are these Louers to part a sunder, but the causes beeing vrgent, they are constrained to make a vertue of necessitie:[476] wherfore taking their leaue of the Knight of the Isle, as also of all the Lords and Barons that so freendlie bare them company all this while, after many amorous and ceremoniall courtesies, accompanied with sighes, teares and sorrowfull lookes,[477] and they had brought them halfe a dayes iourney on the waie, *Palmendos* and *Ozalio* rode toward the seaside, where they had left order that their Shippe shoulde meete them. The Queene and her Daughter, without any trouble to hinder their iourney, arriued at the Cittie of *Constantinople*, sending one of her Knightes to the Emperour to let him vnderstande the cause of her comming, as also the discourse of all that had happened. The Knight discharging his duetie as he was commaunded, his Maiestie requested to know his name, who had so fortunatly deliuered *Francelina*. Dread Lord, answered the Messenger, hee is called *Palmendos*, the most valiant and courteous Knight in[a] all these parts of the worlde. Much good haue I heard of the man, said the Emperor, but commeth he now [S1v] in company with the Queene? No my Lorde,

[a] in] of P2, P3

replied the Knight, because the future deliueraunce of our King, hath procured his iourney into *Turkie.* Then the Emperor commaunded *Primaleon* and his Barons, to goe accompanie the Queene and her Daughter to the Court, which they with all diligence performed, for that the fame and renowne spred of her thorow all those regions,[478] encreased their desire to behold her. *Arnedes* likewise would haue gone with them, but that as[a] yet he was not perfectlie recouered,[479] and beside hee wered dailie verie melancholie, seeing the Embassadours of *Fraunce* staied so long, nor coulde he heare anie tyding[b] of his Cozin *Recinde.*[480] The Queene of *Thessalie,* and her Ladies came attired in mourning blacke,[c] expressing her sorow for the King her Husband: but *Francelina* like glorious *Cynthia*[481] in her cheefest pride, clothed (as you haue heard) in most statelie ornaments, drew every eye to admire[d] her beautie. *Primaleon* hauing saluted the Queene, gaue her place and rode with the Princesse her Daughter, when caried awaie in conceit with her surpassing feature, he entred into these speeches. Mee thinkes (Madame) the Fairies were ouermuch[e] iniurious, to locke vppe in prison such admirable beautie, in that anie gentle hart beholding you, would the sooner aduenture for the King your father, hauing such a gracious reward set downe for his trauaile: wherefore *Palmendos* hath good occasion to boast, if Fortune permitte him to deliuer[f] the King[g] of *Thessalie.*[482] And I, quoth *Francelina,* account my happines nothing inferiour, gaining thereby the most valiant and debonaire Knight, that euer entreprised actions of Chiualrie, which makes mee esteeme the Fairies wise and discreet, by enclosing me in the enchaunted Castell: for verie few wold haue thrust their liues in perrill hauing once seene me, where contrariwise to get honor by the aduenture, they made proofe of that which was onely destenied for *Palmendos,* hee beeing the man that iustly may be called the flower of Knightes. In this matter I will not contende with yee,[h][483] aunswered **[S2r]** *Primaleon,* for the vertues and graces of your beloued is such, as no

[a] that as] as P2, P3

[b] tyding] tidings P2, P3

[c] blacke] back P2

[d] admire] behold P2, P3

[e] ouermuch] too much P2, P3

[f] to deliuer] not to deliver P2

[g] King] K. P3

[h] yee] you P2, P3

man may woorthilie[a] bee compared with him, wherefore you haue good reason to affect him: and he likewise is bounde to constant permanencie, if your diuine lookes haue peirced his hart as they ought.[484] The Emperour and the Empresse, with *Philocrista* and their other daughters, came to the Pallace gate to welcom the Queen, when shee and her Daughter alighting[b] from their Palfraies, with humble reuerence saluted his Maiestie, who with his Empresse honourably entertained them, conducting them into the great Hall, where the Queene began in this manner.

Most mightie and inuincible Monarche, *Palmendos* the onelie[c] Iewell of knighthoode, by vs kisseth the hande of your imperiall Maiestie, hauing sent yee[d] this young Princesse, to be kept vnder your protection, till he returne from Turkie, with my espoused Lord the King of *Thessalie*, if Fortune graunt his deliueraunce from the cruell Infidels, for which I continue in hourely deuotion, as wel for the great desire I haue to see the King my Husband, as also to see the Knights speedie returne, who onely dedicateth his trauailes to your highnes seruice.[485] With these wordes she deliuered her Daughter to his Maiestie, and the Emperour receiuing[e] her vey graciously, shewed himselfe exceeding ioyfull for their arriuall, desiring them to vse his Court as their owne, and to be as frollike there as if they were in *Thessalie*. Beside, hee prayed God so to direct *Palmendos* in his attempt, as hee might deliuer the King her Husband from captiuitie: withal, that if he had requested assistaunce in the cause, he shoulde haue had his Maiesties power at commaund, then taking *Francelina* by the hand, he said. To you[f] Daughter *Philocrista*, I committe the honourable charge of this young Princesse, vntill such time her Knight be returned. My Lorde, answered *Philocrista*, I shall right willinglie fulfill your commaundement, beeing no lesse glad of such a companion, then to haue the Ladie **[S2^v]** present with me, for whom such rare deedes of Chiualrie haue beene performed. The Empresse tooke the Queen by the hande, and *Philocrista* her charge *Francelina*, they all sitting downe vnder a sumptuous Canapie, where the Knights regarding them, especially the Empresse

[a] may woorthilie] worthily may P2, P3

[b] alighting] alighted P2

[c] onelie] noble P2, P3

[d] yee] you P2, P3

[e] receiuing] received P2

[f] you] your P2

and the two Princesses, imagined a second iudgement for the Apple of beautie. And admit we *Arnedes* for the gentle sheepeheard *Paris*, yet hee imagined his *Philocrista* to bee most perfect,[486] although *Francelina* was very farre beyonde her, al the Knights concluding, that they had neuer seene more choyse beautie, except the Empresse when shee was in the flower of her youth. But *Philocrista* neuer attained her Mothers perfections, albeit shee had two Sisters named *Flerida* and *Bazilia*, (which by the Author of *Palmerin* are named *Belisa* and *Melicia*,) that came verie neere her in resemblaunce,[487] especiallie *Flerida*, of whom we shall haue occasion to speake heereafter, when wee come to the noble Prince *Edward* of *England*.[488]

The Emperour intreated *Francelina*, to tell him (if she coulde) of whence *Palmendos* was, whereto the Princesse modestlie[a] thus aunswered. Dreade Lorde, I can reueale no further of him, then that hee is commaunder of a Kingdome, and diuers other Signories of great estate: what els I knowe of him, I am to be excused till his comming, when himselfe will manifest his Countrey and originall,[489] not his valour and courtesie, for that is blazed through moste partes of the world. For this discreet aunswere, shee was greatly commended by the Emperour, who noting her comelie gestures and behauiour, esteemed her discreete and well aduised: and seeing the Ring on her finger that *Palmendos* gaue her, he thought it very much resembled hys owne Ring, which the Queene of *Tharsus* gaue him at his departure.[490] Now coulde hee not containe himselfe, but demaunds of her, of whom she had that costly Iewell, so like one that he held in great estimation. She aunswered that *Palmendos* gaue it her, after her deliueraunce from the Isle **[S3ʳ]** of *Carderia*, wherat his Maiestie greatlie meruailing, imagined this[b] Knight to be the Queene of *Tharsus* Son. Now was he much more desirous to see him, then before, remembring what kindnes shee shewed him in the Realme of *Pasmeria*: then causing his owne Ring to bee brought, and compared with that the Princesse wore, they were founde in euery point so like and conformable, as hardly could the one bee knowne from the other. Indeede they were made both by one workman, and magicallie charmed like in resemblaunce, as the perfect signall to discouer the originall of *Palmendos*: which made the Emperour conceiue some suspition, that this vnknowne Knight shoulde be his Son,

[a] modestlie] modesty P2

[b] this] the P2, P3

especiallie when he called the Queenes darke speeches to memorie, which she vsed after her acquaintance with him.[491] Yet woulde he not reueale this doubt to anie one, but past it ouer with fresh welcomming the Queene and her daughter, and deliuering in speeches, that hee was glad *Belcar* kept not the Bridge, when it was *Palmendos* fortune to arriue there, yet was hee sorrie for *Tirendos* mishap: albeit he commended the courtesie of the Conquerer, in exacting no further on the Prince of *Mecaena*.[a][492]

But leaue we *Palmendos* and *Ozalio* trauailing toward *Turkie*, and speake a little of *Recinde* the *Castilian* Prince, beeing one of them that followed in his search.

[S3v] CHAPTER XXIIII.

Howe Recinde *pursuing the search of* Palmendos, *reskewed a Merchaunt from fiue Theeues, whom he dyscomfited on the mountayne. And how by the meanes of an Archer that bent his bowe against him, hee came to the mouth of a deepe Caue, where hee kylled a Lyon that kept it, and deliuered thence a Lady, which was enchaunted into the shape of a Serpent.*

Recinde leauing *Constantinople*, for the same cause as the other Knights did,[493] happened to the same place where *Palmendos* lodged the night before,[494] demanding of his Hoste, if he had seene anie such man, who made this answer. Verilie the same man that had the honour of the Tourney, was my gueste this last night, and neuer did I see a more courteous Gentleman, which makes me hope he wil ende the aduenture of *Francelina*, whether he is gone as he tolde me he woulde. With these words the *Spanyard* was well contented, minding to follow him to the Isle of *Carderia*, and ryding by the way,[495] he heard a verie lamentable cry, which caused him to looke about, when he espied one hanging on a Tree by the armes, and fiue[496] uillaines[497] harde by making a fire, to dresse some foode they had killed on the Mountaine. Comming to the man that hunge in this wofull plight, he cut him downe, and vnderstanding that these villaines had robd and so[b] misused him: caused[c] the Merchaunt[498] to take his weapon, and so they setting vpon the Theeues, slew three of

[a] *Mecaena*] P2; *Mecana* P1

[b] so] *om.* P3

[c] caused] he caused P2, P3

them, dryuing [S4r] the other to flight, by which meanes the Merchaunt had most of his treasure againe, for which hee thanked the Prince, and mounting on horsebacke accompanied[a] him on the waie.[499] Not farre had they gone, but they met a Knight vnarmed, of huge constitution and euill fauoured, hauing a *Turkie* Bowe[500] in his hand, and a Quiuer hanging by his side full of Arrowes, of whom they desired to knowe which way they should get foorth[b] of the Forrest. The discourteous Knight (without making any answer) let flye an Arrow at them, wherewith hee killed the Prince *Recindes* horse,[501] he beeing not a little mooued at this mishap, grewe into great choller against him, who made no longer staye, but ranne from them so fast as hee could. *Recinde* and the Merchaunt still pursued, till hauing lost the sight of him, and meruailing where he should be hidden, at length they founde the mouth of a very dark Caue,[502] which they suspected the Knight had taken for refuge: whereuppon the Prince intreated the Merchaunt to staie there without, because hee intended to search the Caue, and be reuenged on the Knight[c] that had so wronged him. Not farre had he gone vnder the earth, but hee hearde a pittifull voyce crying for helpe, which caused him to returne backe againe, when at the entraunce of the Vaute he behelde a mightie Lyon, which came foorth with the Knight, and ran vppon the Prince exceeding furiouslie: but he who could not bee frighted with matters of greater moment, so valiantlie defended himselfe against the Beast, as in short time hee layde him dead at his foote. Now ranne the Knight backe againe into the Caue, and the Prince after him so fast as he could, till at length he came into a goodly Hall, which was hanged rounde about with gorgious Tapistrie, and therein might one beholde all such as passed by the mouth of the Caue, as if they had discernd the same in a Glasse. While he stoode beholding this beautiful prospect, he saw the Knight comming towarde him Armed, and drawing his Sworde, thus spake to the Prince. [S4v]

Wretched Knight, ouermuch foolish hardines hath brought thee to this place, for I shall let thee see the daunger encurred by thy presumption. More indiscreetly (quoth the Prince)[d] hast thou behaued thy selfe, in killing my horse without anie occasion of offence. Heerewith they Combatted

[a] accompanied] he accompanied P2, P3

[b] foorth] out P2, P3

[c] the Knight] him P2, P3

[d] More indiscreetly (quoth the Prince)] P2; More indiscreetly, (quoth the Prince, P1

a long while together, till the Knight seeing himselfe vnable to resist the Prince, woulde haue saued himselfe in the Chamber he came from, offering to keepe the doore against him as his defence: but *Recinde* thrusting after him into the Chamber, behelde[a] a great and hidious Dragon lying there, the sight wherof made him somwhat amazed,[b] yet seeing the beast stirred not against him, continued[c] his former quarrell with the Knight, bringing him at length into such subiection, as[d] with his Sword he smote his heade from his shoulders. The Serpent terrefied with extreame feare, began to shrinke backe, when *Recinde* lifting vp his Sword to strike, the Serpent spake in this manner.

Sir Knight, for Gods sake pittie me, and seeke not to shed my bloode, hauing no way offended ye: for shall I bee perpetually bounde at your commaundement, for deliuering me from this cruell Knight, who hath forcibly kept mee heere the space of sixe yeeres. The Prince hearing these wordes, helde downe his Sword, when the Serpent thus proceeded. I am no Serpent Sir, as happily I seeme in your eye, but a most infortunate and abused Damosell,[503] hauing suffered the most miserable life that euer Woman endured, lyuing (against my will) in the custodie of thys trayterous Knight. If thou art a humaine creature, aunswered *Recinde*, I meruaile thou shouldest haue the shape of such a deformed beast. I know sayd the Damosel, what representation I haue in your iudgement, but I dare assure ye[e] on my life, that I am no Serpent or any thing els but a most distressed Woman. Which well she might affirme, because the Knight nowe slayne, (to conceale her the more cunningly) made her to resemble so by Arte magicke, as you shall vnderstand the whole at large. **[T1r]**

He loued this Damosell so extreamelie,[504] shee beeing the Daughter of an auncient Widdowe dwelling not far off, as seeing he could not obtayne her in mariage, by reason of his badde manners and euill[f] fauoured bodie:[505] so laboured with a Magitian a freende of his, to cause her resem-

[a] behelde] he beheld P2, P3

[b] made him somewhat amazed] somewhat amazed him P2, P3

[c] continued] he continued P2, P3

[d] as] that P2, P3

[e] ye] you P2, P3

[f] euill] ill P2, P3

ble[a] a Serpent to any but himselfe. Her Mother and Bretheren ignoraunt[b] of this trecherie: seeing such an ougly Serpent among them: affrighted[c] at this strange Metamorphosis, presently fled[d] foorth[e] of their Castell. The Mayden[f] following to vnderstand the cause of their feare, wandred sorowfully after them thorow the fields,[506] where she was supprised by her Louer, and brought to the Caue prepared by the Sorcerer, appointing she[g] should continue in that apperaunce, till[h] one of the best Knights in the world should arriue there, and valiantly winne her out of his custodie, only by his death to be deliuered, and sixe yeeres shee had abode in that place, seeming a beautifull woman to her Louer onelie, and to all other[i] a monstrous Serpent. *Recinde* driuen into wonderfull admiration, bemoning her cause, thus spake.

In sooth, this is the most strange accident that euer I heard of, but seeing your Louer is dead, bodlie may yee depart this[j] Chamber, and returne home to your Mother againe: for in time (perhaps) this hidious shape will forsake yee.[k] My Lord, quoth she, I haue manie times stryuen to get foorth of this pryson, but all my labour hath beene in vaine: for by like sortiledge hath the Knight bounde mee heere, as he got me from my Mothers Castell. So am I perswaded, aunswered the Prince, wherfore seeing of your selfe ye[l] cannot depart, I will trie if my strength will release yee of this seruitude. Then taking his Arming gyrdle from about him, hee made it fast about the Serpents middle, and forciblie thought to pull her out of the Chamber, but the strength of the enchauntment ouer-maistring him, when he had gotten her to the verie doore, would violently pluck her back againe. Yet *Recinde* beeing all hart **[T1^v]** and courage, gaue not ouer

[a] resemble] to resemble P2, P3

[b] ignoraunt] being ignorant P2, P3

[c] affrighted] were so affrighted P2, P3

[d] presently fled] that they fled presently P2, P3

[e] foorth] out P2, P3

[f] Mayden] Damosel P2, P3

[g] she] that she P3

[h] till] untill P2, P3

[i] other] others P2, P3

[j] this] the P2, P3

[k] yee.] you. P2, P3

[l] ye] you P2, P3

for all these resistaunces, but at length by exceeding labour and trauaile, hee gotte her into the open[a] Hall, and then she seemed a verie beautiful Woman, who falling downe at his feete, intreated him not to forsake her, till[b] he had brought her to her Mothers Castell. So going foorth of the Caue, she told the Merchaunt all that had happened, which made him aunswere her in this sort.

Madame, bothe you and I are highly beholding to this Knight, for he hath miraculously recalled[c] you from a lamentable sufferaunce, and not onelie hath he saued my life, but holpe me to my goods againe which were vtterlie lost, wherefore wee haue good cause to thinke that hee is the onelie Paragon of Chiualrie. So breaking off these speeches, they tooke the Knights horse, because hee had slayne the Princes, and mounting the Damosell behynde him, brought her home to her Mothers Castell, the auncient Ladie, beeing not a little ioyfull to see her Daughter, whom shee reputed vtterlie lost: likewise her Bretheren were verie glad to see their Sister restored home againe. As for their freendlie entertainment, you may iudge it by the cause, which beeing of nature, must needes surpasse all other whatsoeuer.[d507]

[T2r] CHAPTER XXV.

How Recinde *arriued at the Isle of* Carderia, *where vnderstanding that* Palmendos *had ended the aduenture, he went to seeke* Belcar *at Macedon: and of the Combat he had with him, by the false perswasion of the Damosell, that followed the reuenge of her bretherens death.*[e]

Foure daies[508] staied *Recinde* and the Merchant at the olde Ladies Castell, and then taking theyr leaue, the Prince committed[f] the Merchaunt to his owne occasions, and hee rode straite toward the Isle of *Carderia*, desirous to trie his fortune in the aduenture, as also to finde the Knight hee sought for: but beeing there arriued, he vnderstoode

[a] open] *om.* P2, P3

[b] till] till that P2, P3

[c] recalled] called P2, P3

[d] whatsoeuer.] *om.* P2, P3

[e] death.] deaths. P2, P3

[f] committed] commended P2, P3

how *Francelina* was deliuered, *Palmendos* gone toward *Turkie*,[509] and *Tirendos* abode at the Castell with *Lypes* and his Sisters, from whence he sent a Squire to *Macedon*, to certifie *Belcar* what had happened, as also to intreate him staie there for his comming.

As for the Prince *Belcar*, he beeing now with *Alderina* his chosen Mistresse, to speake of all circumstaunces entercoursing between them, woulde bee more laboure to me then pleasure to you.[510] Shee accuseth him with a great manie articles of vngentlenes, that he would trauaile for *Francelina*, beeing before her vowed Knight,[511] and he excuseth al vnder this point, that what he did in a place of such triall, was onelie to eternize the name of *Alderina*, and nothing to the aduantage of *Francelina*, nor could the greatest **[T2v]** Monarch on the earth haue commaunded him from that seruice, but only the gracious Letter sent by her, wherfore he desired to returne thether againe, to make her more famous til the aduenture were ended.[512] To stay her aunswer, and appease his hote desire, at that very instant the Courrire arriued sent from *Tirendos*, whose message being heard, highly was the Princesse contented, but *Belcar* ouercome with exceeding greefe, because fayne he would haue tryed his fortune against *Palmendos*.[513]

Nowe come we to the Damosell againe, that pursued *Belcar* for the death of her Bretheren, according as you sufficientlie heard before,[514] she vnderstanding that hee was in the Court of *Macedon*, so highly loued of the[a] King, Queen, and the whole nobilitie, she was out of hope to worke him iniurie[b] there: wherefore she intended to returne home againe, and by the way she happened to meet with the Prince *Recinde*, when beginning her accustomed complaints, she deliuered the same discourse which she had doone to *Cardino* and *Tirendos*,[515] saying that the Knight who had so trayterously slain her brethren, soiourned in the Court of *Macedon*. *Recinde* desirous to win honor by succouring the distressed, and hoping he might find the Knight he fought for at *Macedon*, answered her in this maner. If it be Damosel as you say, that the Knight in such trayterous sorte slewe your bretheren, I promise ye, by the faith I beare to Chiualrie, that to my power I will reuenge your wrong, because all Gentlemen receiuing this order, are bounde by dutie to assist Damosels, iniuriously wronged by disloyall varlets. The crafty deceiuer fel at the Princes feete, affirming

[a] the] *om.* P3

[b] iniurie] any injury P2, P3

what she had saide with many others. Goe then with me (quoth *Recinde*) to shew me the Knight, and either I will loose my life, or make him confesse his villainy. The effronted palliard mounted on her Palfray, and such speede they made in trauaile, as at length they arriued at *Macedon*, when entring the great[a] Hall, they founde there the King, *Belcar* and diuers noble Barons,[516] whereupon the Damosel **[T3r]** thus spake to *Recinde*. See here my Lord, the Knight that slew my Brethren. I beseech yee[b] make him knowe before the King, the treason[c] he committed against harmeles men:[517] for his Maiestie not knowing the enormitie of the case, reputeth this offendour one[d] of the most courteous Knights in his Court, as my selfe perceiued at my last beeing here. *Recinde* hauing with humble reuerence saluted the King *Florendos*, turned to *Belcar* with these speeches. Sir Knight, this Damosell hath sworne to mee that you haue trayterouslie slaine her two bretheren,[e] after you had been freendlie entertained at her fathers house: if yee[f] did so, surelie it was an act far vnbeseeming you, and by force of Armes I shall make ye[g] so to confesse it, if you haue the hardines to enter the field with mee. *Belcar* greatly offended to heare himselfe so charged, and euermore by one that sought to bring his life in danger, in anger thus replied.

In sooth Knight, I cannot but think thy discretion very simple, in saying if I haue the hardines to enter the fielde with thee, and thy presumption is as insolent, as this Damosell is trothlesse and disloyall, in accusing mee without anie cause: notwithstanding, I hope to recompence ye[h] for light beleefe, and that false woman likewise the instrument of thy follie.[518] After these speeches, he went and Armed him selfe for the Combat, which the King many waies laboured to hinder, but *Recinde* continued so resolutely against *Belcar*, as[i] the King could not diswade the matter, wherfore he thus spake to *Recinde*. Seeing you wil not at my intreatie giue ouer this

[a] great] *om.* P3

[b] yee] you P2, P3

[c] treason] P2; teason P1

[d] one] to be one P2, P3

[e] her two bretheren] two of her brethren P2, P3

[f] yee] you P2, P3

[g] ye] you P2, P3

[h] ye] you P2, P3

[i] as] that P2, P3

rashnes, let me vnderstand the name of him that will not graunt so smal a matter,[519] specially to one that is able to yeeld thanks therfore. I am, quoth *Recinde*, a Knight of a strange Country, who came to the Emperors Court at *Constantinople*, meane while the nuptialles of the *Hungarian* Prince were sollemnized, whether likewise came a Knight vnknowne, bearing a siluer flower in hys Sheeld: hee hauing wun the honor of the Tourney, departed secretely from the assembly, which made me followe in **[T3ᵛ]** searche of him:[520] and in respect I am but a poore Knight errant; I desire no wrong may be offered me in the battail. Be therof assured, answered[a] the King, that none shal meddle with you but your aduersary onlie: and trust me it greeueth me to the very hart, that comming from the Court of the Emperour *Palmerin* my Sonne, you should heere enter the fielde against *Belcar*, who is one of his Maiesties cheefest fauourites. When *Recinde* heard *Belcar* named, on the one side it displeased him, that he was to deale with a Knight so famous and renowned: on the other side it greeued him as much, when he considered the neere alliaunce betweene him and *Melicia*,[521] whom he loued as his verie soule, so that willinglie he would haue forborne the Combat, but that he could not with honor gaine say it.[522]

Nowe the King desires the Duke of *Pontus*, and another of his cheefest Barons, to iudge the fight according to conscience, and without any exception of person.[523] Soone after the Champions enter the Listes, where breaking theyr launces brauelie in the carrire, they were both dismounted, notwithstanding they quicklie recoured themselues, and drawing their Swordes fell to the Combatte. Long while they continued a most furious fight, sharpe and cruell woundes being deliuered on either side, that iudgement could not be giuen who was in greatest daunger: but his Maiestie seeing *Belcar* were very[b] feeble, and that it was like this fight would ende bothe their liues, as one loth to see the death of eyther, he threw his[c] staffe of peace between them: then[d] comming downe from the window where hee stoode into the field, he desired them at his request to giue ouer the fight. My gracious Lord, aunswered *Recinde*, that may we not consent vnto, vnlesse the Damosell that complained of *Belcar*, will first

[a] answered] said P2, P3

[b] very] *om.* P2, P3

[c] his] the P3

[d] then] and P2, P3

remit the iniurie he hath doone her. My selfe will thereto perswade her, said the King, in meane while doo you trauaile no further in this controuersie, seeing you haue bothe shewen sufficient and haughtie Chiualrie. So went the King to the Damosell, who was [T4r] wonderfull glad to see *Belcar* in such daungerous estate, as no Knight before had brought him in the like. Damosel quoth[a] he, seeke not the death of two so good Champions as these are, but (for my sake) pardon *Belcar* if hee haue in ought offended, and I shall cause him to make such amendes, as your selfe shall like well thereof: beside, such courtesy shal ye[b] find at my hand,[c] as happilie shal yeeld occasion of thanks while yee[d] liue. Heereto will I neuer consent though I die, quoth she, and more wold the present death of *Belcar* content me, then if the whole Monarchie of the world were vnder my puissaunce: considering the enorme and detestable treason, wherwith hee villainously wronged[e] my Father and Bretheren, which makes mee I cannot discharge my Knight of his[f] promise. The King with great instance intreated her againe, and so did all the Lords attending on him: but all was in vaine, shee was so resolutly grounded in her wickednes, as shee accounted it pleasure to be selfe-willed therein. Wherupon, the Queene (hartily sorie to see *Belcar* so sore wounded) vnderstanding the obstinate refusall of the Damosell: she accompanied with the Duchesse of *Pontus*, and the Princesse *Alderina* her Daughter, came altogether and desired her, to discharge her Knight of his promise, and the Queene would entertaine her among the Ladies of honour in her Court. But[g] these prayers and requests nothing auailed, to mooue any pittie in this inexorable Damosell, which the Queene perceiuing, and that she continued[h] so obstinate in crueltie: she made a sollemne othe, that if she did not presently pardon the two Knights, (hearing a murmuring among the people, how her accusations against *Belcar*, were false and slaunderous) that her selfe should die a most shamefull death.[524] The Damosel seeing the Queene so displeased

[a] quoth] said P2, P3

[b] ye] you P2, P3

[c] hand] hands P2, P3

[d] yee] you P2, P3

[e] villainously wronged] hath villainously wronged P3

[f] his] this P3

[g] But] All P2, P3

[h] continued] P2; continned P1

was afraid of her cause, and beside she greeued to beholde the teares of faire *Alderina*, wherfore she alighted from her Palfray, and falling at the Queenes feete, desired her not to regard her great errour of ingratitude, which she had shewed to the King her husband, [T4v] in denying a matter consisting in her power: but for her Maiesties sake, shee was content to pardon both the Knights. The Queene embraced her in signe of thankes, sending word to *Recinde*, that hee shoulde[a] proceede no further in battaile, so the Damosell went with the Queene and her Ladies to the Pallace, and bothe the Champions accompanied the King, who bringing them to their Chambers, commaunded that his cheefe Physitions and Chirurgions should giue dilligent[b] attendaunce to see their wounds healed.

Dailie woulde the Queene, accompanied wyth the Duchesse of *Pontus*, and the fayre Princesse *Alderina* her Daughter, come to visite them, so that at length they reconciled the two Princes to amitie, and shortly after, the Queene (in regarde of her promise) caused the Damosell to bee very honourablie married, when *Belcar* made her openly confesse, that her accusations were most false and vntrue,[525] in respect that hee neuer sawe any of her Bretheren, before that night wherein hee was intreated by her Father to lodge at his Castell. But leaue we these, and let[c] vs nowe returne againe to our noble Knight *Palmendos*, whom we left preparing his voyage towards *Turkie*.[526]

[U1r] CHAPTER XXVI.

Howe after Palmendos *and Ozalio were embarqued for Turkie, they landed at a port neere the Castell of Albayzo, where the King of Thessalie was kept prisoner: and howe* Palmendos *intended to bee at the Tourney, which was prepared for the marriage of the Captaines sonne, and what was his successe.*

After that *Palmendos* and *Ozalio*, had left the Queene of *Thessalie* and her daughter *Francelina*, they posted with al speed to theyr Ship: the Marriners hauing in the time of their abode there, happened on a Turke left there in the Hauen by reason of extreame sicknes,[527] wherefore they of *Tharsus*, knowing him to bee a Moore, tooke him

[a] shoulde] would P3

[b] dilligent] very diligent P2, P3

[c] let] now let P3

into their ship, and by the time of the Princes arriuall, he had verie well recoured his health.[528] He vnderstanding that *Palmendos* woulde saile into *Turkie*, desired to graunt him passage thither, and in recompence of that gentlenes, hee would direct him whether hee pleased, because hee knewe all the portes and creekes of the Countrey, and most of the Citties and Townes on[a] the land. *Palmendos* ioyfull of this good hap, accepted him for his patrone, and without concluding to what place they would first saile, hee wylled them to make toward the neerest port to the Cittie of *Tubant*:[529] demaunding of the Turke, if he knew any harbour of suretie neere that place. My Lord (quoth the Turke) I will conduct ye[b] if you please, into a straight of the Sea, which is verie secret, where oftentimes ride diuers great vessels, and no other place of lodging is neere at hand, but **[U1v]** my fathers house onely, which standeth a daies iourney from *Tubant*, and the like from the Castell of *Albayzo*, where the great Turke at this present keepes the king of *Thessalie* and all his treasure,[530] vnder the charge of a good Knight who is the Captaine of the Castell, and this place hee reputeth as the strongest holde in all the Countrey. Moreouer this I dare[c] auouch Sir, that there is no part so little in all that Countrey, but I knowe it as well by night as by day, euen as perfectly as the porte whereof I tell ye: there may you abide in assuraunce, and doe what best your selfe shall please, vncontrouled by any, this wyll I make good for the great curtesie I haue found. *Palmendos* seing how Fortune fauoured him, committed his conducting to the Turke, who was named *Orycano*, when at length they came to the porte neere *Tubant*: then *Oricano* went on shore with the Knightes, to take some order for their good entertainement, but finding not his father at home, entreated his mother and two breethren, who were not a little glad of his safe return, to vse those Gentlemen so curteously as might be, expressing what kindenesse hee had found at their hands. *Palmendos* reioyced that they were in a place so sure and secret, and neere *Albayzo* Castell, where the King of *Thessalie* was detained in captiuitie, yet kept he on his right black Armour, which the Faeries left for him at the Castell of *Carderia*, his good sworde likewise hee had by his side, wherewith hee could enchaunt and bring asleepe anye one by drawing it foorth.[531] It was large and short as a woodknife or Fauchion,[532] most artificially damasqued and garnished with three sortes of Diamonds, the whole

[a] on] in P3

[b] ye] you P2, P3

[c] I dare] dare I P2, P3

sheath beeing composed of one, the mosse-barre and pomell of an other, and the handle of the crost rare and pretious Calamite that euer was seene, the blade of the finest tempered steele that coulde bee in any sworde, in breefe, the like weapon was hardly to be found through the worlde. By this time *Orycanos* father was come home, who reioycing to beholde his Sonne, shewed **[U2ʳ]** very louing countenance to the princes for his sake: when among other talke, *Palmendos* requested to knowe of the olde man whence he came so late, whereto the poore man humblie thus answered. I come Sir, from a Town not far hence, whether I went in the morning to sell fish, because greate number of Knightes are assembled there, against the mariage of the Lordes daughter, with the son to the Captaine of *Albayzo* Castell: and I staied the longer, to see the Bridegroome and his Sister, who is reported to bee the fairest woman in the worlde. By manie great Princes she hath beene requested in mariage, but she hath refused euery one, saying she will neuer be married, but with him that can winne her by Martiall prowesse:[533] for which cause many braue and gallant Knights are come thither, and on the third daye of the feast, haue appointed a Tourney for her loue, the resort being so great to see this Ladie, as if the great Turke with all his Bassaes[534] and Ianizaries[535] kept Court there. *Palmendos* attentiuely noting this tale, considered with him selfe, that if hee could by subtill traines entice this Ladie to loue, hee might easily get into *Albayzo* Castell,[536] where he should the better compasse the stratageme, to set the King of *Thessalie* at libertie: for this cause he determined to be present at the Tourney, and in bedde acquainted *Ozalio* with his whole intent, who thought it the onely waye to woorke their enterprise. On the morrowe *Palmendos* tolde the Fisher, that he would make one in the Ioust: so giuing him good store of money, prayed[a] him to regarde his Ship and Marriners till hee returned, and so hee set forwarde with *Ozalio* and *Orycano*, who serued them faithfullye during all this busines. Not farre had they rid, but they met with a Page that attended on *Iffida*, for so was the beautifull virgin named, the Captains Daughter and occasion of this triumphe: *Palmendos* asketh[b] him, if the Tourney held the day following. It doth Sir, answered the Page, by generall agreement, and so please yee[c] to bee **[U2ᵛ]** there, you shall see many valiant Knights enter the fielde, where I hope the

[a] prayed] he prayed P2, P3

[b] asketh] then asked P2, P3

[c] yee] you P2, P3

pertakers of *Ripole*, for so was the Bridegroome called, shall beare away the honour of the day: and sundrie braue champions will aduenture for the loue of *Iffida* my Mistres, wherby they may gaine the better meane to offer her[a] their seruice, intending therfore to bee on her brothers side, who is the chiefe man in this enterprise.

The Prince calling to minde the perfections of *Francelina*, breathed foorth a sigh that came from his very soul,[537] on[b] the other side, he was marueilous glad, that he had so fortunately met with the Ladies Page: and desirous[c] to gaine some acquaintaunce with her, hee speaketh[d] to the youth in this manner. Gentleman, I thinke the graces of your Mistresse to be so amiable, as in one instant they are sufficient to captiuate al such as beholde her, and therfore I can assure ye,[e] that with the better will and more sincere affection, is he prouided to her seruice that neuer saw her: which I speke on mine own behalfe, who abandoning the place of my original, haue with insupportable trauels crost many Countries, onely to come let[f] her vnderstande my extreame deuotion, to be her perpetuall and faithfull seruant, whereto the renown of her beautie induced me, which I thinke is spread ouer the face of the whole earth. And seeing my hap was so good to meete with you, albeit you know mee not, nor haue I yet deserued any thing at your hand: yet let me intreat ye[g] to do one fauour for me, the issue wherof, beside your atchieuement of notable reputation in debonaire coutesie, which all of your young yeeres ought to haue in singuler commendacion: I hope shall[h] let ye sufficiently perceiue, that you deale not for an ingratefull person, nor wil ye mislike your trauaile in the cause. What would you haue me do? answered the Page, in respect you seeme a man of vertue and quality:[538] if it bee a thing possible for me and honourable, I will with al my heart accomplish it. A thousand thankes for your friendlinesse, **[U3^r]** answered *Palmendos*, and for nothing els is my sute, but that

[a] her] up P3

[b] on] and on P2, P3

[c] desirous] being desirous P2, P3

[d] speaketh] spake P2, P3

[e] ye] you P2, P3

[f] let] to let P3

[g] ye] you P2, P3

[h] shall] I shall P2, P3

you would say to your Ladie Mistresse, how[a] a strange Gentleman, which came into this countrey onlie to see her graces and vertues, most humbly commends him selfe to her fauourable opinion, earnestlye desiring that she would accept him as her Knight in the Tourney, where to morrow hee intends to shewe him selfe, as one that will ouer ballance her most fauoured in weight of affection, and will be accounted second to none in exploits of armes, hauing no better meane, whereby to acquaint her with the insupportable burthen of his heart: and that she may well perceiue it, I will not bee on her brothers side, but against them that take his part, hoping to send them vanquished out of the fielde, or make them gladde to take their heels, by the strength and hardines her diuine beautie shall giue mee, so please her to graunt mee the aforesaid fauour, and which will cause me to account my selfe the happiest[b] Knight, on whom the planets haue breathed their celestiall influence. The Page seeing *Palmendos* faire and so richly armed, imagined him to be some great personage, wherefore he modestly thus replied. My Lord this dare I not doo for any man liuing, without I knewe the partie to haue some familiaritie with my Mistresse: neuerthelesse, beeing a matter of so small consequence, and that you deserue much more then this on my behalfe; I shall deliuer her this message, for your sake who haue so importunatly requested it. *Palmendos* requited the Page with many thanks, and to make him more[c] forward in the matter, hee tooke a bracelet of golde from his arme and gaue it him: so beguiling the time with other speeches, at length they arriued at *Prissa*,[539] for so was the Town called where the Triumphes were appointed, the field being couered all ouer with costly Pauilions, wherefore *Palmendos* made choise of a conuenient place, and there commanded his rich Tent to be presently erected. Meane while the Page curteously tooke his leaue, and entering the town, **[U3^v]** went straight to his Mistresse lodging, where hauing first dispatched the answere sent from her Sister, and seeing her so conuenientlie apart from her Damosels, he rehearsed all that *Palmendos* had saied vnto him. I woonder, (quoth she) what the Knight should bee, that durst send mee such a presumptuous message, seeing he saieth he is a straunger, and for my loue hath forsaken his Countrey. Beleeue me Madame, answered the Page, nor doo I know him, but he seemeth to bee discended of great parentage, and is one of the goodliest personages that euer I saw: as for

[a] how] how that P2, P3

[b] happiest] most happy P2, P3

[c] more] the more P2, P3

his courtesie and liberalitie,[540] beholde Mistres, what a costly Bracelet hee hath giuen mee, that neuer did anie thing for him in all my life.[541]

Me thinks this is verie straunge, replied *Iffida*, that this Knight should come from farre Countries to see me, and verie ingratefull might I be reputed, if I shoulde not thanke him for so great paines:[542] therefore faile not but shewe me him to morrow, so soone as he dooth enter the Listes, that I may giue good heede to his behauiour. Herein, (quoth the Page) will I accomplishe your commaund, because right well I know him by his rich Armour, as also the lustie Courser hee rode on yester day. Thus made the Page a train for loue, which afterward reached to the heart of his Mistresse, where hauing kindled the fire her selfe, shee felt the sparkes so to leape about her imaginations, as all this night she could enioy no rest, for thinking on the Knight that came from far Countries.[543]

[U4r] CHAPTER XXVII.

How Palmendos *came to the Tourney appointed for* Iffida, *where he wonne her by his Knightly chiualry, and by that occasion obtained her loue. And how they spake together by the meanes of their Ambassadour, so that* Palmendos *and* Ozalio *easilie entred the Castell of* Albayzo.

On the morrow, which was the appointed day of the Triumph: *Iffida* decked her selfe in moste sumptuous ornaments, and after dinner came with the Bride and diuers other Ladies, to the Scaffoldes and Pauilions prepared for them in the field. Then assembled the Knightes[544] on all sides, and entered the Lists ech one to shewe his prowesse, but because the greater part were on the Bridegroomes side, therefore the contrarye went apace to wracke,[545] and the other were verily iudged to beare the Prize out of the fielde, if *Palmendos* and *Ozalio* had not suddainlie arriued. For they knew better how to handle their weapons, then the Knightes of this Countrey did, and that they made them verie well perceiue, chieflie *Palmendos* who did marueilous exployts, as *Iffida* (without any instruction of her Page) knew well inough the man that sent her the message, whereat both she and al the beholders were amazed, to see him so play the Deuil[a] among the Knights,[546] as[b] no one dealt with

[a] so play the Deuil] play the Devil so P2, P3

[b] as] that P2, P3

him but was vnhorssed. When they saw there was no more worke to doo, they with-drewe themselues into their Tent, and would not vnarme them selues, least some treacherie should bee practised against them, as often-times at such occassions it [U4v] happeneth, when the vanquished attempt vnhonourablie against the Conquerours. When *Ripole* saw his Knights so[a] discomfited, he was exceedinglie agreeued therewith, because he entirely loued his Sister *Iffida*, and doubted shee would now conuict him of great dishonour: but shee whose minde was no where els, then on the Knight to whom the victorie was due, extolled his admirable magnanimity to the heauens, as the rest of her Historie will plainely discouer,[547] and knowing no better meane to worke by, she called the Page aside, whome the Prince had imploied as his Ambassadour, and thus shee spake to him. Vnspeakable (in mine owne opinion) is the generositie of the Gentleman straunger, who hath right well perfourmed the resolution, whereof by thee he[b] assured mee yester-day:[548] very necessarie is it[c] therefore, that thou goe thanke him on my behalfe, for his long iourney and great paines taken for my sake: beside, as he hath sufficiently shewen me his fortune in deedes of armes, soo doo I desire secretly to see his person, in which request to satisfie me, if he wil this night come to my brothers banquet, which is prouided for the newe maried couple, I shal not fail to esteeme him among my cheefest fauourites.

While euery one was busilie censuring on the conquerour, the messenger from *Iffida* came to *Palmendos* Tent, where breeflie discharging what he was commaunded, and the Prince marueilous glad of this good fortune, thus answered.

Gentleman, I desire ye[d] to tel your Lady, that nothing shall make me disapoint her pleasure, because the onely occasion of my long trauaile, was extreame desire to offer her my seruice, and right happye shall I account my selfe, if she will imploy me in any thing to her content. To bee at the Bridegroomes banquet, me thinkes should argue ouer much boldnesse, in respect of the slender acquaintaunce and habitude, which as yet I haue with him or any of hys company: Notwithstanding, I would willinglie bee there [X1r] after the banquet, to guide mine eies to the place, where they

[a] so] *om.* P2, P3

[b] he] *om.* P3

[c] is it] it is P2, P3

[d] ye] you P2, P3

might feede on the celestial and gracious countenance of your Mistresse,[549] yet with this entreatie before hand, that I would not be knowne to any what I am.[550] And if it happen I may conferre a little with her in secret, I wil tel her such thinges, as all the rest of her life-time shall yeelde her contentation, wherein likewise if you will bee loyall and fauourable to me, to compasse both her good and your own: your guerdon happily will be such, as you will a hundred and a hundred times thinke the hower fortunate, when by so good chance you met me on the way, for though you see me here but in simple equipage, and as a Knight errant, I am the Lorde of many Prouinces, great estates and wonderfull riches. My Lord answered the Page, right willingly will I aduenture my person, in dooing you all the faithfull seruice can be deuised, the actions no way stretching to the dishonour of me and my Lady:[551] and such good order will I likewise take, as you shal not be knowen to any, but onely her that longeth to see you.

Hereupon *Palmendos* vnarmed him selfe, and putting on a Turkish mantle, taking his good sword vnder his arm,[552] hee and *Ozalio* went with the Page into the great Hall wher the banquet was: afterward they closely got to a conuenient place, where both *Iffida* and he might behold each other, which he did but with faint and deluding looks, onelie to adde some grace to his subtill determination, which he had practised for the King of *Thessalies* deliuerance. And while in this counterfeit contemplation he busied his eies, the Page cunninglye went to *Iffida*, and wispering in her eare, saied. See Madame the conquering Knight of the Tourney, who desires you very instantly, to conceale hym onely to your selfe, in that his trauaile hither was to no other end, but to see if your gracious gifts and beauty, were aunswerable to the renowne blazed thereof so far hence in his Countrey, hoping to compasse the matter so, (for to me he hath opened the very secrets of his heart) that when you **[X1v]** haue further knowledge of him: you shall not onelye haue occasion to loue him, but account your selfe likewise beholding to him, in respect of the voluntary paine he hath suffered for your sake. The rest of his speeches I shall tel you[a] at better leasure, in place more conuenient for suche discourse.

Iffida who was prudent and well aduised, forbare[b] to conferre longer with her newe solicitour, least her looue should be lightly espied by any:[553] then secretly shee glaunceth on *Palmendos*, whose thoughts were

[a] tel you] acquaint you with P2, P3

[b] forbare] did forbear P2, P3

busie to compasse his intent, and seeing him so pensiue, she immediatly interpreted this *Saturnine* taciturnitie to her own aduantage, thinking it proceeded from the rauishment of her beautie, as her Ambassadour had before perswaded her: herewith she iudged in him, more elegancie of fourme and sweetnes of complection, then in any other knight whatsoeuer, which made her so esprized with his attracting regard, as to allay the extreamitie of this heat, she desired nothing more then to speake with him, that she might bee resolued of whence and what he was. *Palmendos* stirred not from his place, nor thought he long of his stay there, because hee hoped to gather some fruite thereby: but warily markes the amorous lookes of *Iffida*, and how her eie was the messenger of her inward desire,[554] all which he couertly imparted to *Ozalio*, who mooued not one foot from his deere friend.

They fearing least their long staye would cause suspicion, went their way, which made *Iffida* likewise repaire to her Chamber, and calling the minister of her looue aside, began in this maner.

Ah Page, how trulie didst thou discouer the perfections of the straunge Knight, whose behauiour and discreet modestie, ioyned with his rare and martiall prowesse, makes mee repute him for the cheefest man, that euer came into this Countrey. Madame answered the young Counceller, if you would see innumerable vertues conioyned in one body, I beseech yee[a] hasten your speaking with him, and **[X2r]** let not the happye houre miscarrie through your default, which the fatall destinies haue so graciously appointed: hys loouely speeches shall acquaint yee[b] with his endowments,[c] which you may beholde so correspondent in euery point, as you can wish for nothing but is to be found in him. How should I speake with him, saied *Iffida*, without impeach to mine honor, which hithertoo I haue carefully regarded, vnlesse it be by thy meanes in some secret place, free from the hurt of suspected persons, wherewith the worlde is nowe mightily stored? I shall tell ye[d] how Madame, replied[e] the Page, you know

[a] yee] you P2, P3

[b] yee] you P2, P3

[c] endowments] indowment P2, P3

[d] ye] you P2, P3

[e] replied] answered P2, P3

my Lord your father willed yee[a] the other day, that yee[b] should returne home[c] to him with all possible speed, which will serue as a fit occasion, to take your honest farewell of this company: if then you will depart hence to morrowe towarde euening, you may lodge by the way at my mothers house: whether I will go before with the two Knights, and cause her to say[d] they be both her Nephewes, who now are friendly come to visite her, so may ye[e] confer togeather at your pleasure. The inuention[f] is good aunswered *Iffida*, yet must ye[g] be very circumspect herein, that the drift of our intent be not discouered.

The complot thus concluded, the Page went in the morning to *Palmendos*, and making him not a little glad with these[h] newes, caused both the frends to mount on horsbacke, and set forward with him to his mothers house, seated in a pleasant place betweene *Tubant* and the Castell of *Albayzo*. When the Gentlewoman saw the two knights, she was much abashed, but her Sonne soone resolued her in euery point: and that shee might boldlye call them her Nephewes, her selfe being a straunger borne far from that Countrey. The mother beeing thoroughly enstructed by her Sonne, desired their intent might take good successe, whereupon the Page returned to his Mistresse, who had in this while so well ordered her departure, as the new married nor any other could gather suspicion: then forwarde she sets, for her iourney had hast, so surely had Loue seazed **[X2v]** on her hart, hauing no other company with her, then her foure waiting Damosels and two Squiers of her fathers.

Nowe is she come to[i] the long desired place,[555] where being very graciously entertayned, both by *Palmendos* and *Ozalio*, as also the Pages mother. *Iffida* beeing not to learne her lesson, desires to know what Knights they were that so friendly saluted her.[556] They are quoth the Pages mother, my two Nephewes, who hauing not seene mee of long time, are

[a] yee] you P2, P3

[b] yee] you P2, P3

[c] home] *om.* P2, P3

[d] say] say that P2, P3

[e] ye] you P2, P3

[f] inuention] intention P3

[g] ye] you P2, P3

[h] these] this P2, P3

[i] to] unto P2, P3

come to know if they may stand me in anie steede: as also to offer their seruice to my Lord your father, if in any thing it shall please him to imploy them. Right hartly welcome are they, aunswered *Iffida*, and of dutye I must needs thanke them, for the good will they beare my Lorde and Father: for which cause, as also their neere alliaunce to you, I loue them as they were my proper Bretheren.

Palmendos comming to her with great reuerence, gaue her humble thanks for her honourable kindnes, and while they spent the time about other familiar conferences,[a] supper was set on the table in a pleasant Arbour, where *Iffida* cold digest no meat, her eies were so busied in beholding her Champion,[557] afterwarde they walked vp and downe the Garden, and shee seeing the Pages mother was deepe in talke with *Ozalio*, as one loth to loose so good an oportunity, she beginneth with *Palmendos* in this manner.

I cannot but maruaile at myselfe, (Sir Knight) that being nothing touched with the loue of sundry gentlemen, which heretofore haue diuers times offered mee theyr seruice: my heart should by you (whome I neuer saw before these two daies past) so vehemently be prouoked to loue, so that I cannot heare or think on any thing, but it is broken or reiected by the remembraunce of you: let mee then intreat yee,[b] not to repute me as carelesse of my chastitye, or forgetfull of the modestie beseeming a Virgin. For the worthy behauior, I see couched in your incomparable personage, hath fatally depriued mee of my former libertye, and **[X3ʳ]** yeelded me wholie your Captiue: not doubting but you wil so esteeme of your conquest, as not to impeach the same by any vnhonourable[c] attempt, considering my noble birth and parentage. And to satisfie my earnest longing desire, onelie adicted to haue further knowledge of your estate, acquaint me with the secret consideration of your heart, and what you wil commaund me, in guerdon of the paines you haue taken for my sake: wherein (mine[d] honour defended) I will yeeld that willingly to you, which none els but you can haue of me.[558]

Madame aunswered *Palmendos*, I cannot expresse my high good fortune, finding such grace and courtesie at your hands, beeing on my part no

[a] conferences] conference P2, P3

[b] yee] you P2, P3

[c] vnhonourable] dishonorable P2, P3

[d] mine] my P2, P3

way as yet deserued, but tyme may yeeld the due to euery gentle minde, and make mee able to requite such extraordinary fauour. And thinke not sweet Goddesse of my heart, that in pittying the insupportable burthen of mine[a] oppressions, you shall any waye encurre the detection of lightnes, but rather of honorable and wel gouerned care, when you shal beholde the place wherto I hope safely to bring you: for Madam, setting aside my simple outward appearance, I am a King borne, and Gouerner of sundry famous Prouinces, and this attempt proceeded onely of religious zeale, to make you Lady of mee and mine, as your woonderful fame at first tooke the soueraigntie of my heart.[559]

How can I woorthy Lord, quoth *Iffida*, but stand amazed, that you being a King, and a man of so rare fortune in mannaging arms, shold come hither for so simple a Damosel as my selfe, not woorthy to cast mine eies to such preferment? yet not to dissemble with yee[b] as concerning my resolution, without my fathers consent, I neither may or will goe hence with yee,[c] because it were both disobedience and iniurie to nature.

Notwithstanding, one thing I will doo for yee,[d] which neuer heretofore I offered to any Knight, I will bring you to my Father, and tell him you are one of this Gentlewomans **[X3v]** Nephewes, she being my nursse in the time of mine infancie: to him must yee[e] offer your seruice, and no sooner shall he beholde your Knightly chiualrie, but he will gladly accept yee[f] as his Sonne.

So with my Parents consent you may conuaie mee hence, and in meane while I shall keepe secret your estate, albeit it were good you[g] tolde[h] him the trueth. *Palmendos*, who desired nothing but to get into the Castel, and to compasse the same by any way he could, thus replied.

Madame, such is the extreamitie of my vehement passions, as no one can recure them, but she from whome they tooke their originall, nor doo my vitall spirites receiue anie force to execute their office, but from your

[a] mine] my P3

[b] yee] you P2, P3

[c] yee] you P2, P3

[d] yee] you P2, P3

[e] yee] you P2, P3

[f] yee] you P2, P3

[g] you] that you P2, P3

[h] tolde] tell P2, P3

gracious and gentle disposition: therefore I will go with you when you please to your Father, and say what you can best imagine, for the peaceable assuraunce and fruition of the good pretended. These wordes hee vttered with very cheerefull countenaunce, by reason of the hope wherewith his heart was encouraged, seing the practise of his negotiation stand nowe on the tearmes himselfe desired:[560] the Ladie on the other side was so rauished with his loue, as[a] she could not bee satisfied with beholding him, or consent to forsake his companye, till time of constraint came that they must to their lodgings, where *Iffida* could not sleepe thorough the whole night, her slumbers were so broken by the aboundance and plurality of amorous discourse, which chased all other imaginations from her spirit.

In these extreames poore *Iffida* was tormented, a disease cleane contrarye to that which troubled *Palmendos*, who only sought by dissimulation to recouer the good king of *Thessalie*, whereof he conferred in bed with *Ozalio*, what stratagems and subtilties hee must compasse in the action: intreating him most affectionatlie, they hauing once gotten enteraunce into the Castell, to shewe him selfe hardie and valiaunt, putting euery one to the sword when the watchword shold be giuen. When the morning was come, *Iffida* **[X4r]** decked her selfe in her braue accoustrements, and comming into the Garden, found there the two Knightes armed except their helmets, she praying them to go with her to the Castell of *Albayzo*, that she might haue the honour of presenting them to the Captaine her Father.[561]

This matter being soone concluded, they all mounted on horsebacke, and about noone arriued at the fortresse, the foundation and structure whereof caused *Palmendos* to woonder, in that it was placed on a high and mightie rock, and storred with such munition for war as it was thought impregnable. Beeing come to the gate, *Iffida* lighted from her haqueney and entred taking the Knights by the hand, the Arches permitting them quietly to[b] passe, without any feare or further enquirie what they were, seeing them so well acquainted with faire *Iffida*, whome the Castilian[c][562] loued so well, as none might gaine-say what shee commaunded.

[a] as] that P2, P3

[b] to] *om.* P2, P3

[c] Castilian] Captain P2, P3

Afterward the Bridges were drawen, and the gates strongly barred according as they were woont to bee, so the Princes entering the great[a] Hall, *Palmendos* diligentlie looked about him, thinking eche hower a yeare till the skirmishe were fought in this strong holde, thanking the heauens that had so well guided them thither.[563]

[X4ᵛ] CHAPTER XXVIII.

Howe Palmendos *and* Ozalio *slewe the Captaine of Albayzo Castell, and all the Guard that then kept it, taking the King of Thessalie forth of the Tower, where hee had remained captiue twentie yeeres: and what happened to*[b] *them in the meane while.*

When the Captaine of *Albayzo* Castell, (who was an honourable olde man, and put in cheefe trust with the great Turkes treasure) saw his Daughter accompanied with two such braue Knights, hee was thereat exceedingly amazed: as if this occurrence had alreadye presaged the conflicte and cruell slaughter, which was immediatlie to followe in the Castell, wherefore he said. Why Daughter? How chaunceth it that you are come without your Brother? My Lord, quoth shee, the desire I had yester-night to see yee,[c] hastened my returne in company of your two Squires, my foure waiting Damosels, and these two knights, who are both Nephews to my nursse, where I found them as I passed by that way: and heereof bee assured good father, that this Knight (pointing to *Palmendos*) is one of the most hardie and curteous Gentlemen that euer ye[d] knewe. Whereof his victorie in the Tourney at my Brothers mariage, hath giuen me euident example, as also the honest speeches he had vsed to mee this morning, declaring his earnest desire to offer you his seruice: vnder hope whereof I haue beene his guide hither, esteeming the acquisition of such a man rare and of great consequence, and will chiefly helpe the strength of your charge. [Y1ʳ]

He is the better welcome, answered the Captaine, and in recompence of his good will, hee shall commaunde any courtesie at my hand.

[a] great] *om.* P3

[b] happened to] did happen unto P2, P3

[c] yee] you P2, P3

[d] ye] you P2, P3

For all these wordes, he had other matters in his minde, and because his Daughter praised him so much, so much the more willinglye could hee haue spared his companye in the Castell, for that his presence made him misdout and feare somewhat: yet to dissemble the matter, and take away all occasion of contrary mistrust, with a counterfeit merrie countenaunce he said.

Goe Daughter and salute thy mother, meane while these Knights shalbe vnarmed: which[a] he spake to bee assured of their Armour and weapons, intending they shold not haue them againe till they were foorth of the Castell. But *Palmendos* hearing these wordes, began to misdoubt their interpretation: and therefore thought best not to vse anye more speeches, but going with *Iffidaes* Page into a faire Chamber: in steede of vnarming them selues, they clasped on their Helmets, and taking their Shields with resolued courage, came foorth hauing their good swordes readie drawen, *Palmendos* intending[b] to trie the vertue of his enchanted swoord, or els to put both their liues in danger. The Page seeing this sudden alteration, driuen into as great a quandarie as if he had beene new metamorphised, began to crie out very pitifully, terming this act abhominable and scelerous disloyaltie: wherewith he ran downe to aduertise the Guard thereof, but they themselues were not farre behinde him, because *Palmendos* knew this enterprise was not to bee deferred, therefore hee and *Ozalio* came into the Castell Court, where they found the Captaine threatning the Guarde, that they had so lightly suffered the Knights to enter: but they excused them selues on *Iffida* who brought them with her, wherwith the Captaine turning about, and seeing them come in such furie, hee cried to the Guard, saying. Take Armes my loyall and faithfull Knights, and let vs murther these false villaines, who haue beguiled vs so treacherously. **[Y1ᵛ]**

Palmendos hauing instructed *Ozalio*, to keepe sure the Gate that none might issue foorth, or more reskewe come in, remembring his sweete Ladie *Francelina*, determined to die or deliuer her father from imprisonment.

Now makes he prooue of his Swoord charmed by the Fairies,[564] which as hee lifted about his head, caused euerie one that came against them sleepely to stagger, and when they offered to strike with their weapons, they fell down as though they had beene in a sound sleepe, beeing all

[a] which] which words P2, P3

[b] intending] now intending P2, P3

in that case depriued of their liues, both the Captaine, the Guard, and the rest that could be found, except the Turke who guided them by Sea, and the Page that came wyth these newes to *Iffida*, saying.[565] Alas Madame, wee are all betraied, by the false Knights that entred the Castel with vs: right worthy am I of a thousand deaths, in that your Father and all the Guarde haue lost their liues by my meanes.

When *Iffida* and her mother heard these vncouth newes, they came downe as women distracted of their wits, and seeing this lamentable massacre, she fell downe on her fathers dead bodie, saying.[a] Ah my good Lorde and Father, pardon mee that was the cause of this thy death and seeing innocently I haue beene so circumuented by a false Traitour: my life shall presently followe thee at the[b] heeles, to accomplishe thy obsequies with more solemne[c] pompe and ceremonies. Herewith she offered to run her head[d] against a marble piller, but *Palmendos* came and staied her, when shee beeing greatly offended thereat, raging against him, thus spake.

Thou cruell, false and disloyall Knight, seeing thou hast slaine my Father and his chiefest friendes, why doest thou not[e] send me to beare them company?[566] Tell me thou bloodlie *Barbarian*, what mooued[f] thee to repaye my faythfull loue with such extreame rigour? How durst thou deceiue me so trecherously, considering what fauour I shewed thee on so small acquaintaunce? With guilefull and dissembling **[Y2ʳ]** speeches, thou secretly saydst thou wast a King: but if thou bee one, it is of robbers and theeues, and art come hither to steale the great Emperours treasure. Miserable and vnhappie that I was, in giuing credite to such false perswasions, the ende whereof sorteth to such monstrous effect.

If such as heretofore haue knowen me, imagined me wise and discreetlye inclined, hencefoorth they maye well tearme me a disloyall Daughter, being the onely cause of my fathers death: but though vnwittingly I haue beene deceiued, yet will I complaine on[g] Fortunes instabilitie that by the report of I know not what, friuolous and vain ostentation

[a] saying.] uttering these words. P2, P3

[b] the] his P3

[c] solemne] P2; selemne P1

[d] head] P2; he ad P1

[e] not] not also P2, P3

[f] mooued] did move P2, P3

[g] on] of P3

should so easily change my heart.[567] But what will the mightie Emperour of *Turkie* say, when hee shall vnderstand the trueth of this slaughter, wrought onely for the stealing hence of this treasure? Foolish and miserable Girle that I am, why did not I remember the sundry iniuries, his Maiesties brother sustained by the Emperour *Palmerin* of *Constantinople*, when he trauailed the world as a Knight errant?[568] had I but remembred those stratagems, they would haue forwarned me from affecting this stranger: yet if the fatal decree made me so soone subiect to him, why could he not fauour mee with my fathers life? *Palmendos* litle regarding her iniurious speeches, desired her to be better pacified, promising[a] if she would depart thence[b] with him, to sette the Crowne of *Tharsus* vppon her head, which he would giue to his Cozin *Ozalio*, and ioyne her in mariage with him if she pleased.[569]

Moreouer, he assured her, that he would not take any thing out of the Castell but the King of *Thessalie*, whose deliuerance could not bee compassed by any intreaty, and therefore he ransommed him with the liues of so many. O Mahomet, cried *Iffida* at these wordes, why sufferest thou Christians to make such incursions on thy people and Countries? Why didst thou creat and appoint women so neer to men, seeing that for them they passe thorough innumerable **[Y2v]** torments? The brother to our great Emperor the Turke, was cruelie murthered by the meanes of a woman,[570] and now by me is his Captaine my father brought to the like end, his prisoner likewise the King of *Thessalie* thereby deliuered: how can I but loath and despise my life, beeing hemmed in on euere side with such monstrous affliction?

Needlesse is it now to remember mortal incombrances, or to thinke on the warres which *Hesione* and *Helena* caused betweene the *Greekes* and *Troyans*:[571] *Lauinia* betweene *Aeneas* and *Turnus*,[572] or *Deianira* between *Hercules* and *Acheolus*, and afterward among the *Centaures*:[573] for those[c] which will spring by these newe occasions ere long time bee spent, I feare will bee so horrible and infamous, as[d] they will deface the memorie of them doone so long agoe. Afterward the mother and her daughter ran furiouslie on *Palmendos*, labouring to doo him what iniurie they could,

[a] promising] promised P2, P3

[b] thence] *om.* P2, P3

[c] those] the Wars P2, P3

[d] as] that P2, P3

but he (vnwilling to hurt them) suffred their violence, til *Ozalioes* Squier seeing their impacience, and fearing with their kniues they would in the end murther him: tooke vp one of the Guardes hatchets, and therewith depriued the mother of her life.[574]

Iffida extreamely raging at this greeuous spectacle,[575] rent her haire from her head, and with her nailes cruelly[a] martyred her faire face, then beeing suddainly supprized with a raging apoplexie, presentlie[b] died without vsing anie more speeches.[576] The Page greeuing to behold this woful accident, determined not to liue any longer after her: but first vpon the wall he wrote certaine dolorous verses, which afterward were conuerted to a funerall ditty, in this manner.[577]

[Y3r] *Dead is the bud of Beauties cheefe delight,*
The fairest flower whereon[c] *the Sunne did shine:*
The choyce belou'd of many a famous Knight,
The pride of honour, precious and diuine.
The louely Maid, of whome the Nimphes did sing:
That Nature neuer fram'de so rare a thing.

Had Paris *seene this wonderous peece of art,*
Proud Venus *had not caried beauties prize:*
Pallas *and* Iuno *would haue stood apart,*
To see their gifts one Virgin royallize.
In euerie point surpassing curious:
Had Fate and Fortune beene as gracious.

Vngentle starre that domineerd the day,
When first my Lady Mistres breath'd this aire:
What angry obiect stood then in the way,
To crosse the course that was begun so faire?
You lowring heauens, why did ye oppresse:
The Saint whome you so many waies did blesse?

But wretch, why stand'st thou charging these with guilt,
And art thy selfe the Authour of this ill?

[a] cruelly] most cruelly P2, P3

[b] presentlie] she presently P2, P3

[c] whereon] on whom P2, P3

Thou haplesse Boy thy Ladies blood hast spilt,
Thy Maister and his seruants thou didst kill.
When first thou trauaild for this trothlesse man:
Euen in that hower these miseries began.

But Soueraigne Loue, immortal and diuine,
Whose gracious name did shaddow this abuse:
Canst thou permit before thy holy eien,
This hainous deede exempt from all excuse?
O mightie Loue, what will thy Subiects say:
If foule offence goe vnreueng'd away?

[Y3^{v}] *Stand I expostulating this or that,*
When on my backe the weightie burthen lies?
Waste no more time with vaine and idle chat,
But for this fault be thou a sacrifice.
Faire Iffida, *thy Page doth follow thee:*
The onely engine of this tragedie.[578]

These verses fixed on the wall by the Squire, hee ran hastily and caught vp a Sword from one of the slaine Knightes, and setting the point thereof against his heart, said. If you (Madame) by my meanes haue receiued this harde[a] fortune, reason requires that for your sake I should endure as much:[b] and with these wordes hee fell vpon the Sworde.[579]

This was the second act of the tragicall comedie begun at *Prissa*, and thus after continued in the Theater of *Albayzo*,[580] where all they of the Castell miserably ended their liues, except three or foure Damoselles, and their waiting women: who likewise were so amazed at this lamentable spectacle, as they thought them selues halfe depriued of life. *Palmendos* beeing stricken in a dump by these accidents, stood a good while not able to speake a word:[581] which his Cosin *Ozalio* perceiuing, and marueiling at his alteration, he came and comforted him in this sort. My Lord, you must now abandon[c] all dumpish musing, and reioyce for your good successe in this attempt: neuer trouble your thoughts with other imaginations,

[a] harde] *om.* P2, P3

[b] as much:] P2; asmuch: P1

[c] abandon] leave P2, P3

but let vs determine our departure hence, before the matter bee further manifested, otherwise we may fall in daunger a hundred times more to be feared, then were we enclosed in the inextricable Labyrinth.

Your reason is good, Cosin, aunswered *Palmendos*, wherfore presently we will go seeke for the prison: wherin my Lord the King hath beene kept so long: After they had searched a good while in vaine, at length they found him **[Y4r]** in a strong[a] Tower, bound with huge barres of yron, he being so leane, wrinckled, pale and wan, as they marueiled to see him so withered away.

Palmendos beholding him in this greeuous plight, remembring this was the father to his best beloued *Francelina*, compassion caused the teares to trickle down hys cheekes: but the King not perceiuing this humanitie, rather amazed to see their Swordes so bloodie, thought they were come to end his miserable and distressed life, wherfore he willingly prepared himselfe therto, saying. Soueraign redeemer of humain nature, to thee I commend my soule, which must nowe leaue this loathsome prison, be thou then my intercessour to thy mercifull Father, hauing so paciently for my sinnes suffered punishment in this wretched place. And seeing hee hath reputed my bodie vnworthy[b] longer being in this life, be thou my gracious mediatour for my soule,[582] that in his iudgement it bee not bannished from eternall felicitie promised to the good.

This prayer hauing stopt the passage of *Palmendos* speech, *Ozalio* vsed these wordes to the King. My Lord, bee not dismayed, wee come not hither to offer yee[c] anie outrage, but to deliuer you from this thraldome, and cary yee[d] with vs to *Constantinople*: where you shall finde your Queene and faire Daughter *Francelina*, by whose means your troubles haue[e] nowe taken end, and there they staye onely for your comming.

Afterward he declared the whole successe of the action, and breaking the barres of the little wicket, tooke him foorth of that darke prison, wherein hee had remained twentie yeeres, such marueilous hatred did the great Turke beare him. Yet could hee not bee certainelye[f] resolued of

[a] strong] P2; stong P1

[b] vnworthy] unworthy of P2, P3

[c] yee] you P2, P3

[d] yee] you P2, P3

[e] haue] hate P3

[f] Bee certainelye] certainly be P3

his libertie, till he sawe the Captaine and the rest that were slaine, when embracing the Knightes, hee thanked GOD and them for his happie deliuerance.

Palmendos thought it necessary to make no longer stay **[Y4v]** there, wherfore commanding one of their Squires to fetch a good horsse out of the Captains stable, they caused the king to mount thereon: then remembring the former speeches of *Iffida*, he would not suffer any thing els to bee carried from[a] the Castell.[583]

CHAPTER XXIX.

How the King of Thessalie departing with Palmendos *from the Castel of Albayzo, they met the great Turks Daughter by the way, whome the Prince carried thence by the vertue of his Sworde. And how* Ripole *hauing taken order for the buriall of them that were slaine, hee went to complaine thereof to the great Turke.*

Palmendos remembring his returne to *Constantinople*, and deuising how hee might safelie get awaye from the Castell of *Albayzo*, he caused all the gentlewomen that were left aliue to bee locked in one Chamber: and so soone as it wared[b] darke, leauing the great Gates wide open, and the Bridges downe, they all rode away: *Orycano* being their guide as he was before. About midnight they came to the Pages mothers house, where among the trees in the Garden, they espied diuers lighted Torches, and a sumptuous bed in the middest of the Arbour, at which sight not marueiling a little, they staied there awhile: but *Palmendos* desirous to bee further satisfied heerein, gaue his horsse to *Orycano*, and drawing his vertuous Sworde, charmed all that were in the Garden fast asleepe,[584] by which meanes hee came to the **[Aa1r]** rich beds side, wherin he saw a very beautifull Ladie. Her name was *Marencida*, eldest daughter to the great Turke, and wife to the King *Ocurites* of *Culaquin*, whom *Palmendos* found neere the Gulfe of *Tanais* and *Meotides*:[585] she nowe iournying to recreate herselfe with her Mother, at a fayre Castell not farre from this place, whether she went three daies before in great anger from the Courte, because the great Turke loued another of his concubines better then her.[586]

[a] from] out of P3

[b] wared] was P3

Marencida mourning for the taking of the King her Husband, craued leaue of the great Turke her father, that she might goe visite her Mother for seauen or eight daies, where with her she might beare a share of her greeue and heauines: so parting from the Courte honourably accompanied, and alighting at this pleasant bower to refreshe[a] her selfe, because the night suddainly preuented her, shee commaunded the Groomes[b] to prepare her bed for that night in the Arbour, her Ladies, Gentlewomen and Guard, beeing all there about her. *Palmendos* hauing charmed with his Sword[c] all her attendants a sleepe, approched neere the beddes side, when the Princesse thinking on her Husbands imprisonment, gaue many greeuous sighes from the depth of her hart, cursing the Knight that tooke him, as also *Constantinople* for vniustly detayning him, and to these mournfull regrets added these speeches.

My noble Lord, Oh that I had some sure and loyall person, that might conduct me to the place where thou art, to the ende my longing mind might be satisfied with sight[d] of thee, and these two sources of teares stayed from further streaming ouer: for liuing here, my greefes grow intollerable, and I abide the most desolate Ladie in all *Asia*.[e] Other lamentable speeches she vttered, till nature no longer able to outstand[f] the charges of drowsines, caused her to fall fast a sleepe: and *Palmendos* hauing heard what had[g] passed, imagined her to be[h] the great Turks Daughter, Wife to the King *Ocurites*, whom he sent to *Constantinople*. Wherfore seeing all her Guarde soundly sleeping, he folded down **[Aa1ᵛ]** the bed clothes, and because the precious Calamite in hys Sword, by nature draweth the body of man or woman to it, as the Adamant dooth the yron: the Ladie presently arose into his Armes, so[i] beeing kept[j] a sleepe by his enchanted Sworde, lay as quiet in his armes, as fayre *Daphne* did with *Phaebus*, when

[a] refreshe] P2; refeshe P1

[b] Groomes] Groome P3

[c] charmed with his Sword] with his sword charmed P2, P3

[d] sight] the sight P2, P3

[e] Asia.] P2; ~ , P1

[f] outstand] withstand P2, P3

[g] had] was P3

[h] her to be] that she was P2, P3

[i] so] and P2, P3

[j] kept] so kept P2, P3

Iupiter conuerted her into a Baye tree.[587] Wrapping her costly Mantle about her, hee departed safely from the Guarde, and comming where *Oricano* stayed with his horse, made such shift as he mounted into the saddle, and so galloped to the rest of his company, who meruailed not a little that he had got so good a bootie. Great hast they made till they got on ship-boord, when *Palmendos* laying her vpon his bed, and vsing her reuerently because she was of such honor: he put vp his vertuous sword into the sheathe, when very soone after *Marencida* awaked, and seeing herselfe in the company of straungers, crying out with feare, she said. Alas where am I? what? haue I no one about me that I know? How came I so strangely into this place? why Fortune? hast thou not yet afflicted me enough? are my starres grown into such hatred towarde mee, as in my sleepe to seeke my destruction? And what are you that haue beene so bolde as to take me out of my bed? this audacious behauiour will returne you no other guerdon, then the very sharpest death that can be deuised. Madame, answered *Palmendos*, from that wee shall keepe our selues so well as we may, as for my selfe, I am a Knight of a Countrey far hence, and hearing by chaunce what mone ye[a] made, for the captiuitie of the King your Husband, as also howe desirous you seemed to see him in *Constantinople*, I was greatly mooued to pittie your affliction, and as one willing to pleasure yee[b] heerin, as also what other thing you shall commaund mee, I tooke yee foorth of your bed, promising ye[c] by my religious vowes to Chiualrie, not onely to shewe you the King *Ocurites*: but also to guarde your chastitie incontaminate, as free from the least spot of dishonour, as when yee[d] happened into my custodie.[588] **[Aa2r]**

False and disloyall Knight, quoth shee, how can I but receiue shame and infamie by this treacherie, hauing in such sort beene taken from among my Guarde? If I desired to see the King my husband, it was only to content my minde, which is thereto mooued with vehement affection: yet might my meaning be far enough from my words, because I could not doo it without my Fathers licence, and more willingly woulde I ende my life in this place, then goe with thee of whom I canne imagine no good thought, but as thou hast fellоniously stollen mee from my bedde, so wilt

[a] ye] you P2, P3

[b] yee] you P2, P3

[c] ye] you P2, P3

[d] yee] you P2, P3

thou heereafter trayterously murder me. I am neyther Theefe or Traytour, aunswered *Palmendos*, but a Knight readie at your commaundement, if so you take my seruice in good worth: and seeing you are now in my puissaunce,[a] determine to goe with me willinglie or perforce, and thinke not I intend your death, for it is farre from my thought I promise you.

Then began *Marencida* to teare her haire, which seemed as the Golden wyer, and beate her faire handes so white as the Alablaster, with out-cryes as a Woman depriued of her sences: when the Prince pittying these feminine importunities, drew his Sword, and to ease these extreames charmed her a sleepe againe. During thys time, *Ozalio* had tolde the King of *Thessalie* the whole newes of his Daughter *Francelina*, whereto hee gaue good attention, because since the time of his imprisonment, he had not heard any thing as concerning the affaires of his Realm, or that the Queene his wife had any such Daughter, wherefore the teares trickling downe his face, he came and embraced *Palmendos*, saying. In sooth my Sonne, al the greeuous torments I haue heertofore endured, seeme nothing in respect of the comfort I nowe feele, that my vnknowne Child shall[b] enioy a man so vertuous: and for this Ladies taking I am likewise glad, because by this meane I shall be reuenged sufficiently[c] on the Turke. Thus dooth God, aunswered *Palmendos*, shewe himselfe a iuste Iudge, and **[Aa2v]** the true directour of all humane actions, limitting euerie occasion according as best him pleaseth: but we were best to make what speed we can hence, els may we repent our comming among these inexorable Tyrants. *Marencida* awaking againe, and not perswaded with all the courteous intreaties[d] the Prince[e] could deuise, shee still continued her former acclamations,[f] not vnlike *Ariadne* at the comming of *Bacchus*, when she was found forsaken by *Theseus* at the sea-side:[589] in like sort did she renew her maledictions, inuocating on *Neptune* and *Thetis*,[590] as also the *Tritons* their Herralds,[591] Monsters, Nimphes and Sirens, that shee might suffer shypwracke in the Sea, and the Fishes feede on her vnhappie carcasse. But *Ozalio* pittying her dollorous complaints, and finding his hart somewhat espryzed with

[a] puissaunce] power P2, P3

[b] shall] should P3

[c] reuenged sufficiently] sufficiently revenged P2, P3

[d] intreaties] entertainments P2, P3

[e] the Prince] he P2, P3

[f] acclamations] P2; acclama tions P1

her loue, intreated *Palmendos* to graunt him one request, which aboue al things else he required at his hands, when the Prince yeelding to[a] any thing his Cozin woulde demaund, *Ozalio* proceeded in this manner.

My sute is worthy Lord and Cozin, to enioy this Lady as my Wife, to whom I know the destenies haue fatallie reserued mee,[592] considering the suddaine chaunge and inexplicable controuersie my hart endureth: wheras the continual accompanying of beautiful Ladies heertofore, could neuer mooue my frozen affections, and nowe I feele them not warme but boyling. Easilie may yee[b] (quoth *Palmendos*) obtaine this demaund of mee, if nothing els stande in the way to hinder it, and as[c] much doo I desire your aduauncement, as any waie I can be couetous of mine own, hoping while I liue to see no diuorce between vs, but that our estates shall continue equally together, and in witnes of my worde, I deliuer yee[d] the charge of this Princesse, heereafter to dispose of her according to your desires.[593] *Ozalio* now vseth all decent courtesies to *Marencida*, wherby[e] to gaine fauour in her conceit: yet all was in vaine, for she would not affoorde him any good countenaunce, but remained[f] in her wonted obstinacie. **[Aa3[r]]**

When the poore Fisherman vnderstood by his Sonne *Orycano*, how his guests had deliuered the King of *Thessalie* out of *Albayzo* Castell, hee thought it no longer tarrying for him in *Turkie*, wherefore hee came and intreated the Prince *Palmendos*, that he might saile with him vnto[g] Christendome, which sute was very soone obtained, for hee, his wife and familie did all come[h] aboord the Ship, the Prince promising to reward their gentlenes liberallie.

Nowe let vs come to the Guarde and them that attended on *Marencida*, who waking and not finding their Ladie in her bed, began to chafe and rage in most extreame manner: some renting[i] their haire and beardes violentlie, others running mad among the Trees, thinking she had

[a] to] unto P2, P3

[b] yee] you P2, P3

[c] as] *om.* P3

[d] yee] you P2, P3

[e] wherby] thereby P2, P3

[f] remained] remain P2, P3

[g] vnto] into P2, P3

[h] did all come] came all P2, P3

[i] renting] rending P2, P3

beene metamorphized in the Garden, nor coulde they imagine how to escape the daunger when the great Turke shoulde heare of this mishap. These comfortles creatures thus amazed, not daring any one of them[a] to goe tell the Emperor heerof, they determined to flie the Countrey, and returne no more to the Courte, leauing *Marencidaes* Ladies and Gentlewomen mourning in that vnhappy place, where (about noone) *Ripole* Brother to *Iffida* arriued, returning from the wedding with his wife and diuers braue Knights: but when he vnderstood the cause of their sorrow, hee was strooken into such a quandarie, as hee woulde passe no further before hee enquired more of this[b] euent. In meane[c] while he sent a Squire to *Albayzo* Castel, to aduertise his Father of his comming, and the Squire prauncing vp to the Fortresse, meruailed to see the Gates wide open, but[d] much more when he saw the slaughter of the Knights, and the Captaine himselfe lie slaine among them: nowe was he surprized with such feare, as hee had not the hart to tarrie there any longer, but trusting to the speedy succour of his horse legges, galloped with all speede to his Maister, where standing awhile as a man beside himselfe at length he thus spake. Pardon me, my Lord, in declaring a bloodie and tragicall report, your worthy Father and all the Guard **[Aa3v]** of the Castell, lye cruellie murdered in the base Courte, and because I founde the greate Gates open, I doubt the Treasure and riches in the Castell, hath occasioned thys massacre by some robbers and theeues. *Ripole* hearing these vnlooked for newes, terrified in such sort as he coulde not tell what to say, mounted[e] on a lusty Courser and[f] rode to the Castell, the Gentlemen bringing his wife faire and softlie after: but when he beheld this woful spectacle, and what a butcherie *Palmendos* Sworde had made, his Seruaunts feared he woulde haue followed in this harde fortune. Nor can I heare set downe the rufull mones, which *Ripole* made ouer his Father, Mother and Sister, no doubt they were as strange and yrkesome as this accident: but when they had searched through the Castell, and founde nothing wanting but the King of *Thessalie*, they iudged the Authors of this tirannie to be Christians, and that they likewise had

[a] daring any one of them] any one of them daring P2, P3

[b] this] the P2

[c] meane] the mean P2, P3

[d] but] *om.* P3

[e] mounted] but mounting P2, P3

[f] and] *om.* P2, P3

caried awaie the Queene *Marencida*. After he had taken order for interring the deade, he rode immediatlie toward the great Turke, hauing heard of *Iffidaes* Nursse, all that had past[a] betweene her and the two Knights, and beeing come before the Emperour, he fell at his feete, deliuering the signes of an afflicted spirite, which onelie sought for grace and mercie. At length he declared the substaunce of this wreakfull occurrence, as well that of *Marencida* his Maiesties Daughter, as the other of hys Fathers death, and deliueraunce of the King of *Thessalie*, affirming his Sister *Iffida* as[b] onely cause thereof, and by what traynes she had beene beguiled, himselfe beeing altogether innocent of the treason:[594] notwithstanding, hee freely offered himselfe at his gracious disposition, to abide whatsoeuer he would assigne him. These wordes so wounded the Turke to the hart, as hee remained silent a great while, anger had[c] so locked vp the passage of his speeche: yet furiously at length starting from his Chayre, hee rayled on the Gods, starres, deuils and all the infernall powers. Ah Mahomet, quoth he, doubtlesse thou art angry with mee, **[Aa4r]** or els dost take but little care of thy seruaunts, that euermore haue extolled thee aboue all other Gods and Prophets: but much I wonder thou woldest thus forget me, vnlesse thou wilt haue mee thinke thee extreamely offended, or that the hope is vaine and frustrate which is reposed in thee. You starres, not inclined to fauour me, but rather affecting my totall ruine, wherin haue I so haynously offended, that you shoulde take so sharpe and rigorous vengeaunce on me? what may this presage to me heereafter, but some great misfortune and suddaine mutation in *Asia*? yet will I so carefully foresee these affayres, as the sedicious performers of this villainie, shall not cary it away so lightlie. Like sorrowes made this Infidell for his mishap, when many of his Knights, without attending other commaundement, got ready Foystes, Gallyes and other vessels for[d] warre, to pursue the causers of this tragicall accident, but their labour was spent in vayne, albeit not long after they hearde the trueth of all: which procured such hatred betweene the *Turkes* and the *Grecians*, as they ceased not till with hostilitie they had inuaded *Greece*. But it was not during the raigne of the Emperour *Palmerin*, or anie of his race or next posteritie, for while they liued the *Turkes* durst not stirre against them:

[a] past] hapned P2, P3

[b] as] to be the P2, P3

[c] had] hauing P2, P3

[d] for] of P3

yet long time after, when *Ottoman* a fierce and proude Prince gouerned, infinite euilles happened in *Europe*, where he tooke and sacked many good Cities, Townes and Castels.[595] Now would the great Turke not suffer *Ripole* to bee further tormented, because he was found altogether innocent in the action, but sent him back to the Castel of *Albayzo*, making him Captain therof as his father was before. And long time continued he sad and mellanchollie, thinking hee had reciued wonderfull dishonour by the losse of his Daughter *Marencida*: nor shold he euer recouer the same, til *Greece* were beaten flat to the grounde, and the Emperour *Palmerin* with all his kindred vtterly destroyed: where in these ragings we wil leaue him, and returne to our purpose.

[Aa4v] CHAPTER XXX.

Howe Palmendos *with his company arriued at Constantinople, where the Emperour came and receiued them at the Porte. What speeches hee had with the Queene* Marencida, *after they were come to the Pallace, howe ioyfully likewise the Queene of Thessalie and* Francelina *her daughter, welcommed home the King her father.*

The Marriners cheerefully hoysing their sailes, left the coaste of *Turkie* and launched into the maine Sea, hauing the winde and weather so fauourable, as without anie impeachment they attained the Bosphor of *Thrace*, where *Palmendos* sent his Cozin *Ozalio* before to the Emperour, that the King of *Thessalie* might bee entertained with honour beseeming so great a Prince.[596] *Ozalio* making speede in a swift little Pinnesse,[597] beeing landed went directly to the Pallace, and finding the Emperour in the great Hall, conferring with his Lordes about the enchaunted Birde, which that morning had deliuered manie pleasant notes, wherfore hee expected some comfortable newes,[598] when *Ozalio* falling on his knee, began in this manner.

Dread Lord, I am the seruaunt and freend to the noble *Palmendos*, whose renowne hath heeretofore been blazed in this Court, and he humblie intreateth your highnes by mee, that you woulde entertaine the King of *Thessalie*, whom he hath brought from *Turkie*, with such grace and honour as beseemeth his dignitie. By this time I thinke they are entred the Hauen, in that they were not farre off **[Bb1r]** when I left them, I beeing sent before to acquaint your Maiestie heerewith. The Emperour exceeding ioyfull at these newes, rose and embraced *Ozalio* very graciouslei, and causing all his Knights and Barons to prepare themselues, said, he[a] would goe to the Port in person to welcom them. Right soone were these tydings bruted through the Court, wherwith the Empresse and her Ladies were highly pleased, especially the mourning Queen of *Thessalie* for her Husbands returne, and faire *Francelina* for her loouelie freende, whose absence made her imagine euery howre a yeere: wherfore in haste they got them before to the Porte, attended on by their Ladies and Gentlewomen, where *Palmendos* being new[b] come on shore with the King, thus spake to[c] him. Behold my good Lorde, your Queene and Daughter, who are ioyfullie come to salute your arriuall: but when he looked on *Francelina*, the whole quire of heauen was present in his thoughts. The Queene very earnestlie beheld the King her husband, when seeing his haire and beard so strangelie ouer-growne, beside, his skyn and complexion so wonderfully altered, as doubtfull in minde, she came to him with these wordes. Are ye[d] (my Lord) the king of *Thessalie*, for whom my hart hath suffered exceeding greefe? I praie ye[e] resolue me presentlie, without holding me in longer[f] suspence, in that your deformed estate hath greatlie peruerted[g] my remembraunce.

Madame, aunswered the King, it is no meruel though you know me not, considering the long time since ye[h] sawe me last, which the integrity of our loue hath made vs imagine of greater compasse, although the accustomed reuolution of yeeres, neither[i] deminish or increase one moment in their naturall course: notwithstanding, I am the same King your Husband, who haue felt more passions for your absence, then anguish or torment in my miserable captiuitie. But seeing the immortall bountie hath suffered mee once againe to see you, before my soule forsake this passible bodie, which was my continuall desire during my tribulation: **[Bb1v]** nowe care I not though Death presentlie doo his duetie,[599] for seeing the circle of

[a] he] that he P2, P3
[b] new] newly P2, P3
[c] to] unto P3
[d] ye] you P2, P3
[e] ye] you P2, P3
[f] in longer] longer in P3
[g] peruerted] perplexed P2, P3
[h] ye] you P2, P3
[i] neither] do not P2, P3

your armes haue embraced me, I am the readier for my mother Earth to receiue me. Nowe are ioyfull teares plentifullie powred foorth on all sides, and embracings so vehement, as though they should neuer vnfold againe, the libertie of speeche beeing hindred all this while, for *Palmendos* and *Francelina* were transported into a second heauen, where the outward ceremonies serued to confirme the inward contentation, at length the Queene taking *Francelina* by the hande, thus spake to the King. See heere my Lord your Daughter, of whom I was but newlie conceiued when you went from *Thessalie*,[600] happie and fortunate may she iustly bee tearmed, in that her destenie hath deliuered you from prison, restored me my former ioy, and giuen her the most perfect Knight that euer bare[a] Arms.[601] When the King behelde his Daughter so faire and gracious, he tooke her in his armes, expressing with silent fauours his hartie ioy: and in this while the Emperour came with his traine, alighting from his horse to welcome the King of *Thessalie*, whom when he behelde so spent and disfigured, the teares fell from his eyes, and embracing him in his armes, sayed.

My noble Brother, heauen haue the honour for deliuering ye[b] from our common enemie, where albeit I was heeretofore[c] glad of your reskewe, yet was I agreeued at your imprisonment, beeing then my selfe (as you know) in the Turkes power, although hee gaue mee more libertie then you, in hope I would haue ayded him with my vttermost abilitie: my desire then to get from his seruice, constrayned me to deale somewhat hardlie against you, an errour too notable, and I confesse worthy reprehension:[602] but God pardoning the offences of the repentaunt, hath in pittie regarded vs both, and by his inexpuisable goodnes, directed all thinges to a happy ende. My Lorde, replyed the King, the whole discourse thereof haue I heard by *Palmendos*, which giues me reason not to thinke any fault in you, **[Bb2r]** when yee[d] coulde not otherwise helpe the same: but let vs leaue occasions past, seeing heauen hath so miraculously deliuered me,[603] that I should come my selfe to present the entire affection, wherwith I am bound to your highnes seruice. Nor could anything in the world, said the Emperor, more delight me, then your comming with the Knight I haue so long desired to see: with whom I cannot but be

[a] bare] bore P3

[b] ye] you P2, P3

[c] I was heeretofore] heretofore I was P2, P3

[d] yee] you P2, P3

offended, (these words he merily vttered) in that hee hath taried so long time from mee: then *Palmendos* falling on his knee, modestly answered in this maner. Dread Lord, if heertofore I haue provoked your displeasure, I confesse such punishment is due to me as you shall ordaine, and wyllinglie will I endure it, to fashion mee the better to your seruice, wherein I woulde employ my selfe according to your appointment, although it were to fight against the Gates of death: wherof I gladly could affoord some proofe so please your highnes to enioyne me such a taske, as may expresse my zeale and forwardnes. And that you may know the name of your voluntarie Seruaunt, I am that *Palmendos*, who was since the howre of my birthe destenyed to follow your vertues, humbly intreating to discharge your remembraunce of any discontentment I haue heeretofore occasioned: in that mine owne minde still perswaded me, I wanted worthines to come before your excellencie.

The Emperour beholding him of such gallant stature, did not a little meruaile at his rare perfections, wherefore taking him graciously in his armes, desired he would commaund him any thing wherein he might stand him in sted, for he was not able to requite his high deseruings. Afterward came *Primaleon* and courteously entertained him, the like did *Abenunco*, signifying how much he was bound to him for his happy deliueraunce: then came *Arnedes* with the other Lordes and Knights, all of them embracing the hardie Champion that went away with the honour of the Tourney.[604]

By this time had *Ozalio* brought *Marencida* on shore, **[Bb2v]** shee wondring to behold such state and royaltie, wherefore she desired to know the place of her landing. Madame, answered *Ozalio*, this Cittie is called *Constantinople*, and among this florishing troope of Princes, who haue vouchsafed their coming hether to this Porte, there may yee[a] behold the famous Emperour *Palmerin*, who is heere in person to receiue the King of *Thessalie*, and the worthy Knight that deliuered him from prison: your selfe likewise wil esteeme him a vertuous Prince, by the good entertainment you shall enjoy, when once hee vnderstandeth your state and calling, so that I hope you will not repent this voyage, were it but to haue knowledge of him alone.

How miserable and vnfortunate am I, quoth she, to fall into the mercy of my Fathers capitall enemie? howe can my greefes but growe

[a] yee] you P2, P3

into an exceeding surplusage? If I see the King *Ocurites* my husband, the meeting will bee with meruailous hart breake on either side, beeing both of vs captiue to the very worst enemy we haue.[605] The Emperour and his Lords kindly saluted her: but shee would not once bowe herselfe or make any aunswer, whereat the standers by very much wondred, tearming her a Woman of rough and vnseemely behauiour, saying nature might much better haue made her a man.[606] Mounting all on horseback, in most comelie order they rode to the Pallace, where the Empresse and her Ladies met them in the Court: and[a] to tell the courtesies, gratulations and welcome there vsed, would aske a world of time, yet little[b] to the purpose, let it suffise then, they are so well entertained as you can anie way imagine.

Palmendos taking *Marencida* by the hande, brought her to the Princesse *Philocrista* with these speeches. I desire you Madame, to accept this Lady into your company, and giue her such good counsell as you can best deuise, for she is discended of royall blood I tell ye.[c] Sir *Palmendos*, replyed the Princesse, I must obey what you commaunde me, for the looue I beare to you and your sweete Freende,[607] **[Bb3r]** and I imagine my selfe fortunate, hauing such a precious gage from a Knight so perfect, nor shal she be worse intreated then mine owne selfe.

Marencida hearing these gracious speeches, and what courtesie *Palmendos* vsed to the Princesse, perceiued that she was the Emperours Daughter, wherefore she gaue her many thankes, shewing better countenaunce then before she did to any:[608] which *Philocrista* tooke very kindlie, and mounting vppe the steppes with her into the Hall, shee came to *Francelina* with these wordes. Thys Ladie, Madame, dooth now supply your place, seeing Lorde *Palmendos* is returned, for now your company with me must discontinue, because reason and your fatall loue dooth so commaunde,[d] notwithstanding, I hope our amitie shal continue.

Fayre Princesse, answered *Francelina*, wee are bothe so farre yours, and so good part haue ye[e] in my Lord, as you shall finde your selfe no lesse contented then abashed when ye[f] knowe all: therefore feare not that I will

[a] and] *om.* P2, P3

[b] little] but little P2, P3

[c] tell ye] assure you P2, P3

[d] commaunde] command me P2, P3

[e] ye] you P2, P3

[f] ye] you P2, P3

forget your freendly familiaritie, rather will I continue your louing Sister, as our further assuraunce of our mutuall agreement. Sundry other speeches passed betweene the two young Ladies, in meane while *Marencida* looking about her, and remembring the great pompe, state and riches of her Father, shee made but slender account of the Emperours Courte, which was not at this time so well stored with Knights as it was wont to bee, whereupon shee gyuing a great sigth, thus vttered her minde.

You knowe, Emperour of *Constantinople*, that the sumptuous royaltie of my Fathers Court, dooth exceede the greatest Princes in the whole world, as also howe manie mightie Lordes serue him with homage and fidelitie,[a] because heeretofore you haue seene the same, where if yee[b] were so aduenturous and hardie, to kill[c] without feare of them (as the whole worlde knoweth) the mightie Emperour mine Unckle, thinke I pray you, what miserable case **[Bb3v]** the Ladie is in, so traiterously brought from her owne natiue[d] Countrey, and now deliuered captiue into your custodie, wherein me thinkes, in respect of the renowne spread abroade of you, you should take example by my aduersitie, and rather greeue then glorie therin, as I see you doo, considering that inconstant Fortune is still variable, and doth not alwaies allowe men felicitie. This I speake not, whereby to gaine the more fauour or honour in your Court, because death would be much more welcome to mee, then to liue in the uexation of mind I doo: wherfore I intreate ye[e] againe (if intreatie may beseeme an aduersarie) heereafter to conserue your reputation in such sort, as I may receiue no impeach to mine honour, and you shall comfort mee better therein, then all the commendation of your fame can doo.

To these words shee added many rufull complaynts, as the Emperour beeing therewith mooued to compassion, replyed in this manner. I vnderstande, Madame, full well what ye[f] haue said, and knowe beside, that the feminine choller which gouerneth your spyrite, maketh you vse such kinde of language, as is cleane exempt from all the rules of womanlie modestie:[609] nor am I now to learne, that the strength of earthlie Kinges

[a] fidelitie] fealty P2, P3

[b] yee] you P2, P3

[c] to kill] as to kill P2, P3

[d] natiue] *om.* P2, P3

[e] ye] you P2, P3

[f] ye] you P2, P3

and Pontentates is lesse then nothing, when God is bent repugnaunt against them, whereby we are all to resolue, that we can doo no good acte without his assistaunce.[610] According to his direction came I to[a] your Unckles Courte, before whom I protest, and craue no mercie in the day of uengeaunce, if I slewe him, or euer thought to doo it, beeing too farre caryed away from minding anie such intent, by the honour I had before receiued at his highnes handes. Yet was I priuie to his forcible detayning of the Ladie, and laboured to restore her to her Lorde and Husbande, shee beeing Daughter to the renowned King of *Englande*, and Wife to the nowe famous Emperour *Trineus* of *Allemaigne*:[611] **[Bb4r]** heerein (mee thinkes) I committed no offence, hee keeping her moste vniustlie, profaning thereby the sacred Lawes of royall equitie.

And because the wyse haue euermore patiently endured their fortune, beeing either good or badde, I verilie perswade my selfe Madame, that you wyll forbeare to complaine and lament in this vnseemely manner, knowing your selfe to bee conquered by the most courteous and debonaire Knight that this daie lyueth in *Europe*, euen he that in *Hellespont*[612] ouercame the King *Ocurites* your Husbande.[613]

These newes so greeued *Marencida* to the harte, when she heard the Emperour say, that the King her husbande and shee herselfe were taken bothe[b] captiue by one Knight, as franctick-like shee coulde haue eaten her fleshe with anger,[614] but the young Princesse *Philocrista* conducting her to her Chamber, appeased her furie with diuers freendly speeches and curteous behauiour. But let vs nowe[c] returne againe to the Prince *Palmendos*, who in this time vnarmed himselfe, that the Emperour might at more pleasure beholde him.

[a] to] unto P2, P3

[b] taken bothe] both taken P2, P3

[c] let vs nowe] now let us P3

[Bb4v] CHAPTER XXXI.

What courteous conference Palmendos *had with the Emperour, the Empresse and* Primaleon*: And how beeing afterward baptized, hee was affianced to his Lady.*

After that *Palmendos* had put off his Armour, hee throwe[a] a rich Turkish robe about him, imbrodered all ouer with oriental pearls, which he brought from *Tharsus* with him, according to the moderne custome vsed among the most magnificent Kings of *Asia*, intending to were it when he shold come in[b] the Emperours presence.[615] Beeing returned into the great Hall, and eche one couetous to vnderstand his originall, *Primaleon* tooke him by the hande and sate downe, when the Emperour began in this manner. My noble friend *Palmendos*, longer must ye[c] not conceale your selfe, your renowne being so lauishly bruted thorow all Countries: tell me then I pray ye,[d] of what parents ye[e] are issued, as also what yee[f] thinke els conuenient to acquaint vs withall.

Gracious Lord, answered *Palmendos*, with you whome I so reuerence by honour, I maye not dissemble in anie point, for that I were vnworthie your presence, if I shold deale double with so great a state. Knowe then mightie Emperour, that I am Sonne to the Queene of *Tharsus*, the affectionate seruant and vowed friend to your Maiestie, forsaking my Countrey by a strange occasion, so soone as I vnderstoode where my father remained,[616] which long before was concealed from me. The cause of my comming into your highnes Court, was the fame and praises I heard [Cc1r] of *Francelina*, to whose seruice the fatall destinies enioyned me at my very essence, in that I neuer affected any other Ladie, yet reputing my selfe, vnwoorthy[g] her grace and fauour, or to be seene in this honourable Court. To this he added the discourse of the olde woman, that appeared

[a] throwe] threw P2, P3

[b] in] into P2, P3

[c] ye] you P2, P3

[d] ye] you P2, P3

[e] ye] you P2, P3

[f] yee] you P2, P3

[g] vnwoorthy] unworthy of P2, P3

to[a] him in the Pallace at *Tharsus*, and how she blamed him for his idle and slothfull life:[617] yet hiding how she assured him to bee his Sonne, because further opinion should passe till that were discouered. But quoth he, as hitherto I haue liued according to the law of Mahomet, so now would I willingly receiue Christian Baptisme, which I faithfully promised for my good successe, when heauen made me able to deliuer this woorthy Princesse.[618] When the Emperour heard these thinges, hee presently iudged *Palmendos* to be his Sonne, by the suddaine and summarie supputation he made of his age, and of the time he was in *Pasmeria*, where the Queene his mother came subtilly[b] acquainted with him.[619] Bashful herof he was when he looked on the Empresse, as his vermilion colour plainly discouered, yet did he discreetly shadowe the same: notwithstanding, the Empresse misdoubted somewhat, remembring her dreame of the Queene of *Tharsus*, and what the Emperour himselfe had told her before,[620] yet made she no shew of any such matter, wisely gouerning her thoughtes from outward suspition, whereupon the Emperour thus began againe.

In sooth my especiall good friend *Palmendos*, I nowe loue and esteeme yee[c] much better then before, vnderstanding that you are Sonne to the Queene of *Tharsus*, who did mee so great honor in her Countries, her very name maketh me remember[d] my trauailes in those parts: so that I know not howe to expresse my ioy, hearing your selfe so well resolued, to forsake the Ethnicke paganisme of your blasphemous[621] Gods. Wherefore I am thus aduised, not to prolong so good an occasion, but to morrow you shall receiue the holy charracter of Christianitie,[622] and be likewise **[Cc1v]** affiaunced to your Lady *Francelina*: for reason requireth[e] herein to hasten your right, seeing for her you haue endured such daungerous trauailes, and forsaken a Realme of so great estate, the riches and fertility whereof I am wel acquainted withall. The King and Queene of *Thessalie* were not a little glad, when they heard that *Palmendos* was heire to a kingdome, but much more was their ioye, vnderstanding his original, whereof the Emperor would not as yet make further inquirie, till he were better assured of the certaintie: and good occasion falling out so wel, as the Empresse, her

[a] to] unto P2, P3

[b] subtilly] so subtilly P2, P3

[c] yee] you P2, P3

[d] remember] to remember P2, P3

[e] requireth] required P2, P3

Ladies and euerye one departing to their Chambers, leauing the Emperor and *Palmendos* secretly conferring together, of matters concerning the Ile *Delphos* and such like,[623] but at length his Maiestie opened his minde, saying that[a] he imagined him to be his Sonne, wherefore he was desirous to be therein resolued. In respect, my good Lord, answered *Palmendos*, that truth must and will come foorth at length, know then mighty Prince and my gracious father, that in the Realme of *Pasmeria*, you begot me your Sonne, the night before you departed from the Queene my mother, for shee being aduertised of your rare perfections, became impacient in her amorous affections, and compassed[b] the meane of your acquaintance, by a charmed drinke prouided for that purpose.[624] And heere beholde the effect of this action, my selfe your humble son and obedient seruant, yet did my mother giue mee a further testimonie hereof, hauing her selfe giuen you the like at your[c] departure: but *Francelina* hath the same nowe in possession, for to her I tooke[d] it after her deliuerance.[625] And euermore she concealed this matter from me, till miraculously I was enfourmed both thereof, and as concerning *Francelina*, because she feared I would forsake my Countrey, to come and serue in your highnes Court. As concerning my behauiour since that time, somewhat I am sure hath happened to your hearing, yet of such small and slender valewe, as they neither beseemed this place or your **[Cc2r]** person. The Emperour rauished with conceit of this report, knew not which way best to signifie this ioy, for considering the straunge course of the action past, and what the successe thereof now prooued, his spirites were carried away with woonderfull imaginations.

Ah my noble Sonne *Palmendos*, quoth he, full well am I assured of what thou hast said, although nature hath shaped thee not much vnlike me, and giuen thee such heroycall courage as I had in my younger daies: and albeit the Empresse may well be offended with me, when shee shall be thus thorowly resolued, yet is her wisedoome and modestie such, as she will not mislike what I allow. With these wordes the Emperour tooke him by the hand, going with him presently[e] to the Empresse Chamber, and after his Maiestie had kindly kissed her, hee entered into these speeches.

[a] that] *om.* P2, P3

[b] compassed] composed P2, P3

[c] your] her P2, P3

[d] tooke] gave P2, P3

[e] presently] immediately P2, P3

I know well Madame, that heertofore you haue held good opinion of my loyaltie, and that I euer loued you entirely, as your selfe could desire no better proofe thereof: but the cause why I vse these wordes at this instant, is a little scruple that long since entered my minde, and I fear wil offend yee[a] when the same is knowen. Yet least further doubtes should trouble your thoughtes, I protest before him[626] who is the only searcher of hearts, and I sweare by all the diuine assistaunts about his tribunall, that neuer with my will and knowledge did I contaminate our wedlocke-bedde, much lesse haue I infringed the laws of mariage, or polluted the inuiolable faith I solemnely gaue yee.[b627]

Notwithstanding such hath been my former fortune, that another woman beside your selfe, by charmes obtayned what was your right, then must you not (Madame) be so seuere and rigorous, as not to pardon mee, seeing I haue voluntarily confessed mine[c] offence, beside, the fault not proceeding from me, deliuers my cause to be more innocent. **[Cc2v]**

Remember then Madame, what sometime you tolde me concerning the Queene of *Tharsus*, your dreame I perceiue was not altogether in vaine: in that shee had suche knowledge of mee, by meanes of an enchaunted drinke I receiued vnawares, as engendered *Palmendos* this gentle Knight. My Lord, answered the Empresse, with a smyling countenance, at the first time I beheld *Palmendos* I was perswaded what you haue tolde me, so liuely doth he resemble ye,[d] in countenance and personage:[628] wherefore I not onely pardon ye,[e] being ignoraunt of begetting such an excellent and perfect creature, but thanke heauen that you were the father to a Son so famous.[629] As for *Palmendos*, he shal now accept me as his mother, and I will loue him no lesse than mine owne Sonne *Primaleon*. With sundrie other speeches were these ioyes confirmed, and *Palmendos* right louingly imbraced by the Empresse, at length *Primaleon* came, and hee being thoroughly acquainted with the matter, tooke the Prince in his armes thus speaking.

Hath the mighty gouernour of the heauens appointed, that the onely flower of chiualrie should bee my brother? wherein can I more

[a] yee] you P2, P3

[b] yee.] you. P2, P3

[c] mine] my P2, P3

[d] ye] you P2, P3

[e] ye] you P2, P3

honour that superexcelling bountye, then confirming my thanks to him by kindnes to the worthy copartner of my vitall bloode, drawen from the selfe same source where I receiued my originall? Assure your selfe therefore my moste noble brother, that *Primaleon* is vowed to imitate your rare fortunes, and treading the selfe same steps you haue doone, to eternize the name of our renowmed[a] father:[630] continuing in the meane time so readie at your commaund, as hee that honoreth you with most zealous affection. Might I enter the boldnes, answered *Palmendos*, as to title you by the name of my brother, the second step of my desires were attained, and thogh I dare not striue to coequall[b] my self with you in kindnes, yet wil I ouer pace ye[c] in dutie and affection: continuing the seruant of *Primaleons* welfare, while the starre of my birthday vouchsafeth mee breathing. **[Cc3r]**

Here is occasion offered mee of large discourse, concerning the seuerall salutations of the courtly personages, so soon as these[d] news happened in their ears, how the Lords and knightes came to gratulate this newcome sonne, and the Ladies likewise striuing to excel them in curtesie: but it were needlesse labour, considering the King and Queen of *Thessalie* concerne this present occasion, and with their daughters ioy vnite them altogeather, preparing for the religious obseruations, to bee vsed on the morrowe at the christning of *Palmendos*.[631]

On the morrow, the Emperour and all his Barrons, mounted on horsebacke, the like doth the Empresse withal[e] her Ladies, and in most honourable manner they ride to this solemnitie: so passing in this pompe through the Cittie, they allighted at the Church of S. *Sophie*,[632] where *Palmendos* was religiously[633] baptized, and afterward affianced to *Francelina* by the reuerend[f] Archbishop,[634] she beeing attired in as sumptuous ornaments, as when *Andromachye* was espoused to the valiant *Hector* of *Troy*,[635] or *Cleopatra* Queene of *Aegipt*, when shee contended in magnificence with *Marke Anthonie* the *Triumuirate* her husband,[636] drinking one of the pearles that hung at her eares, esteemed woorth two hundred and fiftie thousand crownes. For euen as the Carbuncle, the most rich and

[a] renowned] P2; renowmed P1

[b] coequall my self] coequal *om. om.* P2, P3

[c] ye] you P2, P3

[d] these] this P2, P3

[e] with al] withal P1

[f] reuerend] religious P2, P3

precious of all the Orientall stones, dooth in the darke giue such a cleere and illustrious splendour, as not onely illuminateth all the place, but also setteth the regarders eies to woonder thereat: of no lesse vertue seemed *Francelina* in the Temple, as the onely and perfect Phenix[637] of her time. In like pompe and royaltie they returned to the Pallace, there beeing such a sumptuous feast prepared, as beseemed the time of so general reioycing, where wanted no honorable deuises to accompany the same.[638] And during the time of this their honorable whole[a] pleasure, heere thinke I good to pause a little, while you consider on[b] the discourses passed, and I haue more leasure to perfect the rest of this Historie.[639]

[Cc3ᵛ] *Next (Gentlemen) followeth the historie of* Primaleon, *wherin (what you see wanting here) is perfectly finished, both* Palmendos *mariage,* Ozalios *loue to* Marencida, Rifaranoes *fortunes, and* Recinde *his returne to* Constantinople.[640] *But this I must tel you with al, that now* Primaleon *beginneth his chiualrie,*[641] *and the famous Prince* Edward *of* England[642] *the course of his aduentures, which are briefly touched in my book of* Palmerin of England,[c643] *who was his Son: what woonderfull stratagems both he and* Primaleon *performed together, attend till the next tearme and you shalbe resolued. And to accompany this discourse, I hope to send ye the first booke of* Amadis *of* Fraunce,[644] *that when ye are wery of the one, you may delight your selfe with the other: so wishing ye no worse then to my selfe, I ende.*

Yours to his poore power:
Anthony Monday.

Honos alit Artes.[645]

[a] whole] *om.* P2, P3

[b] on] of P3

[c] England] Egnland P1H

Explanatory Notes

[1] *Patere aut abstine*. The motto "Patere aut abstine" ("suffer or desist") appears on the title pages of most of Munday's translations, in contrast with "Honos alit artes" ("Honour comes from art"), which he normally included in the title pages of other literary works (Hill, *Anthony Munday and Civic Culture*, 49). According to Louise Wilson, this motto appeared in the printer's device of Etienne Groulleau, successor to Denis Janot, who had published most of the latter's French editions of the Palmerin and Amadis romances doubtlessly consulted by Munday ("The Publication of Iberian Romance in Early Modern Europe," 211).

[2] **Francisco Draco**. Francis Drake (1540–1596): a pirate, sea captain and explorer, knighted by Elizabeth I in 1581. For further information on *Palmendos*'s dedication to Drake, see note 108 in the introduction.

[3] **Herculeas columnas**. The Pillars of Hercules or the promontories between which lies the Strait of Gibraltar.

[4] **Minyas**. The Minyans or Argonauts were the companions of Jason, so called from their ancestor Minyas, a king in Thessaly.

[5] **Dulichium**. An island of the Ionian Sea, southeast of Ithaca, belonging to the kingdom of Ulysses.

[6] **Dulichiumue ducem**. Ulysses, king of Ithaca, famed among the Grecian heroes of the Trojan War for his craft and eloquence.

[7] **Amphitryoniadem**. Heracles or Hercules, the son of Jupiter and Alcmena; after his deification, the god of strength, and the guardian of riches; he was also guide to the muses. Amphitryon was his putative father.

[8] **Iason**. Son of Aeson, the legitimate king of Iolcos, Jason was the leader of the Argonauts in their quest for the Golden Fleece.

[9] **Penelopesque virum**. Ulysses.

[10] Munday compares his publication of *Palmendos* to a sea venture that will end happily—i.e., with the best reception among his readers—thanks to Drake's protection.

[11] **Zolius**. A severe critic at the time of Ptolemaeus Philadelphus; a censurer of Homer.

[12] **Codrus**. A wretched poet, hostile to Virgil.

[13] [To the most strong and skilful man of the navy, the golden knight, Sir Francis Drake. / Stop vain Greece admiring Hercules's pillars / Or the Mynians, or the head of Dulichius. / You surpass Amphitryonidas, most powerful Drake, and Jason and his comrades, and Penelope's husband. / Neptune entrusts his trident to you, / And willingly renders his authority and rule over the sea. / Palmendos, happy and safe under such a patron / Ventures to fly to innumerable hands. / Let Zoilus feel envy and Codrus's flanks break, / Palmendos will be safe under Drake's protection. / It goes, flies and ventures, and despises menacing words, / For you, Drake, are used to despising swollen menaces.]

[14] Munday indicates that his translation will not follow the rhetorical style of his (French) source. For a comparative analysis of Munday and Vernassal's methods of translation, see the section in the introduction titled "Translating Spanish Romances in Sixteenth-Century England: Munday's Method of Translation in *Palmendos*."

[15] He refers to *Palmerin of England* (bef. 1585), *Palmerin d'Oliua* (1588), and *Palladine of England* (1588).

[16] *The First Booke of Primaleon of Greece* was entered in the Stationers' Register to John Charlewood together with *Palmendos* on January 9, 1589 (*SR*, II, 513). Apparently, Munday did not keep his promise, as the first edition of *Primaleon* was not published until 1595. According to Wilson, Munday's publishers seemed to be confident enough that the Palmerin and Amadis series would be highly profitable and often entered in the Stationers' Register different titles at the same time, thus emulating their French predecessors ("The Publication of Iberian Romance in Early Modern Europe," 210). This practice helped influence the readers' approach to these texts as serialized literature.

[17] Cripplegate was a popular area, home to many printers and stationers. Munday and his publishing agents—i.e., John Charlewood, James Roberts, and William Jaggard—lived and worked there.

[18] Munday signs his letter to the reader on February 5 and reckons that he should have *Primaleon* finished by "the next Tearme." He must be referring to Easter, which in the legal and academic calendar came after the Hilary term running for three or four weeks from January 14 (St. Hilary's day) onwards.

[19] **Palmerin d'Oliua**. Main hero in the first book of the Palmerin cycle, *Palmerin d'Oliua*. Both in the title and head title of *Palmendos*, Munday tells his readers that this book is a sequel to *Palmerin d'Oliua*. Munday approaches both books as a textual unit, which helps explain the numerous intertextual references to *Palmerin* in *Palmendos*.

[20] **sonne to the famous Palmerin d'Oliua, Emperour of Constantinople, and the Queene of Tharsus**. For the episode of the begetting of Palmendos, see *Palmerin d'Oliva* II.20. This chapter narrates that the Queen of Tharsus gave Palmerin a magic drink prepared for her by a magician. The hero fell fast asleep and was taken by the Queen and her ladies to her bed where she would lie with him. This episode recalls the begetting of Galahad in Malory's *Le Morte Darthur* XI.2, in which Lancelot was given a poison and led to believe he was lying with Guinevere, when it was actually Elaine, the daughter of King Pelles, he was having sex with. The result of this sexual intercourse was Galahad, a pure knight destined to find the Holy Grail. In both cases, the heroes' sons excel their fathers, a commonplace in the chivalric romance tradition.

[21] *Trineus*. Son to the German emperor and Polinarda's brother in *Palmerin d'Oliva* (I.25). Numbers in parentheses indicate the book and chapter in which the character's name first appears.

[22] *Aurecinda*. The Sultan of Persia's younger sister in *Palmerin d'Oliva* (II.53).

[23] *Macedon*. An area situated between the Balkans and the Greek Peninsula.

[24] **Not long after the destruction of the magnificent and proud Monarchie of the *Romaines*, was erected a new Empire in *Greece*.** He refers to the rise of the Byzantine Empire after the fall of Rome in the fifth century.

[25] **paradoxes**. The *OED* defines paradox as a phenomenon or occurrence "that exhibits some contradiction or conflict with preconceived notions of what is reasonable or possible" (s.v. *paradox*, n.5). Munday sticks to its meaning as employed by the French, as it refers to the "hautes & paradoxes cheualries qu'il fit pour la conquest & defense d'vn tel estat" (Vernassal, A1^{r-v}; Fr., the high and mervaillous acts of chivalry that he (Palmerin) did for the conquest and defense of such a state). Jean Nicot defines "paradoxes" in his *Thresor de la Langue Françoise* (1606) as "choses merueilleuses et admirables, qu'un n'a point accoustumé d'ouir" (Fr., marvellous and admirable things one is not used to hearing). Nicot's dictionary can be consulted online in the *Dictionnaires d'Autrefois* database.

[26] **In which discourse alreadie extant**. He refers to *Palmerin d'Oliua*. Munday presents both books as genealogical romances, and so *Palmendos* will complete the narrative about the foundation of Palmerin's dynasty in *Palmerin d'Oliua*.

[27] Munday translates almost literally from the French, and so he resorts to Vernassal's implicit comments to stress the relevance of military discipline in courtly education. His words recall those in Ramón Lull's *The Book of the Ordre of Chyualry* (1275–1276): "kniȝtes ouȝt to take courses to juste & to go to tournoyes . . . For in doyinge these thynges the knyȝtes excercyse them to armes / for to mayntene thordre of kniȝthode" (31). This reference to the tournaments held annually at Palmerin's court may also evoke the Accession Day tilts organized by Sir Henry Lee since 1561, in which Elizabeth's knights jousted before her to mark the anniversary of her accession to the throne; by 1580, those tilts had become highly sophisticated.

[28] **to bee there educated**. Added by Munday.

[29] *Frysoll*. Nephew to Tarisius, the King of Hungary in *Palmerin d'Oliva* (I.1).

[30] *Hungaria*. A Christian kingdom in central Europe founded in 1000.

[31] **Duke *Eustace* of *Mecaena***. Son to the Duke of Mecaena in *Palmerin d'Oliva* (II.40).

[32] Both princes' births are mentioned in *Palmerin d'Oliva* II.58 and II.67.

[33] Munday also situates *Palmendos* in the "mirror" tradition, as his words here recall those on the title page of *Palmerin D'Oliua The Mirrour of nobilitie, Mappe of honor, Anatomie of rare fortunes, Heroycall president of Loue: VVonder for chiualrie, and most accomplished Knight in all perfections*. The English translator had already followed this same tradition in his *Mirrour of Mutabilitie, or Principall Part of the Mirrour for Magistrates* (London, 1579) and *The Paine of Pleasure, Describing in Perfect Mirror, the Miseries of Man* (London, 1583).

[34] In the late Middle Ages, it was common to receive one's knighthood from a knight widely acknowledged as a man of valor and prowess. A person knighted by such prominent knight would partake of his honor (Keen, *Chivalry*, 77).

[35] Munday omits "le lundy matin de pasques flouries" (Vernassal, A1[v]). This reference also appears in the Spanish—"otro día después de la Pascua de cincuesma" (Marín Pina, 3)—and in Barley—"On the Monday morning next after Easter day" (B1[r]). In his description of the rituals of knighthood, Ramón Lull recommends that the ceremony should coincide with a great religious feast, such as Christmas or Easter (*The Book of the Ordre of Chyualry*, 67). However, this practice was not common in the late Middle Ages, when the ritual of knighthood could take place at a solemn court, a coronation, or the eve of a battle. Munday's Spanish and French sources keep the old medieval tradition and situate Belcar and Tirendos's knighthood at Easter. Munday may have omitted this reference to prevent his heroes from being associated with former Catholic practices.

[36] **embracing him in his armes.** "le baisant en la ioue" (Vernassal, A1[v]; Fr., kissing his cheek).

[37] Belcar reflects on the nature of true nobility, a traditional theme in medieval and early modern romances. This question, whose origin goes back to the classical period, was a matter of debate in the Middle Ages and the Renaissance, when two different approaches were adopted: that of the Aristotelian and scholastic school, who considered nobility in strict relation to lineage and inheritance; and that of the early humanists, led by Erasmus, who associated *vera nobilitas* with the individual's virtue. In chivalric literature both competing notions of nobility (blood vs virtue) coexist, as lineage is thought to rely not just on birth but on the past achievements of the family. The main heroes in *Palmendos* follow this pattern. For the concept of virtue and true nobility in the late Middles Ages and the Renaissance, see Keen, *Chivalry*, 143–61; Schmitt et al., *The Cambridge History of Renaissance Philosophy*, 390–448; and Skinner, *Visions of Politics*, 2:203–44.

[38] **for thine example**. Added by Munday.

[39] **in the Isle of *Carderia*.** This isle has not been identified. Possibly, a fictional place familiar to the reader, as it had first featured in *Palmerin d'Oliva* II.41.

[40] **as was declared in the History of *Palmerin d' Oliua*.** Added by Munday. He refers to the episode in which the King of Thessaly was kept in perpetual prison by the Turk. The three enchantresses that had protected Palmerin in his quest decided to take the King of Thessaly's daughter, Francelina, whom they imprisoned in a tower on the Isle of Carderia; she would then be freed by a knight who would marry her and save her father from the Turk (*Palmerin d'Oliva* II.41).

[41] **Kingdome of *Thessalie*.** Thessaly. A region in ancient Greece.

[42] Mary Patchell describes the deliverance of a lady or knight from an enchanted castle or tower as a "stock adventure" in the Palmerin romances (*The Palmerin Romances in Elizabethan Prose Fiction*, 42). For similar episodes, see *Palmerin of England* I.10, II.60, and III.30.

[43] **Heauen fauour and further his attempts, directing all his actions in such sort, as no tongue may controll his noble forwardness.** Munday rewrites the French and substitutes the word "God" for "heauen," a recurrent practice in his translation method: "ie prie Dieu qu' ainsi soit, & luy plaise diriger & si bien

fortuner la generosité qu'on voit reluire en luy, qu'il en puisse raporter honneur & auancement" (Vernassal, A2[r]; Fr., "God graunt it may be so, and may he fortunatly direct him in his courses, and so well prosper the generous forwardnesse, that all men may beholde shining in him, that he maie winne thereby honour and aduauncement, such as his heart desireth" [Barley, B2[r]]).

[44] ***Belcars* departure was liked of euery one**. The development from the impersonal to personal construction of the verb "to like" occurred in ME, as the original accusative or dative came to be taken as a nominative. "Of" was also the most popular preposition indicating agency in connection with a passive verb in ME and EM English up to the seventeenth century (Mustanoja, 434–35, 442). For other examples of personal constructions of this verb in the text, see "hee rode which waie him liked best" (B1[r]).

[45] **modest speeches**. "la faconde & affabilité don't il enrichissoit assez bien son parler" (Vernassal, A2[v]; Fr., "his eloquence and affability wherewith he much enriched and graced his language" [Barley, B2[v]]). There is no reference to Belcar's rhetorical abilities in the Spanish original, as it only pays attention to his physical attractiveness—"tan apuesto" (Marín Pina, 4; Sp., so good-looking). Manuals on civil courtesy proliferating in sixteenth-century Europe presented good manners, beauty, and attire as important personal qualities in a courtier (Peltonen, *The Duel in Early Modern England*, 19–25), for according to Castiglione, he must have "not onely a wit, and a comely shape of person and countenance, but also a certaine grace, and (as they say) a hewe, that shall make him at the first sight acceptable and louing vnto who so beholdeth him" (*The Courtier*, C1[v]–C2[r]).

[46] **as he had great pleasure to sitte and talke with him**. Munday and Vernassal stress conversation as a positive quality in the courtly hero. Thus, they echo the notion of "civil conversation" largely expanded in the main courtly manuals published in Italy in the sixteenth century—i.e., Castiglione's, and also his successors Giovanni della Casa's *Il Galateo* (Venice, 1560) and Stefano Guazzo's *La civil conversatione* (Brescia, 1574); those two latter manuals were translated into English in 1576, 1581, and 1586 (STC 4738, 12422, 12423).

[47] **Now must I let you vnderstand**. Added by Munday.

[48] Munday summarizes this violent encounter, which takes much longer in the French version (Vernassal, A2[v]–A3[r]). He keeps, though, Vernassal's last ironic remark—"de sorte qu'il ne fut besoing d'appeller Chirurgien pour le penser" (A3[r])—absent in the Spanish (Marín Pina, 4).

[49] **and the others happe so good**. Munday omits the verb "to be," probably for the sake of brevity. The clause would read as "and the others happe was so good." The lot of the other knight was so good (for Belcar) that he (Belcar) was only slightly injured on his arm. In private conversation, Juan Antonio Prieto-Pablos has suggested a different reading, as he considers that "happe" and "good" could respectively work here as a verb and an adverb.

[50] **whose pryde and arrogancie had thus caused their owne death**. Cf. "yf a knyght in as moche as he is prowd mayntened chyualry / he corrupted his ordre

whiche was begonne by Iustyce and humylyte for to susteyne the hūble ayenst the prowde" (Lull, *The Book of the Ordre of Chyualry*, 44).

[51] This character's tears are presented as something negative by Vernassal and the English translators, as they associate tears with excess, and therefore with some kind of irrational behavior—see "Madness from grief" in *Motif-Index* (F1041.8.2). Excessive display of emotions was generally considered feminine in medieval and Renaissance England. According to the Galenic theory of humors, women were colder and moister and therefore more inclined to extreme passions.

[52] See "Sister avenges brother's death" and "Innocent person accused of murder" in *Motif-Index* (P253.5; K2116). Munday and Vernassal suggest contemporary concerns about female grief and its potential for violence. Moved by such revengeful feelings, this character will persecute Belcar up to the end and will become a serious threat to several knights at Palmerin's court. For the resolution of this conflict, see chap. 25.

[53] **King *Florendos*.** The King of Macedon's son in *Palmerin d'Oliva* (I.1).

[54] ***Denisa*.** Griana and Florendos's daughter in *Palmerin d'Oliva* (II.58).

[55] ***Thrace*.** Ancient Thrace comprised the part of Europe lying on the north of Greece.

[56] ***Caniano*.** Son to Remicius, eighth emperor of Constantinople, in *Palmerin d'Oliva* (I.1).

[57] See "Hero finds maiden at fountain" and "Fountain as lovers' rendezvous" in *Motif-Index* (N715.1; T35.1). Palmendos will meet his beloved Francelina for the first time at a fountain in a beautiful garden (chap. 20). For further examples, see also *Primaleon* II.11.

[58] Alderina sees Belcar and loves him instantly. This reference focuses on the medieval notion of the eye as the *locus* of love. Eyes are channels through which love is activated, in this case just by looking at the beloved.

[59] In medieval romance, heroines often show their sexual attraction to their beloveds and are clearly assertive when defending their interests. Alderina sees Belcar first and takes the initiative when approaching him despite his initial carelessness. Their first encounter takes place in a forest, a *locus amoenus* that allows her to acknowledge her attraction to him. Alderina talks to him first and will do so in future meetings with Belcar. For the relevance of female rhetoric in romance literature see Hackett, *Women and Romance Fiction*, 122–29.

[60] **the Iousts and Turnament which was nowe prepared.** Tournaments were common entertainments on major royal occasions in late fifteenth- and sixteenth-century Europe. In addition to their entertaining appeal and their military character, tournaments played a relevant social and political role in Renaissance courts as perfect sites for diplomatic relations. In Spanish chivalric romances, they often take place on the occasion of weddings and coronations; the knights who participate in them prove their chivalric worth (Goodman, "European Chivalry in the 1490s," 47–55; Patchell, *The Palmerin Romances in Elizabethan Prose Fiction*,

31). For other examples in the Palmerin cycle, see *Palmendos* 12, *Primaleon* I.12, *Palmerin d'Oliva* I.1, and *Palmerin of England* I.

[61] **freendlie together**. "deuisans de plusiers de choses" (Vernassal, A4^r^; Fr., "talking of many matters" [Barley, C1^r^]). The French and English translators omit Belcar's last sentence in this conversation as it features in the Spanish: "En el nombre de Dios –dixo Belcar–, todos iremos juntos fasta allá" (Marín Pina, 6; Sp., In God's name, we'll go there all together). Vernassal often omits or turns conversational exchanges in the Spanish original into narrative, thus leaving out many of the characters' invocations to God.

[62] **as might be thought worthie the loue of this Ladie**. "qu'il en peust aquerir l'amour de ceste Damoiselle" (Vernassal, A4^r^; Fr., "that he might purchace the loue of this Ladie" [Barley, C1^v^]). Barley reproduces Vernassal's words literally and translates "aquerir" as "purchace." This verb, which in sixteenth- and seventeenth-century England could stand for "obtain" or "gain" (s.v. *OED, purchase*, n.4.a), was also understood as "buy" in the same period (s.v. *OED, purchase*, n.6.b). This possible association with money may have prevented Munday from using this word in his version. While Barley's translation may seem disturbing as it could suggest some economic interest in Belcar's love for Alderina, Munday tries to make it clear that his hero's feelings for this lady are honest.

[63] Munday does not refer to the feast at Denisa's wedding: "dont la feste fut grande et magnifique en toutes choses" (Vernassal, A4^r^) (Fr., "whose solemne feaste was great and magnificent in all things" [Barley, C1^v^]). By dispensing with this reference, Munday does not omit any basic information and instead emphasizes the fact that the bride was always accompanied by other ladies up to the wedding night, thus indicating that she had preserved her virginity.

[64] **assaulte**. Assault of arms (also *assault at arms*) or "an attack made upon each other by two fencers, etc., as an exercise or trial of skill; and, in a wider sense (after French *assaut d'armes*), a display of hand-to-hand military exercises" (s.v. *OED, assault*, adj.1.b.).

[65] **nor was he knowne to anie**. See "Unknown knight" in *Motif-Index* (R222). This motif was largely, though not exclusively, associated with the "Fair Unknown" stories of the Arthurian cycle, in which the anonymity of knights and their later recognition were common narrative devices. Their names could only be revealed after they had tested themselves in multiple adventures and had proved worthy of their lineage. Two main fair unknowns in the chivalric tradition, Gareth and Lybeaus, succeed in liberating and marrying their respective ladies, a pattern also followed by Belcar and later by Palmendos, in their quest for Francelina.

[66] **which hath receiued such an impression of obeysaunce to her**. "lequel se sent deia si affectioné à luy obeïr" (Vernassal, A5^v^; Fr., "which feeleth it selfe so much affectioned to obey her" [Barley, C3^v^]). In the French and English editions the hero promises to come back and offer his heart to his beloved. In the Spanish text, Belcar simply promises to come back and serve her: "yo vendré a servilla"

(Marín Pina, 8). Munday's version is more elaborate, as he indirectly alludes to the love-imprint medieval motif. See note 69.

[67] Belcar's answer follows the basic principles of courtly love according to which the knight must show faithful devotion to his lady by performing deeds that will make him worthy of her love.

[68] **religiously.** "affectueusement" (Vernassal, A5^v^; Fr., "very cordially" [Barley, C4^r^]). By introducing this change, Munday underlines Belcar's religious devotion to his lady according to the courtly-love code.

[69] The love-imprint is a late medieval poetic *topos* based on Aristotelian principles according to which love was a physiological condition brought about through a precise bodily mechanism. The process consists of several stages: first, the beloved's image enters the eyes of the lover. This image is then processed by a number of mental functions in the brain producing a phantasm which is later imprinted on the heart. Finally, the contemplation of this internal image makes love arise (Singer, *Blindness and Therapy in Late Medieval French and Italian Poetry*, 24, 23–53). Alderina's falling in love with Belcar is described in these terms: she looks at him, feels attracted to him, and cannot think about anything else but him once his image has been imprinted on her heart.

[70] According to Helen Hackett, love becomes the primary cause that justifies "the otherwise potentially morally dubious behavior of sexually compliant heroines" (*Women and Romance Fiction*, 73). Alderina is a virgin but has openly shown her sexual attraction to Belcar. This behavior may have been considered improper according to Renaissance codes of female chastity. She might appear to have been influenced by medieval models of female conduct, which are less stringent, while observing the Renaissance rules of decorum when she promises constant love to her beloved. As Hackett indicates, "a notion of chastity is not discarded as the paramount female virtue; rather it is redefined as constancy in love" (73). Her virginity is not endangered and so, it is not bodily continence but continence of emotional display that turns her into a chivalric romance heroine.

[71] "et ne fit ce iour là guere plus de trois mil, qui fut seulement pour s'eslongner de la cour" (Vernassal, A6^v^; Fr., "and rode that day little more than three mile, onely to dislodge himselfe from the court" [Barley, C4^v^]). Absent in Munday.

[72] **and by the dutifull repentaunce fitting a Knight, recouer the note of thy former blemishe.** "et luy monstrer par efait rien n'estre l'innocente mesprison, où fuit de pres la repentence et satisfaction de l'offense commise" (Vernassal, A6^v^; Fr., "and shew her in effect that the innocent mistaking of dutie is nothing, where repentance and satisfaction for the offence committed presently ensue" [Barley, C4^v^]). Vernassal adds this part to his translation and thus shows some uneasiness about the hero's behavior towards Alderina. In general, both the French and English translators pass judgement on their hero's attitudes and offer clear standards for readers to follow. Belcar has promised to serve Alderina, and so his attempts to save Francelina can only be viewed as treacherous. Vernassal forecasts Belcar's

future repentance (see chap. 20) and softens a possible negative reception by his readers. Munday emulates the French translator.

[73] **he concluded (if hee could finish the aduenture of *Francelina*) to make choyse of thys Ladie onelie as his Wife.** See chap. 2.

[74] **Cardino.** "Sergin filz de Cardin" (Vernassal, A6v); "Seregín, fijo de Cardín" (Marín Pina, 9); "Sergin, the sonne of Cardin" (Barley, D1r). Despite the discrepancy with the other editions, Munday is consistent when identifying this character as Cardino, as such is his name in the episode from *Palmerin d'Oliva* that he is alluding to (II.67). There seems to be, however, some misunderstandings about this character, as in chapter 64 of the same book Munday had referred to Colmelio and Sergillo, Cardino's son, as part of the group of knights sent by Palmerin to rescue Prince Olorico from the Turk. It is quite probable that he had mistaken this character's name in chapter 67 and hence this error continued in *Palmendos*.

[75] **as you may reade in the last Chapter of his Historie.** The episode alluded to here occurs at the end of *Palmerin d'Oliva* (II.67). This intertextual reference is added by Vernassal in his French edition: "ainsi que vous auez leu au dernier chapistre de son histoire" (A6v). Munday turns the past tense into present and thus he informs readers that the book is still available and that they may find that episode there.

[76] **the Fayries.** "la Fée" (Vernassal, A6v; Fr., the fairy). Munday is right when using the plural form as he refers to the three faeries that had enchanted Francelina on the Isle of Carderia.

[77] See "Predestined rescuer" and "Fated hero" in *Motif-Index* (R169.8; M361). There is only one hero who has been predestined to liberate Francelina. Palmendos and Belcar will follow almost a similar procedure to succeed in this quest and will prove equal prowess. However, fate will only prove positive for Palmendos, who will finally rescue his beloved from the enchanted castle. This motif has a structural function in the book as it allows for a comparison of the two main plots and their protagonists.

[78] ***Cardino* met the Damosell, who was Sister to the two Bretheren slayne by *Belcar* in the Woode.** See chap. 1.

[79] She features the role of the lady in distress to be attended by chivalric knights, but she also adjusts to the pattern of the lady errant, as she is not confined to the boundaries of an enclosed place and risks instead her virtue to vindicate revenge. This lady, who is never named throughout the narrative, stands as a negative model, in contrast to most other female characters in the book. Due to her deceitful and wandering (and therefore, out-of-control) nature she is portrayed as being dangerous to men.

[80] **her cautelous prosopopey.** "vne cauteleuse prospopeye" (Vernassal, B1r). Henry Peacham defines this figure as "the fayning of a person, that is when to a thing sencelesse . . . we fayne a fit person" (*The Garden of Eloquence*, O3r). Though it was often considered some sort of personification, the term was also related to deceit in the sixteenth century, as George Puttenham acknowledges when he

describes it as "the counterfeit impersonification" in his *Arte of English Poesie* (324). Edmund Spenser seems to suggest this secondary meaning in the title of his satirical poem *Prosopopoia* (1591). Munday employs "prosopopey" in a similar way, as his use of the adjective "cautelous"—"Full of cautels; deceitful, crafty, artful, wily" (s.v. *OED*, *cautelous*, adj.1)—confirms.

[81] **So well could the traytresse couller her speeches, and set such a smoothe foyle on her cautelous prosopopey: as shee imprinted in the hart of *Cardino*, a dutiful regard to reuenge such wrong.** "Tant bien fceut la trahistresse palier ses raisons, et par ce moyen si dextrement bastir et ageancer vne cauteleuse prosopopeye, qu'elle imprima au cueur de Sergin la deuoir venger de telle iniure" (Vernassal, B1r). Munday translates literally, thus introducing the image of the smooth foil as applied to the lady's narrative. "Foil," a thin leaf of metal, is also defined in the *OED* as "anything that serves by contrast of color or quality to adorn another thing or set it off to advantage" (s.v. *foil*, n.1.6). This image serves here to enhance her false nature.

[82] Different notions of treason coexisted in medieval and Renaissance chivalric literature. According to Megan Leitch, in its specific legal sense, treachery involved betrayal to one's king, but it could also be defined more horizontally, as breaking one's oath to a community or a member of a community in which mutual loyalty is expected. In both cases, treachery was considered the antithesis of knighthood (*Romancing Treason*, 1–13). When accusing Belcar of treason, the lady implies he has broken his oath of chivalry that compelled him to be courteous and fair to other knights. In demanding Cardino's help for what allegedly is a just cause, Cardino remains bound to her. If he had refused to assist her he would have broken his oath as well. In both cases, a liar ultimately defines treason, which may imply some uneasiness about how accusations of disloyalty were formulated at the time.

[83] **choller**. "In ancient and medieval physiology one of the four cardinal humours, identified as bile (or as present within bile) and described as hot and dry in nature, and supposed when predominant to cause irritability or irascibility of temper" (s.v. *OED*, *choler*, n.2a). Choleric humor and anger were strongly associated with a more brutal standard of heroic behavior prevalent in sixteenth-century European romance and theatre. In her book *The Art of Frenzy*, Jane Kromm explains the influence of Seneca's drama and Ariosto's *Orlando Furioso* (Ferrara, 1516) in the articulation of furor as "the deranged extreme of heroic prowess" (11). Vernassal's characterization of Belcar and Palmendos responds to this standard, while Munday emulates the French translator and sets these characters in close relation to the Senecan prototype.

[84] **But little to thy profite will it bee, to pursue mee with such false and lying accusations**. Accusations of treason did not have any effect if they were not supported by law and force (that is, if they were not settled in a combat by means of which the status of the man accused could be turned into that of a traitor). However and though an accusation did not have a performative function in itself,

it was very dangerous for the accused because it raised the possibility of damaging his reputation (Leitch, *Romancing Treason*, 20). Belcar's violence would be then justified, as it would be his only option to avoid such menace.

[85] Vernassal describes the damosel's suffering at Cardino's defeat: "sort dolente et couroucée" (B1ᵛ; Fr., "very sorrofull and angrie" [Barley, D2ʳ]). In omitting this reference and silencing this character's frustration, Munday prevents any sympathetic feeling towards her.

[86] **Ah heauen.** "Helas mon Dieu" (Vernassal, B1ᵛ; Fr., Oh, my God).

[87] **the Squire.** "les deux Escuyers" (Vernassal, B1ᵛ; Fr., the two squires).

[88] **of most rare and exquisite perfection.** Cross-reference: *Palmerin d'Oliva*: "Now did the Sisters inclose her in a strong Tower, made of purpose for young Francelina, wherein was the most goodly Garden in the worlde, there was shee attended by her Nursses, and sixe waiting Gentlewomen: and such enchauntments were imposed on the Tower, as no man should euer see her, vnlesse he were *the best Knight of his time*" (II. 493, lines 35–39) (the editor's emphasis). These intertextual references support Javier R. González's arguments, as he thinks the Spanish editions of *Palmerín* and the first chapters of *Primaléon* dealing with Polendos (Palmendos) were written by the same person, who had a unified idea of both texts in mind. See his article "El sistema profético en la determinación del *Palmerín-Primaleón* como unidad textual."

[89] This episode may recall another one in Chrètien de Troyes's *Le Chevalier de la Charrette* (c. 1180), in which Lancelot tries to rescue Genièvre from the land of Gorre, where she has been made captive by King Baudemagu. To get to the land, he must first cross the sword bridge and then fight against Meleagant, Baudemagu's son, who is waiting for him on the other bank of the river. This narrative shows that Lancelot is not the chosen knight to find the Holy Grail. Belcar has not been chosen to liberate Francelina, and so, he will not succeed. A fierce knight is waiting for him at the entrance of the castle.

[90] This episode is not translated by Munday in *Palmerin d'Oliva*.

[91] Munday omits any reference to the sound of this horn, which Vernassal translates as "sonnant lors doucement" (B2ʳ; Fr., sounding very sweetly). Munday avoids any ambiguity when distinguishing between good and evil. In his attempt at simplification, he also does away with the seductive potential of these evil figures.

[92] **so obstinatlie inclined.** Counsel was a pivotal theme in medieval romance and a way to test the hero's knightly competence and maturity (Barnes, *Counsel and Strategy in Middle English Romance*, ix–xii, 1–28). Belcar's thirst for honor makes him forget about listening to good advice or exercising other virtues such as patience or judgement. His incompetence makes him unfit to fulfill the adventure of Francelina.

[93] Munday omits Vernassal's allusion to God: "à Dieu ne plaise" (B2ᵛ; Fr., God forbid).

[94] In spite of everything, Belcar's doubts and fears before the fight contribute to depict him as a courageous knight. Chivalric prowess is not just physical as it also requires determination and strength of will to endure extremely difficult circumstances. Belcar is now aware of his circumstances, and thus he resorts to the virtuous example of his ancestors to overcome his hesitation.

[95] **whose huge stature somewhat amazed *Belcar*, and as he offered to steppe on the Brydge, the Knight very proudely thus spake**. Munday summarizes this part in Vernassal's text and fails to offer any insight into Belcar's psychology. While the French focuses on the hero's fears and willingness to overcome danger, Munday's version turns extremely concise for the sake of the narrative pace. Barley follows Vernassal's version closely instead: "que bien que Belcar fust hardy et valereux, il en eut neanmoins quelque crainte: ia soit qu'il ne le monstra aucunement en dehors, ains se couurant brauement de son escu, auec vne hardiesse demesurée marcha outre pour entrer sur le pont, quand la garde luy va faire barriere disant assez arrogamment" (Vernassal, B3[r]); "he was notwithstanding somewhat afraid, albeit he shewed no signe thereof outwardly, but couering himselfe brauely with his sheild, hardie past wonder marched on forward to enter the bridge, when the garder, came to debar him, saying uery proudly" (Barley, D4[v]).

[96] Failure was indeed a recurrent motif in chivalric romances. Belcar needs to prove his courage and determination, but at the same time he cannot be obsessed with prowess or be too obstinate when listening to good advice. His defeat partly reveals that he is unable to meet all those demands. See Kennedy, "Failure in Arthurian Romance."

[97] Munday reproduces a common motif in chivalric narratives; namely, that of the combat defending a bridge or passage undertaken by the hero to prove his superiority. This same motif appears in *Palmerin d'Oliva* II.47 and *Palmerin of England* I.59. Belcar's commitment to remain at the castle gate to fight other knights is in accordance with the chivalric concept of worship or the knight's continual and public performance of deeds to display his status to others. Belcar will be accompanied by Lipes, who will then act as a witness of his chivalry and will certify his prowess. For a detailed explanation of the notion of "worship" in English medieval romance, see Lexton, *Contested Language in Malory's Morte Darthur*, 1–14, 77–108.

[98] **that he should apprehend great matters by his enterprise.** "qu'il ne soumettoit pas petite chose à son enterprise" (Vernassal, B4[r]; Fr., "that this was no small thing that he did undertake" [Barley, E2[r]]). Munday slightly differs from his source as, through the use of the modal "should," he foretells Belcar's glorious deeds thanks to this new adventure.

[99] ***Trosse.*** Trousse. A feudal signory in Brie (northern France). It became a marquisate in 1615. The use of this title for this character in Munday's text and his source is not accurate.

[100] **and so without any more speeches they fell to the Combat, wherein the Marquesse shewed verie knightlie and gallant behauiour**. Munday does not

describe this combat but underlines the Marquis of Trosse's fighting as "knightlie and gallant." His translation slightly diverts from the French and Spanish, which emphasize this character's physical prowess and resolution (Vernassal, B4^{v}; Marín Pina, 13). The adjectives used by Munday refer to some main tenets in chivalric manuals that insisted on the need for combatants to show mutual respect and behave honorably.

[101] **and vnderstanding the name of his Conquerour**. In chivalric literature it was common for knights not to know their opponents' names when fighting them. However, names were essential in chivalry as they indicated lineage and alliance. The fact that Belcar acknowledges his name after subduing Trousse is significant as by so doing he confirms his worshipful status and implicitly relates it to that of his ancestors. By resorting to anonymity, the hero is able to test himself and find out whether he is worthy of his name before revealing it to his adversary.

[102] **he rode straite to *Macedon*, where he recounted his ouerthrowe by *Belcar***. Belcar's reputation does not increase by simple accumulation of victories. His deeds must be reported to the court of Palmerin (his lord) or to that of King Florendos (where his beloved Alderina is) so that he may be acknowledged as a hero worthy of praise.

[103] **Without question**. "Sur mon Dieu" (Vernassal, B5^{r}; Fr., "As sure as God lives" [Barley, E3^{v}]).

[104] **it was the same Knight that wunne the honour of the Tourney, and went hence secretlie least he shoulde bee knowne**. Cross-reference: chap. 2.

[105] **worthy**. Added by Munday.

[106] **she had bequeathed his remembraunce to the secrete closet of her hart**. "qu'elle auoit miz son cueur et tous ses plus secrets pensemens en luy" (Vernassal, B5^{r}; Fr., "she had set her heart, and all her most secret thoughts vpon him" [Barley, E3^{v}]). Munday resorts to a conventional Petrarchan image, absent in his source: that of the heart as a closet, that is, the inner abode where love and true feelings dwell. This image had become familiar in early modern literary works.

[107] **shee seeing *Cardino* was indifferentlie recouered, tooke her leaue of him**. Munday does not indicate how long the lady stayed with Cardino. Unlike Vernassal, he does not pass judgement on the lady's attitude to Cardino ("humainement") thus preventing any positive reception of this character: "apres qu'elle eust par trois iours seruy sort humainement Sergin le voyant au quatriesme bien amedé, delibera luy faucer honestement compagnie" (Vernassal, B5$^{r–v}$; Fr., "after that she had three daies serued Sergin very courteously, (seeing him on the fourth well amended) she purposed to depart his companie honestly" [Barley, E3^{v}]).

[108] **which made her greefes the more impatient**. "qui l'esmouuoit encore plus a se plaindre et douloir de sa fortune" (Vernassal, B5^{v}; Fr., "which caused him so much the more to greeue and sorrow at her fortune" [Barley, E4^{r}]). Munday translates freely from his source and appeals to patience as a basic virtue.

[109] **These flattering gloses so beguiled *Tirendos*, as hee againe made her promise of his ayde, enquiring of her where the wounded Knight was?** Cross-reference: chap. 3.

[110] The knight is compelled by his oath to assist those in distress, especially if the person who needs help is a knight, as this is regarded as a challenge to their male chivalric comradeship. Tirendos views Cardino's defeat as an affront to their knightly bonds and to their common loyalty to Emperor Palmerin and is therefore ready to avenge him. Their relationship must be assumed as a "compagnonage of the lower degree," a term defined by MacEdward Leach as "the mutual bonds of followers of a common seigneur" (*Amis and Amiloun*, lxx).

[111] **how *Belcar* and hee were bothe Knighted in one daie, by the Emperour of *Constantinople*, from whence hee very suddainlie and secretlie departed.** Cross-reference: chap. 1.

[112] Tirendos does not know that Belcar had put on green armor when leaving the Emperor's court, and so he finds it hard to identify him. See chap. 1.

[113] **The heauens.** "Dieu" (Vernassal, B6[r]).

[114] **thy Brother *Belcar*.** Both characters are presented as sworn brothers, a concept strongly linked to chivalry. The term "brother by oath" was also related to the *comitatus*, a type of social organization common in Germanic tribes, by which warriors swore an oath of affection and service to a chief as if the latter were their father. The warriors participating in this ritual would then become brothers to one another by means of their oath of devotion to their leader (*Amis and Amiloun*, ixv–lxx). Some remnants of this practice could still be found among chivalric knights in medieval romances. In the case of Belcar and Tirendos, both have been brought up by the same knight (chief), Palmerin, and have been later knighted by him in a common ritual, hence their brotherhood link.

[115] **And louing Freende.** Added by Munday. Medieval and early modern discourses on friendship stressed equal and mutual male friendship. Male friends, since they were of the same sex and status, embodied parity, an ideal that could not be accomplished in any other social structure. The idealization of male bonding allowed for two friends to be regarded as each other's other I.

[116] **for your disguised Armour made mee mistake ye.** For Tirendos's reasons not to identify his friend, see note 112.

[117] **and herewith hee rehearsed the whole discourse, according as you haue read it in the first Chapter of this Booke.** Cross-reference: chap. 1. Munday avoids redundancy.

[118] Munday omits Vernassal's "blasmant et maudissant l'effrontée qui les auoit fausement induitz tous deux à la croire" (C1[r]) (Fr., "much blaming and cursing the shameless woman, who had induced them both falselie to beleeue her" [Barley, F2[r]]) and softens Tirendos's reaction, as it may sound improper in a courteous knight. His interest in presenting clear models of conduct prevails.

[119] ***Tharsus*.** A prominent commercial city in the region of Cilicia, on the southeastern coast of Asia Minor.

[120] ***Alfarano***. Admiral of Tharsus. See *Palmerin d'Oliva* II.19.

[121] ***Pasmeria***. According to Jordi Sánchez-Martí in private conversation, the city of Palmyra in Syria.

[122] **worthy**. Added by Munday.

[123] **as you may reade in his worthy History**. Cross-reference: *Palmerin d'Oliva* II.20.

[124] **all the Nobilitie**. "tous ceux du Royaume" (Vernassal, C1[v]; Fr., "all those of the kingdome" [Barley, F3[r]]).

[125] The education of the hero, which normally comes after his birth and childhood, is a basic element in romances. There is then his quest for chivalric adventures, through which he shows his learning and prowess. It is a pattern that goes all the way back to the late classical epic, in which three characters feature preeminently; namely, the hero's mother or some other women in his childhood, a male tutor in his youth, and then a courtier of the king (Cosman, *The Education of the Hero in Arthurian Romance*, 197–98). *Palmendos* follows the pattern, for the Queen of Tharsus is responsible for her son's early years, while his uncle becomes tutor first and then counsellor until the hero achieves his knighthood.

[126] In this idyllic depiction of Palmendos, Munday is inspired by the mirror-for-princes tradition, which stressed the relevance of education as the only means for the prince to reach *virtù*.

[127] **which made him euermore conuersse with the most skilfull that way addicted**. Added by Munday. Palmendos's warlike abilities and subsequent success in arms stress his heroic nature according to the epic tradition. Munday departs now from the humanist line of thought that condemned warfare as a means to acquire fame or glory.

[128] Munday omits Vernassal's ironic remark "De ce beau spectacle" (C2[r]); Fr., "at this goodly spectacle" [Barley, F4[r]]). The English translator, aware of Ozalio's and Palmendos's unsuitable attitudes, avoids being indulgent at such behavior.

[129] **imperious**. Added by Munday.

[130] **lifting her eyes and handes to heauen**. "enleuant se mains vers le ciel" (Vernassal, C2[v]; Fr., "holding vp her hands to heauen" [Barley, F4[r]]).

[131] The old woman's prophecy recalls the visions of Palmerin in *Palmerin d'Oliva* I.12. Through those visions Palmerin learned of his true, royal origins and initiated his quest for his parents and for Polinarda's love.

[132] ***Polynarda***. Daughter of the German emperor and Trineus's sister. She married Palmerin secretly in *Palmerin d'Oliva* I.43. Munday had used this same name for the beloved of the knight fighting in a judicial duel in the first part of *Zelauto* (*Anthony Munday's Zelauto*, 43–50). See also Sánchez Martí, "*Zelauto*'s Polinarda and the Palmerin Romances."

[133] **as with the dexteritie and strength of his bodie, he assaied to gaine the reward which Fortune prouideth for her cheefest fauourites**. Munday translates the French "comble" (summit) as "reward" to emphasize Fortune's compensation for those who follow their fate and behave according to their duty. He

also adds the adverb "imperially," absent in the French, to indicate that Palmerin's reward was the throne. Fortune is a common motif in chivalric literature, as it links the hero's abilities with his righteousness and providential support (Cooper, *The English Romance in Time*, 342).

[134] **for it will redound to thy great shame, beeing Sonne to so rare and inuincible a Knight, not this way to imitate his laborious deedes**. Palmendos's attitude is similar to Belcar's in chapters 1–3. Their ancestors' reputation not only explains their prowess, it also exerts constant pressure on them to emulate their deeds.

[135] "laquelle fit dessors Palmendos Cheualier de l'ordre de Cupido, qui est porter pour enseigne vn cueur nauré d'vne sagete" (Vernassal, C2^{v}; Fr., "who from that time forward, shee dubbed knight of the order of Cupid, who is to carrie for ensigne A wounded heart pierced with an arrow" [Barley, F4^{v}]). Munday omits Vernassal's reference to Palmendos's armor at this stage, though he will include it below in this same chapter. See note 141.

[136] **What may the Ladie be, with whom (at the report of this Woman) I find my selfe so distraughted?** See "Love from mere mention or description" in *Motif-Index* (T11.1). This is a recurrent motif in Palmendos—i.e., the Duke of Feria's love for the temple priest's daughter in chapter 6, Arnedes's love for Philocrista in chapter 13, and Francelina's and Iffida's love for Palmendos in chapters 21 and 26, respectively. For other instances in the Palmerin series, see King Florendos's love for Griana in *Palmerin d'Oliva* I.1 and the Prince of Denmark's for Princess Miraguarda in *Palmerin of England* I.88.

[137] **for his sake**. "pour l'amour de luy" (Vernassal, C3^{r}); "por amor d'él" (Marín Pina, 18); "for his sake" (Barley, G1^{r}). Barley's choice coincides with Munday's.

[138] **which I am ignoraunt in**. Added by Munday.

[139] ***Thalestria*, Queene of the *Amazons*, who for like cause acquainted her selfe with the valiant King *Alexander***. Thalestria traveled for twenty-five days, together with three hundred amazons, to meet Alexander after he conquered Persia. Thalestria asked him to lie with her, and so they spent thirteen days together before she went back to her country, where she died soon afterwards. Their son would be Alexander's heir.

[140] **the heauens**. "Dieu" (Vernassal, C3^{r}).

[141] **and to be called the Knight of *Cupid*, bearing for his deuise an hart wounded with an Arrowe**. Added by Munday, who omitted this reference above (see note 135). Palmendos's figurative representation as the knight of Cupid underlines a basic feature of his personality: he is a lady's man and a seducer, which will help him succeed in subsequent adventures.

[142] **For (as you are not ignorant therof) his Maiestie trauailed alone through the world, opposing his vnconquerable mind against al aduentures whatsoeuer**. Like Belcar in previous chapters, Palmendos will emulate and try to surpass his father's deeds and chivalric virtues. This is a recurrent pattern in Munday's translations.

[143] **yet did the diuine bountie euermore sheeld him from perill and death, and as he, so manie other famous Kings and Potentates.** Fate has been replaced here by Christian providence.

[144] ***Iason*, when he won the Golden fleece in the Isle of *Cholcos*.** See note 8.

[145] ***Theseus*.** Son of Aegeus, King of Athens. Minos, King of Crete, had imposed a tribute on the Athenians, who were compelled to send fourteen youths to be devoured by the Minotaur. Theseus volunteered to be sent to the Minotaur, whom he managed to kill with the help of Ariadne, Minos's daughter.

[146] **In my time (Mother) I haue seene . . . or sustayned other mischaunce.** Munday translates closely from Vernassal, but this reference becomes particularly significant in the English context, as it would have reminded readers of the Armada's defeat in late July 1588. English Protestant accounts viewed such defeat as a clear sign of God's support to England. The weather conditions, which had played against Spain, were one of the arguments used to invoke the role of providence. Munday's implicit allusion to this event is quite plausible, given his dedication of *Palmendos* to Sir Francis Drake, vice-admiral of the English navy against the Spanish Armada.

[147] **because (where ere I goe) Death tracks mee, as my shadowe, and dare not strike till he be commanded.** See "To follow one like his shadow" in Tilley (S263) and "Shadow of death," a biblical expression denoting "the gloom and horror of approaching dissolution" (s.v. *OED*, *shadow*, n.1.b). Munday rewrites the original sentence in the French edition—"puis que nous sommes tous predestinez" (Vernassal, C4[r]; Fr., "seeing we are all predestinate" [Barley, G2[v]])—and, in contrast with Barley, avoids any reference to predestination. He suggests a verse from Psalm 23:4 instead: "Even though I walk through the valley of the shadow of death, I will fear no evil, for you are with me." This same reference seems to have inspired Albrecht Dürer's engraving "Knight, Death and the Devil" (1513–1514) that depicts an armored knight riding through a narrow path flanked by a devil and the figure of death on a pale horse.

[148] This letter was added by Vernassal in his translation from the Spanish. Munday follows Vernassal quite closely, and so he responds to a growing interest in letter-writing by the English reading public. On letter-writing in Munday's chivalric translations, see Sumillera, "The Rhetoric of Letter-Writing."

[149] **Yet can I not repute this chaunce as matter of mis-fortune, seeing the heauenly powers were so benigne, as from that acte proceeded *Palmendos* our onelie Sonne.** The queen describes Palmendos's begetting as divinely sanctioned. In doing so, this character redeems herself from the sin of adultery, which is here rendered necessary to perpetuate Palmerin's lineage. See the case of Rifarano, son to Trineus, in chapter 7.

[150] **The token, often a ring, as a means for recognition is a motif in romances.** See "Identification through broken ring. Parts of ring fit together" in *Motif-Index* (H94.5). For other examples of this motif in Munday's translations, see *Primaleon* III.24 and *Amadis de Gaule* I.11. Rings have also been presented

as signs of commitment and union. Their binding power is acknowledged by the Queen of Tharsus in her farewell to Palmerin in *Palmerin d'Oliva* II.20 (G2[v]).

[151] **looue.** "amitié" (Vernassal, C4[v]; Fr., friendship).

[152] **that hee may yet be some comfort to my following date of time, while I enioy my beeing in this nether Region.** Unlike Barley, Munday consistently omits invocations to the divine providence uttered by pagan characters: "afin qu'on voye passer ioyeusement auec luy le reste du peu de vie, dont la prouidence de noz Dieux enrichira encore en ceste region basse" (Vernassal, C4[v]); "To the end we may passe together ioifullie the rest of this short life, wherewith it shall please our Gods to enrich vs with hereafter in this base region wherein wee liue" (Barley, G4[r]).

[153] **the Isle of *Delphos*.** One of the two islands separated by a narrow channel near Mykonos in the Aegean Sea. As Terence Spenser observes, in the sixteenth century the large island was generally identified with Delos, while the small one was often connected with Delphos, one of the most popular sites of the sanctuary of Apollo. For a thorough clarification, see Spenser, "Shakespeare's Isle of Delphos."

[154] **the Pagans were often wont in ancient time, to come and visite the temple of *Apollo*, as also to consult with his Oracle.** Apollo was broadly known as an oracular god. Delphos was his most important oracular shrine since the eighth century BC.

[155] **in all those three parts of the world.** In ancient and medieval geography, Europe, Asia, and Africa.

[156] Tyrannical rule is normally associated with usurpers in romance literature. By equating tyranny with an illegitimate claim to the crown, romance promotes the idea that rightful monarchs must necessarily be good monarchs, thus enhancing the virtues of good kingship. For further information, see Cooper, *The English Romance in Time*, 340–42.

[157] **certaine villaines.** "deux hommes" (Vernassal, C5[v]; Fr., two men).

[158] **that al those parts lamented to heare of his villanie.** Added by Munday.

[159] **the daungerous Gulfe of *Caribdis*.** Legendary whirlpool thought to be situated within the Strait of Messina off the coast of Sicily.

[160] Vernassal rewrites the description of this character, which appears as a priest, not as a magician, in the Spanish. He also omits the reference to his being worshipped by the islanders: "Y ovo en él un sacerdote muy sabio, tanto que todos lo tenían por dios" (Marín Pina, 19; Sp., and there lived a priest so wise that he was considered a god by everyone). Munday follows the French version closely.

[161] **because her father would not part with her.** Bueno Serrano points to the Priest's incestuous desire for his daughter as his main reason to disapprove her marriage, a recurrent motif in romance literature—see "Jealous father vows to kill daughter's suitor" in Índice y Motivos (489 n. 527) and in *Motif-Index* (E765.4.1). According to Rachel E. Holmes in private conversation, this may also be linked to the hotly debated role that parents should/shouldn't play in the

marriage of their children, a confessional debate which saw Protestants leaning more towards parental involvement (with state powers) and Catholics privileging mutual consent above all else.

[162] The availability of clandestine marriages in late medieval England and early modern England made it possible for young couples to get married without their parents' consent. Any agreement *per verba de praesenti* (of the present tense) and with the mutual, free consent of both members of the couple, or any made *per verba de futuro* (of the future tense) and consummated, constituted a valid marriage, even though they were not necessarily made in the presence of any witnesses or a priest. This practice, however, had been a matter of controversy at least since the twelfth century and so, there had been an insistent advocacy for public and more regulated ceremonies in both the Church and state (Adair, *Courtship, Illegitimacy, and Marriage in Early Modern England*, 143–44; Sheehan, *Marriage, Family and Law in Medieval Europe*, 87–117; Outhwaite, *Clandestine Marriage in England*, 19–50). Consensual abductions (elopements) were also frequent and a form of clandestine marriage, though legislative attempts had further been made to restrict this practice (Dunn, *Stolen Women in Medieval England*, 15–16, 98–119). Though the Duke of Feria and his beloved's plans to escape together and marry secretly could have been tolerated by the readers, Munday successfully echoes contemporary concerns about this question, as, through his use of the words "cunningly" and "steale," he introduces a negative evaluation of both lovers' intentions which is not present in either of his sources. Elopement was also a common motif in romance literature. See "Father opposed to daughter's marriage," "Elopement," and "Eloping with king's daughter" in *Motif-Index* (T97; R225; C567).

[163] **two fierce enchaunted Lions**. In general, lions in romance do not hurt human beings, except when they are enchanted and so moved by an extraordinarily savage force. Recinde will be attacked by a magic lion in chapter 24. For other instances of this situation, see *Palmerin d'Oliva* II.41, *Primaleon* III.1, and *Palmerin of England* III.67.

[164] **as a mad Woman**. "comme vn corps demoniaclé et forcené" (C6^{r}); "como mujer fuera de seso" (Marín Pina, 20); "as a body possessed with a spirit or mad" (Barley, H1^{v}). Munday follows the Spanish and does not describe the lady's madness as devilish, even though she will turn into an evil spirit after her death. Munday does not foretell the fate of this character and just sticks to her madness, which derives from excessive grief.

[165] **her vowed Husband**. "son future espoux" (Vernassal, D2^{r}; Fr., "her future spouse" [Barley, H1^{v}]). The Spanish shows the Priest's daughter's improper behavior, which deserves a sad fate. Vernassal complicates matters and presents her as the victim of her father's jealousy and anger. Vernassal's reference to the Duke of Feria (Duc de Fere) as the lady's "future espoux" serves to approve their conduct. Munday goes beyond Vernassal when presenting them as legal husband and wife

("vowed"). Munday's text builds on Vernassal's by reintroducing ambiguity and making both options valid.

[166] See "Lover commits suicide on finding beloved dead" in *Motif-Index* (N343.4). The form of this damsel's suicide, by the sword, in the Roman manner, contributes to her tragic nature.

[167] **shee wrote twelue mornefull verses in forme of an Epytaph**. George Puttenham defined this genre in his *Arte of English Poesie* (1589) as "a kind of Epigram only applied to the report of the dead persons estate and degree, or of his other good or bad partes . . . and is an inscription such a man may commodiously write or engrave upon a tombe in few verses . . . for the passer by to peruse and judge upon without any long tariaunce. So as if it exceede the measure of an Epigram, it is . . . rather an Elegie than an Epitaph." He then refers to "elegie" as a "long lamentation" basically used in love rather than in death poems, though Renaissance critics did not generally make such distinction (56; cited in Scodel, *The English Poetic Epitaph*, 87). If one sticks to Puttenham's views, this poem here would be an elegy ("mournefull verses"), rather than an epitaph. The fact that he needs to explain the differences between both confirms that the generic boundaries were somewhat blurred.

[168] **martyrdome**. In non-Christian contexts, the killing or sacrifice of a person for the sake of a belief, cause, etc. (s.v. *OED*, *martyrdom*, n.1.b).

[169] **I will leaue some occasion for his too late repentaunce: yet I desire no other recompence, but causing our bodies to bee buried in one Coffin**. "ie luy vueil maintenant laisser telles reliques, qu'il en pourra auoir certain tesmoignage: à quoy d'autant que son repentir arriuera bien tard, ie le prie en recompense, que faisant enseuelir noz deux corps en vn mesme sercueil" (Vernassal, C6^{r}). Munday avoids describing both lovers' corpses as relics that can prompt the priest's repentance, since this imagery would carry clear Catholic connotations. Barley, however, does not censor these allusions and translates almost literally from Vernassal: "I will now leaue him such relikes, he shall haue certaine testimonie thereof. Wherein for that his repentance shall come too late, I pray him in recompence, to burie our too bodies together in one tombe" (H2^{r}).

[170] The poem is added by Vernassal. Munday translates freely from the French, but retains the number of lines and meter (iambic pentameters). Though the rhythm in his poem is more regular than in Vernassal's, he changes the rhyming pattern, which is ababbccddede in the French, and ababcdcdefef in the English.

[171] **it cannot be esteemed as fabulous that loue should cause the death of anie one, because in auncient Histories, we may finde innumerable of recent and moderne examples thereof**. This episode may also recall Princess Ardemia's suicide for love in *Palmerin d'Oliva* II.8. She also writes a poem expressing despair and extreme grief before killing herself (366–68).

[172] **this wofull tragedie**. In her lexical study of the word "tragedy" in the period 1587–1616, Tanya Hagen concludes that though it was basically a theatre term, it was also widely employed outside drama: "Anything 'mournefull,'

'lamentable' or 'deadly' qualifies as tragic" ("An English Renaissance Understanding of the Word 'Tragedy,'" 16).

173 ***Piramus*** **and** ***Thisbie***. Both lovers were next-door neighbors in Babylon. Their parents did not allow them to marry but after speaking to each other through a chink in the party-wall, they arranged to meet at the tomb of Nisus outside the city. Thisbe came first, but as a lion frightened her, she ran away and in her flight, dropped her veil. When Pyramus noticed Thisbe's veil, he assumed that she had been devoured, and so he stabbed himself to death. Thisbe returned of the cave, saw the corpse of Pyramus, and fell upon his sword.

174 **seeing Fortune hath conducted me hether, and will permitte me but to haue a sight of him**. Munday omits Palmendos's invocation to God in the French: "Si m'aid' Dieu ie le veux voir, puis que Fortune m'a icy guidé" (Vernassal, D1^r; Fr., "If God helpe mee I will see, seeing fortune hath guided me hether" [Barley, H3^r]).

175 **huge** ***Colosses*** **without anie soules**. Huge monsters in Greek mythology.

176 **If I woulde acquire prayse and honour immortall, long time must I followe millitarie exercise, as my Father did in his yonger dayes, preuailing against diuers such Monsters, and bringing innumerable enterprises to happy ende**. Palmendos's wish to emulate his father's adventures shows that he is determined to build his own reputation as a knight without betraying his father's name. His thoughts recall those of Belcar in his attempts to rescue Francelina.

177 ***Golias***. A strong, tall Philistine warrior killed by King David of Israel when he was still a young shepherd (1 Samuel 17). In 2 Samuel 21.19 Goliath (Golias) is described as descending from the giants of Gath.

178 **where** ***Palmendos*** **standing formost, the Gyants Sonne thus spake to him**. Munday, unlike Vernassal, does not comment on this speech: "luy commença dire assez arrogamment" (Vernassal, D1^r; Fr., "began to boord him with these prowd speeches" [Barley, H3^v]).

179 **if hee conquer mee**. Munday translates freely from the French and simplifies it: "si ie suis tant fauorisé de Mars et de fortune, que i'obtienne victoire sur luy" (Vernassal, D2^r; Fr., "If I bee so much fauoured of Mars and fortune that I get the uictory" [Barley, H4^v]).

180 **The Prince lothe to waste the time in words**. "Palmendos l'oyant ainsi parler" (Vernassal, D2^v; Fr., Palmendos hearing him speak thus). Munday somehow alters the French source, presenting his hero as a man who prefers action to words. He seems to follow the Spanish, as Palmendos (Polendos) says he wants to stop talking and start fighting (Marín Pina, 22).

181 **as though** ***Vulcan*** **and his** ***Cyclops*** **were at worke with their hammers**. Though he follows Vernassal when introducing this comparison, Munday includes a mythological reference absent in the French: "qu'on eust iugé ouir vne centeine de forgerons batre des lames sur les enclumes de leurs fournaises" (Vernassal, D2^v; Fr., "that you would haue iudged a hundred smithes had ben a(t) worke, beating their yron plates vpon their And-fields" [Barley, I1^r]). He refers to Vulcan, the

Roman god of fire, who was assisted by the Cyclops (one-eyed giants) in forging armor for the gods.

[182] Munday sums up the long, detailed description of this violent encounter, included in both the French (Vernassal, D2^{v}–D3^{r}) and the Spanish (Marín Pina, 22). He, however, stresses the role of providence in Palmendos's victory.

[183] **for which *Palmendos* humblie thanking heauen**. Added by Munday.

[184] Munday omits Baledons's repentance of sins and his farewell to his wife, both of which are included by Vernassal, thus doing away with any positive traces that might prompt sympathy for this character (Vernassal, D3^{r}). The English translator seems to focus on the giant's evil nature only.

[185] **Now see I well, that myne infinite and wicked offences, committed against men without desert, hath throwne this wreakefull sentence on me**. Baledon's tyrannical rule undermines his authority, hence prompting Palmendos's resistance, whose victory seems to be sanctioned by God, as Baledon himself acknowledges. Similarly, Palmerin's action to save Trineus, sentenced to death by the Sultan of Persia, is presented as providential in *Palmerin d'Oliva* II.56; in that case, the Sultan acknowledges his errors and repents (555, lines 1–3). Munday's Baledon does not have the chance to do so.

[186] **I leaue their ioy to the Readers iudgment**. Munday adds a call to the reader absent in his French source.

[187] **as you may reade in the History of *Palmerin d' Oliua***. Added by Munday. Cross-reference: *Palmerin d'Oliva* II.56.

[188] **Princess *Zephira***. Daughter to Onodius, King of Nabor and wife of the Soldan of Persia in *Palmerin d'Oliva* II.42.

[189] **so that beeing of yeeres to receiue his Knighthoode**. The sons of princes reached the legal age to marry at fourteen, and at that moment they could also be knighted (Church and Harvey, *Medieval Knighthood*, 74). Rifarano then becomes a knight at a very early age.

[190] **King *Maulerinos***. Zephira's younger brother in *Palmerin d'Oliva* II.42.

[191] Rifarano's reaction is similar to that of Belcar and Palmendos in previous chapters. Belcar and Rifarano's origins do not differ much from Palmendos's except in their ancestors' degree of excellence. Palmerin's highest heroic status justifies Palmendos's prominence over the other two knights, and so the coincidences among the three in the earlier stages of their chivalric quests enhance the main hero's providential success.

[192] **accompanied with thirtie hardie Knights they tooke shypping**. Cf. with Belcar and Palmendos who went on their quest with almost no company. See chaps. 1 and 5.

[193] Baledon's deceitful cruelty to these knights would be considered treacherous according to chivalric ideals and contemporary warfare standards which showed great concern for the way prisoners were treated. Palmendos's struggle against Baledon must be viewed then not only as an act of resistance against

tyranny but also as a means to restore honorability to the chivalric/military community.

[194] **heereto hee added the whole discourse of their trouble, which you haue heard alreadie.** Vernassal follows the Spanish and introduces a summary of Lecefin and Rifarano's misfortunes in Delphos at this stage (Vernassal, D4v; Marín Pina, 24). Munday cuts off these lines and does not interrupt the pace of his narrative.

[195] **by the fauour of Fortune.** "s'il plaist aux Dieux m'en donner la grace" (Vernassal, D4v; Fr., if it pleases the Gods to give me their grace).

[196] **I woulde haue his eares so acquainted with some actions of account, as might mooue his spirite with the more affection to see me.** Palmendos is aware that his deeds ought to be made public at Palmerin's court, as otherwise he would not obtain fame or worship. His situation is similar to Belcar's in chapter 4.

[197] **the wife and daughter of *Baledon* the Gyant.** "la femme et le filz de Baledon le geant" (Vernassal, D4v; Fr., Giant Baledon's wife and son).

[198] **it is both iust and reasonable, to dispossesse this Island of such bad people, as haue wyth such horrible tirannies so long time abused the same.** Palmendos defends his actions, as they seek justice and reason, two basic arguments against arbitrary, tyrannic rule.

[199] **For I dare say, the people that inhabite this Isle, will more gladly submit themselues to the Emperours regiment, then be held in slauerie by such helhoundes.** Palmendos makes the native islanders partly responsible for their future welfare, as they must choose between slavery and good rule. He resorts again to early modern resistance theories that dwell on the ideal rule in a commonwealth.

[200] **After all the Knights and Gentlemen had armed themselues.** Munday omits eleven lines from the French version, which deal with the deliverance of prisoners, Baledon's agonic death, and his wife's laments (Vernassal, D5r–v). He thus prevents any sympathy for the villains or any possible doubt about Palmendos's moral attitude when observing their suffering.

[201] **the Gyantesse and her daughter.** Munday alters his sources, as both the Spanish and French refer to Baledon's wife, son, and little daughter as being chained by Palmendos's men.

[202] **least they shoulde offer some violence on themselues.** Added by Munday. The use of violent methods against prisoners—in this case, defenseless women—may complicate Palmendos's moral stance. That is why Munday views it as an act of mercy to those women, who had been acting in an irrational, dangerous manner.

[203] **which the God of heauen hath suffered me to conquere.** "que I'ay conquise par force d'armes" (Vernassal, D5v; Fr., "which I haue now conquested by force of Armes" [Barley, I3v]). In contrast with Vernassal and Barley, Munday presents Palmendos's conquest as a providential act rather than a violent military episode. In this sense, he seems to follow the Spanish, which insists on Baledon's

defeat as an act of God: "yo bien creo que seréis todos ledos por vos haver fecho Dios tanto bien de quitarvos de sujeción de Baledón" (Marín Pina, 25; Sp., I think you must be happy that God has liberated you from your subjection to Baledon).

[204] **his Wife and Daughter.** The Spanish and French refer to Baledon's son—"sa femme, filz et fille" (Vernassal, D5[v]; Fr., his wife, son, and daughter); "su fijo" (Marín Pina, 25; Sp., his son).

[205] Munday omits the reference to the islanders' demonstrations of allegiance to Palmendos by kissing his hands (in the French) or feet (in the Spanish). Kissing someone's hand or foot was a sign of humbleness and loyalty in medieval and early modern Europe. By dispensing with these demonstrations, Munday makes Palmendos's position clearer to the reader: he is not the new lord of the land and therefore, he does not "deserve" those gestures. Instead, he will intercede so that the people on the island may submit to their true lord, Emperor Palmerin.

[206] **that which *Hercules* slewe on the Mountaine *Erymanthus* in *Arcadia*.** Hercules's fourth labor consisted in capturing the gigantic boar that lived on mount Erymanthos in Arcadia.

[207] **And when anie one dooth offer to enter the Temple, he commeth forth of his denne, and makes him sure for euer returning againe.** The detailed description of the wild boar's violence is briefly summarized by Munday, who basically underlines that no one had ever escaped alive from its attacks (Vernassal, D6[r]).

[208] ***Palmendos, Ozalio, Rifarano, Lecefin.*** "Palmendos et Ozalio" (Vernassal, D6[r]).

[209] **Yet resolute for all chaunces.** In the Spanish and French versions, Palmendos remained in this place for two days before entering the Temple. During this time he talked to many people who congratulated him on his defeat of Baledon. The Spanish underlines Palmendos's courage even when admitting that it was impossible to reach the Temple on horse (Marín Pina, 26), while the French refers to Palmendos's attempt at concealing his fears (Vernassal, D6[v]). Munday's depiction of Palmendos is closer to the Spanish, as the hero is neither afraid nor worried but resolute to undertake this challenge.

[210] **he commended himselfe to the heauens, and fell to his worke.** Added by Munday.

[211] **And euen as the Bore of *Calydonia*, that was sent to torment the whole Countrey, died by the valour of *Meleager*, who afterward made a present of his head to the fayre *Atalanta*.** In Greek myth, Artemis, the goddess of hunt, sent a wild boar to ravage Calydon as a punishment for its king, Oneus, who had forgotten to offer her a sacrifice in the annual harvest. The king's son, Meleaguer, succeeded in killing the animal, which he offered as a trophy to his beloved Atalanta.

[212] **He had no sooner put off his coate of waxe, which was well loden with the Bores brystles.** Munday summarizes Vernassal's description and omits Palmendos's thanksgiving to the gods for his victory over the wild boar (Vernassal, E1[r]). This act of thanksgiving is also missing in the Spanish (Marín Pina, 27).

[213] **with monstrous Trompets blewe such forcible wind on him.** In the Spanish and French such trumpets blow an extremely hot wind. Vernassal describes such wind as "ardant and sulphuré" (E1r) and so endows it with some sort of devilish power. Both authors describe the place as a furnace whose heat Palmendos can hardly endure (Vernassal, E1r; Marín Pina, 27). Though Munday suggests in chapter 9 that evil forces inhabit this place, he does not dwell any further on such controversial issue as witchcraft.

[214] **two Images of Brasse stoode on eyther side, who with monstrous Trompets blewe such forcible wind on him, as hee was three or foure times carried forth againe therewith.** A similar image is described in *Amadis* II.1. As Mary Patchell observes, their only function is to guard an entrance (*The Palmerin Romances in Elizabethan Prose Fiction*, 49).

[215] **Hauing read the Epitaph.** Added by Munday. Cross-reference: chap. 6 (F3r).

[216] The Spanish and French enhance Palmendos's yearning for the sword: "se venant lor soffrir à son esprit vn extreme desir de la faire sienne" (Vernassal, E1v); "tomó muy gran codicia de ella" (Marín Pina, 28). This reference that may taint Palmendos's characterization is not present in Munday's text. Barley follows the French source instead: "There came into his minde an extreame desire to make it its owne" (K2v).

[217] **and in remembraunce of the accident.** Added by Munday. Palmendos's seizure of this sword could be considered sacrilegious, hence his reinterpretation of the hero's action as a commemorative act.

[218] **and the light caused the precious stones in the Idoll so to glister, as it wold haue rauished anie eye to note the Maiestie thereof.** Munday is very tactful when having to deal with statues, strongly associated by Protestants with Catholic practices, and he omits Vernassal's references to the alleged divine nature of the image found in the Temple: "Au dessouz pendoit grand nombre de lampes d'argent tousiours alumées don't la clarté donnoit vne diuine splendeur à la pierrerie et plusiers petites images, qui estoyent aupres de l'idole auec encensoirs d'or en leurs mains, faisant semblant par representation de diuers signes, de reuerer souuerainement la maiesté de cest idole" (Vernassal, E1v; "Round about on the walles, did hang lampes of siluer always burning, the light whereof did giue such a diuine splendor vpon the pearles and precious stones, that it seemed there was some diuine maiestie before whom they did shine" [Barley, K2v]).

[219] **with her hayre about her eares, and all her garments soyled with blood.** In Renaissance emblematic literature, disheveled hair normally suggested wrath, fury, or madness. Female figures with unruly hair were choleric and aggressive, and therefore extremely menacing (Kromm, *The Art of Frenzy*, 30–39). The blood on the lady's ghost's clothes point to her violent death but it could also be viewed as an item that forebodes the extraordinary violence of this figure.

[220] **which verie sight greeued him to the hart.** "qu'à la voir seulement elle luy donna assez de frayeur" (Vernassal, E2r; Fr., whose very sight frightened him). Munday silences any reference to his hero's fears and instead points to his feelings

of grief or annoyance—the verb "to grieve" contains both senses—when discovering the damsel's ghost.

[221] **With these wordes she ranne violentlie vppon him, and shooke him as if she would haue torne him in peeces.** This episode was apparently troublesome to both English translators: Barley does not translate the beginning of this chapter in the French and Spanish versions (Vernassal, E2[r]; Marín Pina, 28), and so he omits any reference to the sudden appearance of the lady's ghost. Munday translates this part, very likely for structural reasons, but does not include the reference to the devilish giant trying to devour the lady's soul.

[222] ***Chaos.*** "the 'formless void' of primordial matter, the 'great deep' or 'abyss' out of which the cosmos or order of the universe was evolved" (s.v. *OED*, *chaos*, n.2.a).

[223] **whom the olde Woman that told him of so manie thinges at Tharsus.** The narrator refers to Francelina. See chap. 5.

[224] Palmendos's vision of Francelina recalls Palmerin's visions of Polinarda in *Palmerin d'Oliva* I.12. Such parallels enhance the links between both heroes in their respective quests and contribute to the reading of both books as a textual unit.

[225] **for the time will come, when you shall sundry times say, happie was that howre wherein you found me.** Francelina adopts the role of a prophet as she reveals the Christian faith to the hero, prompts his conversion, and urges him to expand Christend*om*. Palmendos's success at the end of the book will confirm her prophetic status.

[226] Munday follows Vernassal when describing the main tenets of the chivalric mission. These narratives retained many secular elements but still paid much attention to the code of the Christian warrior as it had been formulated in medieval chivalry treatises. The hero's commitment to defend Christendom is a recurrent feature in most romances. Palmendos is not a Christian, as Francelina acknowledges, but his pagan faith does not seem to be an obstacle because he is the son of a Christian emperor, and so his conversion is just a matter of time. However, Munday's decision to keep the reference to a monastery in honor of the Virgin Mary is not consistent with the English translator's alleged Protestant faith. Donna Hamilton views this episode as typifying the victory of Catholicism over false religion and as evidence of Munday's Catholic sympathies (*Anthony Munday and the Catholics*, 91–92).

[227] **Nor were these words anie thing els, but fuell to encrease loues fire already burning.** Munday and his sources resort to a stock image in the provençal and courtly love traditions inherited from Greek and Roman literature and present love as a never-ending fire. This same image was employed both in its figurative and literal senses in early modern medical treatises to explain love melancholy.

[228] **for you seeme celestiall, and sent by the Gods into these nether Regions, where hauing discouered the future euent of my Destinies, my hart hath thereby receiued incredible ioy and contentment.** Though the beloved was

often portrayed as a celestial being in the courtly love and Neoplatonic traditions, Francelina's quasi-divine nature is presented here as resulting from her prophetic role.

[229] **in regard of your worthy valour, I loue and esteeme yee aboue all other in the world.** Francelina appeals to Palmendos's excellence of character as the main reason to love him. She thus refers to a basic courtly-love principle when defining true nobility, following Andreas Capellanus in his *Art of Courtly Love*: "A wise woman will therefore seek as a lover a man of praiseworthy character . . . (and) should not seek for beauty so much as for excellence of character . . . it is excellence of character alone which blesses a man with true nobility and makes him flourish in ruddy beauty" (34–35).

[230] **ere it be long we will meete againe, and then shall you vnderstande more of mee, by one request I must make to ye, which as yet may not bee manifested.** She refers to the episode in which she is delivered by Palmendos on the Isle of Carderia. There she will request him to free her father, the King of Thessaly, from his imprisonment by the great Turk in the castle of Albayzo. See chap. 21.

[231] Palmendos offers her love to Francelina in courtly-love terms: he describes himself as a vassal willing to show fealty to his lady by obeying all of her commandments; he presents his oath of allegiance to her as an act of worship ("in that deuotion I haue vowed"); and he finally addresses her as his "freende," thus implying he expects his love to be rewarded sexually—see the *OED* definition of "friend" as a "romantic or sexual partner; a lover" (s.v. *friend*, n.6).

[232] **the old woman arriued . . . who suffered me to be misused before him in *Tharsus*.** Cross-reference: chap. 5.

[233] **for he did as many young Louers doo, shewe themselues fauourable Iudges in their own causes.** Proverbial: "No man ought to be judged in his own cause" in Tilley (M341).

[234] **she whom he had so liuelie imprinted in his hart.** Cross-reference: chap. 5. Palmendos has internalized the image of his beloved as a mental phantasm thus following the conventional process of erotic love (*amor hereos*) described in medical and philosophical treatises since Aristotle. Up to this moment, Francelina does not exist outside his mind, she being just the result of the lover's deranged imagination. This obsession with the internal image of the beloved was regarded as the main origin of erotic melancholy in medieval and early modern medical writings. In Palmendos's case, such phantasm moves him to go on his quest and becomes an object of continuous deferred desire that will test the hero's endurance. For a study on erotic melancholy in Renaissance romance, see Wells, *The Secret Wound*.

[235] This idea of love as an irresistible passion that enslaves the lover and makes him suffer constantly, even to the point of madness, was recurrent in early troubadour poetry. This motif would later become commonplace in courtly love, for according to Capellanus, "Love is a certain inborn suffering derived from the sight of an excessive meditation upon the beauty of the opposite sex, which causes each one to wish above all things the embraces of the other and by common desire

to carry out all of love's precepts in the other's embrace" (*The Art of Courtly Love*, 28). Early modern medical discourse also underlined the lover's suffering and lack of control: "love or erotic passion is a form of dotage, proceeding from an inordinate desire to enjoy the beloved object, accompanied by fear and sorrow" (Ferrand, *Treatise on Love Sickness*, 238).

236 **the *Antipodes*.** The Antipodes, from the Greek ἀντίποδες ("opposite feet"), had been a matter of debate since antiquity, when the term was generally used to refer to distant, unreachable lands. It became a recurrent literary motif, normally associated with legendary, utopian places, all through the Middle Ages and the Renaissance. It was also considered a desirable goal for imperial enterprises in the sixteenth century. Munday may have profited from all those images of the Antipodes: Palmendos and Francelina are enclosed in an idyllic microcosm distant from the rest of the world, thus enhancing their mutual and perfect relationship. See Moretti, "The Other World and the 'Antipodes.'"

237 **Crowne, Scepter and Booke.** Munday translates directly from the Spanish: "corona, cetro y libro" (Marín Pina, 30). The French reads "scepter, liure et couronne" (Vernassal, E3^v).

238 **extolling the happy starre.** "remercians le ciel" (Vernassal, E4^r; Fr., thanking heaven); "davan gracias a Dios" (Marín Pina, 30; Sp., thanked God); "thanked the planet" (Barley, L1^v). Barley seems to emulate Munday in his rewriting.

239 **sauing his conference with the Damosel, because none of them shoulde suspect his looue.** Cf. Capellanus: "The man who wants to keep his love affair for a long time untroubled should above all things be careful not to let it be known to any outsider, but should keep it hidden from everybody" (*The Art of Courtly Love*, 151). The main couples in the book—i.e., Palmendos and Francelina, Belcar and Alderina, and Arnedes and Philocrista—follow this principle.

240 **and so are they sailing toward *Constantinople*.** Munday sticks here to the Spanish original—"en poco tiempo llegaron al Puerto de Constantinopla" (Marín Pina, 31; Sp., in short time they got to the port of Constantinople)—and does not follow Vernassal's longer version: "si qu'en peu d'heure ilz se virent bien auant en la haute mer, où prenans la route de l'Archipelague (pource que la campagne marine estoit calme et bonace) ilz se geterent bien tost en la coste de Trace" (E4^v; Fr., in short time they were on the high seas, where they took the Archipelago way, since the sea was calm and tranquil arriving quite soon at the coast of Thrace).

241 **sonne to King *Frysoll*, and twinne Brother to *Belcar*.** Cross-reference: *Palmerin d'Oliva* II.58.

242 **his courteous and ciuill maners, ioyned with his forwardnes in Armes, gaue hope that he would prooue a valiant Knight hereafter.** Courtly and militarily skills were expected from a chivalric hero, taught in the "liberal" arts—reading, music, law, sports, hunting—and other subjects relating to the practical and theoretical learning of chivalric/military precepts (Cosman, *The Education of the Hero in Arthurian Romance*, 198). The ideals of honor (violence) and civility coexisted in late sixteenth- and early seventeenth-century discourses on nobility, in

what Markku Peltonen has described as "the neat early modern transition from an honour culture to a politeness culture" (*The Duel in Early Modern England*, 10).

[243] *Esquiuela*. Jean Maugin, the French translator of *Palmerín de Olivia*, erroneously translated the name of Asquivela (Esquivela) in the Spanish for Philocriste (*Palmerin d'Oliue*, 138). Munday maintained this error in his English translation (*Palmerin d'Oliva* II.67). Vernassal corrects the mistake in his French translation of *Primaleon*, for Esquivela appears as Esquivele (I3[v]). In *Palmendos*, Munday follows Vernassal and emends his previous error.

[244] **the Soldane of *Babilon* and *Alchidiana*.** Alchidiana was the daughter of Maulicus, the Sultan of Babilon in *Palmerin d'Oliva* II.4. Olorico, the eldest son to the King of Arabia (*Palmerin d'Oliva* II.6) married her and later became the Sultan of Babilon (*Palmerin d'Oliva* II.67).

[245] **his Cozin *Philocrista*, eldest Daughter to the Emperour, deuising with her and her Sister *Melicia*.** The French and English translators make a considerable mess with these characters in relation to *Palmerin d'Oliva*, as Philocrista (Fr., Philocriste; Sp., Esquivella) is daughter to Olorico and Alchidiana; Melicia (Fr., Melicie; Sp., Melisa) to Frisol and Armida, and Belliza (Fr., Bellicie; Sp., Pulicia) to Palmerin and Polinarda (II.67).

[246] **Our Armes we will not leaue, said *Rifarano*, because it ill beseemes an honest Knight to doo so.** In Lull's *The Ordre of Chyualry*, arms are given a spiritual meaning emphasizing the virtues a knight must embody. In the case of offensive weapons, the edges of the sword mean justice and chivalry, while the spear is associated with truth (77). The arms borne by the knight are part of his identity and constant reminders of his chivalry oath, hence Rifarano and Lecefin's resistance to leave them aside.

[247] ***Primaleon*.** Son to Palmerin and his wife Polinarda.

[248] Up to now, both moorish princes act according to chivalric and courtly codes common among Christian knights, and so they alight from their horses and kiss Palmerin's hand as a sign of respect to the emperor and to his heir. By embracing them, Palmerin disclaims any superior status with regard to those princes and their families, as he feels equal to them. For the significance of such gestures, see Burrow, *Gestures and Looks in Medieval Narrative*, 28–29.

[249] Palmerin appeals to his bond of friendship with Trineus to justify his welcoming gestures to both princes. They had been *compagnons d'armes* in their youth (*Palmerin d'Oliva* I.44) and had built and everlasting bond ("indissoluble amitie"). It is this bond that compels Palmerin to love and protect Trineus's family. On the other hand, he shows his affection for Zephira and describes her and her husband as friendly political allies ("Freendes and confederates") but does not go any further.

[250] **that I may goe see the Emperour *Tryneus* my Father, whose Sonne I account my selfe not onelie happie to be, but greatlie accuse my selfe of ingratitude, that I haue so long time deferred this voyage.** Rifarano was begotten in Trineus and Aurecinda's adulterous intercourse. For Aurecinda's seduction

of Trineus, her pregnancy, and the delivery of her son, see *Palmerin d'Oliva* II.55. This episode recalls the begetting of Palmendos after the Queen of Tharsus seduced Palmerin (*Palmerin d'Oliva* II.20). The Queen of Tharsus had, however, resorted to magic in order to have sex with Palmerin, whereas Aurecinda seduced Trineus by her own means, which makes the difference between the two fathers, and therefore, between the two sons.

[251] This letter was added by Vernassal. Munday sums up the first part of the letter but translates the rest very closely from the French.

[252] **perpetuall vowed freende.** Palmerin and Zephira's relation was very close in *Palmerin d'Oliva*: he first helped Zephira protect her lands from the assaults of her evil elder brother, then brought her the magic water necessary to heal her facial wounds and, finally and thanks to the Sultan of Persia's love for her, the fierce war between the Sultan and Palmerin came to an end. See *Palmerin d'Oliva* II.45, II.50–51.

[253] **To the right happy and most fortunate Prince, Palmerin d'Oliua . . . wyshing your increase in all felicitie.** Added by Munday, who follows the English contemporary conventions in letter-writing. For a detailed analysis of epistoles in Iberian romances, see Sumillera, "The Rhetoric of Letter Writing."

[254] **And albeit they deserued greater royaltie for such a voyage . . . and therfore they come no otherwise accoustred.** Zephira's words recall the conversation between Palmendos and the Queen of Tharsus before his departure to Constantinople (chap. 5). Such parallels enhance Palmendos's prowess in contrast with that of other knights, particularly, Rifarano and Lecefin, who fell captive to Baledon.

[255] **Freendes.** "ministers" (Vernassal, E6[r]). The tone of Zephira's letter in the French is more submissive. Munday on the other hand stresses Zephira's friendly bonds with Palmerin.

[256] **And to witnes my bounden duetie in acceptation heereof, I vowe both me and mine euermore to your obeysaunce.** Her son Lecefin, however, would not prove a loyal knight in the following chapters, as his conduct may be considered treacherous when dealing with his rival (Arnedes), his lord (Palmerin), and his own family, who have vowed obedience to the emperor. See chaps. 11–12.

[257] ***Zephira*, Soldanesse of *Persia*.** Persia was often regarded by humanists as a legitimate, powerful kingdom that could help Christian Europe against their common enemy, the Ottoman Empire. Many attempts had been made since the Middle Ages to set up alliances with eastern countries in order to counteract Islamic power, and Persia had been one of them (Meserve, *Empires of Islam in Renaissance Historical Thought*, 1–21, 203–48). Munday and his sources seem to dwell on such trend.

[258] **you are the vndoubted Sonne of the Emperor *Trineus*, because you so liuelie resemble him in face.** See "Recognition by resemblance" in *Motif-Index* (H20). Cf. Polinarda's words to Palmerin when Palmendos reveals his identity

in the last chapter of this book. For other examples, see *Palmendos* 13, *Palmerin d'Oliva* I.14, *Palmerin d'Oliva* II.32, *Primaleon* II.29, and *Primaleon* III.47.

[259] **the mirrour and Paragon of Chiualrie.** The words echo a similar phrase in chapter 1 when describing Palmerin as "the true mirrour and Idea of manhood" (A1[v]).

[260] **without his seconde or match in martiall affaires.** Once Palmendos's worship is publicly acknowledged he can equal his father in prowess, which had been his goal as a knight from the onset (see note 196). He is then presented at Palmerin's court as "one of the best knights of the world," thus fulfilling the prophecy of the faeries in *Palmerin d'Oliva* II.41 (493, line 25).

[261] **the heauens.** "la grace aux Dieux" (Vernassal, E6[v]; Fr., the grace of the gods).

[262] **the Wife and Daughter.** "la femme et le filz" (Vernassal, E6[v]; Fr., the wife and son).

[263] **Without doubt.** "Si m'aid Dieu" (Vernassal, E6[v]; Fr., God help me).

[264] **A Moore borne as I thinke, aunswered *Rifarano*, notwithstanding he well vnderstandeth this language: and such is his braue constitution of bodie, as I thinke a more gallant Gentleman was neuer seene.** Palmendos's moorish origin is not a hindrance, since his valor and gentle nature are presented in the narrative as though they were truly Christian. In this sense, certain medieval notions on the begetting of children are particularly useful. Isidore of Seville, for instance, argues that in sexual intercourse the seeds of both father and mother battle in the mother's womb so that the most powerful of those seeds will prevail and will determine the child's character. According to Ramey, this view may be applied to children whose parents have different religions, for the seed of a Christian parent is supposed to prevail over a non-Christian one (Isidore of Seville, *The Medical Writings*, 48; cited in Ramey, "Medieval Miscegenation," 1, 3). The Aristotelian one-seed theory, which considered that only the father was responsible for the new child, may be useful to explain Palmendos's origin too.

[265] **two costlie Turkish Robes.** A contemporary vogue for Turkish garments, regarded as luxurious and elegant, was partly promoted by various books circulating at the time in Europe. A taste for Eastern fashions developed through the sixteenth century as diplomatic and commercial exchanges with the East increased. This reference to the Turkish robes worn by Rifarano and Lecefin must be viewed in the context of such popular genres as travel narratives and costume encyclopedias. For the significance of the Turkish style see Wunder, "*Western Travelers, Eastern Antiquities, and the Image of the Turk in Early Modern Europe*"; and Smith, "Ottoman Dress in Sixteenth-Century German Printed Costume Books."

[266] **but *Lecefin* regarding the beautie of *Phylocrista*, grew into such conceite of her singuler feature, as she stoode in his thoughts beyond all compare.** Munday rewrites his French source. While Vernassal focuses on the *topos* of the eyes as the *locus* of love and describes the beloved as a quasi-celestial being (F1[r]), Munday omits any neoplatonic reference but mentions Lecefin's internal view of the phantasm of Philocrista ("conceite of her singular feature"), as his obsession

with her image will ultimately drive him mad. In reconsidering his source, Munday succeeds in showing the reason for Lecefin's subsequent violence.

267 ***Flerida, Bazilia* and *Melicia*.** Munday alters the French version, which names "Philocriste, Fleride, et Basilie" (Vernassal, F1ʳ) Palmerin's youngest daughters (Philocrista, Florida, and Basilia, M1ᵛ). Vernassal had previously changed the Spanish "Policia y las otras infantas" (Marín Pina, 34; Sp., Policia and the other princesses). Both revisions prove troublesome later in the text.

268 **Beholding.** A mistaken use for "beholden" originated in the late fifteenth century. It was widely accepted in the seventeenth century (s.v. *OED, beholding,* adj.n.1).

269 ***Xerxes, Iulius Caesar,* or *Alexander* the great.** Xerxes (c. 519–465 BC) was son to Darius the Great and King of Persia from 489 BC. Under the rule of his dynasty (550–330 BC), Persia became the most important empire in the ancient East. Julius Cesar was a Roman general, consul, senator, and dictator (100–44 BC). He conquered Dalmatia, Italy, France (Gaul), Greece, Syria, and Pontus and succeeded in all of his military campaigns through the Mediterranean. Alexander III (356–323 BC) was King of Macedon and leader of the city-states of Greece. He went on a series of military campaigns through Asia and northeast Africa at the rate of one a year, thus expanding his empire, from Greece to Egypt and northern India, one of the largest empires in the ancient world.

270 **yet her Daughter became a Christian, and lyued long time in the Emperours fauour.** Added by Munday. The English translator changes the reference to Baledon's son in the French and Spanish; young Baledon converts to Christianity and becomes a knight at Palmerin's court (Vernassal, F1ᵛ; Marín Pina, 35).

271 **I thinke this Booke can bee opened by other, then him onelie that conquered it, let it therefore bee carefullie kept till his comming.** Cross-reference: *Primaleon* I.2 (C3ʳ⁻ᵛ). The book includes an image announcing the fall of Constantinople at the Turk's hands.

272 **Nowe call I to minde the Damosels wordes, that departed so suddainlie without aunswer: and verilie I am perswaded this Knight is the man shee spake of, who hath sent vs this Treasure from the Isle of *Delphos*.** Cross-reference: *Palmerin d'Oliva* II.67. This woman's prophetic message was the following: "Noble Emperor Palmerin, I haue more delighted to behold thy Chiualrie, then any of the Princes on the earth: but a time shal come, that the renowne of them and thee, shall be vtterly abolished by Strangers, chiefely by one, whose vertue and bountie shall be such, as thy selfe shalt account him the best that euer bare Armes" (594, lines 41–43 – 595, lines 1–2).

273 **which in the end was transferred to one of *Palmendos* Sonnes.** No allusion to Palmendos's son has been found in any of the following books in the cycle. A reference to his daughter Vilisarde, who will eventually marry King Tarue of Lacedaemonia in *Primaleon* III.38, has been found instead. Nothing is said about Delphos in this chapter, though.

[274] **Culaquin.** This reference, which has not been identified, may allude to a fictional kingdom.

[275] **causing religious obseruations to bee vsed in the Temple.** Both English translators omit the reference to the bishop's blessing in the church and to the image of the Virgin Mary in the French and Spanish (Vernassal, F2[v]; Marín Pina, 35). Though Barley is consistent with his previous proceedings—he did not translate the reference to the Virgin in chapter 9 (K3[v])—Munday's omission now differs from his previous decision to retain it in H2[v] (see note 226).

[276] ***Aeolus.*** King of the island of Aeolia and son to Hippotas, dear to the gods, Aeolus was given by Zeus the command of the winds. He was later known as the god of the winds.

[277] ***Sestus* and *Abydos.*** Sestus was a city in Thrace on the coast of the Hellespont, between the Aegean Sea and the Sea of Marmara; it lay on the European side, facing Abydos in Asia.

[278] **when the Soldane of *Babylon* and *Alchidiana* vnderstoode the mariage intended by the Emperour, betweene their daughter and *Dytreus* Prince of *Hungaria*.** Cross-reference: chap. 10.

[279] ***Ocurites.*** "ce Corsaire" (Vernassal, F3[r]; Fr., "this Rouer" [Barley, M3[r]]).

[280] **streamers.** According to the *OED*, "a flag streaming or waving in the air; *spec.* a long and narrow pointed flag or pennon" (s.v., *streamer*, n.1).

[281] **knowing the King by his rich Armour.** Traditionally, the armor and insignia were necessary for recognition in the field. By the thirteenth century they were also markers of distinction and symbols of pride of lineage for the nobility (Keen, *Chivalry*, 125–32).

[282] Munday omits the reference to Palmendos's use of the sword taken from the Temple of Delphos (Vernassal, F3[v]; Marín Pina, 37). Such omission affects the characterization of Palmendos, whose victory over Ocurites is worthier in Munday's, as it is simply due to the hero's very prowess.

[283] **but *Ozalio* stept betweene him and his purpose, still labouring him with so manie hardie strokes, as at length he smote his head from his shoulders.** In the other versions Palmendos himself kills Ocurites's cousin (Vernassal, F4[r]; Marín Pina, 38). In giving Ozalio some agency in their fight against the Turks, Munday enhances his role as the *compagnon* of Palmendos, ready to fight and die for his friend.

[284] **Tyrant *Ocurites*.** By describing Ocurites as a heathen, tyrannical barbarian, Munday seems to relate Christianity to civility and good rule. This book does in fact advance both the causes of a united Christendom against the Turk and England's colonial expansion.

[285] **requesting that this auncient Christian enemie may be safelie kept.** Palmendos insists on the need to treat a captive enemy ethically, which is the conduct expected in a conqueror. Thus, if unchristian and uncivil manners would justify an attack, the civil conduct of the attacker is judged according to similar standards. See Lockey, *Law and Empire in English Renaissance Literature*, 35–36.

[286] **he determined to goe thether secretlie, without making himselfe known to anie, but as a strange Knight to aduenture his fortune among other.** Palmendos follows the same pattern as Belcar, who also hid his identity when participating in the tourney held in Macedon to celebrate Princess Denisa's wedding.

[287] **yet woulde not hee accept of anie.** Cross-reference: chap. 8. See note 205.

[288] **commaunding hee should haue all thinges necessary for hys health, and a Page to attende on him least he shoulde offend himselfe.** Palmerin treats his enemy in a civil manner, as expected from a good ruler/conqueror, but it is also a courtesy token to thank Palmendos for his exploits in his honor.

[289] **which vnited a faithfull league of amitie betweene them, hoping one day to trauell as companions in Armes together.** Abenunco will convert to Christianity the night before being knighted. Since Primaleon and Abenunco will be knighted in the same ceremony, they will become companions of arms. See *Primaleon* I.11. In Goran Stanivukovic's view, Palmerin intends to bring together not only two young knights-errant, but also "two princes from the opposite sides of the religious line, one from the West, the other from the East," as romances "exploit the possibility of such relations, in which the emotional and the somatic mingle, for political purposes, especially in shaping the empire in the Ottoman Mediterranean" (*Knights in Arms*, 153–54).

[290] Munday's and Vernassal's view of Babylon as a splendid country differs from that of contemporary religious works that describe it as an enemy to Christianity. Munday likens the Babylonian Empire to Greece ("the best state in Christendome"), thus promoting their alliance against the Turk. A similar view of Persia is presented in chapter 10.

[291] **the fift day.** Munday alters Vernassal's text—"le quinziesme iour" (Vernassal, F6^{v}; Fr., the fifteenth day). The French had previously changed the Spanish: "ocho días" (Marín Pina, 40; Sp., eight days).

[292] **Among other came thether *Lynedes* the Lorde of *Lique*, he that hazarded himselfe so farre in the aduenture of *Francelina*, beeing (in sooth) reputed one of the most valiant men at Armes in all *Greece*.** Cross-reference: chap. 3 (C3^{r-v}). Lynedes had been the only one to fight against the knight defending the first turret in Francelina's castle before Belcar arrived.

[293] **the Duke of *Pera*.** A knight of Palmerin's court. Pera was the ancient name for Galata, the land north of the Golden Horn opposite Constantinople.

[294] **for when one thing continuallie beateth on a mans conceit, hee imagineth euerye thing conformable to the same.** Proverbial: "Every Man is wise in his own conceit" in Tilley (M127).

[295] **who is more desirous to fight with his Sworde then his tongue.** Proverbial: "He that strikes with his Tongue must ward his head" in Tilley (T385).

[296] **otherwise you offer iniurie to the order, which euery noble minde preferreth as his proper life.** Cf. "A knyght ought more to doubte the blame of the people and his dishonoure / than he shold the perylle of dethe / & ought to gyue gretter passion to his corage than hongre ne thurste / hete ne cold maye gyue to

his body . . . For to stele or take awey thonour / is to gyue euyll fame & renommee / & to blame that thyng whiche is worthy to haue praysyng and honour" (Lull, *The Book of the Ordre of Chyualry*, 62, 50). Renaissance manuals recommended the use of arms as the only means for noblemen to defend themselves from offensive speech (Peltonen, *Duel in Early Modern England*, 53–59). Lynedes's challenge alters the course of the tournament, now viewed as a duel to cleanse his honor after his accusation of perjury against Rifarano.

[297] **they seemed good and hardie Champions, discended of some great birthe, in that they were so woorthilie accompanied, with women of choyse and singuler beautie, as also Gentlemen of ciuill behauiour**. Munday echoes contemporary debates on true nobility that comprised not only virtue ("good and hardie Champions") and lineage ("discended of some great birthe") but also civility. The term "civility" was increasingly used in sixteenth-century courtesy manuals in relation to good manners.

[298] **but others came in meane while and altered their intent, as you at large shall perceiue heereafter**. Munday refers to Arnedes, son to the King of France, and his cousin Recinde. Cross-reference: chap. 13.

[299] **they determined vpon an alliaunce by marriage . . . as the like might not be found thorow the whole worlde**. Cross-reference: *Palmerin d'Oliva* II.61. The exact words of the French king were "Our first Nephewes and Neeces may match togither in marriage, therby to continue the honour of their predecessours" (573, lines 26–28).

[300] **which Prince *Lewes* promising his dying Father to performe, with exceeding sorrow accomplished his funeralles, and making choyse afterward for his owne fancie, in hope to fulfill his Fathers desire in his issue**. Munday slightly alters the French—"Le Prince l'asseura d'ensuiure reueremment en cela et toutes autres choses sa derniere volunté comme vn diuin Oracle" (Vernassal, G2r; Fr., The Prince promised him to accomplish that and any other thing according to his will like a Divine Oracle). He then focuses on Lewes's humane nature ("with exceeding sorrow") and resolution ("making choyse afterward for his owne fancie") in his efforts to fulfill this promise. Such additions can help understand Arnedes's conduct here and in the following chapters.

[301] **hee maried with the daughter to the King of *Castile*, by whom hee had three Sonnes and two Daughters that were borne at a byrth**. Munday chooses something in between the plain Spanish narrative—"y el ovo de su mugger, la fija del Rey de España, tres fijos y dos fijas" (Marín Pina, 42; Sp., And he had three sons and two daughters from his wife, the daughter of the King of Spain)—and the elaborate description in the French (G2r), and so he omits any description of the princess or the little infants born from this union. He follows the French when he replaces "España" for "Castile" perhaps to avoid mentioning a country that was then enemy to both France and England.

[302] ***Recinde***. Son to the King of Castile, brother-in-law to the King of France. According to Donna Hamilton, the family ties between these two continental

powers add a European perspective to the book, which supports her thesis about Munday's irenic defense of a unified Christian Europe (*Anthony Munday and the Catholics*, 92).

303 **that they swore an inuiolable league of amitie betweene them twain, neuer to forsake eche others companie in matters of Armes.** Through this vow the two friends accept mutual loyalty under all circumstances, thus becoming sworn brothers. Brotherhood by oath was the highest level of binding between two friends who committed themselves to share equally in all things. This was a recurrent topic in medieval romances and the main theme in the ME narrative *Amis and Amiloun*, in which the standard elements of this oath are clearly outlined. Both friends thus swear that "While þai mi3t liue & stond / Þat boþe bi day & bi ni3t, / In wele & wo, in wrong & ri3t, / Þat þai schuld freely fond / To hold to-gider at eueri need, / In word, in werk, in wille, in dede" (lines 147–152).

304 **nowe aged sixteene yeeres.** "agée de quinze à seize ans" (Vernassal, G2r; Fr., "of age betweene fifteen and sixteene yeares" [Barley, N4r]). Munday avoids imprecision. Women usually married for the first time at their mid or late teens (Sheehan, *Marriage, Family, and Law in Medieval Europe*, 188), so the King of France is right when considering this as the appropriate moment to solicit Philocrista's hand for his son.

305 **these eyght Spheres.** In the Ptolemaic universe, the Moon, Mercury, Venus, the Sun, Mars, Jupiter, Saturn, and the fixed stars.

306 **wise and aduised in concealing his owne desires.** Added by Munday.

307 **so that fayne would hee compasse a secrete iourney to *Constantinople* . . . as the honourable prayse of them should compasse his loue.** Arnedes follows the same pattern as Belcar and Palmendos in their quest for their respective beloveds.

308 **which in secrete he imparted to his Cozin *Recinde*.** "lequel il communiqua moult voluntiers à Recinde" (Vernassal, G2v; "which he imparted very willingly to Recindos his cousin" [Barley, N4v]). Munday shows his didactic concern when replacing Vernassal's "moult voluntiers" for "in secrete," hence stressing the importance of discretion when dealing in love affairs.

309 **imagining it no wisedome to iugle with his Father.** Added by Munday.

310 **not doubting but by our vertuous behauiour, to yeelde you content by our voyage, and our selues good report.** "pourtant n'ayez aucune crainte de nous, car I'espere que Dieu (duquel dependent toutes choses vertueuses) nous guidera et dirigera si bien noz pensées en ce voyage, que rien n'y será fait contre sa volunté" (Vernassal, G2v; Fr., and so do not be afraid, because I hope that God [on whom all virtuous things depend] will guide us in our voyage and nothing will be done against his divine will). Munday rewrites his sources and does not introduce any reference to providential help, probably because both youths are acting against parental authority, and so a reference to God's protection could be troublesome. Instead, Munday underlines the two knights' commitment to behave virtuously.

[311] **this Emperour of *Constantinople* . . . pursueth in ambush the steppes of the woorthiest**. These words recall those in the introduction to Palmerin's court in chapter 1, in which, according to the narrator, knights from all over the world came to the emperor's court to learn about arms and civility from him, "the true mirror and Idea of manhood" (A1[v]). Palmerin's court becomes a military and diplomatic center for various Christian peoples regardless of their linguistic or cultural differences.

[312] **and which much more wyll redownde to your disaduantage**. Arnedes will suffer the treacherous attacks of Lecefin and will nearly die. His misfortunes and long wait for his father's consent to his marriage will drive him deeply melancholic. See chaps. 17–18.

[313] ***Marseilles***. Located on the southern coast of France, it was an important commercial center in the Mediterranean since antiquity.

[314] **three**. "trois ou quatre" (Vernassal, G3[r]; Fr., "three or foure" [Barley, N4[v]]). Munday avoids imprecision.

[315] **accompanied with none but his Cozin *Recinde*, his Dwarffe and three other**. The best heroes in the book leave their home countries with almost no retinue—i.e., Belcar and Palmendos in chapters 1 and 5.

[316] **braue Tryumphes were ordayned at the Courte**. Those organized to celebrate the marriage of Ditreus. See chap. 12.

[317] **before the sports were ended**. Unlike Barley, Munday translates freely from the French: "auant que les noces de Ditreus et d'Esquiuele se celebrassent" (Vernassal, G3[r]; "before the mariage of Ditreus and Esquiuela were celebrated" [Barley, O1[r]]).

[318] **the Countie**. The County of Pelada, cousin to Lynedes, Lord of Lique. See chap. 12.

[319] **hee had aduisedlie marked theyr Armes, when immediatly hee iudged them to bee *Frenchmen***. In medieval and Renaissance times, four main regions had specific military dress—i.e., armor and arms—different from the rest: England/France, the Iberian Peninsula, the Holy Roman Empire/Italian city-states, and Eastern Europe. Beside their obvious military function, arms served to be identified at the battlefield (Jaritz, "Dress, Jewels, Arms and Coat of Arms"). Munday and his sources, aware of those differences, use them to identify the two characters who appeared *de incognito* at Palmerin's court. Munday also rewrites the French at this point—"quand il fut auerty qu'ilz descendoyent du seigneur de l'isle de Liquie, qu'il vainquit à la conteste du Sagitaire" (Vernassal, G3[r]; Fr., "after he knew they were descended of the lord of the island of Liquia, whom he vanquisht in his conquest of the Sagitaire" [Barley, O1[r]])—and omits the reference to the episode of the Sagitaire, which he did not translate in his *Palmerin d'Oliva*.

[320] **eache of them breaking theyr staues gallantly without any further daunger**. The adverb "gallantly"—defined in the *OED* as "in gorgeous style, showily" (s.v. *gallantly*, n.1)—highlights the theatrical nature of the tournament. In the late Middle Ages and the Renaissance, tourneys had become, primarily,

courtly spectacles and sites for social gathering, though their original use as military training had not disappeared. The courtly behavior of both knights in the tournament prevails over their military abilities, which enhances Munday's didactic interests and his apparent concern with violent display.

[321] ***Lynedes* was very chollericke.** Lynedes's reaction contrasts with the previous gallant attitude of Arnedes and the County of Pelada. The heated irritability associated with this humor could easily turn into furious madness, a potentially dangerous force for its destructive and uncontrollable nature. When Lynedes eventually acknowledges his failure, he seems to be sending the reader the message that those extreme passions ought to be kept under the rule of reason.

[322] In his summary of Vernassal's description of the tournament (G3^{v}), Munday omits any violent allusion and does away with many details of the tourney. He does not mention Palmerin's suspicion that the unknown knight might be Palmendos, either.

[323] **But *Arnedes* he remayned fresh and frollick, as though he had yet doone nothing at all.** Castiglione insists that the good courtier must be admired by others and recommends an easy-going attitude when carrying out difficult tasks: "to vse in euerye thing a certaine disgracing to couer arte withal, and seeme whatsoeuer he doth and saith, to doe it without paine, and (as it were) not minding it" (*The Courtier*, D5^{r}).

[324] **embracing them graciously in his armes.** "ilz s'offrirent à luy baiser la main: mais il ne le voulut onc permettre, pource qu'il ne les cognoissoit, ainçois les embrassa tous deux" (Vernassal, G4^{r}; Fr., "when they offered to kisse his hand: he would not permit, because he did not know them, but embraced them both louingly" [Barley, O1^{v}]). Kissing Palmerin's hand is a gesture a submission which, if accepted, would commit the emperor to hold his authority over them. As long as their identity is unknown, Palmerin cannot accept that submission, and so he resorts to a greeting gesture—embracing them—often used between relatives but also between knights, which would not have any further meaning apart from being a courtesy token.

[325] **Fraunce.** Munday follows the Spanish—"Francia" (Marín Pina, 44)—whereas the French reads "les contres Galliques" (Vernassal, G4^{r}; Fr., the Gallic lands).

[326] **King *Lewes* his eldest Sonne.** "son prochain parent" (Vernassal, G4^{r}; Fr., his close relative). Munday avoids imprecision.

[327] **I am King *Lewes* his eldest Sonne, therfore I am the more like to him.** In his book *A History of Intelligence and Intellectual Disability*, Christopher Goodey observes that the concept of primogeniture changed throughout the sixteenth century, and from the mere legal notion it developed into an abstract idea served to explain the natural order (111). Arnedes concludes that he resembles his father most because he is his eldest son. In doing so he appeals to Renaissance order theories that established the authority and virtue of the primary elements in the chain of being. In his case, being the eldest implies he has naturally inherited not only his father's countenance but his innate virtue as well.

[328] **because heeretofore I receiued by him and his Brother very great honour**. Cross-reference: *Palmerin d'Oliva* I.36–39.

[329] "partirent auec quatre Escuyers seulement pour leur seruice" (Vernassal, G5^{r}; Fr., "departed with foure squiers onely for their seruice" [Barley, O2^{r}]). Absent in Munday.

[330] **hauing made a quicke dispatch, they rode till they came to the house of an auncient Knight**. Munday simplifies his text and omits any detailed reference to time or place: "Si cheminerent deux iournées vers la cour, et la troisiesme hebergerent au pie d'vne colline en la maison d'vn vieil Cheualier" (Vernassal, G5^{r}; Fr., They traveled for two days to the court and on the third day they spent the night at the foot of a hill, in the house of an old knight).

[331] **an auncient Knight, poore in goods, but noble of harte and person.** The poor honorable knight is a commonplace topic in chivalric literature. One of the earliest chivalric texts that opened the debate on money, class, and chivalry is the popular thirteenth-century prose romance *Lancelot do Lac*, in which the poor knight is finally rewarded for his prowess. Elspeth Kennedy points to this work as a determining influence on Geoffroi de Charny's manual *Liure de Cheualerie* (comp. 1350–1351), in which the author appealed to those living honorably on the profession of arms regardless of their economic or social status (*The Book of Chivalry of Geoffroi de Charny*, 34).

[332] ***Palmendos* likewise was somewhat prouoked, seeing his eyes ouerbusied with bathing in the floode of delight, which the presence of thys Damosell onelie procured**. The lady's gaze arouses Palmendos's desire. According to Marsilio Ficino's theory of fascination, the spirits or substances flow from the lover's heart though his eyes to those of the beloved person, who will be influenced by them. A similar event takes place when the beloved looks at the lover and so he/she exchanges his/her spirits with him/her (*De Amore* 7.4, cited in Wells, *The Secret Wound*, 50–51).

[333] Cross-reference: chap. 4.

[334] ***Palmendos* hearing the name of *Francelina* . . . and his very soule was touched with the word *Francelina***. The permanent imprint of Francelina's image in Palmendos's mind can move him just as when he first saw her: now, that mental image makes the spirits from his heart flow to his brain, and the other way round. The excess of those hot substances inside his body makes itself present in his very countenance.

[335] **the two Tropiques of heauen**. In the *OED*, "each of the two points on the celestial sphere at which the sun reaches its greatest distance north or south of the celestial equator and begins to move back towards it again" (s.v. *tropique*, n.1.b).

[336] **Daughter to the King of *Thessalie* . . . but by the meanes of some perfect accomplished Knight**. Cross-reference *Palmerin d'Oliva* II.41.

[337] **for hee that shall deliuer the Ladie, must enioy her as his Wife, next heire after the death of the captiue King**. See "Princess as reward to most valiant knight" and "kingdom as reward" in *Motif-Index* (T68.7(B); Q112.0.1).

Palmendos's fulfillment of this mission will certify he is the rightful heir to the throne of Thessaly, which will be accomplished by his marriage to Francelina.

[338] **alreadie set downe in the Booke of *Palmerin d'Oliua*.** Added by Munday.

[339] **Now he remembers the olde Womans wordes, and sawe there was some likelihoode of trueth in them, thinking because shee had spoken so much of *Francelina*.** Cross-reference: chap. 5.

[340] **Then commaunded he one of his Squires to bring a great bagge of Gold and Iewels . . . and furnish her with all things beseeming such a beautifull Bride. Largess is a main virtue in chivalric knights.** Palmendos's generous presents contribute to depict him as the chosen hero, in contrast with Belcar's frugality at the poor knight's home in chapter 1. In this passage, Belcar behaved courteously but did not give or promise any reward to this poor lord and his family, thus failing to prevent the treacherous behavior of the sons.

[341] **and would haue kissed his hande: but he very kindly tooke them vppe in his armes.** Palmendos does not accept the old knight's submissive gesture (kissing his hand), thus showing a humble attitude towards him. His humility and charity to the poor present him as an ideal Christian knight, even though he has not yet converted.

[342] **without making himselfe knowne to anie one.** Palmendos follows the same procedure as Belcar in chapter 3 and Arnedes in chapter 13, and he will conceal his identity and prove his prowess in the tournament. Palmendos's worth is thus enhanced by comparing him to other heroic figures in similar circumstances.

[343] **to whom he hadde religiously dedicated his hart.** Munday substitutes the military metaphor in the French for the courtly-love motif of the religious worship of the lady: "celle à qui il sentoit la maistrise de son cueur deia vouée" (Vernassal, H1^{r}; Fr., "her to whom the conquest of his heart was already vowed" [Barley, O4^{r}]).

[344] **For euen as the Sunne, the most excellent of all the Planettes.** The sun was not considered a star until the nineteenth century.

[345] **For euen as the Sunne . . . and altred the iudgement of *Arnedes* in such sort.** The sun was often viewed by Neoplatonic writers as an image of God, hence, the beloved's radiant beauty pointed to her divine nature. Just as the sun's rays dazzled the human eye, so the beloved's own beams dazzled and confounded the lover.

[346] ***Paris*.** "Paris Alexandre" (Vernassal, H1^{v}).

[347] **the Goddesse, that appeared to the Sheephearde *Paris* on the Mountaine of *Ida*, when of him she was iudged to bee fayrest of the three.** He refers to the Greek legend of the Judgement of Paris. Eris, the goddess of discord, attended the wedding of Peleus and Thetis bringing with her a golden apple from the Garden of the Hesperides. The apple would be awarded to the most beautiful goddess present at the ceremony. Athena, Hera, and Aphrodite claimed the apple and asked Paris, a handsome Trojan shepherd from Mount Ida, to decide who was fairest.

[348] ***Barbarie*.** A region in northern Africa, comprising modern-day Morocco, Algeria, Libya, and Tunisia.

[349] **caparisons.** In the *OED*, "A cloth or covering spread over the saddle or harness of a horse, often gaily ornamented" (s.v. *caparison*, n.1.a).

[350] **loue.** "Cupido" (Vernassal, H1[v]).

[351] ***Lecefin* who looued her more aduisedlie . . . that he might contemplate her beautie more easily.** While the Spanish text offers a negative view of Lecefin's love, due to its excessive nature (Marín Pina, 47), Vernassal alludes vaguely to the two lovers' equal love for this lady (O4[r]). Munday holds an even more positive view and presents Lecefin's feelings as being more moderate and wiser than those of Arnedes who, unable to control himself, breaks the rules of courtly decorum. By introducing these two different conducts, Munday seems to support manners in order to preserve order. Arnedes's rude behavior will ultimately damage himself and Lecefin, while his lack of self-control will result in his subsequent melancholy state.

[352] **In breefe.** Munday omits sixteen lines in Vernassal (H1[v]); it is a conversation between Arnedes and Recinde on the beauty of their beloved ladies.

[353] **the nuptialles of *Peleus* with the Goddesse *Thetis*.** Peleus, king of the Myrmidons of Thessaly, married sea-nymph Thetis; their son was Achilles.

[354] **a fitte occasion for Louers to commune with their Ladies, yet dyssembled with such cunning modestie, as the eye and action were cheefe messengers of the hart.** Cf. Castiglione's advice on how to woo a lady: "Therefore (in my minde) the way which the Courtier ought to take, to make his loue knowne to the woman me think should be to declare them in signes and tokens more than in words. For assuredly there is otherwile a greater affection of loue perceiued in a sigh, in a respect, in a teare, than in a thousand words. Afterwarde, to make the eyes the trustie messengers, that may carrie the ambassades of the hart" (*The Courtier*, Ff1[v]). The image of the eye as the messenger of the heart is added by Munday; he shortens Vernassal's longer description (H2[r]).

[355] **and so committed to enioy her whom he had so long desire.** Added by Munday. He is always tactful about sexual matters so this explicit allusion to sex may be due to his concern for social duty, as the expression "committed" seems to suggest.

[356] **the iudgement of fayre *Philocrista*.** Munday's translation is closer to the Spanish—"qué seso es el de Policia" (Marín Pina, 47; Sp., what Policia's judgement is) than to the French—"le sçauoir et prudence d'esprit de Philocriste" (Vernassal, H2[r]; Fr., "the knowledge and wisdome of the spirit of Philocrista" [Barley, P1[r]]).

[357] **trie if the iudgement of fayre *Philocrista*, bee aunswerable to her excelling beautie, and if the inward vertue agree with the outward singuler perfections.** Arnedes seems to take into account one of the basic principles of the courtly love tradition—i.e., that the beloved's excellence should be both outward and inward, the former being a sign of the latter. Capellanus stresses the beloved's excellence of character: "If you see a woman too heavily rouged you will not be

taken in by her beauty unless you have already discovered that she is good company besides" (*The Art of Courtly Love*, 34).

[358] **the Bride and the young Princesses.** "les nouueaux mariez, qui furent conduits par les trois Infantes" (Vernassal, H2^v; Fr., "the new married couple, who were conducted by the three infants" [Barley, P1^v]).

[359] **the Goddesse of his thoughts.** "sa chere Dame Philocriste" (Vernassal, H2^v; Fr., "his deare Ladie Philocrista" [Barley, P2^r]).

[360] **so disguised as *Abenunco* and *Rifarano* could not knowe him.** In contrast with Munday, Vernassal presents an accurate description of Palmendos's coat of arms: "(Palmendos) portant vne cotte d'armes rouge, et sur un escu à champ de sinople peinte vne petite fleur d'argent: ce qu'il deuisa en telle maniere, pour n'estre cogneu d'Abenunque ny de Rifaran, qui l'auoyent veu souuent en l'autre equipage" (H3^r); Fr., "carrying a coat of armor red, and vpon a shield in a greene fled painted with a little flower argent, which he deuised for this purpose, because hee would not be knowne of Abenunq nor of Rifaran, who had seene him often in the other equipage" [Barley, P2^v]).

[361] **Soueraigne Creator.** "Souuerain Dieu createur" (Vernassal, H3^r); "Soueraigne God" (Barley, P2^v).

[362] **continually hauing *Francelina* in his minde.** Cf. Castiglione's rule of love number 30: "A true lover is constantly and without intermission possessed by the thought of his beloved" (*The Art of Courtly Love*, 185).

[363] **wherfore he vowed to be reuenged, or hee woulde die the death, and so diuers other Knightes that murmured against the Conquerer, did the like.** The taking of solemn vows in tournaments was a widespread practice in late medieval England, often linked to the defense of a lady's honor. Despite their extravagant, flamboyant nature, they were not void of serious intention (Keen, *Chivalry*, 200–218). A tournament was a privileged occasion for knights to attain worship through their deeds. If victory brought honor, defeat could only bring dishonor. Arnedes's and the other knight's vows to take revenge on Palmendos underline their willingness to regain their lost honor, especially in the case of the French prince, who tried to show his prowess both to Palmerin and Philocrista.

[364] **very sufficient Chiualrie.** "grand valeur et preudhomie" (Vernassal, H4^v; Fr., "their great valor and chiualrie" [Barley, P4^r]); "sus grandes bondades" (Marín Pina, 50; Sp., their great merits).

[365] Munday speeds up the narrative pace and omits various lines from the French and the Spanish that deal with Palmerin's father-like attitude and largess to his knights, and Palmendos's fame at his father's court (Vernassal, H4^v; Marín Pina, 50).

[366] This oath and the subsequent quest for Palmendos, with the help of Palmerin's best knights, open up another plot line. The interaction of those knights with the main hero will enhance Palmendos's supremacy, and therefore the lady's prophecy on the coming of a stranger to the emperor's court who will surpass all will eventually come true. On this prophecy, see *Palmerin d'Oliva* II.67.

[367] **I referred to such as are desirous to breake the Ise of their amorous passions, to them that hold them in so seuere seruitude.** Added by Munday, who summarizes this description in Vernassal (H4[v]). The lovers' servitude to love was a common Petrarchan motif largely employed since the fifteenth century.

[368] **bashfull modestie with-helde him a while from making anie aunswere.** Modesty was a highly recommended courtly and chivalric virtue. Ramón Lull includes it in a list of knightly virtues (*The Book of the Ordre of Chyualry*, 90), while Capellanus considers it suitable to courtly lovers (*The Art of Courtly Love*, 82). In the late sixteenth century and the seventeenth, modesty was progressively likened to civility. Arnedes's bashful modesty is also an effect of his love for Philocrista, which turns him dumb. The silent-lover motif was often taken up by those late Elizabethan poets who advocated a plain style as a marker of truth.

[369] **your diuine perfection.** In the Neoplatonic tradition, God projects his divine nature on the beloved's beauty, thus endowing it with his own divine perfection, and so its contemplation ultimately leads the lover to his subsequent union with God. For a different instance of Neoplatonic speech employed to praise Philocrista's beauty, see note 345.

[370] **my libertie.** "l'heur" (Vernassal, H5[r]; Fr., the fortune); "lo que perdí" (Marín Pina, 50; Sp., what I lost); "my Fortune" (Barley, Q1[r]).

[371] **the labor to *Sisiphus* in rolling the restlesse stone.** In Greek myth, Sisiphus, king of Ephyra (Corinth), was punished in Hades to roll an enormous stone up a hill only to see how it rolled down again. He was condemned to repeat this action eternally.

[372] **The heauens.** "Dieu" (Vernassal, H5[r]); "Dios" (Marín Pina, 50); "God" (Barley, Q1[r]).

[373] **in extreame iealouzie.** Lecefin's jealousy arises from his impossibility to attain the object of his desire. His jealous feelings are not far from those of the melancholy lover, as in both cases there is a clear refusal to accept the loss of the beloved, driving the lover to despair. Whereas melancholy despair becomes self-destructive, jealousy turns the lover violent.

[374] **because the league of amitie betweene him and *Primaleon* enforced him to stay.** Cross-reference: chap. 12.

[375] "Telle largesse monstroit il fort liberalement, d'autant qu'il se reputoit le plus heureux Prince qui regna on ces contrées de Germanie, mesmes oyant raconteur les choses amirables que Belcar son autre filz faisoit en Macedone: pour la prosperité duquel il prioit iournellement Dieu le vouloir preserver de tout encombre" (Vernassal, H6[r]; Fr., "Such largesse shewed he very liberally, for he esteemed himself the most fortunate prince who euer reigned in the countrie of Germanie, in that he heard of the wonderfull chiualries that Belcarin his other sonne did in Macedon: for the prosperitie of whom, he praied God dayly to preserue him from an euill incombrance" [Barley, Q2[v]]). Absent in Munday. Apart from his silence on the King of Germany's liberal display, Munday does not make any reference to Belcar and focuses on Palmendos's central role as the protagonist of the main plot.

The German prince does not have a narrative function in this passage and so the translator can dispense with him easily. For practical reasons, this omission may be interpreted as a means of preventing further confusion in the reader.

[376] **if they saw not a Knight in redde Armour, hauing a little Siluer Flower for his deuise in his Sheeld.** Munday's reference is inconsistent since he did not describe Palmendos's armor in his account of the tourney in chapter 15. Therefore, his readers know nothing about it.

[377] Munday summarizes thirteen lines from the French which describe Arnedes's mood and thoughts about his beloved lady. Munday, following the Spanish, does not indicate the time it takes the knight to reach the hermit's home. This reference is added by Vernassal—"deux iours" (H6^{v})—and retained by Barley—"two daies" (Q3^{r}).

[378] **at the foote of a Mountaine.** Munday radically changes Vernassal's information—"sur la croupe d'vne petite montaigne" (H6^{v})—which Barley translates literally: "vpon the top of a little hill" (Q3^{r}). It is missing in the Spanish.

[379] Medieval hermits were characterized by their hospitality. Their strict aestheticism, piety, and counseling capacity made them respectable. Stock figures in chivalric literature, hermits often help knightly heroes. See Kennedy, "The Hermit's Role in French Arthurian Romance."

[380] **bidding his Hoste courteously farewell.** The two English translators omit any reference to the mass, present in both the French and the Spanish: ("apres auoir ouy deuotement la messe du saint homme" (Vernassal, H6^{v}; Fr., after devoutly hearing the mass said by this saintly man); "el ermitaño dixo missa y Arnedos se detovo por la oír" (Marín Pina, 51; Sp., and this hermit said the mass and Arnedos stopped to hear it).

[381] **that I may discharge my promise heerein to his Maiestie.** Cross-reference: chap. 16. See also "Promise is debt" in Tilley (P603).

[382] **as for my selfe, in respect of my looue to the Emperour, I woulde be lothe to Combat with yee.** Arnedes resorts to combat as the only option left to defend his honor, since he has been unable to fulfill his oath to the emperor. Palmendos accepts out of respect for Palmerin and his knight.

[383] **came downe the Mountaine.** Munday translates directly from Vernassal, but the result is internally inconsistent, as he had previously indicated that the hermit's place was at the foot, not at the top, of the mountain. See note 378.

[384] **he reputed it for an act of great humanitie, in not kylling him outright, his life standing at his mercie.** Chivalric literature, aware of the problems that the pursuit of prowess could bring about, had already set a series of rules to channel violence in combats. In this context, courtesy and mercy were promoted as key virtues: knights had to combat in equal conditions; an opponent could never be attacked when despoiled of his weapons and when defeated, it was compulsory for the winner to show mercy. Palmendos's attitude to Arnedes ensures the former's prowess and reputation. On courtesy in military encounters, see Kaeuper and Bohna, "War and Chivalry," 277–82.

[385] **to him**. "nostre seigneur" (Vernassal, I1^{v}); "a Dios" (Marín Pina, 52); "our Lorde" (Barley, Q4^{v}).

[386] **idle and vndecent thoughtes**. Munday is more precise than his sources—"ces discours" (Vernassal, I1^{v}; Fr., these discourses); "las cosas" (Marín Pina, 52; Sp., the things). He shows his didactic intention as he considers Arnedes's thoughts and words to be improper in a virtuous knight.

[387] **a Moore, and therefore the more inexorable**. A moor, according to Elizabethan stereotypes, was supposed to be irrational, vengeful, and sexually unrestrained. All of these vices apply to Lecefin, whose violent lascivious nature is the result of his moorish origins. His obsession with Philocrista may also illustrate his melancholy spirit (Wells, *The Secret Wound*, 245). Lecefin's disappointment is projected on Arnedes, and ultimately on himself. On the moor stereotype in Elizabethan literature, see D'Amico, *The Moor in English Renaissance Drama*, 59–66; and Matar, *Turks, Moors, and Englishmen in the Age of Discovery*, 12–17. See also "Hot Love: Hasty Vengeance" in Tilley (L482).

[388] **disloyall Traytour**. In attacking Arnedes and killing the hermit, Lecefin subverts various basic chivalric principles. According to Ramón Lull, "Thoffyce of a knight is to mayntene and deffende wymmen / wydowes and orphanes / *and men diseased and not puyssaunt ne stronge*," as well as "to *mayntene and deffende the holy feyth catholyque*" (*Book of the Ordre of Chyualry*, 39, 24; the editor's emphasis). His lack of mercy to harmless people and his murder of a religious man contradict the model conduct set out for a knight. He is also accused of treason. On the other hand, Arnedes follows the chivalric agenda when attempting to avenge the killing of the hermit for "Thoffyce of a trwe knight is to accuse a traytor / & to fight ageynst hym" (*Book of the Ordre of Chyualry*, 51–52). On medieval notions of treason see Leitch, *Romancing Treason*, 62–63, 163–64.

[389] **In a happy howre arriued there *Pernedin***. "Là monstra le souuerain dominateur de ceste ronde machine vne aventure fort miraculeuse y faisant arriuer tout appoint pour son salut Pernedin" (Vernassal, I2^{r}; Fr., "There did the Soueraine dominator of this round Machine, shew a most miraculous aduenture, bringing thether iust at that hower Pernedin" [Barley, R1^{r}]); "Mas Dios traxo por allí a Pernedín" (Marín Pina, 53; Sp., but God brought Pernedin there). Munday is more selective in his references to Providence, which he focuses almost exclusively on Palmendos.

[390] **Why how now Gentlemen?** Munday translates from the Spanish, which has no invocation to God: "¡Ay, cavalleros!" (Marín Pina, 53). He omits the French—"Dieu eternal et qu'est cecy?" (Vernassal, I2^{r}), translated literally by Barley: "Eternal God what meaneth this?" (R1^{r}).

[391] **by my Sworde, did not my looue to *Rifarano* ouer-rule mee . . . but I shall declare this treason before the Emperor and his Barons**. Cross-reference: chap. 7 (G2^{r}). Though the chivalric code encourages knights to punish traitors, Pernedin cannot challenge Lecefin because this action would bring dishonor to Rifarano who, as Lecefin's brother of arms, would have been compelled to avenge

the latter. The only honorable option left then is to ensure that the treacherous knight will be tried at Palmerin's court.

[392] **knowing hee had notoriously blemished his honour: wherefore he went to a Monasterie of Nunnes neere at hande, to haue his woundes bounde vp that he had receiued by *Arnedes*.** Lecefin's amoral behavior does not fit into the moral standards required from the knights at Palmerin's service. His public shame and subsequent departure stress his isolation and self-imposed banishment. Exile was, in fact, a common punishment for traitors in late medieval England (Leitch, *Romancing Treason*, 101–2). There is no further reference to Lecefin in this book. The first allusions after this passage are found in *Primaleon* I.4–5. In those episodes he encounters Rifarano and fights him; when Rifarano is about to kill him, he acknowledges his true identity and is pardoned. As from this moment, he sticks to Rifarano and tries to adjust to true knightly principles.

[393] **that alwaies attended on the olde Father**. Munday omits any reference to the mass, present both in the French and Spanish: "qui seruoit tousiours l'Hermite à la messe" (Vernassal, I2^{v}); "que le ayudava a missa" (Marín Pina, 54). Barley translates directly from the French: "who helped daily the old Hermit to masse" (R1^{v}).

[394] **applying soueraigne salues . . . they should goe straite to the Cittie of *Constantinople*.** Herbs and charms were commonly employed with medicinal purposes in the Middle Ages. These practices, mostly of monastic provenance, were associated with magic and were largely criticized by theologians who warned against their use. Magic medicine, however, remained popular for centuries. See Saunders, "Bodily Narratives."

[395] **Well may *Lecefin* resemble the Soldane his Father, a man full of trecherous and ignoble practices**. Cross-reference: *Palmerin d'Oliva* II.52. The chapter deals with the war between the Sultan of Persia and the King of Nabor. The sultan had demanded a tribute from the king and had tried to impose his (illegitimate) rights on the realms of Grisca and Romata. As the king rejected the sultan's demands, a war broke out; Palmerin sided with the king, captured the sultan and sent him to the court of Nabor, where the latter fell in love with princess Zephira. The sultan and Zephira eventually got married, thus bringing the war to an end and making Palmerin the sultan's ally. However, Palmerin's negative comments on the sultan's tyrannical past cast some serious doubts on the new alliance. Palmerin seems to imply that Lecefin's irrational and treacherous attitude has been inherited from his father.

[396] In the other versions, Palmerin worries about a possible violent encounter between Belcar and Palmendos and asks God to prevent it: "Dieu vueille pourtant (si ainsi est) garder mon neueu Belcar de ses mains" (Vernassal, I3^{v}); "A Dios plega de guardar a Belcar de sus manos" (Marín Pina, 54); "If so it bee, God keepe my nephew Belcarin out of his hands" (Barley, R2^{v}). Munday omits this reference, thus avoiding too negative a view of the main hero.

397 Vernassal emphasizes Philocrista's chastity. Both English translators follow Vernassal almost literally and thus stress this same virtue, so valued in late Elizabethan moral and political discourse. Philocrista's need to preserve her chastity does not only involve her virginity, essential in a marriageable woman, but behaving according to the conventional female virtues of wisdom, discretion, and gentleness. Arnedes and the dwarfs' attempts at persuading Philocrista to accept the French prince have a clear structural function in the plot and, at the same time, are attempts at compromising her chastity.

398 **for the great mishappe had befallen his Maister**. The omission of the relative pronoun in nominative position was very common in EM English, especially when the antecedent clause was incomplete.

399 ***Amenada* meruailing at these words . . . and therefore she labored *Bruquell* with intreaties**. Dwarfs acting as servants to heroes and heroines were conventional in medieval chivalric literature. The exchanges between male and female dwarfs, usually assumed as comic, were realistic alternatives to the Neoplatonic outbursts of lords and ladies. See Daniels, *The Function of Humour in the Spanish Romances of Chivalry*, 23.

400 **so shall she gyue cure to hys woundes, and make him the most fortunate Champion that euer entred the fielde for his Ladie**. Munday dwells on the duality body-mind to explain a lover's disease. Thus the lover turns sick when unable to attain the object of his desire, but if his desire were satisfied, he could recover his health. Philocrista is then the only possible remedy to cure Arnedes's wounds.

401 **Pigmey**. According to certain Greek traditions, a race of dwarfs who lived close to Oceanus, in Egypt and India.

402 **the two *Pithagorick* companions**. The term "Pithagorick" refers to Pythagoras, a Greek philosopher and mathematician (569–475 BC). Munday uses this adjective instead of "Greek" to stress the origin of the characters he mentions.

403 ***Orestes* and *Pyllades***. Pyllades was son to King Strophius and Queen Anaxibia of Phocis in ancient Greece. He grew up with his cousin Orestes and became friendly with him. The pair Orestes-Pyllades was recurrently mentioned in sixteenth- and seventeenth-century works, just like those of Damon and Pithias, or Theseus and Pirithous. For famous pairs of friends see "Faithful Friend and Doting Lover," in Norton, "The Homosexual Pastoral Tradition."

404 ***Nisus* and *Eurialus***. Two close friends fighting under Aeneas's command in Book 9 of Virgil's *Aeneid*.

405 **two thoughts afflicted with one kind of martirdome, receiue together more consolation, then they coulde by anie other that feele not the like torment**. Proverbial: "It is good to have company in trouble (misery)" in Tilley (C571).

406 **promise in requitall of his hard sufferings, to accept of him as my loyall Husband**. Difficulty and pain were necessary to test the true nature of love. Arnedes's extreme suffering makes his love true and worthier in the eyes of his

lady, who eventually accepts him. It was a common romance and courtly-love motif, for according to Capellanus: "The easy attainment of love makes it of little value; difficulty of attainement makes it prized" (*The Art of Courtly Love*, 185). See also "We love that dearly that costs us dearest" in Tilley (L562) and "Love is the reward of love" in Tilley (L515).

[407] **dittie.** "chanson" (Vernassal, I5r; Fr., song); "sonnet" (Barley, S1v).

[408] Munday paraphrases Vernassal's poem, which consists of ten lines rhyming ababbccdcc (I5v). Barley also paraphrases the French and keeps the same number of lines though rhyming in couplets (S1v). Munday's changes are more innovative as he adds two more lines, thus making up three quatrains rhyming ababcdcdefef. There is no poem in the Spanish.

[409] **Sundry times.** Munday rewrites his source: "lendemain" (Vernassal, I5v; Fr., "on the morrow" [Barley, S2r]).

[410] **and nowe in the euening.** Munday's information is less precise than that provided by the French: "au septiesme enuiron l'heure de vespres" (Vernassal, I6r; Fr., and after seven days in the evening).

[411] The dwarf is here presented as a weak person. Dwarfs and women are in fact variants of the literary type of the helpless (Índice y Motivos, 485, 517) and as such feature in romance—"Dwarfs seek human help in their fights and troubles" in *Motif-Index* (F451.5.23). Both woman and dwarf are explicitly linked here due to their vulnerable nature, and so Rifarano's subsequent fight for their cause responds to his knightly duty to "deffende wymmen . . . and men diseased and not puyssaunt ne stronge" (Lull, *The Book of the Ordre of Chyualry*, 39). However, the dwarf's role as lord and true lover departs from the tradition and points to a different topic—namely, virtue as the marker of true nobility.

[412] **of whom hee enquired likewise as concerning the Knight.** Munday avoids redundancy and omits the reference to the knight's armor present in the French: "auquel il demanda s'il auoit point veu en celle contrée nul Cheualier qui portast vne fleur blanche sur son escu trassé de verd" (Vernassal, I6r; Fr., of whom he demanded if he had seen a knight with a shield painted green with a white flower on it).

[413] **I shall pray.** "ie prie Dieu" (Vernassal, I6r; Fr., I pray to God).

[414] Munday does not indicate when the lady has been kidnapped by the evil knight: "il y a ia plus de deux mois" (Vernassal, I6v; Fr., over two months ago).

[415] **there tooke my Wife perforce from me . . . he will come kill me with his owne hande in my Castell.** In medieval English law *raptus* could be associated both with rape and with abduction or kidnap—that is, the taking illegally a woman from their husbands or fathers. Both senses are considered in this passage in which the *raptus* of the dwarf's wife is presented as a serious offense against the honor of her husband, who resorts to Palmerin's help. A similar incident is found in *Amadis de Gaule* I.28, as the hero frees a lady who has been kidnapped by her uncle Gasinan. Amadis defeats Gasinan but does not kill him because the lady finally agrees to remain with her kidnapper. In both episodes, the damsel's

consent is crucial to define *raptus* as a crime. For another case of *raptus* in *Palmendos*, see chap. 24. For further information, see Saunders, "A Matter of Consent"; and McSheffrey and Pope, "Ravishment, Legal Narratives and Chivalric Culture in Fifteenth-Century England."

416 Rifarano's attitude recalls Palmendos's in chapter 8, when he did not accept the presents of the people of Delphos after delivering them from Balendos. In the French and Spanish, both heroes behave humbly and make it clear they act on behalf of Palmerin (Vernassal, I6^{v}; Marín Pina, 58). By omitting this reference, Munday enhances the figure of Palmendos, while Rifarano's attitude, though praised, is never compared to that of the protagonist.

417 **that tall fellowes loue**. Though keeping the same derogatory sense, Munday adds a sarcastic tone absent in his sources: "la femme du desastre" (Vernassal, K1^{r}; Fr., the wife of that disaster); "la mujer d'esse enano" (Marín Pina, 58; Sp., the wife of that dwarf).

418 **two or three words**. In general, Munday's references are more precise than those present in his sources, though there are some exceptions to this rule: "trois motz" (Vernassal, K1^{r}; Fr., three words); "una cosa" (Marín Pina, 58; Sp., one thing).

419 **I had not thought, replyed the Knight of the Castell, that thy indiscretion had beene so great, as to thinke I would win a thing so hardlie, and deliuer it from me so lightlie**. Added by Munday, who omits the references from the French and Spanish to the evil knight invoking God, and his love for the lady, which will make him keep her (Vernassal, K1^{r}; Marín Pina, 58). Munday avoids any sympathy for this character and offers a negative view of him.

420 **to hinder his embracings**. Added by Munday.

421 **but the Dwarffe espying him, cryed out**. Added by Munday. By including this reference Munday provides the dwarf with an agency absent in the French and Spanish, for he warns Rifarano against the assaults of his enemy.

422 Munday omits the dwarf's gestures of submission to Rifarano and the latter's refusal to accept them (Vernassal, K2^{r}; Marín Pina, 59). Cross-reference: chaps. 8 and 19.

423 **and by the way he succoured a distressed Countesse . . . hee lost his life in that bad attempt**. Munday omits chapter 20 in the French and offers instead a very brief summary of its contents.

424 **because wee haue too long forgotten our cheefe Knight *Palmendos***. Added by Munday.

425 **Not long since you vnderstoode, how after *Palmendos* had vanquished *Arnedes***. Cross-reference: chap. 17.

426 **and very soone after it was his chaunce to arriue there**. Munday expands the text: "le lundy d'apres heure de none" (Vernassal, K6^{r}; Fr., on Monday afternoon).

427 **and as a sacrifice after victorie, he promised to offer his soule to the holy caracter of Christianitie, and to be baptized so soone as he could**. Palmendos's conversion is one of his promises to Francelina, as it was made clear

at his meeting with his beloved's ghost in chapter 9. The infidel's conversion to Christianity, usually through a love-relationship with a Christian, was a common motif in Catholic romance; it was a means for outsiders to become members of the Christian community. As Dennis A. Britton observes, baptism and conversion had the power to eliminate "the religious significance of racial signifiers." Such change was often contested by Protestant theologians, who demystified the "miraculous" transformative function of baptism. Instead, they argued that there would always be certain natural differences between infidels and Christians. Those distinctions would be rather racial than religious (Britton, *Becoming Christian*, 8–9, 21–22). Munday cannot do away with all pre-Reformation ideological assumptions present in his sources. Palmendos commits himself to receiving baptism before undertaking Francelina's adventure, and so, his future success is closely linked to his conversion. The English translator, however, has already stressed Palmendos's crypto-Christian behavior in previous chapters, which suggests that the hero is biologically determined by his father to become a Christian. In this sense, Munday combines both Catholic and Protestant views on conversion and the new, modern theology of race.

[428] **At this time *Belcar* kept not the passage of the Bridge**. Cross-reference: chap. 4.

[429] The contents of this letter are briefly summarized in reported speech in the Spanish (Marín Pina, 62). The letter as such is Vernassal's invention (K6^{r}). Munday paraphrases, sums up, and, in other instances, translates almost literally from the French.

[430] **And if you woulde exactlie consider . . . and dedicated to none but onely you**. Alderina's excessive love for Belcar derives both from her active desire for him and from the internalization of her beloved's image. Her use of the adjective "violent" to describe her feelings points to the early stage of the erotic melancholy state she is now going through.

[431] **you seeme a promise breaker, or rather a preuaricatour in looue towardes mee**. Alderina is right when accusing Belcar of breaking his vow of service to her, as is clear from the knight's words to Alderina's attendant in chapter 2: "Thou maist also assure her from me, that henceforth I shall serue as her deuoted Knight: hoping vnder fauour of her name to gaine such account, as I and mine shall remaine perpetually bound to her excellencie" (B3^{v}). Belcar's decision to defend Francelina's castle brings dishonor to Alderina as her knight has not carried out chivalry deeds on her behalf and so has failed to keep his word. Alderina's letter is the only means to have her honor restored as no one else, except for her page, knows about her relationship with Belcar. This hero's sudden departure to meet Alderina reveals his anxiety about being accused of breaking this vow, an act that, if made public, would endanger his honor as well.

[432] **I pray you come hether with what speede you canne . . . which in looues unquenchable fyre my hart suffereth by your occasion**. Alderina resorts to a traditional Petrarchan motif when playing the role of the martyred lover—i.e.,

Petrarch lamenting his "brief solace for so long a martyrdom" and "the years I have lived tasting this golden martyrdom" (*Petrarch's Lyric Poems*, 48–49; 592–93).

433 The subscription in Vernassal's letter (K6^{v}) is a quatrain that consists of six-syllable lines with alternate rhyme. Munday turns it into two hexameters rhyming in couplets. The English translator retains the iambic rhythm of his French source.

434 **but other matters happened vnto him which excused that labour, according as you shall reade hereafter.** For this information, see *Primaleon* I.4.

435 **because the last of the three Fayries that caused the enchauntment in the Fortresse . . . as you haue hearde before.** Cross-reference: chap. 5.

436 **Wheron thinkest thou *Palmendos*? . . . and followe thine intent though thou die therein.** Palmendos's fear before assailing the castle recalls Belcar's in chapter 3 (C4^{r}). While the latter invoked his ancestors' example to gain strength for the battle, Palmendos is confident that God and Fate will be on his side. Both paralleled scenes underline Palmendos's role as the chosen hero.

437 **what.** "What" was used instead of "who" in predicate position from Old English up to the late seventeenth century (Mustanoja, 182).

438 **because the Fairies . . . in recompence of his aduenturous trauayles.** Cross-reference: *Palmerin d'Oliva* II.41.

439 **And as the Pilot long perplexed with outragious tempests, mounts to the toppe to see if any Hauen for reskewe is at hande: so this Lady tossed to and fro in the roughe billowes of looue.** Cf. Petrarch: "As in the force of the winds the tired helmsman at night lifts his head to the two lights that our pole always has, thus in the tempest I endure of love those shining eyes are my constellation and my own comfort" (*Petrarch's Lyric Poems*, 170).

440 **In breefe.** Munday omits Vernassal's elaborate time reference: "Deia les rayons de la grande planete coulans plus viste que de coustume faisoyent place à la lueur de Phebe sa seur" (Vernassal, L3^{v}; Fr., "By this time the beams of the great planet, running swifter then they were woont to doe, gaue place to the light of Phebe his sister" [Barley, U2^{v}]).

441 **he beeing entred the Garden, as you haue heard already.** Cross-reference: chap. 20. The explicit address to the reader is added by Munday.

442 **beeing second to none that at this day beareth Armes.** Palmendos's success here fulfills the prophecy of the three faeries in *Palmerin d'Oliva* II.41 (493).

443 **as if *Herebus* had sent his Daughter to hide the day light, spreading darke night all ouer the Hemisphere, so were great store of Torches and Tapers alighted.** In Greek mythology, Herebus or Erebus was the primordial god of darkness. His daughter Hemera scattered her father's darkness at dawn, thus bringing about the new day.

444 ***Apollo, Orpheus, Arion.*** Apollo was the god of music and poetry in Greek and Roman mythology. Poet Orpheus helped the Argonauts withstand the lure of the Sirens; he could tame wild beasts and make plants and rocks arise at the sound of his lyre. Arion was a seventh-century-BC Greek lyric poet; according to old

legends he was dumped into the sea by certain thieves, but his singing charmed a dolphin that carried him back to land.

[445] References to flowers, music, and the joy of the senses help place Francelina's garden within the conventional *locus amoenus* and *hortus conclusus*, both associated with pastoral romance. While a chivalric quest implies a linear narrative, such pastoral setting introduces a circular plan by means of which Francelina will set up the conditions to fulfill their main goal. Starke views it as a "journey inside the self" both for the lady who remains enclosed and for the male hero, whose experience there will utterly transform him (*The Heroines of English Pastoral Romance*, 7–8). Palmendos's contemplation of Francelina's Neoplatonic beauty is the first stage in his transformation. The lady's agency relies now on her ability to restrain her and his desire until Palmendos has fulfilled his mission. Despite its static nature, love, essential in a pastoral setting, will encourage action.

[446] **Fortune.** "le Seigneur Dieu" (Vernassal, L4[r]); "Dios" (Marín Pina, 66); Barley "the God of heauen" (U3[v]).

[447] ***Leander* and *Hero*.** Leander, who lived in Abydos, was in love with Hero, a priestess from Sestus, on the opposite shore. Leander would swim across the Hellespont every night to meet his beloved; he was guided by the light from a tower, but one night there was a terrible storm, the light was put out and Leander drowned. When Hero found her lover's dead body she went mad and threw herself into the sea.

[448] **these louers.** "les deux vassaux du filz de Cytherée" (Vernassal, L4[r]; Fr., "the two vassals of the son of Citherea" [Barley, U4[r]]). Cytherea was another name for Aphrodite.

[449] **But these louers coulde eate verie little . . . and makes them feed on his louely deuises.** Lack of appetite was a symptom of love in medieval and Renaissance literature. As Marsilio Ficino puts it, "The entire affection of a lover's soul is devoted to continuous thought (*assidua cogitatione*) about the beloved. And to this all the force of the natural complexion is directed. For this reason the food in the stomach is not digested perfectly . . . As a consequence, all parts of the body become thin and pale because of the scarcity and crudity of food" (*De Amore* 6.9; in Wells, *The Secret Wound*, 48). Those "louely deuises" refer to the mental images of the beloved—see the definition of "device" as "inventive faculty; invention" or "the manner in which a thing is devised or framed; design (s.v. *OED*, *device*, n.1.a, 1.b)—and to the lovers' obsessive dependence on them.

[450] **Hence proceedeth the pleasure . . . engraues on the hart the perfect portrait of the thing beloued.** Munday paraphrases Vernassal's text (L4[r]), which he follows closely. Both authors stress the role of both heart and stomach in the process of impressing a mental image of the beloved on the lover's body. The Aristotelian notion that the heart, as the seat of the sensitive soul, prevailed over other organs of the body was widespread in the Middle Ages and the Renaissance. The stomach, regarded as the seat of emotions, was assumed to be the "most literal site of human inwardness" (Schoenfeldt, *Bodies and Selves in Early Modern England*,

25–33, 63). The fact that the beloved's image goes through those main organs regulating physiological, intellectual, and emotional functions highlights its capacity to possess the lover entirely.

451 **the brandon of *Venus*.** Venus was the goddess of profane wine. The Roman wine festival *vinalia urbana* held on April 23 was dedicated to her and Jupiter. She was also dedicated the *vinalia rusticia*, the old Roman festival of wine, vegetable, and fertility held on August 10.

452 Munday omits Vernassal's reference to the hero's taking the beloved by the hand (L4^{v}) which Barley includes in his translation (U4^{r}). In the Spanish, the protagonist kisses his lady's hand (Marín Pina, 66). Munday is tactful when alluding to physical contact between lovers.

453 **now find I that for truth which you told me in the Temple at *Delphos*.** Cross-reference: chap. 9.

454 **the foure elements lodged neere the celestial region.** In the Ptolemaic universe, the four elements—earth, water, air, and fire—were located in a sublunary region between the earth and the moon. The perfect and immutable celestial region was beyond the moon.

455 **in sooth at the age of three yeeres I was fatally enclosed in this Castell.** Cross-reference: *Palmerin d'Oliva* II.41 (P4^{v}).

456 **til you first haue rescued the King of *Thessalie* my father, from the long imprysonment wherein the Turke hath kept him.** In the plan set up by the three faeries for Francelina, her father's deliverance was the first and main demand she was expected to make. See *Palmerin d'Oliva* II.41 (494, line 2).

457 Munday omits Vernassal's Palmendos's reaction to his beloved's words (L5^{r-v}). He also disposes of the latter's reference to Palmendos holding Francelina in his arms. The Spanish even alludes to various sexual games between the lovers that do not, however, sully Francelina's chastity (Marín Pina, 67). Barley follows Vernassal (X1^{r-v}).

458 **Then did he giue her the Ring, which hee receiued of the Queene his Mother when he came from *Tharsus*.** Cross-reference: chap. 5. In Vernassal Palmendos kisses Francelina before giving her this ring (L5^{v}).

459 **which.** It was commonly used in reference to persons instead of nominative "who" in ME (Mustanoja, 199). Its use here may be a remnant of that usage. The *OED* cites further examples up to the late nineteenth century (s.v. *which*, pron.9). It is only dialectal now.

460 Munday summarizes Vernassal's version, which abounds in figurative speech, classical allusions, and various descriptive details (L6^{r}). Munday follows the Spanish more closely: "Demasiadamente fue alegre Francelina cuando supo que era fijo del Emperador, y toda la noche no durmieron fablando en las cosas que le convenían fazer" (Marín Pina, 67; Sp., Francelina was very happy when she heard that he was son to the emperor, and they could not sleep, for they spent all the night talking about what should be done).

[461] **Nowe shined faire *Francelina* . . . as the valewe thereof was imagined inestimable.** Munday sums up Vernassal's description of Francelina (L6v). This sun-like portrait of Francelina recalls that of Philocrista in chapter 15 (M4r–v).

[462] The lovers hold their hands both in the French and the Spanish (Vernassal, L6v; Marín Pina, 67). Barley retains it (X2v), but Munday does away with any allusion to physical contact.

[463] **Father to the three Fairies.** "parent des Fées" (Vernassal, L6v; Fr., "kin vnto the Faeries" [Barley, X2v]). Munday mistranslates the French, which alludes to a relation, not to a "father." The father of these fairies is dead as it is acknowledged in *Palmerin d'Oliva* I.16 (152, line 11).

[464] **if you be either Father, Vncle, or allied to those noble Dames.** At this point Munday translates Vernassal word for word and contradicts himself, as he had previously stated that this man was the three faeries' father.

[465] **who on the Bridge attendeth your comming.** Cross-reference: chap. 21.

[466] **for till you haue brought her Daughter ouer the Bridge . . . when *Francelina* came first hither.** In the French, the queen is required to wait for Palmendos and Francelina at the other side of the bridge. Vernassal also marks that, once the magic spells end, the castle will remain in its former state as a memorial to Francelina's imprisonment (Vernassal, M1r). The French translator slightly rewrites the Spanish original, which mentions a tower, not a castle (Marín Pina, 68). There is no allusion to this requirement in Munday, who also omits the idea of the memorial. Barley follows Vernassal closely (X3r).

[467] In Vernassal's text, Palmendos refers to the time he has spent in the castle—"dix ou douze iours" (M1r; Fr., "ten or twelve daies" [Barley, X3v]).

[468] The description of the mother-daughter encounter, more melodramatic in the French source, takes ten lines (Vernassal, M1r).

[469] **but heerein I consented to the perswasion of the Fairies . . . whether theyr words will sort to effect or no.** Cross-reference: *Palmerin d'Oliva* II.41. In this chapter Munday also explains the queen's reasons to give away her child to the faeries: "Wee neede not doubt that the Queene was heereat amazed, yet the loue of the Mother to her infant, cannot conquer the loue of the Wife to her Husbande, which among all loues is the most honest and loyall: so that in hope to free him againe, on whom depended her wealth and welfare, shee gaue her Childe to the Damosell" (493, lines 26–30).

[470] **I haue determined to loose my life . . . and thereby confirmed you my gracious Mother.** Munday rewrites his sources and emphasizes that Palmendos's future marriage to Francelina will be sanctioned by God and, consequently, the Queen of Thessaly will become a mother to him. In this answer, Palmendos accepts his mission not only as a commitment to his beloved, but also as an act of obedience of a son to his mother. This is absent both in the French (Vernassal, M1v) and the Spanish (Marín Pina, 68).

[471] **Which *Palmendos* perceiuing . . . whereby it might be the better inhabited.** Palmendos's chivalric aims go hand in hand with his colonial projects. Old

romances were often the pretext for contemporary discourses on expansionist policies. Colonial narratives were often arranged as chivalric quests in which the hero was finally rewarded with the property of new lands. This reference to Palmendos's plans was added by Vernassal, who actually employs the word "colonie" (M1ᵛ); Barley, who translates literally, retains that very word (X4ᵛ), while Munday, who follows the French closely, omits the term. There is no indication of the hero's colonial aims in the Spanish text.

[472] **Gracious Madame and mother.** "Madame" (Vernassal, M2ʳ); "Señora" (Marín Pina, 69). See note 470.

[473] **I wil take no other company . . . into the fielde.** Palmendos is consistent with his decision to carry out his quest almost on his own, as this is a requirement to prove his prowess and attain honor. Cross-reference: chap. 5 (E3ᵛ).

[474] **I beeing on the Sea not long since . . . at *Constantinople*.** Cross-reference: chap. 11.

[475] **faire *Francelina*, not doubting but her Lord and Husband woulde soone returne, and knit vp all their ioyes with the presence of the King her Father.** In his brief summary of Vernassal's text, Munday omits any reference to the lovers' sexual desire for each other. He does not mention Francelina's future loss of her virginity (Vernassal, M2ʳ). Though the French version softens the Spanish explicit description of Francelina yielding to Palmendos's (Polendos's) wishes (Marín Pina, 69), Vernassal's emphasis on the sexual needs of the young couple seems a problem for Munday in his attempt to convey a clear didactic message to young readers.

[476] **to make a vertue of necessitie.** Proverbial in Tilley (V73). Added by Munday.

[477] **accompanied with sighes, teares and sorrowfull looks.** They were commonplace symptoms of Petrarchan love and, at the same time, clear signs of loss in melancholy lovers, both in medical and literary discourses. Palmendos and Francelina's self-control and patient endurance of their temporary loss contrast with Arnedes's insane conduct, as described below.

[478] **thorow all those regions.** "par toutes les regions de Leuant" (Vernassal, M3ʳ; "all the regions of the Leuant" [Barley, Y2ʳ]).

[479] **as yet he was not perfectlie recouered.** Cross-reference: chap. 17.

[480] **beside hee wered dailie verie melanchollie, seeing the Embassadours of *Fraunce* staied so long, nor coulde he heare anie tyding of his Cozin *Recinde*.** Arnedes's despair can be viewed as the result of a melancholy passion he is unable to control. Though he enjoys Philocrista's presence, his inability to consummate his sexual desire makes him feel worse. This sense of loss is increased because Recinde, his vowed brother in arms, is away.

[481] **Cynthia.** The Moon. A Greek goddess and an emblem of beauty and chastity. Francelina was also compared to Cynthia in *Palmerin d'Oliva* II.41, when she was taken by the three faeries at the age of three, since her beauty began to show itself "as fayre Cynthia dooth among the Starres" (493, line 34).

[482] **if Fortune permitte him to deliuer the King of *Thessalie*.** The narrative of this chapter suggests that the hero is predestined to fulfill his mission. That might be a Catholic bias, since Protestant romance fiction usually dispenses with any sort of supernatural agencies in the success of its characters.

[483] "A Dieu ne plaise" (Vernassal, M3[r]); "No quiera Dios" (Marín Pina, 70); "God forbid" (Barley, Y2[v]).

[484] **and he likewise is bounde to constant permanencie, if your diuine lookes haue peirced his hart as they ought.** Primaleon's courteous words to Francelina dwell on the constancy vow she made to Palmendos in the previous chapter. Her resistance proves that she is honest and keeps her promises.

[485] **who onely dedicateth his trauailes to your highnes seruice.** This sentence recalls that of Palmendos in chapter 21: "I will leaue you to the Emperours charge, the Prince whom I loue and desire to serue" (R2[v]).

[486] **where the Knights regarding them . . . yet hee imagined his *Philocrista* to bee most perfect.** Munday follows Vernassal and resorts to the image employed to describe Arnedes's fascination for Philocrista in chapter 15.

[487] **shee had two Sisters named *Flerida* and *Bazilia*, (which by the Author of *Palmerin* are named *Belisa* and *Melicia*,) that came verie neere her in resemblaunce.** Munday follows Vernassal and offers a confusing description of those characters: "elle eut deux seurs nomées Fleride et Basilie (que l'autheur de Palmerin a voulut apeller Belicie et Melicie) qui luy ressemblerent assez" (M4[r]). The Spanish author mentions Philocrista's—Policia in the Spanish—two sisters but does not indicate their names (Marín Pina, 71). Barley omits this reference (Y3[v]).

[488] **especiallie *Flerida*, of whom we shall haue occasion to speake heereafter, when wee come to the noble Prince *Edward* of *England*.** Cross-reference: *Primaleon* I.24. The last clause, "when wee come to the noble Prince *Edward* of *England*" has been added by Munday, who introduces this advertising technique to increase his readers' expectations about the following book in the series.

[489] **I can reueale no further of him . . . his Countrey and originall.** Francelina keeps her promise not to reveal her lover's identity. Cross-reference: chap. 21 (R2[v]).

[490] **he thought it very much resembled hys owne Ring, which the Queene of *Tharsus* gaue him at his departure.** Cross-reference: *Palmerin d'Oliva* II.20.

[491] **especiallie when he called the Queenes darke speeches to memorie, which she vsed after her acquaintance with him.** Cross-reference: *Palmerin d'Oliva* II.20. After lying with the Queen of Tharsus under the effect of a magic drink, Palmerin had a dream in which his beloved Polynarda accused him of disloyalty and commanded him to abandon the court immediately. At his departure, the Queen of Tharsus said these enigmatic words to her beloved: "Noble *Palmerin*, my heart attainted with such extreame greefe, as the sight of you doth somewhat remedie, expected further hope of ease by your presence: but seeing your departure may not bee withstood, I pray you vouchsafe to weare this Ring for my sake, and keep it safely, till my messenger bring you another like vnto it . . .

Go then in the safe protection of the Gods, quoth shee, for thou hast left me such a recompence, as all my life time will be ioyfull to mee" (406, lines 27–31, 34–36). Though Palmerin did not understand her words at that point, he showed his explicit commitment to satisfy her request: "I will not denie you so small a request, that I may the better fulfill the bond of allegiaunce, wherein I stande bound to you while I liue" (406, lines 33–34). The reference to the Queen of Tharsus's dark speeches to Palmerin is added by Vernassal (M4^{r}). Both English translators follow the French (Barley, Y4^{r}).

[492] **that hee was glad *Belcar* kept not the Bridge . . . the Prince of *Mecana*.** Cross-reference: chap. 20.

[493] **for the same cause as the other Knights did**. Recinde abandoned Palmerin's court to search for Palmendos after the latter had won the tournament. Cross-reference: chap. 16.

[494] **happened to the same place where *Palmendos* lodged the night before.** Cross-reference: chap. 14. Munday's time reference "the night before" differs from the French: "auparauant" (Vernassal, M5^{r}) (before). Vernassal, in his turn, had previously changed the Spanish version, which states that Palmendos had spent two nights at that place (Marín Pina, 72). Given the number of adventures undergone since that time, Munday's choice does not seem to be appropriate. Barley translates literally from Vernassal (Y4^{v}).

[495] **ryding by the way**. Munday shortens his source texts, omitting all references to time and place, according to which Recinde got to a mountain at night and, unable to find his way, decided to sleep there till morning (Vernassal, M5^{r-v}; Marín Pina, 72). Barley does not translate the episode included below.

[496] **fiue**. "quinze" (Vernassal, M5^{v}; Fr., fifteen).

[497] **uillaines**. Munday does not incorporate the background information on these characters found in his sources—i.e., that they were thieves and assassins responsible for numerous murders in that part of the country (Vernassal, M5^{v}; Marín Pina, 72). So, he offers a slightly different view of his hero's actions; for instance, when Recinde kills those thieves, only the merchants benefit from it; in the Spanish and French versions, Recinde favors all the people from that land.

[498] **the Merchaunt**. A traditional figure in chivalric books; middle-class readers would have identified with him.

[499] In summing up this violent encounter, Munday introduces certain changes. Recinde kills all the villains in the Spanish and French, but only three deaths are mentioned in the English version, which sounds more realistic. Recinde's horse is killed by the murderers in the sources, but Munday blames it on the mysterious knight, thus giving Recinde an excuse to seek revenge (Vernassal, M5^{v}–M6^{r}; Marín Pina, 72–73).

[500] **a *Turkie* Bowe**. A powerful medieval weapon of Turkish origin, consisting in a bow with a sharp curvature (s.v. *Merriam-Webster's Collegiate Encyclopedia*, "bow and arrow," 220).

[501] The merchant's horse in the French and Spanish sources (Vernassal, M6[r]; Marín Pina, 73).

[502] **a very dark Caue.** See "Entrance to lower world through cave/cavity" in *Motif-Index* (F92.6). Caves were normally presented as mysterious and supernatural places in chivalric literature. In this case, it is the entrance to an enchanted palace. See also *Primaleon* I.19, II.26.

[503] **I am no Serpent Sir, as happily I seeme in your eye, but a most infortunate and abused Damosell.** See "Transformation: serpent to person" and "Magic change to different appearance" in *Motif-Index* (D391, D52). The serpent-transformation motif is particularly relevant in the fourteenth-century verse romance *Lybeaus Desconus* in which Lybeaus frees a lady who had been turned into a worm with a woman's face by magicians Jrayne and Mabon. When the hero kills the magicians, the lady kisses him, and she regains her original shape. See *Lybeaus Desconus*, 197–99, lines 2067–2108. For other examples of serpent-transformation in the Palmerin cycle, see *Palmerin of England* III.4, III.83 and *Palmerin d'Oliva* II.66.

[504] **He loued this Damosell so extreamelie.** See "Hot Love: Hasty Vengeance" in Tilley (L482) and Capellanus's warning against loving or being loved exceedingly: "A man who is vexed by two much passion usually does not love" (*The Art of Courtly Love*, 185).

[505] **by reason of his badde manners and euill fauoured bodie.** This description recalls that of the evil knight in chapter 19, through which Munday insists on virtue and civility as essential requirements in a true lover. Though the traditional equation of virtue and beauty is reverted in that chapter, Munday resorts here to the convention that evil nature parallels physical ugliness.

[506] **wandred sorowfully after them thorow the fields.** The fields become now a liminal space between life in the castle and her imprisonment in the cave. Her wandering through those lands stresses her exposure to danger. Though Recinde revenges on his rival for his previous behavior, the delivery of the lady, though unintended, makes him more noteworthy.

[507] **As for their freendlie entertainment, you may iudge it by the cause, which beeing of nature, must needes surpasse all other whatsoeuer.** Added by Munday. He omits, however, the account of the three characters going to the lady's castle (Vernassal, N1[v]; Marín Pina, 75–76). The expression "of nature" is defined in the *OED* as "by virtue of the character or essence of a thing or person" (s.v. *nature*, n.P3).

[508] **Foure daies.** "six iours" (Vernassal, N2[r]); "seis días" (Marín Pina, 76).

[509] **but beeing there arriued, he vnderstoode how *Francelina* was deliuered, *Palmendos* gone toward *Turkie*.** Cross-reference: chap. 22.

[510] **As for the Prince *Belcar* . . . then pleasure to you.** Added by Munday. His tone reveals his concern that his readers might grow weary if he had to repeat Alderina's arguments stated in chapter 20 (Q1[v]–Q2[r]), and also his intention of shortening this episode to make it more lively.

[511] **Shee accuseth him with a great manie articles of vngentlenes, that he would trauaile for *Francelina*, beeing before her vowed Knight.** Munday recalls the scolding tone employed by Alderina in her letter to Belcar and thus departs from the French, in which the lady sounds less strict while asking her beloved not to return to Carderia. Both sources include a lengthy dialogue in which she declares her love for him and reminds him that if he married her he would inherit her father's lands (Vernassal, N2^{r-v}; Marín Pina, 76). Alderina does not mention Belcar's apparent breach of his oath, alluded to in the French and the Spanish. Her tone is gentle and persuasive instead. Munday's rewriting of his sources reveal certain uneasiness about Alderina's lenient attitude to her beloved and his desire to present her as a model of virtue.

[512] **wherfore he desired to returne thether againe, to make her more famous til the aduenture were ended.** Belcar's reasons for his return to Carderia differ from those in the French and Spanish: "Madame, que ie ne m'en puy deporter sans maculer quelque peu mon honneur, veu que ie l'ay promis et confirmé deuant tant de gens, qui me le pourroyent cy apres reprocher et imputer veritablement à couardie" (Vernassal, N2^{v}); "sabed que la guarda de Francelina yo no la puedo dexar porque lo he prometido delante muchos buenos cavalleros y terníanme por perjuro si otra cosa fiziesse" (Marín Pina, 77). Barley offers similar arguments: "As touching my returne to the garding of the castle of Celestina (Francelina), Madame you know I cannot surcease without somewhat impairing mine honour, seeing I haue made promise and vowed before so many, which may hereof reproach me and impute it to my disgrace" (Z1^{r-v}). Belcar has sworn both to serve Alderina and to guard Francelina's castle, but those oaths almost cancel each other. In the other versions, the second one prevails over the first, because the oath was taken in the presence of other knights. Belcar's commitment to Alderina is unknown to everyone, and so breaking it would have less impact on the hero's reputation. Munday omits the second oath, thus assuming that it would pose a serious challenge to Belcar's devotion to his lady.

[513] **but *Belcar* ouercome with exceeding greefe, because fayne he would haue tryed his fortune against *Palmendos*.** Belcar seeks fortune in *Primaleon* I.8. In this episode, both knights fight each other in the tournaments held at Palmendos and Francelina's wedding. At his defeat, Belcar finally acknowledges his rival's superiority and declares his admiration and respect for him (K1^{v}–K2^{r}).

[514] **Nowe come we to the Damosell againe, that pursued *Belcar* for the death of her Bretheren, according as you sufficentlie heard before.** Cross-reference: chaps. 1, 3–4. Munday adds the adverb "againe" and the last clause "as you sufficientlie heard before." Munday is weary of such repetitions, which he omits for his readers' sake, thus briefly summing up the encounter between those two characters (Vernassal, N2^{v}–N3^{r}; Marín Pina, 77).

[515] **she deliuered the same discourse which she had doone to *Cardino* and *Tirendos*.** Cross-reference: chaps. 3–4.

[516] **they founde there the King, *Belcar* and diuers noble Barons.** Munday omits the reference to the mass found in the French: "trouuant que le Roy venoit de la messe acompagné de Belcar" (Vernassal, N3[r]). Barley retains it: "meeting the King as he came from masse accompanied with Belcarin" (Z2[r–v]).

[517] **I beseech yee make him knowe before the King, the treason he committed against harmeles men.** This confrontation is presented as a judicial combat to settle an accusation of treason when there are no witnesses, so that the winner may be considered righteous according to God's judgement. It had been a common practice amongst the nobility in the early Middle Ages, but it went into decline as from the fourteenth century. Such duels already had little value in the sixteenth century (Bartlett, *Trial by Fire and Water*, 103–26).

[518] **I hope to recompence ye for light beleefe, and that false woman likewise the instrument of thy follie.** Once the accusation is made, the accused must either accept it or reject it. A rejection would imply that the defendant acknowledges his guilt and subsequent punishment (Bloch, *Medieval French Literature and Law*, 50). Belcar's sole option here is to accept the challenge.

[519] **let me vnderstand the name of him that will not graunt so smal a matter.** It was customary for both parties to identify themselves. Unlike other combats in which knights hid their identities in order to prove that they were worthy of their names, the judicial duel only seeks to vindicate truth, and so they must acknowledge their names.

[520] **a Knight of a strange Country . . . in searche of him.** Cross-reference: chaps. 13, 15–16.

[521] **when he considered the neere alliaunce betweene him and *Melicia*.** Melicia is King Frysol's daughter and Belcar's sister. This family link is made explicit in Munday's sources: "pour estre son enemy frere de l'Infante Melise" (Vernassal, N3[v]); "porque era hermano de Melisa" (Marín Pina, 78); see also Barley, "because his enemie was brother to Melissa" (Z3[r]). Munday's vague reference may be the result of his confusing allusion to Melicia in chapter 10; he now follows Vernassal and presents Melicia as sister to Philocrista. Vernassal amends the error, but Munday's imprecise reference does not completely contradict his previous statement. See notes 267 and 487.

[522] **so that willinglie he would haue forborne the Combat, but that he could not with honor gaine say it.** Since Recinde has already accepted to become this lady's champion, he is not free to break the bond, as that would challenge the chivalric code. The combat between those knights is, rather than a means to find out the truth, a matter of honor.

[523] **Nowe the King desires the Duke of *Pontus*, and another of his cheefest Barons, to iudge the fight according to conscience, and without any exception of person.** Judicial combats were witnessed by the barons at court and controlled by a judge, who listened to the accusations and pronounced sentences. For further information on the ritual concerning judicial duels, see Bloch, *Medieval French Literature and Law*, 46–53.

[524] **she made a sollemne othe, that if she did not presently pardon the two Knights . . . that her selfe should die a most shamefull death.** As the judicial duel ultimately relies on God's judgement, a false accusation is thought to bring God's wrath upon the accuser, who then deserves punishment. In chapters 3 and 4, the damsel was not punished because although the struggle between the knights had been provoked by her, it was a matter of honor. In this case, the queen reminds the lady of the serious consequences of her dishonesty. A trial by ordeal is divinely sanctioned, and so a false accusation, which is a direct affront to God, cannot go unpunished.

[525] **the Queene (in regarde of her promise) caused the Damosell to bee very honourablie married, when *Belcar* made her openly confesse, that her accusations were most false and vntrue.** Belcar's honor can only be restored when his innocence is publicly acknowledged. The lady, after having admitted the truth, is no longer a threat to Belcar or anyone else. The queen's decision to have her married shows the ruler's merciful nature.

[526] **But leaue we these, and let vs nowe returne againe to our noble Knight *Palmendos*, whom we left preparing his voyage towards *Turkie*.** Added by Munday.

[527] Munday omits the episode in which a Turk becomes the victim of a group of Christians (Vernassal, N5^{r}; Marín Pina, 80). The Spanish author tries to justify those Christians but does not quite succeed: "que lo avían echado ahí una nao de cristianos, cuando vieron ansí malo, pensando que sanaría" (80; Sp., that a Christian ship had left him there, as they saw he was sick, thinking that he would recover). No reference to that is found in Munday's version.

[528] **happened on a Turke left therein the Hauen by reason of extreame sicknes . . . he had verie well recoured his health.** The mariners from Tharsus are here described as good, merciful Christians, for they help the sick person recover. See the works of mercy in Matthew 25.34–46. By contrast, the Turk and his followers are shown as cruel, merciless people, and this negative attitude will help present Palmendos throughout the narrative in a more positive light.

[529] ***Tubant*.** This location, which has not been identified, is the seat of the Great Turk's court in *Palmerin d'Oliva* (P4^{r}).

[530] **the Castell of *Albayzo*, where the great Turke keepes the king of *Thessalie* and all his treasure.** Cross-reference: *Palmerin d'Oliva* II.41.

[531] **his right black Armour, which the Faeries left for him at the Castell of *Carderia*, his good sworde likewise hee had by his side, wherewith hee could enchaunt and bring asleepe anye one by drawing it foorth.** Cross-reference: chap. 22 (R3^{r}).

[532] **Fauchion.** In the *OED*, "a broad sword more or less curved with the edge on the convex side" (s.v. *falchion*, n.1.a).

[533] **saying she will neuer be married, but with him that can winne her by Martiall prowess.** See "Suitor contest: bride offered as prize" in *Motif-Index* (H311). A recurrent motif in Arthurian romances, it was also largely employed

in Spanish chivalric books. With regard to the Amadis and Palmerin cycles, see *Amadis de Gaule* II.19 and *Primaleon* I.13, I.16, I.19.

[534] **Bassaes.** Pashas or high-rank Turkish officers (s.v. *OED, parsha*, n.1).

[535] **Ianizaries.** The main part of the Turkish infantry; they also constituted the Sultan's guard (s.v. *OED, janizary/janissary*, n.1).

[536] **that if hee could by subtill traines entice this Ladie to loue, hee might easily get into *Albayzo* Castell.** Palmendos is a seducer, a "Knight of Cupid," as he himself acknowledges in chapter 5, in which he adopts the figurative elements traditionally associated with the god of love, namely, a heart wounded with an arrow. His main characteristic feature is precisely his sex appeal, which becomes the means to succeed in his final and most important challenge. Munday regards Palmendos's proceedings as "subtill traines." "Subtile" is defined in the *OED* as "crafty, cunning, sly" and "treacherous" while "train" is associated with "treachery, guile, deceit, trickery" and "prevarication" (s.v. *subtile*, adj.1.a; *train*, n.1.1.a).

[537] **The Prince calling to minde the perfections of *Francelina*, breathed foorth a sigh that came from his very soul.** Far from leading to a melancholy state, the permanent thought of Francelina encourages the hero to carry out his mission. Munday now presents Palmendos as a faithful lover, forever devoted to his lady. By highlighting the hero's loyalty to his beloved, Munday tries to cast the hero in a more favorable light, especially at this stage, when readers will have to put up with such troublesome incidents as those taking place in the following chapters.

[538] **you seeme a man of vertue and quality.** The page, after listening to Palmendos's speech and watching his outward look, concludes that he embodies such noble values as virtue and lineage—c.f. the hostess's comments on the hero's nobility in Munday's *Zelauto*: "First, the outward apparaunce of this gallant Gentlemans humanitie: maketh ample discouerie of true nobilitie" (*Anthony Munday's Zelauto*, 81). Beauty, elegance, and fine speech were central to late sixteenth-century courtly manuals of good manners (Peltonen, *Duel in Early Modern England*, 24–36).

[539] ***Prissa.*** An unidentified, possibly fictional location.

[540] **courtesie and liberalitie.** Courtesy was always considered of paramount importance in knights; and so was liberality: "And what it shal be tyme of necessite to make largesse / his hondes must gyue and dispende after that it apperteyneth to his honour" (Lull, *Booke of the Ordre of Chyualry*, 85). In the courtly love tradition, liberality is one of the requirements of true lovers; Andreas Capellanus underlines its practical value: "Nothing is considered more praise-worthy in a lover than to be known to be generous, and no matter how worthy a man may be otherwise, avarice degrades him, while many faults are excused if one has the virtue of liberality." Capellanus also stresses courtesy and nobility as pivotal virtues that must guide the lover's conduct: "he must keep in mind the general rule that lovers must not neglect anything that good manners demand or good breathing suggests" (*The Art of Courtly Love*, 52).

[541] Munday omits a parenthetical phrase from the French that describes the presents the page has been given as "les arres de leur mort sans que l'vn ny l'autre y pensast" (Vernassal, O1^r^); Barley translates directly from the French and refers to them as "the earnest of their deathes, albeit neither of them thought thereof" (Aa4^r^). Munday does not anticipate the resolution of this episode, thus sticking to the narrative pace.

[542] **Me thinks this is verie straunge, replied *Iffida*, that this Knight should come from farre Countries to see me, and verie ingratefull might I be reputed, if I shoulde not thanke him for so great paines.** Iffida's words recall those of Philocrista in chapter 18: "thou (her dwarf) shalt then goe to Arnedes, and tell him from me, that I meruaile he would thrust himselfe into so manie perils, for which I account my selfe beholding to him, and promise in requital of his hard sufferings, to accept of him as my loyall Husband, if my gracious parents will so permit it" (P1^v^). Both Iffida and Philocrista fall in love with their respective lovers through the agency of their servants. The parallels between both episodes may have disappointed readers, as they may have compared the main hero to faithful Arnedes.

[543] **Thus made the Page a train for loue . . . for thinking on the Knight that came from far Countries.** Capellanus includes sleeplessness among the symptoms of love, as he warns against thinking excessively of the beloved ladies: "He whom the thought of love vexes eats and sleeps very little" (*The Art of Courtly Love*, 185). Insomnia and permanent restlessness were thought to hinder imagination and bodily functions.

[544] Both the French and Spanish sources specify that there were two thousand knights assembled (Vernassal, O1^v^; Marín Pina, 82). Munday almost systematically omits such references to quantity.

[545] **went apace to wracke.** The expression "go to wrack" was of frequent use from c. 1560 to 1680. Its meaning was close to the contemporary "go to rack" or "fall into a state of total neglect, disrepair, or ruin" (s.v., *OED*, *wrack*, n.2.b. and *rack*, n.9.1).

[546] **to see him so play the Deuil among the Knights.** "il sçauoit encore manier et voltiger tant bien son cheual" (Vernassal, O2^r^; Fr., "yet he knew better to manage and voltidge his horse, so well" [Barley, Bb1^r^]); "porque Polendos dava tan esquivos golpes a diestro y siniestro" (Marín Pina, 82; Sp., because Palmendos gave so many strokes to everyone there). Munday rewrites Vernassal's sentence adding a colloquial English phrase, "to play the Devil"—"to do mischief, make havoc or ruin" (s.v. *OED*, *devil*, n.22.k)—just to make his text more accessible to English readers. In doing so, he emulates the Spanish version, which uses the idiom "a diestro y siniestro."

[547] **as the rest of her Historie will plainely discouer.** Munday misreads both the French and the Spanish. In Vernassal, Iffida, fascinated by Palmendos's prowess, "eust bien voulu entendre tout le reste de son histoire" (Vernassal, O2^r^; Fr., would have liked to hear all the rest of his account). The French translator follows

the Spanish, in which the lady "deseava saber quién era" (Marín Pina, 83; Sp., she wanted to learn who he was). Munday's mistaken use of "her" instead of "his" suggests that he misunderstood his sources, which might have led him to rewrite the text. Instead, Barley translates quite directly from the French text: "Faine would she haue vnderstood the whole processe of his historie" (Bb1v).

548 **whereof by thee he assured mee yester-day**. Cross-reference: chap. 27.

549 **I would willinglie bee there after the banquet, to guide mine eies to the place, where they might feede on the celestial and gracious countenance of your Mistresse**. The food-of-love motif was also employed in chapter 21, as Palmendos and Francelina had supper together in the garden. Palmendos's use of this same motif to express his counterfeit devotion to Iffida suggests a possible criticism on the artificiality of Neoplatonic language.

550 **that I would not be knowne to any what I am**. Though the "fair-unknown" motif is recurrent throughout the book, its use here is somewhat different. Rather than being the way to show personal prowess and worth, anonymity is now a cunning, practical means for Palmendos to carry out his design.

551 **the actions no way stretching to the dishonour of me and my Lady**. The page's care for his lady's honor underlines his loyalty; by focusing on him, Munday highlights his victimized position, thus complicating the view readers may get of Palmendos.

552 **taking his good sword vnder his arm**. The magic sword left by the three faeries in the castle of Carderia has the power of making people fall asleep. Cross-reference: chap. 22.

553 ***Iffida* who was prudent and well aduised, forbare to conferre longer with her newe solicitour, least her looue should be lightly espied by any**. Iffida is described in the same terms as Francelina, "discreete and well aduised" (S2v) and Philocrista—who behaved "wisely and discreetly as became a sober virgin" (O3v). No difference is made between Christian and non-Christian ladies who, up to this point, stick to the same social and moral standards.

554 **and how her eie was the messenger of her inward desire**. The motif of the eye as a gateway to the soul was largely employed in Renaissance love literature; it helped explain the way lovers exchanged their spirits (Wells, *The Secret Wound*, 50–51).

555 **Nowe is she come to the long desired place**. Vernassal offers a pathological description of Iffida's desire, as she has obsessive thoughts ("fantasie") about Palmendos (O3v). Her lack of restraint shows her vulnerable nature, which anticipates her tragic end. By omitting this reference, Munday presents a more discreet portrait of the lady.

556 ***Iffida* beeing not to learne her lesson, desires to know what Knights they were that so friendly saluted her**. Munday summarizes his sources adding a critical comment on Iffida's irresponsible attitude ("beeing not to learne her lesson"). He omits the fact that the page's mother regards Iiffida as her own daughter, which the Spanish mentions (Marín Pina, 84), and the French explains by

presenting the old lady as Iffida's wet nurse (Vernassal, O3[v]). Munday, however, inserts a warning against young women who secretly act against their family's wishes.

[557] **where *Iffida* cold digest no meat, her eies were so busied in beholding her Champion.** Munday omits Vernassal's detailed description of Iffida's contemplation of Palmendos (O3[v]). The Spanish text refers to Iffida's passionate love for Palmendos but does not explore its reasons: "tan bien le parescía, tanto que lo començó de amar muy afincadamente" (Marín Pina, 84; Sp., he looked so graceful that she began to love him intensely). Munday emulates the Spanish and ignores Vernassal's addition. The French tries hard to present Iffida as a victim of erotic melancholy, so that her excessive reaction to Palmendos's betrayal may be better assumed by the reader. Munday does not dwell on her sickly state, though.

[558] Iffida's behavior recalls Alderina's in chapter 2. Both ladies openly show their sexual desire and take the first step when addressing their beloveds. They speak freely, as they feel free and away from the social constraints of court. Although the outspoken lady had been a recurrent character in medieval romance literature, it might have looked troublesome to late sixteenth-century readers. That is why both Iffida and Alderina get into serious trouble, thus delivering a clear moral message to female readers.

[559] **I am a King borne, and Gouerner of sundry famous Prouinces, and this attempt proceeded onely of religious zeale, to make you Lady of mee and mine, as your woonderful fame at first tooke the soueraigntie of my heart.** Munday completely rewrites his sources (Vernassal, O4[r]; Marín Pina, 85). Palmendos does not commit himself to marrying Iffida, either in the Spanish or in the French, as he only promises to give her his lands. In the French, Palmendos also swears permanent amity, while letting the reader know about Palmendos's real intentions—to marry her to Ozalias and make them both king and queen of Tharsus. So, though Palmendos's speech in the French and Spanish is deliberately ambiguous, it cannot be deemed dishonest. Munday makes Palmendos lie to Iffida, as he promises "to make you Lady of mee and mine." He clearly commits perjury; the lack of references to the hero's real intentions complicates matters even further.

[560] **on the tearmes himselfe desired.** For the use of the reflexive pronoun "himself" for the third person pronoun "he" in subject position, see *OED*, *himself*, pron.3.a.

[561] "[Iffida] dit que son pere seroit tres aise de leur venu" (Vernassal, O4[v]); Fr., "[Iffida] said her father should be right glad of their comming" (Barley, Cc1[v]). This comment, a clear instance of dramatic irony, was added by Vernassal and translated literally by Barley. Munday omits it.

[562] ***Castilian.*** "chastelain" (Vernassal, O5[r]; Fr., lord of the castle); "padre" (Marín Pina, 86; Sp., father); Barley "lieutenant" (Cc2[r]).

[563] **thanking the heauens that had so well guided them thither.** Palmendos's success is presented as being sanctioned by God. By providing him with divine

support, Munday counterbalances the negative aspect of the hero's actions here and in the following chapter.

[564] **Now makes he prooue of his Swoord charmed by the Fairies.** Cross-reference: chap. 22.

[565] Munday completely rewrites his sources. In the French and Spanish, Palmendos does not use the magic sword to get rid of Iffida's father and his men, for he, with the help of Ozilio, manages to kill them all, without having to resort to magic (Vernassal, O5[v]–O6[r]; Marín Pina, 86–87). Barley translates almost literally from the French (Cc3[r–v]). Munday stresses the predestined status of the hero and tries to correct the inconsistencies in the Spanish and the French, in which Palmendos is given a magic sword in chapter 22 precisely to deliver the King of Thessaly; he omits any reference to Palmendos's reluctance to attack Iffida's father (Vernassal, O6[r]; Marín Pina, 87; Barley, Cc3[r–v]).

[566] **Thou cruell, false and disloyall Knight, seeing thou hast slaine my Father and his chiefest friendes, why doest thou not send me to beare them company?** Iffida is right when accusing Palmendos of disloyalty as he has not fulfilled his promise—"to make you Lady of me and mine" (chap. 27; X3[r]). Andreas Capellanus warns women against false lovers: "Women should therefore take great care not to bind themselves to lovers of this kind, because from such a love they will get no true joy, but will be exposed to innumerable troubles and infinite griefs. Therefore, when a woman is asked for her love, before she grants it she should make every effort to find out the character and the good faith of the man who is asking, so that there will be nothing she does not know about him" (*The Art of Courtly Love*, 161). In spite of her being a victim, she is held responsible for her disgrace as she has not been cautious enough about Palmendos's intentions.

[567] **If such as heretofore haue knowen me . . . friuolous and vain ostentation should so easily change my heart.** Bad faith or ill intention was a basic principle to define treason in medieval literature. Iffida pleads ignorance of Palmendos's stratagems to defend herself from accusations of disloyalty to her father. By blaming Fortune for her misery she adopts the role of a tragic heroine while exonerating Palmendos of his responsibility. If the previous chapters had offered a troublesome view of the hero's dealings, Munday tries now to dissociate his protagonist from any charge of treason. He offers instead a more humane portrait of Palmendos, one that his readers may sympathize with.

[568] **why did not I remember the sundry iniuries, his Maiesties brother sustained by the Emperour *Palmerin* of *Constantinople*, when he trauailed the world as a Knight errant?** Cross-reference: *Palmerin d'Oliva* II.41, 43. Palmerin and his men were attacked by Olimaell, the general of the Turkish fleet and, given their inferiority in number, decided to surrender and offer their service to him. Palmerin declared then that this decision was "sound dissimulation" as he expected that "Fortune will better teach vs the way to recouer our losse, and reuenge us on our enemies to their confusion" (490, lines 30–32). Later Palmerin helped Olimaell in his spoils of Christian towns so as to gain his and the Great

Turk's trust. Once at the Great Turk's court, he remained close to the ruler while devising the means to escape.

[569] **promising if she would depart thence with him, to sette the Crowne of *Tharsus* vppon her head, which he would giue to his Cozin *Ozalio*, and ioyne her in mariage with him if she pleased.** The Spanish author and Vernassal only refer to Palmendos's promise to make Iffida the Queen of Tharsus if she accepts to go with him (Vernassal, O6[v]; Marín Pina, 87). Neither of them mentions her possible marriage to Ozalio, as both texts have provided this information in the previous chapter. The fact that Munday omits this reference in chapter 27 and includes it here, once Palmendos's strategy is fully known, can affect the hero's characterization. In the English text, Palmendos's proposal sounds less cunning, the result of a rash decision, given the tragic climactic moment in which it is made.

[570] **The brother to our great Emperor the Turke, was cruelie murthered by the meanes of a woman.** Cross-reference: *Palmerin d'Oliva* II.43. At their arrival at the Turkish court, the Great Turk is soon attracted to beautiful Laureana, a Christian lady Olimaell has captured in one of his spoils. At the same time, Palmerin finds out that the Great Turk has married Agriola (his friend Trineus's wife) and so he commits himself to freeing her. Both ladies, together with Palmerin and the Duke of Pontus, plan a sexual encounter between Laureana and the Great Turk; when he comes into her room alone, the Duke kills him and cuts his head off. Palmerin, the Duke, and both women escape from the court straightaway. These references allow for certain parallels between Palmerin's and his son Palmendos's adventures at the Turk's court.

[571] **the warres which *Hesione* and *Helena* caused betweene the *Greekes* and *Troyans*.** In the first destruction of Troy, the Greeks captured Hesione, daughter to the Trojan King Laomedon. Hesione's brother Priam tried unsuccessfully to negotiate with the Greeks to bring her back to Troy. Priam then decided to send his younger sons Paris and Deiphobos with a huge fleet to attack Greece and recover Hesione, but instead, Paris took away Helen, wife to King Menelaus of Greece. Menelaus would then declare war on the Trojans (Guido delle Colonne, *Historia destructionis Troiae* (c. 1287), Books IV–VII, cited in Thompson, *The Trojan War*, 123–40).

[572] ***Lauinia* betweene *Aeneas* and *Turnus*.** Lavinia was the daughter of King Latinus. Though previously betrothed to Turnus, she married Aeneas, which made Turnus declare war on the Trojan prince. Turnus was defeated by Aeneas and died at his hands.

[573] ***Deianira* between *Hercules* and *Acheolus*, and afterward among the *Centaures*.** Deianira was loved by both Acheolus and Hercules, who fought for her. Hercules succeeded and married her. According to another legend, Centaur Nessus tried to rape Deianira, who was finally delivered by her husband. Nessus died in his fight against Heracles.

[574] **Afterward the mother and her daughter ran furiouslie on *Palmendos* . . . and therewith depriued the mother of her life.** Iffida's and her mother's

deeds recall those of the Lady at the Temple of Delphos in chapters 6 and 9, or Baledon's wife's in chapter 10. As both women refuse to accept the loss of their beloved men, they become melancholy and eventually go mad. Palmendos, as he had to put up with those women's violent mood, is shown in very positive light. He even caresses Iffida when in the French text he tries to appease her (Vernassal, $P1^{r}$). However, his paralysis suggests he is undergoing a process of mental collapse that can eventually drive him melancholy too. The squire plays here an important role, as he not only protects his lord from the violence of those women but saves him from his own melancholy fits as well.

575 **this greeuous spectacle**. Added by Munday. The translator insists on the dramatic appeal of the episode.

576 ***Iffida* extreamely raging at this greeuous spectacle . . . presentlie died without vsing anie more speeches**. Self-destructive actions were common symptoms of madness in sixteenth- and seventeenth-century literary works. Felix Plater explains in *A Golden Practice of Physick* (1662) that mentally diseased people "pull out their hairs, tear their cloaths and sometimes hurt their own body by biting," a conduct he describes as beastly and extremely threatening, for "they endeavor to scratch them (people trying to control them), bite, strangle and kill" (28). See also Marencida's reaction when kidnapped by Palmendos in chapter 29.

577 The poem is added by Vernassal. In the French, it consists of eleven quatrains with enclosed rhyme (Vernassal, $P1^{r-v}$). Barley's poem is a series of rhyming couplets; he paraphrases the French and introduces some slight differences ($Dd1^{r-v}$). Munday has six sestets all of which insert a final rhyming couplet. In his translation, he retains the general sense of Vernassal's text but completely rewrites it.

578 **tragedie**. Added by Munday. The translator employs this term in the episode on the Lady of the Temple at Delphos in chapter 6 ($F3^{r}$). See note 172.

579 Iffida's page commits suicide by the sword in the Roman manner, thus enhancing the tragic appeal of this episode. The Lady of the Temple at Delphos committed suicide in a similar way.

580 **This was the second act of the tragicall comedie begun at *Prissa*, and thus after continued in the Theater of *Albayzo***. Munday translates literally from Vernassal, who uses the term "tragicomedie" ($P2^{r}$). By the time Vernassal and Munday issued their respective translations, the term "tragicomedy" was not yet fully established. In general, these plays were characterized for their combination of high and low characters and their mixing comic and serious episodes. Marvin T. Herrick has noted other more specific features, such as "intricate plots," "improbable situations," "atmosphere of evil," "extravagant passions," and "highly emotional language" (*Tragicomedy*, 263). The use of the term here seems in accordance with Herrick's definition. The death of Iffida's servant also reveals the mixed nature of this passage in which a lower-class character can die a tragic death thus prompting the reader's admiration and pity. For a similar use, see also *Anthony Munday's Zelauto*, 65.

[581] ***Palmendos* beeing stricken in a dump by these accidents, stood a good while not able to speake a word.** Vernassal explains Palmendos's reaction as a sign of his remorse at what he had done (P2[r]). That would indicate that he was fully aware of his actions, which would complicate matters if he was going to be shown as a Christian hero. In doing away with this sentence, Munday avoids those problems.

[582] **be thou my gracious mediatour for my soule.** In the Spanish, the King of Thessaly commends his soul to the Virgin Mary, whom he considers an intercessor between him and God (Marín Pina, 88–9). Vernassal reconsiders this prayer which he addresses to Jesus Christ (P2[r]). Both English translators follow the French (Barley, Dd2[r]).

[583] **then remembring the former speeches of *Iffida*, he would not suffer any thing els to bee carried from the Castell.** Cross-reference: chap. 28 (Y2[r]).

[584] **and drawing his vertuous Sworde, charmed all that were in the Garden fast asleepe.** Palmendos was given his magic sword expressly to deliver the King of Thessaly, but it should not be employed for any other purposes. His use of magic to kidnap a lady and retain her as war booty is not heroic and can only be viewed in the context of war against the Turk. In private conversation, Juan Antonio Prieto Pablos has suggested that this could be interpreted as a way to prevent bloodshed.

[585] ***Ocurites* of *Culaquin*, whom *Palmendos* found neere the Gulfe of *Tanais* and *Meotides*.** Cross-reference: chap. 11. Tanais was an ancient Greek city located in the delta of the River Don. This delta reached Lake Maeotis in the northern part of the Azov Sea in southeastern Europe.

[586] **because the great Turke loued another of his concubines better then her.** This reference to the Great Turk's polygamy stresses his excessive desire and associates him with sexual practices largely condemned in early modern Europe, which could justify Palmendos's dubious dealings against him.

[587] **as fayre *Daphne* did with *Phaebus*, when *Iupiter* conuerted her into a Baye tree.** Nymph Daphne asked her father Jupiter to save her from Phoebus (Apollo), who wanted to rape her. She was then transformed into a bay tree.

[588] **I was greatly mooued to pittie your affliction . . . as when yee happened into my custodie.** Palmendos conceals his political and economic reasons and justifies his kidnapping of Marencida by pretending to be merciful to her. By presenting Palmendos's violent deeds as charitable acts to the weak, Munday explores the perverted use of chivalric discourse to justify military aggression. However, the hero's personal commitment to preserve the lady's chastity contrasts with the Great Turk's sexual harassment of Laureana and Agriola in *Palmerin d'Oliva* I.65; II.1–2, 41, 43. Palmendos's self-restraint underlines his manliness and moral principles.

[589] **Not vnlike *Ariadne* at the comming of *Bacchus*, when she was found forsaken by *Theseus* at the sea-side.** Ariadne helped Theseus kill the Minotaur and find his way out of the Labyrinth. Theseus had promised to marry her, but

once on the isle of Naxos he forsook her; she was then found by Bacchus, who eventually married her.

[590] ***Neptune* and *Thetis*.** Sea nymph Thetis was Achilles's mother. Neptune had been in love with her, but since he had been foretold that her son would become greater than his father, he rejected her, and she ended up marrying Peleus, a mortal.

[591] ***Tritons*.** Mythological creatures half human, half fish. They descended from Triton, the sea messenger.

[592] **to enioy this Lady as my Wife, to whom I know the destenies haue fatallie reserued mee.** Ozalio's willingness to marry Marencida even though she is already married recalls the Great Turk's marriage to Agriola in *Palmerin d'Oliva* II.2. While the Turk's attitude was then considered an act of violence against a prisoner, and she could only preserve her chastity thanks to divine intervention, providence seems to be now on Ozalio's side, thus sanctioning his desire for her. The Turkish lady then becomes an object of economic, political, and sexual exchange for Christian or proto-Christian heroes.

[593] **hoping while I liue to see no diuorce between vs . . . heereafter to dispose of her according to your desires.** Palmendos's disregard for Marencida's loyalty to her husband reveals his violent war-like attitude towards the people he has conquered. Marencida and Ozalio's marriage will finally occur in *Primaleon* I.3. In this chapter, Marencida is given the chance to say goodbye to her husband Ocurites, who at the news of his wife's future wedding, gives up eating and eventually dies. Ocurites's tragic end is there explained as God's punishment for his pride. His death ultimately justifies Marencida and Ozalio's marriage against any accusation of bigamy on her part.

[594] **affirming his Sister *Iffida* as onely cause thereof, and by what traynes she had beene beguiled, himselfe beeing altogether innocent of the treason.** Cross-reference: chap. 28 (Y2[r]).

[595] **which procured such hatred betweene the *Turkes* and the *Grecians* . . . and sacked many good Cities, Townes and Castels.** Munday refers to the conquest of the Byzantine Empire by the Ottomans in 1453, when Constantinople was taken by Mehmed II. The "fierce and proude Prince" probably refers to Suleiman I the Magnificent, who ruled the Ottoman Empire from 1520 to 1566 when it reached its economic, political, and military zenith and became a real threat to European rulers.

[596] Both the Spanish and the French authors describe the King of Thessaly's feelings and his unsuccessful attempts at learning about Palmendos's identity. The Spanish author also informs about his age when he was captured, eighteen to twenty years old, and so makes clear he is still "muy apuesto y muy sesudo" (Marín Pina, 93; Sp., very handsome and intelligent). Marencida, though sad at her state, also begins to appreciate Ozalio's service and shows some favor to him (Vernassal, Q1[r]; Marín Pina, 93). Munday omits these lines; he does not explore the psychological insight of these characters, for the sake of the narrative pace.

[597] **Pinnesse.** "A small sailing vessel" (s.v. *OED*, *pinnace*, n.1).

[598] **conferring with his Lordes about the enchaunted Birde, which that morning had deliuered manie pleasant notes, wherfore hee expected some comfortable newes.** See "Magic Bird" in *Motif-Index* (B172). Thanks to the sweet flowers and the magic bird he brought from the Castle of the Ten Rocks, Palmerin was able to cure Zephira's wounds in *Palmerin d'Oliva* II.51. In that chapter, the Persian wise man Muzabelino explained the prophetic abilities of that bird, which would remain with Palmerin up to his death. As Muzabelino said, "If any knight or Ladie shall enter your [Palmerin's] court, either with intent of treason, or bringing ill newes, the Birde shall giue such fearefull shrikes, as she did at the time when you [Palmerin] tooke her in the Arbour: but if the newes be of ioy, and for your good, then shall she sing more sweetly" (T1[r]). This prophetic bird will also appear in *Primaleon* I.11, II.27–29, III.52, and *Palmerin of England* II.64, thus becoming a recurrent motif in the cycle. For an analysis of this motif in the Spanish Palmerin cycle, see González, "El ave profeta de *Palmerín de Olivia* y *Primaleón*"; and Ciapparelli, "La relación intertextual entre *Las mil y una noches* y el *Palmerín de Olivia*," 35–38.

[599] **nowe care I not though Death presentlie doo his duetie.** Munday omits the classical reference present in the French: "vienne la mortelle Atropos quand bon luy semblera" (Vernassal, Q2[r]; Fr., "let mortal Atropos come now when he pleaseth [Barley, Ee3[r]]).

[600] **See heere my Lord your Daughter, of whom I was but newlie conceiued when you went from *Thessalie*.** Cross-reference: *Palmerin d'Oliva* II.41 (493, lines 11–12).

[601] **happie and fortunate may she iustly bee tearmed, in that her destenie hath deliuered you from prison, restored me my former ioy, and giuen her the most perfect Knight that euer bare Arms.** The King of Thessaly lists the three main deeds that had been prophesied by the three faeries in *Palmerin d'Oliva* II.41 (493, lines 24–25).

[602] **yet was I agreeued at your imprisonment . . . and I confesse worthy reprehension.** Cross-reference: *Palmerin d'Oliva* II.41, 43. In those chapters, Palmerin planned to befriend the Great Turk so as to gain his confidence and escape from the Turkish court. No reference to any evil-doing by Palmerin against the King of Thessaly has been found. However, the fact that he did not include him in the group that eventually managed to escape may explain Palmerin's remorse.

[603] **Seeing heauen hath so miraculously deliuered me.** The King of Thessaly's delivery does not result from Palmendos's heroic prowess but from his predestined nature.

[604] **all of them embracing the hardie Champion that went away with the honour of the Tourney.** Cross-reference: chap. 15.

[605] **If I see the King *Ocurites* my husband, the meeting will bee with meruailous hart breake on either side, beeing both of vs captiue to the very worst enemy we haue.** Cross-reference: *Primaleon* I.3. Munday omits Ozalio's

words of consolation to her. In general terms, the translator shows no interest in the love relationship between these two characters, and so he omits the passages about Ozalio's courtship. There will be no further reference to their being together up to *Primaleon* I.3.

[606] **The Emperour and his Lords kindly saluted her . . . saying nature might much better haue made her a man.** Marencida's silence and rude conduct reveals her melancholy state, which alienates her from any social codes. She shows contempt for her captors and actively refuses to submit to their power; Munday, however, regards that attitude as unnatural and perverted. The fact that neither Palmendos nor Ozalio has exerted any open sexual violence on her contributes to that idea. By insisting on the courteous behavior of those two men, Munday invites the reader to compare Marencida's opposition with Agriola's self-defense in *Palmerin d'Oliva* I.65. In that chapter, Agriola resisted the Turkish captain Olimaell's attempts to embrace her by exerting extreme violence, to the extent that she almost strangled her captor (333, lines 1–2).

[607] **and your sweete Freende.** Francelina.

[608] **wherefore she gaue her many thankes, shewing better countenaunce then before she did to any.** As in previous cases—see, for instance, the Queen of Macedon's intervention in Recinde and Belcar's judicial duel in chapter 25—female diplomacy proves more effective than male violence.

[609] **that the feminine choller which gouerneth your spyrite, maketh you vse such kinde of language, as is cleane exempt from all the rules of womanlie modestie.** Choler was an important feature of antisocial conduct in early modern literature, especially among certain women (Kromm, *The Art of Frenzy*, 64). Palmerin's reference to Marencida indirectly links her to such stereotypes as the unruly woman, thus prompting a negative response from his readers.

[610] **that the strength of earthlie Kinges and Pontentates is lesse then nothing, when God is bent repugnaunt against them, whereby we are all to resolue, that we can doo no good acte without his assistaunce.** Munday rewrites the sentence in the French source, altering somewhat its meaning: "ne pouoir faire aucun bon acte que selon sa volunté" (Vernassal, Q4v; Fr., "that we cannot doe any good act but according to his will" [Barley, Ff3r]).

[611] **if I slewe him, or euer thought to doo it . . . and Wife to the nowe famous Emperour *Trineus* of *Allemaigne*.** Cross-reference: *Palmerin d'Oliva* II.43. Munday follows Vernassal (Q4v) but adds the allusions to the lady who is daughter to the King of England and wife to Trineus, thus making it easier for his readers to identify her. In his literal translation of the French, Barley fails to make this reference clear (Ff3v).

[612] ***Hellespont*.** A strait between Thrace and Abydus in Asia Minor which connected the Aegean Sea to the Marmara Sea.

[613] **euen he that in *Hellespont* ouer-came the King *Ocurites* your Husbande.** Cross-reference: chap. 11.

[614] **as franctick-like shee coulde haue eaten her fleshe with anger.** This action was considered then a symptom of frenzy and wrath. In James Mabbe's *The Spanish Bawd* (London, 1631), Calisto uses a similar expression to refer to those ladies who consume "their bodies as their lives with envy, being ready to eat their own flesh for vey anger, still augmenting martyrdoms to themselves, thinking to equal that perfection by art which Nature had bestowed upon her (Melibea) without any labour" (*James Mabbe, The Spanish Bawd*, 164). Robert Burton suggests that it is an ungodly action, and associates it with man's deep melancholy after the fall: "How much altered from that he was, before, blessed and happy, now miserable and accursed; he must eat his meat in sorrow, subject to death and all manner of infirmities" (*The Anatomy of Melancholy*, 122).

[615] Vernassal describes the way people admired Palmendos's handsome demeanor and his resemblance to Palmerin (Q5^{v}). Barley translates this part literally (Ff4^{v}), but Munday disposes of this description and omits the reference to Palmendos's similarity to his father.

[616] **forsaking my Countrey by a strange occasion, so soone as I vnderstoode where my father remained.** Cross-reference: chap. 5.

[617] **To this he added the discourse of the olde woman, that appeared to him in the Pallace at *Tharsus*, and how she blamed him for his idle and slothfull life.** Cross-reference: chap. 5 (E1^{r-v}).

[618] **so now would I willingly receiue Christian Baptisme, which I faithfully promised for my good successe, when heauen made me able to deliuer this woorthy Princesse.** Cross-reference: chap. 20 (Q1^{r}).

[619] **and of the time he was in *Pasmeria*, where the Queene his mother came subtilly acquainted with him.** Cross-reference: *Palmerin d'Oliva* II.20.

[620] **remembring her dreame of the Queene of *Tharsus*, and what the Emperour himselfe had told her before and what the Emperour himselfe had told her before.** Cross-reference: *Palmerin d'Oliva* II.23 (419–20). In their first meeting after Palmerin's adultery with the Queen of Tharsus, Polinarda told her husband that she had had a vision in which he betrayed her with a queen; this queen acknowledged Palmerin's love for his wife but added too that he would "leaue some part of his loue with me" (420, lines 1–2). Palmerin confessed then that he had been given a magic drink by the Queen of Tharsus that had made him lose his senses (420, lines 11–14).

[621] **blasphemous.** Added by Munday.

[622] **but to morrow you shall receiue the holy character of Christianitie.** Neither of the English translators includes the reference to the mass which features in the Spanish and French (Vernassal, Q6^{r}; Marín Pina, 97).

[623] **of matters concerning the Ile *Delphos* and such like.** Cross-reference: chaps. 6–9.

[624] **in the Realme of *Pasmeria*, you begot me your Sonne . . . by a charmed drinke prouided for that purpose.** Cross-reference: *Palmerin d'Oliva* II.20 (403, lines 11–15; 405, lines 40–41).

[625] **yet did my mother giue mee a further testimonie hereof, hauing her selfe giuen you the like at your departure: but *Francelina* hath the same nowe in possession, for to her I tooke it after her deliuerance**. Cross-references: chaps. 5, 21.

[626] **him**. "Dieu" (Vernassal, R1v); "Dios" (Marín Pina, 96); "God" (Barley, Gg3r).

[627] **I sweare by all the diuine assistaunts about his tribunall, that neuer with my will and knowledge did I contaminate our wedlocke-bedde, much lesse haue I infringed the laws of mariage, or polluted the inuiolable faith I solemnely gaue yee**. Palmerin defends his innocence by arguing that he was not fully aware that he was committing adultery. His present argument recalls his words to Polinarda in *Palmerin d'Oliva* II.23: "I sweare to you Madame, by the religious vowes of our loue, that neuer did I commit such wrong against you: if the Queen of Tharsus of whome you haue spoken, did not one night deceiue me by an enchaunted drinke, which unwillingly I receiued as I sate at supper, causing me to loose both sence and understanding" (420, lines 10–14).

[628] **at the first time I beheld *Palmendos* I was perswaded what you haue tolde me, so liuely doth he resemble ye, in countenance and personage**. See "Recognition by resemblance" in *Motif-Index* (H20).

[629] **wherefore I not onely pardon ye, being ignoraunt of begetting such an excellent and perfect creature, but thanke heauen that you were the father to a Son so famous**. Polinarda had already forgiven Palmerin in their encounter after he had committed adultery with the Queen of Tharsus; she argued that Palmerin had indeed been deceived by the Queen (*Palmerin d'Oliva* II.23, 420, lines 15–18). Now she goes still further as she accepts Palmendos as God's blessing. The adultery itself is committed within a providential framework which exonerates the man from any moral condemnation, as it serves to perpetuate the hero's lineage.

[630] **Assure your selfe therefore my moste noble brother, that *Primaleon* is vowed to imitate your rare fortunes, and treading the selfe same steps you haue doone, to eternize the name of our renowmed father**. In introducing Primaleon's intentions to emulate his brother Palmendos's prowess, Munday indirectly alludes to his future book in the series, which deals with Palmerin's second son's adventures. *Primaleon* will be openly advertised in a brief section following this last chapter.

[631] This passage is more detailed in the French and Spanish, as they also refer to Ozalio's concern about Palmendos's baptism and his willingness to remain at Palmerin's court. In those sources, Ozalio foretells the Queen of Tharsus's eventual disappointment about her son's behavior (Vernassal, R2v; Marín Pina, 99). Barley includes a brief summary of this part (Hh1r), but Munday does away with it. In chapter 5, Palmendos had promised his mother to come back to his kingdom after meeting his father. By the end of the book it is clear he is not going to

keep his promise. By omitting this passage, Munday eliminates any trace of misconduct that might cast a shadow on the readers' perception of the hero.

[632] **the Church of S. *Sophie*.** Built under Emperor Justinian I in 527–565, it was the seat of the Byzantine Church up to 1453, when the Ottomans invaded Constantinople and turned it into a mosque. By setting Palmendos's baptism at St. Sophia's, Munday and the authors of his sources symbolically recover this space and provide it with the religious functions it enjoyed in the pre-Ottoman period. The hero's defeat of the Turk and subsequent baptism in this church allow for an optimistic view on contemporary European affairs, especially those regarding the Turkish menace.

[633] **religiously.** Added by Vernassal: "catholiquement" (R2[v]; Fr., "catholicklie" [Barley, Hh1[r]]).

[634] **and afterward affianced to *Francelina* by the reuerend Archbishop.** A betrothal had been considered a binding contract as from ancient times. In the English tradition, it was a solemn contract agreed on in the presence of witnesses and a clergyman, and it was sanctioned by the Church (Yalom, "Betrothal: Overview"). Palmendos and Francelina's betrothal follows this tradition, thus serving as if it were a real marriage. The wedding ceremony will take place in *Primaleon* I.12.

[635] ***Andromachye* was espoused to the valiant *Hector* of *Troy*.** Hector, the eldest son of King Priam of Troy, had traditionally been viewed as an emblem of courage and honor, and as such he featured on the list of the worthies in both medieval and Renaissance literature. His wife Andromache was considered a model of faithfulness (Brumble, *Classical Myths and Legends in the Middle Ages and Renaissance*, 151–52). Greek poetess Sappho describes in her poem 44 "The Wedding of Hector and Andromache," in which she portrays the newly married couple as god-like figures.

[636] ***Cleopatra* Queene of *Aegipt*, when shee contended in magnificence with *Marke Anthonie* the *Triumuirate* her husband.** Despite contemporary negative interpretations of Cleopatra and Antony's passionate relationship, Munday follows the medieval tradition of noble lovers which presented those two characters as emblems of faithful love. For a detailed study of this tradition, see Hamilton, "Anthony Munday and *The Merchant of Venice*," 245–47.

[637] **Phenix.** According to an ancient myth, the phoenix was a bird that lived long, burnt itself to ashes, and then was born again. It was often associated with renewal, and as such it became a symbol of Christ's resurrection first and then an allegory of perfect female love. In Elizabethan times, it was identified with the unique wonderful nature of the beloved (Brumble, *Classical Myths and Legends in the Middle Ages and the Renaissance*, 273–74). Munday employs it as a stock image to praise the ladies' exceptionality. He also describes Gridonia as "the only Phoenix of her time" in *Primaleon* I.21 (Z4[v]).

[638] Vernassal ends this chapter with a long paragraph to describe Arnedes's exasperation at the French ambassadors' delay; the French prince thus becomes

progressively melancholy, as he is unable to consummate his love for Philocrista. Munday omits this account entirely and provides an ending which is consistent with his narrative.

[639] **And during the time of this their honorable whole pleasure, heere thinke I good to pause a little, while you consider on the discourses passed, and I haue more leasure to perfect the rest of this Historie.** Added by Munday. He states his plan to bring the original story of *Primaleon* to an end, just as he introduces a pause so that his audience may read the book on Palmendos while he ends translating the following work in the series. Thus, he molds the reading habits of his audience accommodating them to the demands of serial literature.

[640] ***wherin (what you see wanting here) is perfectly finished, both* Palmendos *mariage,* Ozalios *loue to* Marencida, Rifaranoes *fortunes, and* Recinde *his returne to* Constantinople.** Palmendos and Ozalio's marriage to their respective beloveds occur in chapters 12 and 13; Rifarano's adventures after leaving the Countess of Island are narrated in chapters 4–5, while Recinde's return to Constantinople takes place in chapter 8.

[641] ***now* Primaleon *beginneth his chiualrie*.** Primaleon is knighted in chapter 9. His adventures start at this point.

[642] ***Prince* Edward *of* England.** Eldest son of Frederick King of England and great rival to Primaleon for the love of Gridonia. He first appears in the book in chapter 18.

[643] ***my book of* Palmerin *of* England.** Though the earliest known edition of *Palmerin of England* dates from 1596, there must have been a previous edition printed before 1588 as can be inferred from Munday's words to his readers. At the beginning of the 1637 edition of *Palmerin d'Oliva* he explains the order of composition of both works: "When I finished my second Part of *Palmerin of England*, I promised this worke of *Palmerin D'Oliua*, because it depended so especially on the other" (A4^r). In his address to the reader at the end of the 1616 edition of *Palmerin of England* he concludes: "Thus Gentlemen, I haue finished the second part of this most famous History . . . As for the *History of Palmerin d'Oliue*, which containeth three seueral parts, and should have bin translated before this . . . you shall haue them very speedily."

[644] ***the first booke of* Amadis *of* Fraunce.** *The First Book of Amadis of Gaule* was first published in 1590. Munday had not yet fixed its title when *Palmendos* was published one year earlier.

[645] ***Honos alit Artes*.** A Ciceronian *motto* which Tracey Hill translates as "Honour comes from art" (*Anthony Munday and Civic Culture*, 49). According to Jack Stillinger, Cicero used it as a "lawful excuse for lack of skill," a conventional way for authors to show a false humility (*Anthony Munday's Zelauto*, 189). Hill observes that this motto usually appears in Munday's self-authored works—six times in his *Zelauto* alone—while he normally uses "*Patere aut abstine*" for his translations (49). The case of *Palmendos* is quite exceptional as both *mottoes* appear at the beginning and end of the book respectively.

Textual Apparatus

Editorial Policy

This edition takes as its copy-text the first edition of Anthony Munday's *The Honorable, Pleasant and Rare Conceited History of Palmendos*, printed in 1589 by John Charlewood to be sold by Simon Waterson. There are three remaining copies of this first edition, which are kept at the Huntington Library (62667), the Bodleian (Vet. A1 e.110), and the British Library (C.56.d.10), respectively. Only the Huntington Library copy is complete; the one at the British Library has leaves 84–92 mutilated, and the Bodleian copy lacks the title page, the dedication, and the letter to the reader. The transcription has therefore been made using the Huntington text as a base, and then collating it with the text of the other two issues; all substantive and accidental variants have been recorded. This transcription has also been collated with two subsequent editions of *Palmendos*, published by Elizabeth Alsop in 1653 and by Thomas Fawcet in 1663. Copies of those two editions, kept at the Huntington Library (147050; 147051) and the British Library (12410.bb.6; C.116.b.8) have been examined, together with various EEBO facsimiles. The 1653 text is complete, but that of the 1663 Huntington copy is cropped at foot, so some signatures and catchwords are not perceptible, while in the 1653 British Library copy, leaf A1 is missing. In the historical collation, misprints in the 1589 text have been emended, and substantive variants from the first edition have been annotated. Accidentals, syntactic mistakes, and typographical errors in the seventeenth-century copies have not been recorded.

Spelling

This is an original-spelling edition that aims at being as close to the conjectural original manuscript as possible.[1] For emendations of evident mistakes in the first edition (identified as P1), the second and third editions (identified as P2 and P3) have been consulted. If they correct the error in the 1589 text, the emendation has been incorporated and recorded on the list of emendations. In each of these records, the correct reading appears in

[1] In this sense it complies with many of the editorial principles set out by Fredson Bowers, Ronald B. McKerrow, W. W. Greg, and Thomas Tanselle.

the lemma, within square brackets, followed by the original mistake in the first edition (P1). No reference to any other edition in the record indicates its reading coincides with the lemma. When a mistake is not emended in P2 or P3, the error has been corrected in the present edition. When the emendation is editorial, it is indicated as ED. Other emendations that may be regarded as printing mistakes—that is spacing problems (splitting letters within just one word)—have not been recorded.

Typography

The body of the text is written in black letter in the three extant copies of the first edition, proper names feature in roman type, and placenames are written in italic. The use of typefaces also alternates in the poems and epistles inserted throughout the text. For instance, poems appear in italic, while the four epistles in the text follow the same pattern: italics are used in the introductions and subscriptions; roman is used in the directions, and black letter is employed in the body of the text. Chapter titles feature italics except for proper names, which are printed in roman. Black letter has not been employed in this edition, which has made use of the other two fonts necessary: roman for the body of the text (originally printed in black letter) and italic for proper nouns and placenames.

	1589 edition	**This edition**
Body of the text	Black letter	Roman
Chapter titles (CT)	Italic	Italic
Proper names in the text	Roman	Italic
Proper names in CT	Roman	Roman
Placenames in the text	Italic	Italic
Placenames in CT	Italic	Italic
Poems	Italic	Italic
Epistles (body)	Black letter	Roman
Introduction to epistles	Italic	Italic
Directions in epistles	Roman	Italic
Subscriptions in epistles	Italic	Italic
Munday's final address to readers	Roman	Italic

Other silent changes involve ligatures, abbreviations, and accents. Ligatures such as the aesch (æ), ethel (oe), oo, and ėe have been normalized as "ae," "oe," "oo," and "ee." while the ampersand has been retained only when followed by c. (&c.). The abbreviations qo, y^{e}, and w have been expanded as "quoth," "the," and "with," and suspensions, indicated with a straight macron over a vowel (ō, ē), have been replaced by the same vowel followed by "m" or "n." Chapter numbers abbreviated in the 1589 text have also been expanded—that is, "CHAP. I." as "CHAPTER I."). Other silent changes apply to the long (ſ) and short (s)—the long one has been normalized as short in the text—and to the hyphen in "satiſ-fied," "tranſ-ferred," "miſ-fortune," "diſ-figured" and "succeſ-full." Such hyphen was employed to distinguish between the long ſ and the f in their original spellings. The silent change applied to the long (ſ) clarifies any possible confusion with the spelling and so the hyphen is no longer necessary and has been removed in the spelling of these words in the text ("satisfied," "transferred," "misfortune," "disfigured," and "succesfull"). No further silent changes have been considered.

As a general rule, features added by the printer for decorative reasons, such as the width of typefaces, the symbols of fleurons and asterisks, and head ornaments have been preserved in the transcription of the title page but are not retained in any other parts of the text. Ornamental initials introducing the chapters and the four different epistles have been replaced by plain versals; this printing convention has been partly kept, since it is currently used today. Though the letters following the versals in the original text are always capitalized, they are lower case in this edition, in accordance with contemporary printing practice.

Punctuation

The original punctuation has been kept as long as it is not confusing or misleading. Otherwise the second edition text has been followed, or common sense has just been applied. Changes in this regard have been properly recorded. Evident mistakes such as a comma at the end of a sentence or a parenthesis missing in parenthetical phrases have been corrected and annotated.

Pagination, Chapter, and Paragraph Division

Leaf signatures in the copy-text are given within square brackets throughout this edition. All of them, also those which are signed in black letter in the original, appear in roman type, while typographical errors have been silently emended. Though page division is editorial, both chapter and paragraph divisions present in the 1589 original have been preserved.

Bibliographical Descriptions

1. The First Edition (1589)

TITLE PAGE: [159 × 94 mm; enclosing 120 × 55 mm; within a double rule of lace pattern; fleuron border (Plomer 1924, nos. 19, 86); within a double rule of lace pattern] THE | Honorable, pleaſant | and rare conceited Hiſtorie | of Palmendos. | * | *Sonne to the famous and fortu-| nate Prince Palmerin d'Oliua, Em- | perour of Conſtantinople and the | Queene of Tharſus.* | (·.·) | Tranſlated out of French by *A* [swash]. | *M* [swash]. one of the Meſſengers of | her Maieſties Cham- | ber. | *P* [swash] *atere aut abſtine.* | AT LONDON | * Printed by I. C. for Simon | Waterſonne, & are to be ſold in | Church-yarde at the ſigne of | the Crowne. | *A* [swash] *nno. Domini.* | *1589.*[1]

HEAD TITLE: The hiſtory of *P* [swash it.] *almendos*, ſonne to | the famous Palmerin d' Oliua, Emperour of | Conſtantinople, and the Queene | of Tharſus. | Diſcourſing likewiſe of the Prince Rifarano, Sonne | to Tryneus Emperour of Allemaigne, & Aurecinda, | Siſter to the Soldane of Perſia: theyr Knightly deedes | of Chiualrie, famous aduentures, and | woorthy reſolutions.

RUNNING TITLE: The hiſtory of *P* [swash it.] *almendos.*

[1] There is a slight variant in the title pages of the Huntington and British Library copies of the first edition (the title page of the Bodleian copy is missing). The Huntington copy informs the book can be bought "at the signe of the Crowne" while in the British Library copy such place appears "at the signe of the Crown." In 124 out of the 226 records in the Early English Books Online database of books sold by Watersonne during his career as a professional bookseller (1583–1635), such reference appears as "at the signe of the Crowne" (see STC 37, 1831, 1953–55.5, 3116, 3438, 4523–24, 5756, 6238, 6343.2, 6343.4–5, 6343.8, 6252, 6265, 6302–3, 6646.2, 6889, 7077, 7210, 10857.7, 11075, 11187, 11817, 13226, 13398, 13422, 13429, 13479, 13776, 13783, 13873, 13899, 14023, 14035, 14357, 14734–35, 14738, 14812.a, 17216, 17257, 17615, 17641, 17986, 19011–13, 19088, 19088.7, 19091, 19105.5–19107, 19296, 19383–88.a, 19648–49, 19669–71.5, 19673–75, 19690–91, 19705.4–19706, 19688, 19699, 19725, 19728–29, 19737–38, 19745, 19750–51, 19757.5, 19761.3, 19764, 20010–11, 20025, 20027, 20144, 20773, 21128, 21716–17.5, 21734–37, 22839.3, 23101, 23123, 23135, 23137, 24036, 24947.7, 24947–48, 24952, 25176, 25280, 25673, 25676, 25704, 25759, 25797). No record refers to his shop "at the signe of the Crown." For this reason, the variant state selected for the description of the title page in the ideal copy has been that of the volume in the Huntington library.

COLLATION: 4°: π^{2} A–Cc^{4} [$4 (–B4, R4, T4, Aa4) signed], X4 misprinted as 4, Cc4 missing; [2] 99 leaves, ff. [1] 2–99.[1]

CONTENTS: $\pi 1^{r}$: title page (verso blank); $\pi 2^{r}$: [a section of a fleuron border (Plomer 1924, nos. 19, 86), 78 × 25 mm] "Fortiſsimo, et militiæ naualis Peritiſ- | ſimo viro, Domino Franciſco Draco | Equiti Aurato." ital. with five-line initial 20 × 20 mm; dedication ending: "Antonius Mondaius." $\pi 2^{v}$: "To the courteous | Reader." rom. with eight-line initial; letter ending: "Thine in all courtesie. | *Anthony Monday*." A1^{r}–Cc3^{r}: HT and text; Cc3^{v}: announcement (roman with two-line initial 6 × 5 mm); announcement ending: "*Yours to his poore power*: | Anthony Monday. | Honos alit Artes."

CATCHWORD VARIANTS: D4^{v} abroade [abrode] E1^{r} now [nowe] E3^{r} chance. [chaunce.] G3^{v} daunger [danger] G4^{r} ware, [ware] H2^{r} me, [me.] I1^{r} Belcar, [Belcar.] L3^{v} youthful [youthfull] M4^{v} wyth [with] N2^{r} returne [return] Q2^{r} behol- [the beholders] S4^{v} Hee [He] T3^{r} search [searche] U2^{r} there [there,] Y2^{v} *Dead* [D*Ead*] Bb1^{r} (tribu-) lation, [lation:] Bb2^{r} she [shee] Cc1^{r} affianced [affiaunced] Cc2^{v} Heere [Here] Cc3^{r} Next [NExt]

TYPOGRAPHY: 36 ll., 147 (159) × 85 mm (A2^{r} in 1Bod.); text, black letter (and some roman and italic) 82 mm for 20 ll.; "To the courteous Reader." ($\pi 2^{v}$) and announcement (Cc3^{v}), roman 46 mm for 10 ll.;[2] verse, italic 41 mm for 10 ll. (P2^{r}).[3]

COPIES EXAMINED: Henry E. Huntington Library (62667): complete copy, designated P1H in the critical apparatus; British Library (C.56.d.10): leaves 84–92 are mutilated, designated P1BL in the critical apparatus; Bodleian (Vet. A1 e.110): wanting all before A1 and M4; title page missing, designated P1Bod in the critical apparatus.

STC:18064.

NOTE: Signature markers appear in black letter type except for A4, F4, P2, Q1, S3, Bb4, which are printed in roman. Large white initials in roman type introduce all chapters in the book. They are 5 lines deep and are framed by highly elaborate motifs. They also appear at the beginning of the dedications

[1] Leaf 98 is erroneously numbered as 99 in the Huntington copy.

[2] Larger sizes of the roman type are used in the title page, the directions in the epistles (E4^{r}, Q1^{v}), and in the dedication to Sir Francis Drake ($\pi 2^{r}$). Roman type is also used for proper names.

[3] Chapter titles, toponyms, and subscriptions in the epistles (E4^{v}, I3^{v}, Q2^{r}) also feature this type. Larger sizes of italic are used in the title page and introductions to the epistles.

to Sir Francis Drake and to the Reader. A framed minor white initial 5 lines deep, also in white roman print, introduces the second paragraph in chapter 1 (A1^{v}). Finally, at the beginning of the first paragraph in the epistles appear three smaller initials respectively. The one introducing the epistle in I1^{r} is an outline letter K in arabesque design, 6 lines deep. Those at the start of the epistles in E4^{r} and Q1^{v} are factotums, 4.5 lines deep. In both of them initials (I and E, respectively) are in black letter print. A printer's flower is employed to introduce the three different epistles in the text (E4^{r}, I3^{r}, and Q1^{v}). A part of a bold fleuron border (12 × 84 mm) appears across the top of I3^{r} as well.

2. *The Second Edition (1653)*

TITLE-PAGE: The famous Hiſtory of | PALMENDOS | SON to the moſt Renowned | Palmerin D' Oliva, | EMPEROUR of | CONSTANTINOPLE, | And the Heroick Queen of | THARSUS. | Wherein is likewiſe | A moſt pleaſant Diſcourſe of Prince *Rifarano*, the Son | of *Trineus* Emperour of *Almain*, and *Aurecinda*, Siſter to the | Soldane of *Perſia*. | With their Knightly Deeds, and Acts of Chivalry ; Their | Famous Adventures, and moſt Worthy Reſolutions. Newly | Corrected and Amended, and moſt Profitable and De- | lightfull for all ſorts of People. | [single rule] | type-orn., 9 × 24 mm | [single rule] | *LONDON* : Printed by *E. Alſop*, and are to be ſold at | her houſe in Grubſtreet, near the Upper Pump. | 1653.

HEAD TITLE: [*type orn.*] THE | HISTORY | OF | PALMENDOS: | Son to the famous *Palmerin d' Oliva*, Emperour | of Conſtantinople, and the Queen of Tharſus. Diſcour- | ſing likewiſe of the Prince *Rifarano*, ſon to *Trineus* | Emperour of Almain, and *Aurecinda* ſiſter to | the Soldan of Perſia; their Knightly deeds of | Chivalry, famous Adventures, and worthy | RESOLUTIONS.

RUNNING TITLE: [*rule*] The Hiſtory of *Palmendos*. [*Palmendos*^ BCDEFGHIKLMNOPQRSTVXYZ4^{r}AaBb^{r}] [*rule*]

COLLATION: 4°: A–Bb^{4} [$3 (–A2, S3, Z3, Aa3) signed], F3 misprinted as G3; [*4*] 96 leaves, pp. 1–192 (misnumbering 123 as 321, 162–163 as 166–167, 166–167 as 170–171, 170–171 as 174–175, 174–175 as 178–179).

CONTENTS: A1^{r} (blank except for signature A at the center of a rectangular frame made of type-orns., 31 × 95 mm) (verso blank); A2^{r}: title page (verso blank); A3^{r} [row of type-orns. with floral motifs, 24 × 87 mm] "The Epiſtle to the Reader." rom. with three-line initial 18 × 19 mm; A4^{v}: letter ending: "Thine &c. | *AM.*"; B1^{r} [row of type orns. with floral motifs quite similar to those in A3^{r}, 6 × 88 mm] HT and text; Bb4^{v}: [single rule] "FINIS." [single rule].

CATCHWORD VARIANTS: B4^{r} Chap. 2. [CHAP. II.] D2^{v} (Sa-) gittary, [gittary.] D4^{v} Chap. 4. [CHAP. IIII] E2^{v} (ho-) micide [micide,] E3^{v} Chap. 5. [CHAP. V.] F4^{r} Chap. 6. [CHAP. VI] F4^{v} (de-) fended [defended] G1^{r} (re-) fuſal [fuſall,] G4^{v} child [child.] H2^{r} Chap. 8. [CHAP. VIII.] I1^{v} hereafter [ter] I3^{v} (il-) luſion [luſion,] I4^{r} Chap. 10. [CHAP. X.] I4^{v} Princesse [Princesse:] K1^{r} (for-) most [most,] K3^{r} to [be] K3^{v} (Af-) terwards [terward] K4^{r} shal [shall] M3^{r} (e-) quivalent [quivalent;] N2^{r} Chap. 15. [CHAP. XV.] P1^{r} Chap. 18. [CHAP. XVIII.] P4^{r} They [Then] P4^{v} Chap. 19. [CHAP. XIX] Q3^{r} bridge, [Bridge,] R1^{v} Chap.21. [CHAP. XXI.] S4^{v} Chap. 24. [CHAP. XXIIII.] T3^{r} Chap. 25. [CHAP. XXI.] U2^{r} Chap. 26. [CHAP. XXVI.] U4^{r} (friendli-) neſſe [neſſ] X1^{r} Chap. 26. [CHAP. XXIIII.] X3^{v} Now [be Now] Y1^{r} helmets [Helmets,] Y1^{v} Chap. 28. [CHAP. XXVIII.] Y3^{v} woman, [woman] Y4^{r} Deap [DEad] Z2^{r} journying [journeying] Aa1^{v} Chap. 30. [CHAP. XXX.] Bb1^{v} (Coun-) treys, [treys:]

TYPOGRAPHY: 36 ll., 145 (162 to top rule of headline) × 88 mm (C3^{v} in P2H); text, black letter (and some roman and italic) 82 mm for 20 ll. (C3^{v} in P2H); "Epistle to the Reader," rom. 143 mm for 20 ll. (A4^{r} in P2H); verse, rom. 40 mm for 10 ll. (G2^{r} in P2H).[1]

COPIES EXAMINED: Henry E. Huntington Library (147050): complete copy (designated P2H above); British Library (12410.bb.6): A1 missing (designated P2BL).

Other copies in: Cambridge University Christ's College, Oxford University Bodleian Library, Oxford University Worcester College Library, University of California, William Andrews Clark Memorial Library.

ENGLISH SHORT TITLE CATALOGUE: Wing (CD-Rom, 1996): F377.

NOTE: Signature markers appear in black letter type. Ten three-line deep white initials in roman introduce fifteen chapters in the book. They are framed by simple motifs. A three-line deep white initial also appears at the beginning of the "Epistle to the Reader." Four seven-line deep white initials introduce thirteen chapters. These larger initials are framed by more elaborate motifs. A six-line deep white initial introduces chapter 16, while the same six-line

[1] Italic is used in the chapter titles, while toponyms, proper names, and the introductions and subscriptions in the epistles feature roman type. Toponyms and proper names only feature italics when they appear in chapter titles and epistle introductions and subscriptions.

deep factotums introduce chapters 3 and 19. A three-line deep black initial with no frame introduces one of the epistles (K2^{r}). A double row of acorns (Plomer 1924, no. 67) with fleuron in between appears across the top of A3^{r} 24 × 87 mm; a row of acorns (Plomer 1924, no. 67) appears across the top of B1^{r}6 × 88 mm.

3. The Third Edition (1663)

TITLE-PAGE: The famous Hiſtory| OF | PALMENDOS | SON to the moſt Renowned | Palmerin D'Oliva, | EMPEROUR of | CONSTANTINOPLE, | And the Heroick Queen of | THARSUS. | Wherein is likewiſe | A moſt pleaſant Diſcourſe of Prince *Rifarano*, the Son of | *Trineus* Emperour of *Almain*, and *Aurecinda*, Siſter to the | Soldane of *Perſia.* | With their Knightly Deeds and Acts of Chivalry ; Their | Famous Adventures, and moſt Worthy Reſolutions. | Newly Corrected and Amended, and moſt profitable and | Delightfull for all ſorts of People. | [single rule] | type-orn., 15 × 23 mm | [single rule] | LONDON, | Printed by T. FAVVCET, and are to be ſold by *Fr. Coles* at | the ſigne of the Lambe in the Old Baily, 1663.

HEAD TITLE: THE | HISTORY | OF | PALMENDOS: | Son to the famous *Palmarin d'Oliva*, Emperour | of Conſtantinople, and the Queen of Tharſus, Diſcourſing | likewiſe of the Prince *Rifarano*, Son to *Trineus* Em- | perour of Almain, and *Aurecinda* ſiſter to the | Soldan of Perſia, &c.

RUNNING TITLE: [*rule*] The famous Hiſtory of *Palmendos*. [*rule*] | [Blank A4^{r}; *Palmeodos* B1^{v}, B2^{v}; *Palmendos*^ I1^{r}, I4^{r}, K1^{r}, K2^{r}, L1^{r}, L3^{v}, M1^{r}, M3^{v}, N1^{r}, N3^{v}, O3, P3, Q3; *H*iſtory R3^{r}, R4^{r}; The Hiſtory I1^{v}, I2–I3, I4^{v}, K1^{v}, K2^{v}, K3–K4, L1^{v}, L2, L3^{r}, L4, M2, M3^{r}, M4, N1^{v}, N2, N3^{r}, N4, O1–O2, O4, P1–P2, P4–Q2, Q4–R2, S1–S2, S3^{r}, S3^{v}, S4–Z3; *Palmendas*. S3^{v}].

COLLATION: 4°: A–Z^{4} [$3 (–A1, A2, I3, K3, L3, M3, N3, O3, P3, Q3, R3, S3, T3, V3, X3, Y3, Z3) signed]; [3] 88 [1] leaves, pp. [1] 2–175 [176] (misnumbering 12–13 as 20–21, 16–17 as 24–25, 27 as 31, 28–58 as 32–62, 123 as 119, 124–176 as 120–172).

CONTENTS: A1^{r}: "The Famous History | of | PALMENDOS" [woodcut featuring a knight on his horse; hand-written on the top left corner, "Bellcar"; row of type-orns. with floral motifs, 4 × 84 mm] (verso blank); A2^{r}: title page (verso blank); A3^{r} [double rule; a fleur-de-lys with flowers and fruit 25 × 83 mm] "*The Epiſtle to the Reader.*" rom. with four-line deep initial 20 × 19 mm; A3^{v}: letter ending: "Thine, &c. | *A* [swash] . *M* [swash] ."; A4^{r}–Z3^{v} [double rule] HT [single rule] and text; Z3^{v}: "*FINIS*."; Z4^{r}: "You may have theſe *Hiſtories* with this *Hiſtory* at | the Lamb in the Old-Baily. All theſe in Quarto." rom. (and some italic) with two-line deep initial 7 × 7 mm; Z4^{v}: "PALMENDOS" | woodcut featuring a Knight on his horse.

CATCHWORD VARIANTS:[1] A3^{r} ima- [imagine] B1^{r} chant- [chantment] B2^{r} Gent- [Gentleman] D3^{v} Terendos, [Tirendos,] F2^{r} Pro- [Province] G2^{v} people, as [as] G3^{r} (con-) quer: [quer;] G4^{v} Palmendos [in] I1^{v} *The* [*The*] L1^{r} them [themselves] M2^{r} Coun- [Conntrey] M3^{r} Chap. [CHAP.] N1^{r} Chap. [CHAP.] N4^{v} be [be,] O2^{r} (paſ-) ſions [ſions,] P1^{r} attempt [attempt,] R3^{v} Chap. 25 [CHAP. XXV] T1^{r} Chap. 27 [CHAP. XXVII] V3^{v} Dead [DEad] X1^{r} Chap. 29. [CHAP. XXIX.] Y1^{r} Chap. 30: [CHAP. XXX.]

TYPOGRAPHY AND PLATE: 37 ll., 154 (164 to top rule of head line) × 95 mm (B4^{r} in P3BL.); text, black letter (and some roman and italic) 82 mm for 20 ll. (Q1^{r} in P3BL); "*The Epiſtle to the Reader*," rom. 95 mm for 20 ll. (A3^{v} in P3BL); verse, rom. 41 mm for 10 ll. (F3^{r}).[2] The plate featuring a chivalric knight on a horse in A1^{r} measures 108 × 84 mm The plate featuring the name of "PALMENDOS" above a chivalric knight on a white horse in Z4^{v} measures 132 × 112 mm.

COPIES EXAMINED: Henry E. Huntington Library (147051): A1 missing; cropped at foot, affecting many catchwords and signatures; British Library (C.116.b.8.): complete copy (designated P3BL above). Other copies in: Newberry Library.

ENGLISH SHORT TITLE CATALOGUE: Wing (CD-Rom, 1996), F378.

NOTE: Signature markers appear in black letter type. Most initials are five to six-line deep white initials in roman framed by simple motifs. Larger (seven to eight-line deep) white initials in more elaborate frames introduce chapters 1, 3, 7, and 29. Four-line deep initials in simple frames introduce the epistle to the reader and chapters 24 and 30. A six-line deep black framed initial introduces chapter 9 and two-line deep initials in black letter font introduce the epistles in F1^{r} and I2^{r}. Two four-line and five-line deep factotums appear at the beginning of chapters 6 and 13.

[1] The Huntington copy has been cropped, and many catchwords have been impossible to identify, as those in A3^{r}, B1^{r}, B2^{r}, B3^{r}, B4^{v}, C1^{r}, C3^{r}, C4^{r}, D1^{r}, D2^{r}, D4^{r}, E1^{r}, E2^{r}, E4^{r}, F1^{r}, F2^{r}, F3^{r}, F4^{r}, G1^{v}, G4^{r}, H1^{r}, I1^{r}, L1^{r}, L3^{r}, M2^{r}, R2^{r}, S1^{r}, S4^{r}, S4^{v}, T3^{r}, U1^{v}, Y4^{v}.

[2] Italic is used in the chapter titles while toponyms, proper names, and the introductions and subscriptions in the epistles feature roman type. Proper names and toponyms feature italics only when they appear in chapter titles and in the epistle introductions and subscriptions.

Word Division

I have followed the copy-text when keeping the word division and all hyphenated words within the line. Corrections on words running together or separated in a clearly wrong way have been recorded. For line-end hyphenated compounds, I have retained end-line hyphenation in only two cases: (1) when the two words in the compound appear separated in the *OED* (vpper-hand) and (2) when the word is hyphenated in the *OED* (selfe-willed).

Line-End Hyphenation

Copy-Text List	**Critical Edition List**
Afore-saide	Aforesaide
Cup-boorde	Cupboorde
Euer-more	Euermore
Gentle-man/Gentle-men	Gentleman/Gentlemen
Heere-after	Heereafter
Heer-uppon/ Heere-uppon/ Heere-upon	Heeruppon/ Heereuppon/ Heere-upon
Heere-with	Heerewith
Hence-foorth	Hencefoorth
Here-in	Herein
Her-selfe	Herselfe
Him-selfe	Himselfe
Hither-to	Hitherto
In-to	Into
Mani-fold	Manifold
No-thing	Nothing
Satis-fie	Satisfie
Selfe-willed	Selfe-willed
Som-what/ some-what	Somwhat/ somewhat
Them-selues	Themselues
There-at	Thereat
There-of	Thereof
Ther-fore	Therfore
Vpper-hand	Vpper-hand
Vtter-most	Vttermost
Watch-word	Watchword
Wel-come	Welcome
Wher-at	Wherat
Where-fore	Wherefore
Wher-in	Wherein
Wher-of	Wherof
Wher-to	Wherto
Wher-with	Wherwith
With-out	Without

Figure 1. "Bellcar." Woodcut in Anthony Munday, *The Famous History of Palmendos* (1663), sig. A1r. British Library C.116.b.8. (© The British Library Board.)

Figure 2. "PALMENDOS." Woodcut in Anthony Munday, *The Famous History of Palmendos* (1663), sig. Z4v. British Library C.116.b.8. (© The British Library Board.)

Glossary

THE PRESENT GLOSSARY LISTS all words and expressions that may be difficult to a modern reader. They are: (1) words whose spelling may present some difficulty to readers; (2) archaic, old-fashioned, or obsolete terms; (3) words whose meaning has changed since the sixteenth century. The items are listed in the left-hand column; their spelling, definitions, and leaf signatures are provided in the right-hand column. When there are more than three instances of one and the same term, only the first one (followed by "etc.") is given in the parentheses. All definitions come from the *OED*.

This glossary also aims at illustrating Munday's original, modern vocabulary, as can be appreciated from a series of neologisms and quasi-neologisms here identified by means of various symbols. An asterisk (*) means that a word, or the specific use of a word, predates the first entry in the *OED*. Those neologisms that have not been found in the *OED* are also identified with an asterisk and are defined in accordance with their occurrence in the text. Words whose first entry in the *OED* dates back to 1589 have been marked with a bullet (•). Terms whose first entry in the *OED* dates back to the period 1579–1588 have been identified with two bullets (••). The words whose significance has not changed since the sixteenth century are not provided with a definition. All these items, divided into four different groups, are listed in the table below.

A	
Abate *v.*	1. To put an end to (L2ʳ) 4.a. To lessen or reduce in force or intensity; to moderate (L2ʳ)
Abide *v.*	1.b. To await, remain waiting for; to lie in wait for (U1ᵛ, Aa3ᵛ) 8. To remain, to stay (B1ʳ, C2ʳ, I1ʳ, T2ʳ, Aa1ʳ) 9. To stay habitually in a place; to remain in residence; to reside, dwell (P2ʳ, P3ʳ, T1ʳ)
Abrode *adv.*	Abroad (E1ʳ)

Accessable *adj.**	Accessible (C2^{v}, H2^{v}, R3^{v})
Accident *n.*	5.b. An occurrence, incident, event (E4^{v}, etc.)
Accoustred *adj.*	Accoutred (H2^{v}, I3^{r})
Addicted *adj.*	1.d. Committed (P3^{r})
Aduenture *v.*	Adventure 1.b. To risk oneself, to venture (N3^{r}, P1^{r}, Q3^{r}, S1^{v}, U2^{v}, X1^{r}) 3. To try, attempt to do (something); to undertake (a thing of doubtful outcome); to try (one's luck); to venture, risk, chance (B1^{r}, D2^{r}, K3^{v})
Aduertise *v.*	Advertise. 1. To notify, warn (C4^{v}, etc.)
Aduisedlie *adv.*	Advisedly. 1.a. In a manner indicative of careful consideration or good judgement; judiciously, prudently (L4^{r}, M4^{v})
Affect *v.*1	4.a. To fancy, like, or love (B4^{r}, etc.)
Affection *n.*	2.a. Love (F1^{r}, I1^{v}, K1^{r}, L1^{r}, L3^{r}, P1^{v}, U3^{r}, Cc2^{v}) 3.The state of the mind as regards some specific object; disposition towards something; inclination, bent, penchant (G2^{v}, I3^{r}, N4^{r}, O4^{r}, Q2^{v}, U2^{v}, Bb2^{r})
Affrighted *adj.*	Struck with fear; frightened, alarmed (T1^{r})
Afore *adv.*	Before (M2^{v})
Against *prep.*	10. In anticipation of, in preparation for, in time for (U2^{r})
Agreeued *adj.*	Aggrieved. 1. Affected with grief or trouble; distressed, troubled, annoyed, vexed. (U4^{r}, Bb1^{v})
Alablaster *n.*	Alabaster (Aa2^{r})
Allowe *v.*	Allow. I. To praise, to approve (B2^{v})
Ambrosius *adj.**	Ambrosial (R1^{v})
Amends *n.*	3. Means of obtaining satisfaction, or of amending; remedy (K3^{v})
Amount *v.*	2. To ascend, climb, mount (E1^{r})
Animate/Annimate *v.*	1.a. To fill with boldness, courage, spirit; to encourage (C4^{v}, L3^{v})
Animated *adj.*	4. Mentally moved or excited; inspired, stimulated; incited, encouraged (P1^{v})
Anker *v./n.*	Anchor (F1^{v}, F3^{r}, I1^{r})
Arbour *n.*	2. A garden of herbs or flowers; a flower-garden (X2^{v}, Y4^{v}, Aa1^{r})
Articulate *v.**	3. To come to terms of agreement (L1^{r})
Artificial *adj.*	9.a. Of a thing: skillfully made or contrived; cleverly constructed (C2^{v})
Artificiallie/Artificially *adv.*	1.a. Expertly, skillfully, ingeniously (F1^{v}, U1^{v}) 1.b. With skill directed to hide or deceive (D2^{r})
As namelie *adv.*	As namely. 3.b. For example (R1^{v})
Assistaunt *n.*	Assistant. 1. One who is present, a bystander; one who takes part in an assembly (Cc2^{r})
Astonied *adj.*	1.a. Stunned, stupefied, deprived of sensation; primarily by a blow; insensible, benumbed, paralyzed (B2^{r}, C2^{r}, C4^{r})
Attempt against *v.**	9.c. To make an attack upon the chastity of, to try to ravish or seduce (R2^{r})

Attend *v.*	13.a. To look out for, wait for, await (B2^{v}, etc.)
Auaile *n.*	Avail. 1.a. Beneficial effect; advantage, benefit (F2^{r}, H4^{r})
Auaunce *v. refl.*	Advance. Reflex. 6.b. To move oneself forward (L4^{v})
Auncient *adj.*	Ancient. 6. Aged, old (G3^{r}, M1^{v}, R3^{r}, T1^{r-v})
B	
Banderolle *n.**	Banderol. 2.a. A small ornamental streamer, *e.g.* that attached to the lance of a knight; in *Heraldry* one hanging down from the crook of a crosier, and folding over the staff (K2^{v})
Barbarian *n.**	3.a. A rude, wild, uncivilized person
Bare away *phr. v.*	Bore away, past form of bear away. 1. To carry away as winner (B4^{r}, etc.)
Bason *n.*	Basin (R1^{r})
Battaile *v.*	Battle (D1^{v})
Bear (anyone) company *v.*	3.c. To bring, give, company (A2^{v}, etc.)
Beere *n.*	Bier (A4^{r})
Beholding *adj.*	1. Under obligation, obliged, indebted (I4^{v}, etc.)
Behoue *v.*	1. To have use for or need of, to require; to be in want of (C2^{v})
Bemone *v.*	Bemoan (C3^{r}, F2*v*, O3^{v})
Bequeath *v.*	4.a. To transfer, hand over, make over, assign, deliver (D2^{r})
Bewraie *v.*	Bewray. 5. To reveal the presence of (B2^{v})
Billowe *n.*•	Billow. 1. The swell on the ocean produced by the wind, or on a river or estuary by the tide (Q4^{r})
Blazed *adj.*2*	Published, made famous (L3^{r}, etc.)
Blemish *v.*	1. To hurt, damage, do physical damage or injury to, deface (O2^{v})
Bore *n.*	Boar (G4^{r}, etc.)
Bounden *adj.*	3. Under obligation, legal or moral; obliged, compelled, enforced (I3^{v})
Bountie *n.*	Bounty. 1.a. Goodness in general, worth, virtue (A1^{v}, etc.)
Brandon *n.**	Brandy (R1^{v})
Bravado *n.*•	1.a. Boastful or threatening behavior; ostentatious display of courage or boldness; bold or daring action intended to intimidate or to express defiance (C1^{v})
Brave *adj.*	2. Finely dressed (X4^{r})
Brigandine *n.**	Brigander. n.1. 2. A foot-soldier wearing a brigander (a body-armor) (K2^{v})
Bruite *n.*	1. Noise, din, clamor, sound (H2^{r})
Bruite *v.*	1.c. To noise, report, rumor (D2^{v}, etc.)
Bruted *v.*	Bruited (D2^{r})
Buckle with *v.*	3.b. To close, come to close quarters; to grapple, engage (A3^{v}, Q2^{v})
Buy *v.*	3. To pay the penalty of, suffer the consequences of, "pay for"; to expiate, atone for (D3^{r}, etc.)
Byte in *v.**	Bite in. 7. To repress (what one has to say); to restrain (one's feelings) (E3^{v})

C	
Canzonet *n.**	A little or short song; a vocal solo in more than one movement (R1^{r})
Cap a pe *adv.*	Cap-à-pie: from head to foot (Q3^{r})
Capital *adj.*	2. Of an enemy or enmity: deadly, mortal (Bb2^{v})
Caractre *v.*1	Character. To stamp, mark (E4^{r})
Carire, carrire *n.*••	Career. 1.a. The ground on which a race is run, a racecourse; (also) the space within the barrier at a tournament (A3^{v}, etc.)
Castilian *n.*••	One living in or belonging to a castle (X4^{r})
Cautelous *adj.*	1. Full of cautels; deceitful, crafty, artful, wily (C1^{v})
Censure *v.**	3.a. To form or give an opinion; to judge, estimate (U4^{v})
Certes *adv.*	Of a truth, of a certainty, certainly, assuredly. Used to confirm a statement (B2^{v})
Chat *n.*	2. Familiar and easy talk or conversation (H3^{r})
Chaunce *v.*	Chance. 1.To come about by chance; to happen, occur, fall out, come to pass (F4^{r}, Q1^{r}, X4^{r})
Chirurgion *n.*	Chirurgeon. 1.a. One whose profession is to cure bodily diseases and injuries by manual operation (A3^{v}, etc.)
Choyse *p.pt, adj.**	Choice. Chosen (B3^{r}, F1^{v})
Circumstance *n.*	6. Detailed and hence (formerly) circuitous narration; circumlocution (A3^{r})
Cloy *v.*1	5. To stop up, block, obstruct, choke up (a passage, channel, etc.) (O4^{v})
Clymat *n.*	Climate. 1.b. A region of the earth (H3^{r}, R4^{r})
Coast *v.*	3. To proceed or travel by the coast of (K2^{v}, R4^{v})
Coequall *v.**	Coequal. 1. To be or become coequal with (another) (Cc2^{v})
Comelie *adj.*	Comely. 3.a. Becoming, decent, proper, seemly, decorous (S2^{v}, Bb2^{v})
Commendations *n.**	2.c. Renown, credit, repute (Q4^{r})
Commune *v.*	1.a. To talk together, converse *with* someone; to communicate; to confer, consult (A2^{r}, etc.)
Compass *n.*	Measure (Bb1^{r})
Compass *v.*	1.a. To plan, design, contrive, devise (I1^{r}, U2^{r}) 11.a. To attain to or achieve (an end or object aimed at); to accomplish (L3^{v}, etc.)
Conceit *n.*	1.a. That which is conceived in the mind, a conception, notion, idea, thought (N3^{r}, etc.) 3.a. The faculty of conceiving; conception, apprehension, understanding (H3^{v}, etc.) 4.a. Personal opinion, judgement, or estimation (B3^{r}, Aa2^{v})
Conceiue *v.*	4.a. To become affected or possessed by (an emotion); to form or develop (an attitude or feeling) towards a person or thing (G2^{r}, etc.)
Conclaue *n.*	1.a. A private room, inner chamber, closet (H1^{v})

Condigne *adj.*	Condign. 3.a. Fitting, appropriate; adequate (Q1^{v})
Condiscend *v.*	Condescend. 5. To give one's consent, to accede or agree *to* (a proposal, request, measure, etc.); to acquiesce (A1^{v}, G2^{r}, P4^{r})
Conferre *v.*	Confer. 5.a. To agree, accord, conform (Q1^{r})
Conference *n.*	5. Communication, converse, intercourse (C2^{v}, etc.)
Coniecture *n.*	Conjecture. 6. A ground of reason for conclusion (E4^{v})
Consolidate *v.*	4.a. To cause (the sides of a wound, the parts in a rupture or fracture) to unite or grow together, and so to heal (P1^{v})
Constantly *adv.*	1.a. With mental constancy or steadfastness; steadfastly, steadily, resolutely; with loyal attachment, faithfully (D1^{r}, N3^{r})
Content *adj.*	3.a. Consenting, willing, ready (+ inf.) (A3^{r}, etc.)
Contentation *n.*	3.a./b. Contented or satisfied condition; contentment (I2^{r}, etc.)
Contrarie *v.*	Contrary. 1. To oppose, strive against, thwart (E3^{v})
Conuersse *v.**	Converse. 4.a. To associate familiarly, consort, keep company; to hold intercourse, be familiar with (D4^{v})
Corasiue *n.*	Corrosive (H4^{r})
Corpes *n.*	Corpse (F2^{v})
Couch *v.*	12. To place in a lodging or dwelling; to lodge; *pass.* to be lodged or located (G3^{r}) 13. To hide, conceal; *refl. and pass.* to lie hidden, to lurk (X2^{v})•
Couller *n.*	Color (N1^{v})
Couller *v.*	Color (C1^{v})
Counceller *n.*	Counselor; counsellor (X1^{v})
Count *v.*	Account. 6. To estimate, consider (C2^{v}, etc.)
(out) Countenance *v.*	Countenance out. 3. To face out, persist in maintaining unblushingly or unfalteringly (L1^{v})
Countenaunce *n.*	1.a. Bearing, demeanor, comportment; behavior, conduct (Cc2^{v}) 2.a. Appearance, aspect, look (*obs.* exc. as *transf.* from 4); also, a show or semblance of anything (A3^{r}, B1^{v}, M1^{r}, P1^{r}, X1^{r}) 7. Demeanor or manner towards others as expressing good or ill will; show of feeling or manifestation of regard towards another (Q4^{v}, U2^{r})
Counterbuffe *n.*	Counterbuff. 1. A blow in the contrary direction; a blow given in return; the blow or shock of a recoil (A3^{v})
Countie *n.*	County. Count *n.*2 (K4^{r}, etc.)
Courrire *n.*	Courier (T2^{v})
Courser *n.*2	1.a. A large powerful horse, ridden in battle, in a tournament (M4^{v}, U3^{v}, Aa3^{v})
Craue *v.*	1.a. To demand (a thing), to ask with authority, or by right (I2^{v}, R4^{v})
Cullour *v.*	Color (R4^{v})
Cunning *adj.*	1.a. Possessing knowledge or learning, learned (O2^{v}) 2.a. Possessing practical knowledge or skill; able, skillful, expert, dexterous, clever (N1^{r})

Cunning. *n.*	1. Knowledge; learning, erudition (O3^{v}) 3.a. Knowledge how to do a thing; ability, skill, expertness, dexterity, cleverness (G4^{r}, K1^{r})
Cunningly *adv.*	1. With skill, knowledge, or wisdom; wisely, knowingly (F2^{r}) 2. With skillful art (F3^{r})
Cupboorde *n.*	Cupboard (R1^{r})
Curious *adj.*	2.c. Particular about details (O4^{v}) 7.a. Made with care or art; skillfully, elaborately or beautifully wrought (H2^{r}, N1^{v}, Q3^{v}, Y3^{r})
Curiously/curiouslie *adv.*	3.a. With careful art, skillfully, elaborately, exquisitely, cunningly (H1^{v}, R3^{r})
D	
Daine *v.*	Syncopated form of dedain: deign (B3^{v})
Daintie *adj.*	Dainty. 1. Pleasant, delightful (R1^{r})
Darcken *v.*	Darken (A2^{r})
Dazel *v.*	Dazzle (M4^{r})
Debonaire *adj*	A.a. Of gentle disposition, mild, meek; gracious, kindly; courteous, affable (A4^{v}, etc.)
Deceiue *v.*	1. To ensnare; to take unawares by craft or guile; to overcome, overreach, or get the better of by trickery; to beguile or betray into mischief (Y1^{v}) 3.b. To frustrate (a purpose, etc.), to disappoint (hope, expectation, etc.) (B4^{v}) 4.a. To cheat, overreach; defraud (E3^{r})
Decipher *v.*	6. To represent verbally or pictorially; to describe, delineate, portray, depict (M4^{r})
Deerelie *adv.*	Dearly. 4. At a high price; at great cost (C1^{v}, D3^{r}, O1^{v})
Deface *v.*	4. To destroy the reputation or credit of; to discredit, defame (Y2^{v})
Demaund *v.*	Demand. 10. With cognate object: To ask (a question, etc.) (B3^{v}, D2^{r}, K2^{v})
Deserts *n.*	2.b. A good deed or quality; a worthy or meritorious action; a merit (B3^{v}, L4^{v}, N3^{v})
Desire *v.*	6.c. To express a wish to (a person); to request, pray, entreat (C1^{v}, etc.)
Desseigne *n.*	Design (E2^{r})
Destenied *v.*	Destinied (Q2^{v})
Detection *n.**	2.a. Discovery (of what is unknown or hidden); finding out (X3^{r})
Deuise *n.*	Devise. 5. Familiar conversation, talk, chat (Q4^{r}).
Deuise *v.*	Devise. 3. To assign, appoint, order, direct (Q2^{r}) 14.b. To confer, commune, discourse, converse, talk (I1^{v}, etc.)
Difformed *adj.**	(F3^{v})

Discide *v.*	Decide (D1^{v})
Discomfit *v.*	1. Defeated in battle; beaten, routed; vanquished (A4^{r}, S3^{v})
Discontinue *v.*	1.a. To break the continuity of; to interrupt; to sever, divide (Bb3^{r})
Discouer *v.*	Discover. 3.a. To disclose or expose to view, to reveal, show (D1^{r})
Disdained *adj.**	2. Characterized by disdain; disdainful, scornful (I3^{v}).
Dispayr *v.*	Despair (R4^{r})
Dispose of *v.*	8.a. To make a disposition, ordering, or arrangement of; to do what one will with; to order, control, regulate, manage (Q4^{v}, Aa2^{v})
Distraughted/ Distracted *adj.**	5. Deranged in mind; out of one's wits; crazed, mad, insane (E1^{v}, Y1^{v})
Do *n.**	1. Commotion, stir, trouble, fuss (Q3^{v})
Dogged *adj.*	1.a. In negative sense (of a person, action, etc.): having the bad qualities of a dog; malicious, spiteful, perverse; cruel (O2^{r})
Domineer *v.**	5.a. To govern imperiously, tyrannize over, dominate with absolute sway (Y3^{r})
Doubt *v.*	5.a. To dread, fear, be afraid of (A4^{v}, D2^{v}, H2^{r}, Q4^{v}, U4^{v}, Aa3^{v})
Drift *n.*	4.a. Purpose, intention, object, aim (X2^{r})
Dump *n.*	1. A fit of abstraction or musing, a reverie; a dazed or puzzled state, a maze; perplexity, amazement; absence of mind (Y3^{v})
Durst *v.*	Dares (B2^{r}, etc.)
E	
Effronted *adj.**	Shameless, barefaced, unblushingly insolent (T2^{v})
Effuse *n.**	A pouring out, effusion (A4^{r})
Eien *n.*	Eyes (Y3^{r})
Embassade *n.*	The mission or function of an ambassador (P1^{v})
Emprise *n.*	1.a. An undertaking, enterprise; especially one of an adventurous or chivalrous nature (E3^{r})
Encurre *v.**	Incur. 5. To cause to be incurred; to bring on or upon (someone); to entail (S4^{v}, X3^{r})
Endeuour *n.*	Endeavour (G4^{r})
Endomage *v.*	Endamage (R4^{v})
Enfourme *v.*	Inform (Cc1^{v})
Enioy *v.*	Enjoy. 2.a. To put into a joyous condition; to make happy, give pleasure to (G1^{r})
Enioyne *v.*	Enjoin. 2. To impose (Bb2^{r}, Cc1^{r})
Enorme *adj.*	2. Abnormally wicked, monstrous, outrageous (T4^{r})
Enquire *v.*	1.a. To search into, seek information or knowledge concerning, investigate, examine (C2^{v})
Entercourse *v.**	Course. 1. To exchange, to interchange (H4^{r}, T2^{r})
Enterprise *v.*	1.a. To take in hand (a work), take upon oneself (a condition), attempt or undertake (a war, an expedition, etc.), run the risk of or venture upon (danger) (B1^{v}, B3^{r}, E1^{v})

Entertain *v.*	8. To treat in a (specified) manner (A3r, etc.) 12. To give reception to; to receive (a person) (Aa4v)
Entertainment *n.*	5. Treatment (of persons) (N2v, etc.)
Entrayles *n.*	Entrails. 1.a. The intestines or internal parts generally; the inside (R4r)
Enuy *v.*	Envy. 3.b. With clause as object: to grudge that (something should take place) (O1v).
Equipage *n.*	4.a. Military garb, uniform, accoutrements, trappings (I1v)* 11. Train of retainers or attendants, retinue following (I1v)
Ere *prep.*	Before (P4v)
Errande *n.*	1.a A message, a verbal communication to be repeated to a third party (B2v)
Esprise *v.*	1. To set on fire, enkindle, inflame (with love, etc.); also literary (with flame) (R1v, X1v)
Espy *v.*	1.a. To watch for, look out for (P1r)
Estate *n.*	1.3. A landed property (X1r)* 3.a. Status, standing, position in the world; degree of rank; *especially,* exalted rank or dignity (B3r, etc.) 3.c. Person or persons of estate (B2r) 10. A body politic, a kingdom or commonwealth (A1r, S2v)*
Estraunge *v.*	Estrange. 4. To change, render remote from one's accustomed or normal condition; to make unlike oneself; hence, to put beside oneself, madden (E1v)
Eternize *v.**	(T2r)
Ethnicke *adj.*	Ethnick. 1. Pertaining to nations not Christian or Jewish; Gentile, heathen, pagan (Cc1r)
Euer *adv.*	Ever. I. Always, at all times (G1v)
Exact on *v.*	1.a. To extort. (S3r)
Exceeding *adv.*	Exceedingly (G2r)
Exempt *adj.*	Exempted. 1.a. Taken away, removed *from* (Bb3v)
Exigents *n.*••	2.a. Needs, requirements (G1r)
Expedition *n.*	1.a. Speedy performance or prompt execution (K3r) 2.b. A journey, voyage or excursion made for some definite purpose (K1r)*
Exploit *n.*	1. Favorable outcome (C2v)
Expostulate *v.**	2.a. To complain of (Y3v)
F	
Faine *adj.*	Fain. 2.b. Necessitated, obliged (N2r)
Faine/Fayne *adv.*	Fain. Gladly, willingly, with pleasure (D3r, etc.)
Faint *adj.*	1.a. Feigned, pretended, simulated (X1r)
Fatall *adj.*	Fatal. 1. Allotted or decreed by fate or destiny; destined, fated (H2r, etc.)

Fauchion *n.*	Falchion (U1^{v})
Fauour *n.**	Favor. 7.a. Something given as a mark of favor; especially a gift such as a knot of ribbons, a glove, etc., given to a lover, or in medieval chivalry by a lady to her knight, to be worn conspicuously as a token of affection (N1^{v})
Fayn *v.*	Feign. 7.a. To disguise one's sentiments, practice dissimulation, dissemble (B4^{v}, M1^{r})
Feate *n.*	Feat. 2.a. An exceptional or noteworthy act or achievement; *esp.* a deed of valor; a noble exploit (B2^{r-v}, C2^{r})
Feature *n.*	1.a. Make, form, fashion, shape; proportions, especially, of the body (B2^{v}, I4^{v}, S1^{v})
Fellon *n.*	Felon. 1. A vile or wicked person, a villain, wretch, monster (C1^{v})
Flie *v.*	Flee (Aa3^{r})
Footing *n.*	3.b. The action or an act of walking, running, or stepping; a step. Also in to set (or put) (a) footing: to set foot (*in*, *on* a place); to enter (H1^{r})
Forbeare *v.*	Forbear. 4.c. To avoid (C3^{v})
Forborn *ppt.*	*Ppt.* of forbear. (T3^{v})
Forcible *adj.*	2.a. Strong, powerful (C4^{r}, H1^{r})
Forgerie *n.*••	Forgery. 2. Deception, lying; a fraudulent artifice, a deceit (Q2^{r})
Formost *adj.*	2.a. First in serial order (A4^{v}; etc.)
Foyl *n.*2	Foil. 2.a. A repulse, defeat in an onset or enterprise; a baffling check (M1^{v}, etc.)
Foyl *v.*1	Foil. 1. To tread under foot, trample down (G1^{r}, N4^{v})
Foyle *n.*1	Foil. A leaf (of a plant) (C1^{v})
Foyste *n.*	Foist. 1. A light galley; a vessel propelled both by sails and oars (K2^{r}, Aa4^{r})
Franctick-like *adj.*	Frantic-like, frantic. 1. Affected with mental disease; lunatic, insane (Bb4^{r})
Fray *v.*1	1. To affect with fear, make afraid, frighten (G4^{v})
Frollick *adj.*	Frolic. 1.a. Joyous, merry, mirthful (L4^{v}, S2^{r})
G	
Gaine say *v.*	Gainsay. 4. To refuse (T3^{v})
Gallant *adj.*	1.a. Gorgeous or showy in appearance (E3^{r}) 5.a. Chivalrously brave (D1^{v}, U2^{r})*
Gallant *n.*	1.a. A man of fashion and pleasure; a fine gentleman (N2^{r}, N3^{r}) 2.b. One's military follower (N2^{r}, N3^{r})
Gardant *n.**	Guardant. A keeper, guardian, protector (C3^{r})
Gentile *n.*	Gentile. 2.a. Heathen, pagan (F1^{v})
Goodly *adj.*	1.a. Of good or pleasing appearance; handsome, beautiful, good-looking; comely, fair (Q3^{v}, S4^{r}) 4.a. Splendid, excellent (R3^{r})

Gratifie *v.*	Gratify. 1.a. To show gratitude to (a person) in return for benefits received, *esp.* in a practical manner; to reward, requite (I1^{v}, P2^{r})
Gratulate *v.*	1. To express joy at the coming or appearance of; to welcome, hail; to greet, salute (Cc3^{r})
Gratulation *n.*	3.a. The expression of pleasure or gratification at a person's success, good fortune, or the like; compliment, felicitation, congratulation (Bb2^{v})
Graunt *v.*	Grant. 2.a. To agree to, promise, undertake (B3^{r}, etc.)
Groome *n.*	Groom. 3. A serving-man; male attendant (Aa1^{r})
Grystle *n.*	Gristle. 4. A tender, delicate person (G1^{r})
Guelles *adj*	Gules. Red in color (A2^{v})
Guerdon *n.*	A reward, requital, or recompense (A2^{r}, etc.)
Guerdon *v.*	To reward, to recompense (F3^{v})
Guileful *adj.*	Full of guile; deceitful, treacherous (Y1^{v})
H	
Habitude *n.**	3.a. Familiar relation or acquaintance; familiarity (U4^{v})
Happe/Hap *n.*	1. Chance or fortune (good or bad) that falls to anyone; luck, lot (A3^{v}, etc.)
Happen *v.*	3.b.(b) To find or encounter by chance (U1^{r}) 4.a. To chance to be or to come; to come or go casually (B4^{v}, C2^{r}, S3^{v})
Happily *adv.*	1. By chance, perhaps, possibly (S4^{v})
Haqueney *n.*	Hackney (X4^{r})
Harde by *adv.*	Hard by. In close proximity; nearby (S3^{v})
Hardie *adj.*	Hardy. 1.a. Courageous, daring; bold, resolute (A2^{r}, etc.)
Hardiness *n.*	1.a. Boldness, daring; audacity; hardihood (S4^{v}, etc.)
Hartie *adj.*	Hearty (G4^{v})
Hautie *adj.*	Haughty (K4^{v})
Haynously *adv.*	Heinously (Aa4^{r})
Hazard *v.*	1.b. *Refl.* To expose oneself to risk; to run or incur risks (G3^{v}, L1^{r-v})
Heathenesse *n.**	Heatheness. 2. Heathendom, the heathen world; the lands outside Christendom, including, in Middle English, Muslim lands (K2^{r})
Heed *n.*	1.a. Careful attention, care, observation, regard (U3^{v})
Hemde *ppt.*	Hemmed (F1^{v})
Holde *n.*	10. A fortified place of defense; a fort or fortress (X4^{r})
Holpe *v.*	*Past* and *ppt.* of help (T1^{v})
Howre/Hower *n.*	Hour (R1^{v}, X1^{r})
Hoyse *v.*	Hoise. 1.a. To raise aloft by means of a rope or pulley and tackle, or by other mechanical appliance (F1^{r}, etc.)
Humble *v.*1	*Refl.* 3.a. To render oneself humble; to assume a humble attitude; to do obeisance, bow (P4^{r})

I	
Imagination *n.*	1.b. An inner image or idea of an object or objects not actually present to the senses (B4^{v}, etc.) 2. The inner operations of the mind in general, thinking; thought, opinion (A3^{v}, P1^{r})
Imbrodered *ppt.*	Embroidered (Bb4^{v})
Impeach *n.*	2. Injury, damage, detriment (X2^{r}, Bb3^{v})
Impeach *v.*	3. To challenge, call in question, cast an imputation upon, attack; to discredit, disparage (X3^{r})
Impeachment *n.*	1. Hindrance, prevention, obstruction; impediment, obstacle (Aa4^{v})
Imtomb *v.*	Entomb (F3^{r})
Incombrance *n.*	Encombrance. 1.a. Trouble, molestation, perplexity (Y2^{v})
Incomprehensible *adj.*	1. That cannot be contained or circumscribed within limits; illimitable, boundless, infinite; immense (A1^{r})
Incurre *v.**	Incur. 3. To run into; to move or pass into, on, or against; to come upon, meet with (X3^{r})
In despight *prep. phr.*	In despite of. 5.a. In contempt or scorn of; in contemptuous defiance of (F3^{v}) 5.d. Notwithstanding the opposition or adverse efforts of (a person) (Q3^{r})
Indifferent *adj.*	6.b. Moderate, fairly large (M1^{v})
Indifferently *adv.*	5.a. Moderately, tolerably, fairly (D1^{r}, D2^{r})
Inexplicable *adj.*	2. That cannot be "unfolded" or expressed in words (Aa2^{v})
Inexpuisable *adj.**	Inexpugnable, invincible (R2^{r}) Infinite, inexhaustive (H3^{r}, Bb1^{v})
Infringe *v.*	1.a. To break; to cancel, invalidate (Cc2^{r})
In meane space *prep. phr.*	In mean space. Meanwhile (R2^{r})
In respect *prep. phr.*	P2c.d. Seeing that, in view of the fact that, considering that, since (T3^{r}, etc.)
In sooth *prep. phr.*	3. In truth, truly, really (B3^{r}, etc.)
In sunder *prep. phr.*	4. Into separate parts or pieces (E2^{v})
In their stedde *prep. phr.*	In their stead. 1.b. As his deputy or representative (I2^{v})
Intreat *v.*	Entreat. 7. To sue, plead for (D4^{r})
Intreatie *n.*	Entreaty. 1.a. Treatment (of persons) (Aa2^{v}) 2. Treatment, discussion, investigation (of a question, subject, etc.) (B2^{v}, E4^{r}) 3. Negotiation (Y2^{r})
Inueterate *adj.*	Inveterate. 1. That has existed or continued for a long time; of old standing (K2^{r})
Inuironed *adj.*	Environed (H1^{v})
Iote *n.*	Jot (E2^{v})

Irrecuperably *adv.*	Incurably. From irrecuperable: that cannot be recovered or regained (E4r)
Ise *n.*	Ice (N3r)
Iugle *v.*	Juggle (L3v)
K	
Kinred *n.*	Kindred (B1v)
L	
Labour *v.*	6.a. To burden, overwhelm, oppress, distress (B2v, K3r) 5.c. To endeavor to influence or persuade (a person); to urge, entreat, petition (O4r)
Laciuiously *adv.*	Lasciviously (P3v)
Largesse *n.*	Largess. 1. Generosity, liberality, bountifulness (I4v)
League *n.*	An itinerary measure of distance, varying in different countries, but usually estimated roughly at about three miles (A3r)
Leasing *n.*1	b. A lie, falsehood (L3r)
Like *v.*	1.a. To please, to be pleasing or agreeable to, to suit (someone) (A2v)
Like of *v.*1	7.a. To derive pleasure or enjoyment from (P2r)
Limitrophe *n.**	A border-land (D4v)
Lingering. *adj.**	1.b. Slow, painfully protracted (H4r)
Lustie *adj.*	Lusty. 5.a. Healthy, strong, vigorous (M4v)
Lyste/List *n.**	9.b. A place or scene of combat or contest (B3r, etc.)
M	
Maiest *v.*	May
Maine sea *n.*	Main sea. The high sea (Aa4v)
Make daintie *v.*	Make dainty. To be chary or loth, to scruple (L4r)
Manifold *adj.*	2. Numerous and varied; of many kinds or varieties. Formerly also: numerous, many; abundant (G1r)
Manhoode *n.*	Manhood. 5. Manliness, courage, valor; (esp.) these qualities collectively, perceived as pre-eminently belonging to or characterizing a man (A1v, etc.)
March *n.*3	2.a. A boundary or frontier of a country, district, or region (D4v)
Martyr *v.**	2.b. To inflict wounds or disfiguring blows on (a person); to mutilate; to torment (Y2v)
Marueilous/Meruailous *adv*	Marvelous. Wonderfully, astonishingly; exceedingly (A2v, etc.)
Mary *adj.*	Merry (P3r)
Mauger *prep.*	Maugre. 1.b. In spite of, notwithstanding (Q3r)
Mean *adj.*2	3. Intermediate in kind, quality, or degree (E1r, E3v) 7. Not much above or below the average; moderate (E1r, E3v)

Meete *adj.*	Meet. 2.a. Suitable, fit, proper for some purpose or occasion, expressed or implied (A3^{r}, O2^{v})
Meetelie *adv.*	Meetly. 1. Fittingly, properly, suitably (D2^{r})
Melancholie *adj.*	Melancholy. 1.a. Affected with or constitutionally liable to melancholy as a medical condition; accompanying melancholy (N3^{r})
Mette with *v.*	Meet with. 1. To come across, come upon by chance, find, encounter (a thing or person) (C1^{r})
Middest *n.*	Most central; situated in the middle; middle (C2^{v}, etc.)
Mind *v.*	10.a. To have a mind to do something; to wish, be inclined, purpose, intend to do something (B4^{r}, S3^{v})
Mine/Myne *adj.*	My
Misdeeme *v.*	Misdeem. 1.a. To form a wrong judgement, to be mistaken; to hold a mistaken opinion (B3^{r})
Misdoubt *v.*	2.d. To fear, suspect, or anticipate something evil mistaken opinion (Y1^{r}, Cc1^{r})
Mishap/Mishappe *n.*	Mishap. 1. Bad luck, misfortune (F3^{r}, etc.)
Mislike with/of *v.*	3.b. To be displeased with (N3^{r}) or disapprove of (N2^{r})
Misse of *v.*	Miss of. 1. To fail to accomplish (a design) or realize (a hope); to fail in (an attempt or enterprise) (F2^{v})
Mone *n.*	Moan (F2^{v}, etc.)
Mornefull *adj.*	Mournful (F2^{v})
Morrowe/Morrow *n.*	1. Morning (A3^{r}, etc.)
N	
Nether *adj.*	1. Designating the lower or bottom part (section, component, segment, etc.) of a person or thing (E4^{v})
New *adv.*	1. Newly (B1^{v}, etc.)
Nicromancer *n.*	Necromancer (H4^{v})
Note *n.*1	4. Sorrow, trouble, pain (B4^{v})
No whit *adv.*	Not at all; not in the least (H3^{v})
Nurse *n.*	1.b. That which nourishes or fosters some quality, condition, etc. Also: a place that nurtures or produces people of a specified type (A1^{v})
O	
Obeysaunce *n.*	Obeisance (B3^{v}, H3^{v}, I3^{v})
Obiect *n.*	Object. 9. Something put in the way; an interruption or obstruction; an obstacle, a hindrance (Y3^{r})
Obsequies *n.*	Funeral rites or ceremonies (G2^{r}, Y1^{v})
Occurrence *n.*	1. A thing that occurs, happens, or takes place; an event, an incident (A2^{r}, X4^{r}, Aa3^{v})
Odoriferous *adj.*	Odoriferous. 1. That bears or diffuses a pleasant scent; sweet-smelling; fragrant (R1^{r})

Oeconomie *n.**	Economist. 2.a. A person who manages resources, especially sparingly or effectively (D4^{v})
Office *n.*	4.b. A bodily or mental function as operating; the proper activity of an organ or faculty (E3^{v}, M2^{r}, X3^{v})
Oftentimes *adv.*	Often (C3^{v}, etc.)
Onelie *adj.*	2.a. Alone, sole, lone (B3^{r}, etc.)
Onelie *adv.*	Only (C1^{r})
Original *n.*	1.a. The thing or person from which something springs or is derived; a source, cause; an originator, creator (S2^{v}, S3^{r}, Bb4^{v}, Cc1^{v}) 5.a. Origin, derivation (E1^{v}, H3^{r}, U2^{v}, X3^{v}, Cc2^{v})
Ouerfonde *adj.**	Overfond. 1. Too foolish (N3^{r})
Ouer-spent *adj.**	Overspent, completely spent; exhausted (D4^{v})
Ouertake *v.*	Overtake. 2.a. To encounter or catch up with (a person travelling in the same direction) (B1^{r})
Ouer trauaile *n.*	Over-travail. Overwork (A2^{v})
Ouer-trauaile *v.*	Overtravail. To cause or force to work too hard; to exhaust or oppress with excessive work (M4^{r})
Ought *pron.*	Aught. Anything (T4^{r})
Out *prep.*	1. Out of (D4^{v})
P	
Pacquet *n.*	Packet (N4^{r})
Palfray *n.*	A horse for ordinary riding (as distinct from a warhorse); especially, a small saddle horse for a woman (C2^{r}, etc.)
Palliard *n.*	A. A professional beggar or vagabond. Also in extended use: a person of bad character, a scoundrel (T2^{v})
Paragon *v.*••	1. To compare or equate *with* or *to* (B2^{v})
Parle *v.*	1. To speak, to talk (B4^{v}, M3^{r}, N3^{v})
Pas my worde *v.**	Pass one's word. Give one's word (L4^{r})
Passenger *n.*	3.a. A person who passes by or through a place (A3^{r}, K1^{v})
Passible *adj.*	2. Liable to undergo change or decay (Bb1^{r})
Patrone *n.*	Patron. 7.a. The captain or master of a ship, especially, a galley or carrack (U1^{r}) 7.b. Any captain of a ship in the ancient world (U1^{r})
Peazaunt *adj.*	Puissant. Mighty, potent, powerful (K2^{v})
Peirce *v.*	Pierce (S2^{r})
Pendent *n.*	Pendant (N1^{v})
Penetraile *n.**	Penetral. The innermost part of something (R1^{v})
Peraduenture *adv.*	1. Expressing a hypothetical, contingent or uncertain possibility: perhaps, maybe, possibly (B1^{r})
Perfect *v.*	1.a. To bring to fulfillment or full development (Cc3^{r})
Perforce *adv.*	1. By the application or threat of physical force or violence; forcibly, violently; by force (G2^{r}, etc.)

Peremptorilie *adv.*	Peremptorily. 4. Determinedly, resolutely; obstinately (F4^{v})
Personage *n.*	2.a. The body of a person, especially with reference to appearance, stature, etc.; a person's figure; personal appearance (X2^{v}, Cc2^{v}) 4. The type of person anyone is, or is represented as being; character, status, or bearing (U3^{r})
Piller *n.*	Pillar (G3^{r}, H2^{r}, Y1^{v})
Pinnesse *n.*	Pinnace (Aa4^{v})
Phisition/Physition *n.*	Physician (O3^{r}, T4^{v})
Plight *n.*	1. Peril, danger, or risk (C2^{r})
Portrature *n.*	Portraiture. Portrait (M4^{v})
Post *v.*2	2.a. To ride, run, or travel with speed or haste (U1^{r})
Poste *n.*3	Post. 1. Any of a series of men stationed at suitable places along appointed post-roads, the duty of each being to ride with, or forward speedily to the next stage, the monarch's (and later also other people's) letters and dispatches, and to provide fresh horses for express messengers riding through (H2^{v})
In poste *prep. phr*	In post. In the manner of capacity of a courier or bearer of dispatches; (hence) at express speed, in haste
Praunce *v.*	Prance 1.b. To move, walk, or behave in an ostentatious or arrogant manner (F4^{v})
Presentlie *adv.*	Presently. 1.a. Without delay; at once, forthwith, immediately; instantly; quickly, promptly (A4^{r}, etc.)
Pretend *v.*	10.c. To intend, plan (X3^{v})
Pristinate *adj.*	Pristine (E4^{r}, R2^{v})
Procurde *past and ppt.*	Procurd; procured (F2^{v})
Proper *adj.*	4. Own (E2^{v}, etc.)
Prosopopey *n.*	Prosopopeia (C1^{v})
Proue *v.*	Prove. 7. To have experience of; to go through, undergo (C2^{r}, O3^{r})
Prouince *n.*	Province. 1.1. A country, territory, district, or region; a region of the earth or of a continent (E3^{v}, etc.)
Prowe *adj.*	Prow. Good, worthy; valiant, brave, gallant (F3^{v})
Puissaunt *adj.*	Puissant. Mighty, potent, powerful (A3^{v})
Pulde *v.*	Pulled (K2^{v})
Q	
Queint *adj.*	Quaint. 4.a. Gracious, courteous; courtly, refined (M2^{r})
Quiet *n.*	1.a. Freedom from mental or emotional agitation; inner tranquility; peace of mind (D2^{v}, Q1^{v})
R	
Raunsome *n.*	Ransom (N3^{v})
Rayne *n.*	Rein (L4^{v})
Rayon *n.*2	2. The area within the boundaries or fortifications of a particular place, a precinct (R1^{v})

Reason *v.*	4. To argue, have a discussion, discourse, or talk (D3^{r}, E2^{r}, G2^{v})
Recompence *n.*	Recompense. 2. Retribution for an injury or offence (F2^{v}, F3^{v}, P3^{r})
Recompence *v.*	Recompense. 2.a. To compensate or make up for (a loss, injury, defect, etc.) (A3^{v}, T3^{r})
Recorde *n.*	Record. 1.b. A witness (H2^{r})
Recouer *v.*	Recover. 8.a. To get over, get better from (an illness, misfortune, or injury) (D1^{r}, M1^{v}) 11.a. To get to, reach, arrive at (a place or position) (P4^{v}) 15.d. To rescue or deliver (a person) (K1^{v})
Recure *v.*	4.b. To cure (a disease, sickness, etc.); to heal (a wound or sore) (X3^{v})
Refection *n.*	1.a. Refreshment with food or drink after hunger or fatigue; sustenance, nourishment (O1^{r}, R1^{v})
Referre *v.*	Refer. 2.c. To hand over, give, transfer (E3^{v})
Regard *v.*	2.a. To look after, take care of (U2^{r}) 2.d. To consider, take into account (T4^{r}, Q4^{v}) 3.b. To have a regard for, to hold (a person) in esteem (Bb1^{v}) 4.a. To heed or take into account in determining action or conduct (T4^{r}, Q4^{v}) 4.c. To pay attention to (a person speaking, words spoken) (Y2^{r}) 6.b. To take care to do something (E1^{r})
Without regard of *prep. phr.*	Without taking heed of or giving consideration to (L4^{r})
Regarde *n*	Regard 1.c. Concern, care, or interest directed to some purpose (C1^{v}) 1.d. Care in doing something (M4^{v}) 2.a. Repute, standing; estimation in which a person or thing is held; value, importance (G2^{r}) 2.b. In a person's regard. In a person's opinion, according to a person's judgement (R2^{r})* 6. Aspect, appearance (X1^{v})
Regiment *n.*	1.a. Rule or government over a person, group, or country; governance; esp. royal authority (G3^{r})
Renting *adj.*	1. That tears or lacerates; that causes great emotional pain (O3^{v})
Repose *v.*2	1.a. To take a rest from something; (also) to recover from (H2^{r})
Repugnaunt *adj.*	Repugnant. 1.b. Making or offering resistance or opposition (to a person or thing); hostile, antagonistic (Bb3^{v})
Repute somebody for *v.*	2.c. To take a person for something (I1^{v}, X1^{v})
Requite *v.**	4. To take the place of, replace; to make up or compensate for (D4^{v})
Reskewe *v./n.*	Rescue (S3^{v}, Bb1^{v})

Resolue *v.*	Resolve. 1.c. To melt; to dissolve; to become liquid (H2^{v}) 17.b. To explain, to make clear (B2^{v})* 20.a. To free (a person) from doubt or perplexity; to bring to a clear understanding; to provide with definite information (C1^{r}, etc.)
Resort *n.*	5.b. A gathering of people; a crowd, a throng (D4^{v}, N1^{v}, U2^{r})
Resort *v.*	6.b. To return (D3^{v}) 7.a. To proceed or go to a place (G3^{v})
Reste *v.*3	Rest. 4.a. To remain to be done (B3^{r})
Return *v.*2	Re-turn (P4^{r})
Royalize *v.**	1.b. To make famous, celebrate (Y3^{r})
Royaltie *n.*	Royalty. 1.a. Magnificence, pomp, splendour (A1^{v}, etc.)
Rufull *adj.*	Rueful (F2^{v})
S	
Scant *adv.*	1.a. Hardly, scarcely; barely (D2^{v}, F1^{r})
Scantly/scantlie *adv.*	1.a. Scarcely (A3^{r}, B1^{r})
Scelerous *adj.*	Wicked, villainous (Y1^{r})
Seazed *ppt.*	Seized (I4^{r}, K3^{r}, X2^{r})
Secure *adj.*	3.a. Feeling sure or certain; free from doubt or mistrust (F4^{v})
Sedicious *adj.*	Seditious. Given to or guilty of sedition Sedition. 1. Violent party strife; an instance of this, especially, a factious contest attended with rioting and disorder (Aa4^{r})
Selfesame *adj.*	Selfsame. a. (The) very same, very identical (A1^{v}, etc.)
Selfe-willed *adj.*	Selfwilled. Willful or obstinate in the pursuit of one's own desires or opinions; characterized by self-will (T4^{r})
Semblable *adj.*	1.a. Like, similar (O4^{r})
Seruiceable *adj.*••	Serviceable. 1.b. Of actions or conditions: involving or expressing readiness to serve (I2^{v})
Shadow *v.*	6.a. To conceal (D4^{r}, Cc1^{r})
Sheepeheard *n.*	Shepherd (S2^{v})
Shrike *n.*	Shriek (F2^{r})
Signory *n.*	1. A domain, territory, especially, one held by a feudal lord (S2^{v})
Sigth *n.*2'	Sithe. A sigh (O3^{v}, Bb3^{r})
Singuler *adj.*	Singular. 10. Above the ordinary in amount, extent, worth, or value; especially good or great; special, particular (A1^{v}, etc.)
Sith *conj.*	2.a. Seeing that (E3^{r}, etc.)
Slack *v.*	To delay or retard; to render slower in respect of motion or progress (M3^{v})
Smitt *v.*	Smite. 3.a. To administer a blow to (a person, etc.) with the hand, a stick, or the like; to strike or hit; to beat or buffet (C4^{v}, H4^{r})

Smoother *v.*••	Smother. 2.a. To conceal by keeping silent about; to suppress all mention of (B2^{r})
Smote *v.*	Past form of smite. 13.a. To strike or cut off (the head, a limb, etc.) with a slashing blow (K3^{r}, P4^{r}, S4^{v})
Soldane/Soldan *n.*	1.a. The supreme ruler of one or other of the great Muslim powers or countries of the Middle Ages; specially the Sultan of Egypt (A1^{r}, etc.)
Sore *adv.*	1.a. Severely, violently (C2^{r}, D3^{v}, T4^{r})
Sorie *v.*	Sorry. To grieve, to sorrow; to feel sorry for (E3^{v})
Sort *v.*1	1. To allot, apportion, or assign (R1^{r}) 5. To arrive at, attain to, result in, or reach (an effect, end, etc.) (Y2^{r})
Sortiledge *n.*1	Sortilege. 1. Sorcery, magic, witchcraft (T1^{r})
Soueraigne *adj.*	Sovereign. 3. Of remedies: Efficacious or potent in a superlative degree (O2^{v}, P1^{v})
Sound *v.*2	4.a. To investigate (water, etc.) by the use of the line and lead or other means, in order to ascertain the depth or the quality of the bottom (N1^{r})
Speede *v.*	Speed. 1.a. To succeed or prosper; to meet with success or good fortune; to attain one's purpose or desire (C1^{r}) 1.b. Speed of. To succeed in getting, obtaining, or accomplishing (N3^{r})
Sport *v.*	1.a. To amuse, divert, or entertain oneself; to take one's pleasure, have a pleasant or leisurely time (P3^{r}, R4^{r})
Staffe *n.*	Staff. 3.b. A spear, lance, or similar armed weapon (A3^{v})
Stand *v.*	53.d. To abide by, obey, remain loyal to (an ordinance, etc.) (Bb2^{r})
Stay *v.*1	1.a. To cease going forward; to stop, halt; to arrest one's course and stand still (S1^{v}). 2.a. To base or ground upon, to fix or set firmly in (D2^{v}) 20.a. To detain, hold back, stop (a person or thing); to check or arrest the progress of, bring to a halt; to hinder from going on or going away; to keep in a fixed place or position (H4^{r}, etc.)
Stealing *adj.*	That steals or moves stealthily; that eludes observation; that glides or creeps softly along; that comes on imperceptibly (P4^{r})
Stouped *v.*	Stopped (B3^{r})
Strange *adj.*	1.a. Foreign, alien (E2^{r}, etc.) 8. Of a kind that is unfamiliar or rare; unusual, uncommon, exceptional, singular, out of the way (A2^{r}, etc.)
Stratageme *n.*••	Stratagem. 3. A deed of blood or violence (F2^{v}, U2^{r})
Strike *v.*	1.a. To make one's way, go (M1^{v})
Strooken *ppt.*	Struck (M3^{r})
Subtil/Subtille *adj.*	Subtile. 1.a. Crafty, cunning; sly, treacherous (D3^{v}, etc.)
Subtilly *adv.*	Subtilely; subtly (Cc1^{r})

Subtiltie *n.*	Subtilty 1.a. Cunning, craftiness (R4^{v}, X3^{v})
Suddaine *adj.**	Sudden. 4.b. Quick (Cc1^{r})
Suddainly/Suddainlie *adv.*	Suddenly. 2. Without delay, forthwith, promptly, immediately, directly, at once (C4^{v}, etc.)
Suffer *v.*	13.a. To allow (a thing) to be done, exist, or take place; to allow to go on without interference or objection, put up with, tolerate (C1^{v}, etc.)
Sufficient *adj.*	3.a. Qualified by talent or ability; competent, capable (C4^{v}) 4. Of adequate means or wealth; having a competence, substantial, well-to-do; hence, qualified by means or status for an office or duty (A4^{v}) 5. Of adequate quality; of a good standard; substantial; in good condition (D2^{v}, N3^{r}, T3^{v})
Suffise *v.*	2. Impersonal (E3^{r}, Bb2^{v}) 5.a. To be enough for; to meet the desires, needs, or requirements of (a person); to satisfy (F2^{v}, P1^{v})
Summarie *adj.*••	Summary. 4.a. Consisting of or relating to a mathematical sum or summation (Cc1^{r})
Suncke *v.*	Sunk (H2^{v})
Sundry *adj.*	3.a. Various, (many) different (A2^{r}, etc.)
Superexcelling *adj.*	1. That superexcels; superexcellent (Cc2^{v})
Superintendaunce *n.*	Superintendence, superintendency (H4^{v})
Supprise *v.*	2. To overcome (a person) by force; to overpower, subdue (T1^{r})
Supputation *n.*	1. Calculation, computation, reckoning (Cc1^{r})
Suretie *n.*	Surety. 4.a. Safety, security; freedom from danger (U1^{r})
Surfetting *n.*	Surfeiting. Excessive indulgence, esp. in food or drink; an instance of this (E1^{r})
Susteyne *v.*	Sustain (E3^{r})
Sute *n.*	Suit. 11.a. The action or an act of suing, supplicating, or petitioning; (a) petition, supplication, or entreaty; *especially,* a petition made to a prince or other high personage (C1^{v}, etc.)
Swoune *n.*	Swoon (C3^{r})
T	
Tarrie/Tarie *v.*	Tarry. 4.a. To remain, stay, abide, continue (Aa3^{r}, Bb2^{r})
Tary *v.*	1. To provoke, vex, worry, harass (P4^{r})
Tell *prep.*	Till, until (F3^{r})
Thence *adv.*	1.a. From that place; from there (A2^{r}, etc.)
Thereon/Theron *adv.*	1.a. On or upon that or it (π2^{v}, etc.)
Therewith *adv.*	3.b. With that as cause or occasion; on account of or because of that; in consequence of that (O2^{r}, Bb3^{v})
Therwithall *adv.*	Therewithal. 1. Along with or together with that; besides, or in addition to that (fact, circumstance, etc.); with all that; over and above that (B3^{v})

Think *v.* 1	To seem; to appear. 2. Without expressed subject or with following clause as implicit subject. Always with personal pronoun as indirect object (E2^{v}, etc.)
Thither/Thether *adv.*	1.a. To or towards that place (A2^{v}, etc.)
Thorow *prep.*	Thorough. 1. Through (H2^{v}, etc.)
Title *v.*	6.a. To designate by a certain name, indicative of relationship, character, office, etc. (Cc2^{v})
Tomble *v.*	Tumble (E1^{r}, G4^{v}, N2^{r})
Toole *n.*	Tool. 1.b. A weapon of war, especially a sword (D3^{r})
To the uttermost *prep. phr.*	7. To the utmost, to the extreme or uttermost degree, extent, capacity, or limit (N1^{v})
Toward *adj.*	3. Promising, "hopeful," forward; making good progress in learning or practice; disposed, apt, or willing to learn (G1^{v})
Train *n.* 1	1.b. An act or scheme designed to deceive or entrap, a trick, stratagem, artifice, wile. Also: a lie, a false story (U2^{r}, U3^{v}, Aa3^{v})
Trauaile *n.*	Travail. 1. Bodily or mental labour or toil, especially of a painful or oppressive nature; exertion; trouble; hardship; suffering (B4^{v}, etc.) 7. Travel. A journey (B4^{v}, etc.)
Trauaile *v.*	Travail. 2.a. To exert oneself, labour, toil, work hard (L3^{r}, T2^{r}) 5. To journey (A2^{r}, etc.)
Tribulation *n.*	1.a. A condition of great affliction, oppression, or misery (Bb1^{r})
Trickle *v.*	1.a. Originally said of tears: To flow or fall in successive drops (Y4^{r})
Trustie *adj.*	Trusty. Characterized by confidence or faith in a person, thing, quality, etc.; having or displaying trust; trustful (K3^{r}, N1^{r})
Tryumphe *n.*	Triumph. 4. A tournament (B1^{r}, etc.)
Twaine *adj.*	Two (L3^{r}, P2^{r}, R1^{v})
Tyding *n.*	Tiding. 2.a. The announcement of an event or occurrence; a piece of news (C1^{r}, etc.)
V	
Valewe *n.*	Value (Cc1^{v})
Varlet *n.*	1.b. An attendant on a knight or other person of military importance (T2^{v})
Vaunt *n.*	1. Boasting, bragging. To make (one's or a) vaunt: To boast or brag (E4^{r})
Vaunt courrier *n.*	Vaunt-courier. 1. One of the advance-guard of an army or body of troops; a soldier or horseman sent out in advance of the main body (K2^{v})
Verilie *adv.*	Verily. a. In truth or verity; as a matter of truth or fact; in deed, fact, or reality; really, truly (E2^{r}, etc.)

Vertue *n.*	8.a. Magical power ($Y4^{v}$)
Vertuous *adj.*	6. Endowed with, or possessed of, inherent or natural virtue or power (often of a magical, occult, or supernatural kind) ($Y4^{v}$)
Vivacitie *n.**	Vivacity. 2.a. Vital force or power; vitality ($C2^{r}$) 4. Vigorous or energetic action; activity, energy, vigour; spirit ($C2^{r}$)
Vnawares *adv.*	Unawares. 1.a. Without being aware; unconsciously; inadvertently; unintentionally ($Cc2^{v}$)
Vnbeseem *v.**	Unbeseem. 1. To be unseemly or unbecoming for (a person); to suit (one) badly ($T3^{r}$)
Vncouth *adj.*	Uncouth. 4.a. Of a strange and unpleasant or distasteful character ($Y1^{v}$)
Vndecent *adj.*	Undecent. 1.a. Unfitting, unbecoming, improper ($O1^{v}$)
Vnderstand *v.*	Understand. 4.b. To have knowledge of, to know or learn by information received ($A2^{v}$, etc.)
Vouchsafe *v.*	2.b. To give, grant, or bestow in a gracious or condescending manner. ($Cc2^{v}$)•• 3.b. To receive graciously or condescendingly ($Bb2^{v}$)•
Vpper-hand *n.*	Upper hand. 15.a. The mastery, control, or advantage (of a person, people, etc.) ($P4^{r}$)
Vtensille *n.**	Utensil. 4. A sacred vessel, furnishing, etc., belonging to, and especially used in the services of, a church, temple, or other place of worship ($K1^{r}$)
Vttermost *adj.*	Utmost ($G4^{r}$, $I2^{v}$, $Bb1^{v}$)
W	
Waight *n.*	Weight ($D1^{v}$)
Waighting woman *n.*	Waiting woman ($L1^{v}$)
Wake *v.*	2.a. To stay awake for the purpose of watching or tending ($F2^{r}$)
Wan *adj.*	2. Sad, dismal ($Y4^{r}$)
Watchword *n.*	1.a. A word or short phrase used as a password ($X3^{v}$)
Wared *v.*	Wore, past tense of wear. Wear *v.*1. 19.a. Of time, a period of time: To pass on or advance gradually to its conclusion; to pass away ($G1^{v}$, $Y4^{v}$)*
Warily *adv.*	Watchfully ($X1^{v}$)
Wellgyuen *adj.*	Well-given. Given 2. Well-disposed, inclined ($K2^{r}$)
Wel-willer *n.*	Well-willer. 1. A person who desires the well-being, happiness, or success of another; a supporter ($K2^{v}$)
Were *v.*	Wore, past tense of wear ($G1^{v}$)
Wered *v.*	Wore, past tense of wear. Wear *v.*1. 19.a. ($G1^{v}$)
Weyed *v.*	Weighed ($I1^{r}$)
Wherefore *adv.*	4. On account of or because of which; in consequence or as a result of which ($A3^{r}$, etc.)

Whet *v.*	2. To incite, instigate or urge on to or to do something (F2r)
Will *v.*1	Desire, wish for, want. 2. With object clause (K3r, K4v, X2r)
Will *v.*2	4.b. To pray, request, entreat (R2v)
Wisedoome *n.*	Wisdom (Cc2r)
Withall *adv.*	Withal. 1.a. Along with the rest; in addition; besides; moreover; likewise; as well (B3v, etc.)
Without *adv.*	2.a. Outside (or out of) the place mentioned or implied; especially, outside the house or room; out of doors (S4r)
Without *prep.*	1.a. Outside of, on or at the outside of, in the space external to (R3r)
Wonderfull *adv.*	Wonderful. Wonderfully (T4r)
Wont *adj.*	1. Accustomed, customary, usual (F1r, X4r)
Wonted *adj.*	Wont (π2v, etc.).
Worthy/Worthie/ Woorthy *adj.*	1.a. (Of things) having worth; possessed of value or importance; good; excellent (A1r, etc.) 3.b. Holding a prominent place in the community; of rank or standing (D2r, etc.)
Woulde *v.*	Would. Past form of will. Desire, wish for, want (K2r, etc.) 1.a. With simple object (I3r) 2. With object clause (B2v, E2r, I2v)
Wrapt *ppt.*	Rapt. Rap *v.*4. 1. To affect with rapture, ravish (O3v)
Wunne *v.*	Won, past tense of win (L3r)
Y	
Yeelde *v.*	Yield. 12.a. To give, render, state, declare, deliver, communicate (speech, or something expressible in speech, as a reason, etc.). (B4v) 8.a. To give forth from its own substance by a natural process, or in return for cultivation or labor; to produce, bear, generate (fruit, seed, vegetation, minerals, etc.); to put forth (a bud, shoot, etc.); †to bring forth, give birth to, bear (offspring) (N1v) [† = meaning is obsolete, no longer in use]
Yet *adv.*	3.d. At some time in the past; previously, before (H3r)
Yrkesome *adj.*	Irksome (H4r)

Neologisms

A. Included in the OED

Articulate
Attempt against
Banderolle
Barbarian
Blazed
Byte in
Canzonet
Censure
Coequall
Commendation
Conuersse
Detection
Difformed
Disdained
Distracted
Do
Domineer
Effuse
Encurre
Equipage
Estate
Eternize
Expedition
Expostulate
Fauour
Foil
Gallant
Gardant
Habitude
Limitrophe
Lingering
List
Martyr
Ouerfond
Ouerspent
Pas my worde
Penetrail
In a person's regard
Requite
Royalize
Sigth
Suddaine
Title
Viuacitie
Vnbeseem
Vtensille
Wear

B. Not included in the OED

Accessable
Ambrosius
Brandon
Brigandine
Choice
Entercourse
Heatheness
Inexpuisable
Oeconomie

Quasi-Neologisms

C. Words dating back to 1589 (included in the OED)

Billowe
Brauado
Vouchsafe

D. Words dating back to 1579–1588 (the year of the first record of each of these words in the OED is given in parentheses)

Carrire (1586)
Castilian (1587)
Exigents (1588)
Forgerie (1582)
Paragon (1586)
Seruiceable (1586)
Smoother (1579)
Stratagem (1588)
Summarie (1588)
Vouchsafe (1587, 1589)

List of Characters

THE FOLLOWING IS A list of all characters featuring in *Palmendos*, arranged in alphabetical order. They are briefly described, and both their role in the story and their relationship with other characters are here explained. Chapter numbers refer to the chapters in which characters appear or are mentioned for the first time.

ABENUNCO. Son of the Soldan of Babilon and Alchidiana. He is captured by Ocurites on his way to Constantinople to attend his sister Esquivela's wedding to Ditreus. Palmendos rescues him. He eventually becomes Primaleon's companion. Chapter 11.

ALCHIDIANA. Wife to the Soldan of Babilon and Esquivela's mother. Chapter 10.

ALDERINA. Daughter to the Duke of Pontus and Durace. In love with Belcar. Chapter 2.

AMENADA. A woman dwarf attending to Philocrista. Chapter 18.

ARNEDES. Son to the King of France. In love with Philocrista, Emperor Palmerin's daughter. He fights twice with Palmendos and is defeated on both occasions. He is attacked and seriously wounded by Lecefin, jealous of Arnedes's love for Philocrista. While recovering from his wounds, he declares his love to her, but soon falls into deep melancholy while waiting for his father's permission to marry his beloved. Chapter 13.

AURECINDA. Sister to the Soldan of Persia. Tryneus's wife and Rifarano's mother. Chapter 7.

BALEDON. A giant. He had conquered by force the Isle of Delphos and captured anyone who anchored at Delphos port. Among his victims were Rifarano and Lecefin. Palmendos defeats him in single combat and frees his prisoners and the inhabitants of Delphos. Chapter 7.

BAZILIA. One of Palmerin's youngest daughters. Chapter 10.

BELCAR. One of King Frisol's sons. Knighted by his uncle, Emperor Palmerin, together with Tirendos. Belcar fails in his adventure to rescue Francelina but stays to defend the bridge at Carderia. In love with Alderina, he abandons the bridge when accused of treason by his beloved. Throughout the book he is constantly pursued by a lady who wrongly wants to avenge the death of her brothers. Chapter 1.

BRUQUELL. Arnedes's dwarf. Chapter 12.

CAPTAIN OF ALBAYZO. He guards the castle of Albayzo, where the King of Thessaly has been imprisoned by the Great Turk. He dies when defending the castle from Palmendos's and Ozalio's attacks. Chapter 27.

CARDINO. A knight who had unsuccessfully tried his fortune in the adventure of Francelina. Deceived by the lady who is in pursuit of Belcar, he challenges the latter to a combat in which he is nearly killed. Chapter 3.

DENISA. Daughter to King Florendos and wife to the King of Thrace. Belcar shows his prowess in the tournaments held on the occasion of her wedding. At this moment, Belcar offers his service to Alderina too. Chapter 2.

DITREUS. King Frisol's son and Belcar's twin brother. He marries Esquivela. Chapter 10.

DUKE OF ANEMON. Defeated by Belcar in the tournaments held at Macedon. Chapter 2.

DUKE OF FERIA. A youth in love with the lady at the temple of Delphos. He talked her into marrying him in secret, but her father found out about it and sent two enchanted lions that killed him. Chapter 6.

DUKE OF MENSA. Defeated by Belcar in the tournaments held at Macedon. Chapter 2.

DUKE OF PONTUS AND DURACE. Alderina's father. Chapter 2.

ESQUIVELA. Daughter to the Soldan of Babilon and Alchidiana. She is Abenunco's sister and marries Ditreus. Chapter 10.

FLERIDA. One of Palmerin's youngest daughters. In love with Prince Edward of England. Chapter 10.

FLORENDOS. King of Macedon and father to Palmerin d'Oliva and Denisa. Chapter 2.

FRANCELINA. Daughter to the King of Thessaly. The three faeries enchanted her when she was three years old. She was imprisoned in a tower on the Isle of Carderia. The knight who could free her would also marry her and save her father from the Turk. Palmendos is the knight chosen for this adventure. Chapter 1.

FRYSOLL. King of Hungaria and father to Belcar. Chapter 1.

GRACIAN. Alderina's page. He makes it possible for Alderina and Belcar to meet for the first time. Chapter 2.

GRIANA. Queen of Macedon and mother to Palmerin d'Oliva and Denisa. Chapter 2.

GUILLADOR. An old knight from Delphos who is granted the government of the island by Palmendos. Chapter 8.

IFFIDA. Daughter to the Captain of Albayzo. Her father is in charge of the Great Turk's castle, where the King of Thessaly has been kept prisoner for twenty years. Palmendos seduces Iffida so he may enter the castle and free the King of Thessalia. Chapter 26.

KING OF THESSALY. Francelina's father. Imprisoned by the Turk for twenty years at the castle of Albayzo, he is liberated by Palmendos. Chapter 1.

LAURANA. Duchess of Pontus and Durace and mother to Alderina. Chapter 2.

LECEFIN. Son to the Soldan of Persia and Princess Zephira. He accompanies his cousin Recinde on his way to Constantinople. They are captured by Baledon and then freed by Palmendos. They eventually reach Constantinople where they inform Palmerin of Palmendos's great deeds. In love with Philocrista, he treacherously attacks Arnedes. He then abandons Palmerin's court. Chapter 7.

LYNEDES. Lord of the Isle of Lique. He tried unsuccessfully to get involved in the adventure of Francelina. He is one of the knights that take part in the tournaments held on the occasion of Ditreus and Esquivela's wedding. He is defeated by French Prince Arnedes in one of those combats. Chapter 2.

LYPES. Son to the widow who gives shelter to Belcar on his way to Carderia. He tells Belcar about the risks that the adventure of Francelina entails. Once Belcar fails in his attempt to rescue Francelina, Lypes stands by him, mainly when the former decides to defend the bridge at the foot of the Isle of Carderia, thus preventing the passage of any other knight. Chapter 3.

MARENCIDA. Eldest daughter to the Great Turk and wife to King Ocurites of Culaquin. She is kidnapped by Palmendos and then taken to Palmerin's court. Despite her constant protestations, Palmendos promises his companion Ozalio that he will marry her. Once at court, she is only appeased by Philocrista, who takes care of her. Chapter 29.

MELICIA. One of Emperor Palmerin's youngest daughters. In love with Recinde. Chapter 10.

OCURITES. King of Culaquin, and Marencida's husband; hence, son in law to the Great Turk. He is taken prisoner by Palmendos, who sends him to Palmerin's court. Chapter 11.

ORICANO. A Turk. He is left sick at a harbor near Albayzo. Palmendos and his men rescue him and take care of him until he recovers his health. In exchange, Oricano helps Palmendos reach the castle where the King of Thessaly has been imprisoned. Chapter 26.

OZALIO. Son to Palmendos's uncle and tutor. He has been brought up together with his cousin and acts as a companion to Palmendos in his adventures. Palmendos promises him the kingdom of Tharsus and Marencida's hand. Chapter 5.

PALMENDOS. Son to Emperor Palmerin and the Queen of Tharsus. An old woman, who turned out to be one of the three faeries, revealed his identity and prompted him to carry out the adventure of Francelina. He is the chosen knight who manages to rescue Francelina and her father, the King of Thessaly, from their prison. He ultimately meets his father Palmerin, who acknowledges him and welcomes him at his court. He is baptized and is betrothed to his beloved. Chapter 5.

PALMERIN. Emperor of Constantinople and father to Palmendos and Primaleon. Palmerin acknowledges Palmendos to be his son in the last chapter of the book. Chapter 1.

PERNEDIN. Son to the Duke of Pera, he is defeated by Palmendos in the tourney held in Macedon. Chapter 15.

PHILOCRISTA. Emperor Palmerin's eldest daughter. She is in love with French Prince Arnedes. Chapter 10.

POLINARDA. Emperor Palmerin's wife and mother to Primaleon. She soon realizes that Palmendos is Palmerin's son due to their resemblance. She forgives Palmerin and accepts Palmendos as her own son. Chapter 5.

PRIMALEON. Palmerin's youngest son. Though not yet knighted, he is encouraged by his father Palmerin to follow in Palmendos's footsteps. Chapter 10.

QUEEN OF THARSUS. Palmendos's mother. She has brought him up at her court and is reluctant to let him go. Once Palmendos decides to leave to Constantinople, she gives him a ring, similar to the one she gave to Palmerin when he abandoned her. Chapter 5.

RECINDE. Arnedes's cousin and companion. He travels with him to Constantinople and falls in love with Melicia, one of Palmerin's youngest daughters. Chapter 13.

RIFARANO. Son to Trineus, Emperor of Allemaine and Aurecinda, sister to the Soldan of Babylon. He has been brought up at the Soldan's court, together with his cousin Lecefin. After his mother's death, he and his cousin leave the court and set off for Constantinople but are captured by giant Baledon. Palmendos frees them and they eventually reach Palmerin's court, where they tell the emperor about Palmendos's heroic deeds. Chapter 7.

TIRENDOS. Son to the Duke Eustace of Mecaena. He is knighted, together with Belcar, by Palmerin. He takes offence when Belcar decides to abandon Palmerin's court on his own. Persuaded by the lady who seeks revenge on Belcar, he challenges his companion, unaware of his true identity. Belcar reveals his identity and both friends reconcile. Tirendos defends the bridge at Carderia when Belcar goes to meet Alderina's demands at Macedon. He is defeated by Palmendos. Chapter 1.

ZEPHIRA. Wife to the Soldan of Persia and mother to Lecefin. Chapter 7.

Bibliographical References

Primary Sources

Aesop. *The Fables of Esop in Englishe*, trans. William Caxton. London: Henry Wykes for John Waley, 1570. STC 181.

Amadis de Gaule, Anon. (1619). Translated by Anthony Munday, ed. Helen Moore. Aldershot, UK: Ashgate, 2004.

Amis and Amiloun, ed. MacEdward Leach. London: Early English Text Society, 1960.

Apuleius. *The XI Bookes of the Golden Asse*, trans. William Adlington. London: Thomas East for Abraham Veale, 1582. STC 719a.5.

Ariosto, Ludovico. *Orlando Furioso*. Ferrara, Italy: Giovanni Mazocco, 1516. EDIT16 CNCE 2541.

The Auncient Order, Societie and Unitie Laudable of Prince Arthure, trans. Richard Robinson. London: Richard Jones for John Wolfe, 1583. STC 800.

Averell, William. *A Dyall for Dainty Darlings*. London: John Charlewood for Thomas Hackette, 1584. STC 978.

Bandello, Matteo. *Certain Tragicall Dicourses*, trans. Geoffrey Fenton. London: Thomas Marshe, 1567. 2nd ed. London: Thomas Marshe, 1575. STC 1356.1, 1356.3.

Bandello, Matteo. *The Tragical Historie of Romeus and Iuliet*, trans. Arthur Brooke. London: R. Robinson, 1587. STC 1356.9.

Bibliotheca Curiosa, or, A Choice Collection of Books in English, Latin, French, Italian, Spanish, Greek, and Hebrew in All Volumes. London: s.n., 1697.

Blenerhasset, Thomas. *The Seconde Part of the Mirrour for Magistrates, Conteining the Falles of the Infortunate Princes of this Lande*. London: Thomas Dawson for Richard Webster, 1578. STC 3131.

Boccaccio, Giovanni. *The Ammorous Fiammetta*, trans. Bartolomew Young. London: John Charlewood for Thomas Gubbin and Thomas Newman, 1587. STC 3179.

Bodenham, John. *Bel-vedére or The Garden of the Muses*. London: F. K. for Hugh Astley, 1600. STC 3189.

Bodenham, John. *Englands Helicon*. London: James Roberts for John Flasket, 1600. STC 3191.

Burton, Robert. *The Anatomy of Melancholy*, ed. Thomas C. Faulkner, Nicholas K. Kiessling, and Rhonda L. Blair. Vol. 1. Oxford: Clarendon Press, 1989.

Capellanus, Andreas. *The Art of Courtly Love*, ed. John Jay Parry. New York: Columbia University Press, 1990.

Cartigny, Jean de. *The Wandering Knight*, trans. William Goodyear. London: Thomas East, 1581. 2nd ed. Thomas East for Richard Ballard, 1584. STC 4700.

Castiglione, Baldassare. *The Courtier*, trans. Thomas Hobby. London: John Wolfe, 1588. STC 4781.

Catalogue Containing Variety of English Books in Divinity, History, Travels, Romances, Poetry &c. Which will be Exposed to Sale by Way of Auction at Mr. Bridges Coffee-House in Popes-Head Alley in Cornhill, on Monday the 20th of this instant December, 1686. London: s.n., 1686.

Catalogue of Choice English Books: Consisting of Divinity, Physick, History, Travels, Romances, vol. of Tracts, &c. Which will be sold by auction, on Monday the 6th.of August, 1688. London: s.n., 1688.

Catalogue of Vendible and Useful English and Latin Books on Most Subjects and in All Volumes will be Sold by Auction, on Monday next the 18th instant, 1688/9 at the Three Half Moons in St. Pauls Church-yard among the Woollen Drapers. London: s.n., 1689.

Catalogus librorum tam antiquorum quam recentium in omni facultate insignium, quorum auctio (in gratiam & commodum celeberrima eacademiae Oxoniensis) Oxoniae habenda est Novemb. 9, 1692 apud (The Auction House) prope ecclesiam B. Mariae. Oxford: Distributed by G. West, Joh. Crosley, and Joh. Howell, 1692.

Cervantes, Miguel de. *The History of the Valorous and VVittie Knight-Errant, Don-Quixote of the Mancha*, trans. Thomas Shelton. London: William Stansby for Edward Blount and William Barret, 1612. STC 4915.

Cervantes, Miguel de. *El ingenioso hidalgo don Quixote de la Mancha*. Madrid: Juan de la Cuesta, 1605. IB B9296.

Cervantes, Miguel de. *The Second Part of the History of the Valorous and Witty Knight-Errant, Don Quixote of the Mançha*. London: Eliot's Court Press for Edward Blount, 1620. STC 4917.

Cervantes, Miguel de. *Segunda parte del ingenioso cavallero don Quixote de la Mancha*. Madrid: Juan de la Cuesta, 1615. IB B9306.

Charny, Geoffroi de. *The Book of Chivalry of Geoffroi de Charny: Text, Context, and Translation*, ed. Richard W. Kaeuper and Elspeth Kennedy. Philadelphia: University of Pennsylvania Press, 1996.

Citois, François. *A True and Admirable Historie, of a Mayden of Consolens*, trans. Anthony Munday. London: James Roberts, 1603. 2nd ed. London: James Roberts, 1604. STC 5326–27.

Collet, Claude. *The Famous, Pleasant, and Variable Historie, of Palladine of England*, trans. Anthony Munday. London: Edward Allde for John Perin, 1588. STC 5541.

Colonne, Guido delle. *Historia destructionis Troiae*, trans. Mary Elizabeth Meek. Bloomington: Indiana University Press, 1974.

The Delightful History of Celestina the Faire, trans. William Barley. London: Adam Islip for William Barley, 1596. STC 4910.

Della Casa, Giovanni. *Il Galateo*. Venice: Domenico Farri, 1560. EDIT16 CNCE 47442.

Deloney, Thomas. *Haigh of Devonshire*. London: Thomas Creede, 1600. STC 21081.

De Rojas, Fernando. *The Spanish Bawd*, trans. James Mabbe. London: John Beale, 1631. STC 4911, 4911.2.

Des Périers, Jean Bonaventure. *The Mirrour of Mirth*, trans. Thomas Deloney. London: Roger Ward, 1583. STC 6784.5.

Doni, Antonio Franceso. *The Morall Philosphie of Doni*, trans. Sir Thomas North. London: Henry Denham, 1570. STC 3053.

The Famous and Renowned Historie of Primaleon of Greece, trans. Anthony Munday. London: Thomas Snodham, 1619. STC 20367.

The Famous History of Palmendos, Son to the Most Renowned Palmerin D'Oliva, Emperour of Constantinople, and the Heroick Queen of Tharsus, trans. Anthony Munday. London: Printed by Elizabeth Alsop, 1653.

The Famous History of Palmendos, Son to the Most Renowned Palmerin D'Oliva, Emperour of Constantinople, and the Heroick Queen of Tharsus, trans. Anthony Munday. London: Printed by Thomas Fawcet, and are to be sold by Francis Coles, 1663.

Faye, Antoine de la. *A Breefe Treatise of the Vertue of the Crosse*. London: Edward Allde for Edward White, 1599. STC 24216.

Fernández, Gerónimo. *The Honour of Chiualrie*, trans. L. A. London: Thomas Creede, 1598. STC 1804.

Ferrand, Jacques. *A Treatise on Love Sickness*, trans. and ed. Donald A. Beecher and Massimo Ciavolella. Syracuse, NY: Syracuse University Press, 1990.

The Fift Booke of the Most Pleasant and [D]electable Historie of Amadis de Gaule, trans. Anthony Munday. London: Adam Islip for Hugh Jackson, 1598. STC 542.5.

Ficino, Marsilio. [*De Amore*] *Commentary on Plato's Symposium on Love*, trans. Sears Jayne. Dallas: Spring Publications, 1985.

The First Book of Amadis of Gaule, trans. Anthony Munday. London: Edward Allde, 1590. STC 541.

The First Booke of Primaleon of Greece, trans. Anthony Munday. London: John Danter for Cuthbert Burby, 1595. STC 26366.

Flores, Juan de. *Grisel y Mirabella*. Lérida: Heinrich Botel, 1495. IB 8945–48.

Flores, Juan de. *The Historie of Aurelio and of Isabelle*. Antwerp: Juan Steelsio; Juan Latio, 1556. STC 11092, 11092a. 2nd ed. Brussels: Mommart and J. Reyns, 1608. STC 11093, 11093.5.

Forde, Emanuel. *The Most Pleasant Historie of Ornatus and Artensia*. London: Thomas Creede, 1599. STC 11168.

Forde, Emanuel. *Parismenos: The Second Part of Parismus*. London: Thomas Creede to be sold by Richard Oliue and William Holmes, 1599. STC 11171.2.

Forde, Emanuel. *Parismus, the Renoumed Prince of Bohemia*. London: Thomas Creede to be sold by Richard Oliue and William Holmes, 1598. STC 11171.

Gil Polo, Gaspar. *The Troublesome and Hard Adventures in Love*, trans. Robert Codrington. London: Thomas Creede, 1594. STC 153.3.

Greene, Robert. *Arbasto*. London: John Windet and Thomas Judson for Henry Jackson, 1584. 2nd ed. John Charlewood for Hugh Jackson, 1589. STC 12217–19.

Greene, Robert. *Greenes Vision*. London: Edward Allde for Thomas Newman, 1592. STC 12261.

Greene, Robert. *Gwydonius: The Carde of Fancie*. London: Thomas East for William Ponsonby, 1584. STC 12262.

Greene, Robert. *Mamillia*. London: Thomas Dawson for Thomas Woodcocke, 1583. 2nd ed. Thomas Creede for William Ponsonby, 1593. STC 12269–70.

Greene, Robert. *Morando*. London: John Kingston and John Charlewood for Edward White, 1584. STC 12276.

Greene, Robert. *The Myrrour of Modestie*. London: Roger Warde, 1584. STC 11278.

Greene, Robert. *Pandosto: The Triumph of Time*. London: Thomas Orwin for Thomas Cadman, 1588. STC 12285.

Greene, Robert. *Penelopes Web*. London: Edward Allde for John Hodgets, 1601. STC 12294.

Greene, Robert. *Perimedes: The Black-smith*. London: John Wolfe for Edward White, 1588. STC 12295.

Greene, Robert. *Philomela: The Lady Fitzvvaters Nightingale*. London: Robert Bourne and Edward Allde for Edward White, 1592. STC 12296.

Greene, Robert. *Planetomachia*. London: Thomas Dawson and George Robinson for Thomas Cadman, 1585. STC 12299.

Greene, Robert. *The Spanish Masquerado*. London: Roger Ward for Thomas Cadman, 1589. STC 12309.

Greville, Robert. *Catalogus librorum ex bibliotheca nobiliscu jusdam angli qui ante paucos annos in humanis esse desiit accesserunt libri eximii theologi d. Gabrielis Sangar, adjectis theology alterius magni, dum vixt, nominis libris selectioribus: quorum omnium auctio habebitur*. London: s.n., 1678.

Guazzo, Stefano. *La civil conversatione*. Brescia, Italy: Vincenzo Sabbio, 1574. EDIT16 CNCE 22070.

Guillemeau, Jacques. *The French Chirurgerye*, trans. Anthony Munday. Dordrecht: Isaac Canin, 1598. STC 12498.

Heliodorus. *An Aethiopian History*, trans. Thomas Underdowne. London: Henry Wykes for Fraunces Coldocke, 1569. 2nd ed. London: Henry Middleton for Fraunces Coldocke, 1577. 3rd ed. London: Henry Middleton for Fraunces Coldocke, 1587. STC 13041–43.

The Honorable, Pleasant and Rare Conceited Historie of Palmendos, trans. Anthony Munday. London: John Charlewood for Simon Waterson, 1589. STC 18064.

Humphrey, Laurence. *Interpretatio linguarum*. Basel: Hieronymus Froben and Nikolaus Episcopius, 1559. USTC 666931.

Isidore of Seville. *The Medical Writings*, trans. William D. Sharpe, M.D. Vol. 54.2. Philadelphia: American Philosophical Society, 1964.

Johnson, Richard. *The Most Famous History of the Seuen Champions of Christendome*. London: John Danter for Cuthbert Burby, 1596. STC 14677.

Johnson, Richard. *The Second Part of the Most Famous History of the Seuen Champions of Christendome*. London: Edward Allde for Cuthbert Burby, 1597. STC 14678.

Kidner, Thomas. *Catalogus variorum & insignium librorum selectissimae bibliothecae revendi viri d. Thomas Kidner, a.m. et olim rectoris ecclesiae de hitchin in comitatu Hertfordiensi quorum auction habebitur londini ad insigne capitis regii in vico vulgariter dicto little-Britain, Februarii 6th*. London: William Cooper, 1677.

Kitowe, Robert. *Loves Load-Starre*. London: Thomas Creede, 1600. STC 15026.

Landi, Ortensio. *The Defence of Contraries*, trans. Anthony Munday. London: John Windet for Simon Watersonne, 1593. 2nd ed. London: John Windet for Simon Watersonne, 1602. STC 6467–6467.5.

L'Histoire de Palmerin d'Olive, trans. Jean Maugin. Paris: Jeanne de Marnef pour Jean Longis, 1546. FB 40395–96.

L'Histoire de Primaleon de Grece continvant celle de Palmerin D'Olive Empereur de Constantinople son Pere, trans. François de Vernassal. Paris: Ian [Jean] Longis, 1550. FB 44732.

Libro Segundo del emperador Palmerín en que se recuentan los grandes & hazañosos fechos de Primaleón y Polendos sus fijos. Salamanca, Spain: Juan de Porras, 1512. IB 16739.

Lodge, Thomas. *An Alarum against Usurers*. London: Thomas Este for Sampson Clarke, 1584. STC 16653.

Longus. *Daphnis and Chloe*, trans. Angel Day. London: Robert Waldgrave, 1587. STC 6400.

Lull, Ramón. *The Book of the Ordre of Chyualry*, trans. William Caxton and ed. Alfred T. P. Byles. London: Early English Text Society, 1926. Reprint, Oxford: Early English Text Society, 1971.

Lybeaus Desconus, ed. Maldwyn Mills. London: Early English Text Society, 1969.

Lyly, John. *Euphues: The Anatomy of Wyt*. London: Thomas East for Gabriel Cawood, 1578. 2nd ed. London: Thomas East for Gabriel Cawood, 1579. 3rd ed. London: Thomas East for Gabriel Cawood, 1580. STC 17051–54.

Lyly, John. *Euphues and His England*. London: Thomas East for Gabriel Cawood, 1580. STC 17068–70.

Mabbe, James. *James Mabbe, The Spanish Bawd*, ed. José María Pérez Fernández. London: Modern Humanities Research Association, 2013.

Maisonneufve, Etienne de. *Arthur of Little Britain*. London: Thomas East, 1582. STC 808.

Maisonneufve, Etienne de. *Gerileon of England*, trans. Anthony Munday. London: Thomas Scarlet for Cuthbert Burbie, 1592. STC 17206.

Marche, Olivier de la. *The Travayled Pilgrime*, trans. Stephen Bateman. London: Henrie Denham, 1569. STC 1585.

Martínez, Marcos. *The Eighth Booke of the Myrror of Knighthood*, trans. L. A. London: Thomas Creede for Cuthbert Burby, 1599. STC 18870.

Martínez, Marcos. *The Ninth Part of the Mirrour of Knighthood*, trans. Robert Parke/Parry. London: Stafford for Cuthbert Burby, 1601. STC 18871.

Meres, Francis. *Palladis Tamia: Wits Treasury being the Second Part of Wits Common Wealth*. London: Printed by Peter Short for Cuthbert Burby, 1598. STC 17834.

Mexías, Pedro de. *The Forest*, trans. Thomas Fortescue. London: John Kingston for William Jones, 1571. 2nd ed. London: John Kingston for John Day, 1576. STC 17849–50.

Middleton, Thomas. *The Triumphs of Truth. A Solemnity Vnparaleled for cost, art, and Magnificence at the Confirmation and Establishment of that Worthy and True Nobly-Minded Gentleman, Sir Thomas Middleton, Knight, in the Honorable Office of his Maiesties Lieuetenant, the Lord Maior of the Thrice Famous City of London*. London: Nicholas Okes, 1613. STC 17904.

Millington, Edward. *Appendix to Mr. Charles Mearne's Catalogue of English Books, Chiefly of History, Miscellany, and Law, to be Sold by Auction at Richard's Coffee-House near the Middle-Temple-Gate, on Tuesday February 22d. 1686/7*. London: s.n., 1687.

Montemayor, Jorge de. *Diana*, trans. Bartholomew Young. London: Edmund Bollifant and George Bishop, 1598. STC 18044.

Morais, Francisco de. *The [First] Seconde Part, of the no Lesse Rare, Historie of Palmerin of England*, trans. Anthony Munday. London: Thomas Creede, 1596. 2nd ed. London: Thomas Creede, 1609. STC 19161–62.

Morais, Francisco de. *The [First-] Second Part of the no Lesse Rare, then Excellent and Stately Historie, of the Famous and Fortunate Prince Palmerin of England and Florian de Desart his Brother*, trans. Anthony Munday. London: Thomas Creede and Bernard Alsop, 1616. STC 19163.

Morais, Francisco de. *The Third and Last Part of Palmerin of England*, trans. Anthony Munday. London: James Roberts for William Leake, 1602. STC 19165.

Munday, Anthony. *Anthony Munday's Zelauto: The Fountain of Fame, 1580*, ed. Jack Stillinger. Carbondale: Southern Illinois University Press, 1963.

Munday, Anthony. *The Arraignment and Execution of a Vilful and Obstinate Traitor*. London: John Charlewood for Edward White, 1581. STC 17124.

Munday, Anthony. *A Banquet of Daintie Conceits*. London: John Charlewood for Edward White, 1588. STC 18260.

Munday, Anthony. *A Breefe Answer Made unto Two Seditious Pamphlets*. London: John Charlewood for Edward White, 1582. STC 18262.

Munday, Anthony. *A Brief and True Reporte of the Execution of Certaine Traytour at Tibourne*. London: John Charlewood for William Wright, 1582. STC 18261.

Munday, Anthony. *A Brief Discourse of the Taking of Edmund Campion*. London: John Charlewood for William Wright, 1581. STC 18264.

Munday, Anthony. *The Coppie of the Anti-Spaniard Made at Paris*. London: John Wolfe, 1590. STC 684.

Munday, Anthony. *A Courtly Controversie between Looue and Learning*. London: John Charlewood for Henrie Carre, 1581. STC 18268.

Munday, Anthony. *A Discoverie of Edmund Campion*. London: John Charlewood for Edward White, 1582. STC 18270.

Munday, Anthony. *The English Romayne Life*. London: John Charlewood for Nicholas Ling, 1582. 2nd ed. London: John Charlewood for Nicholas Ling, 1590. STC 18272–73.

Munday, Anthony. *A Gorgious Gallery, of Gallant Inventions*. London: W. How for Richard Iones, 1578. STC 20402.

Munday, Anthony. *The Masque of the League and the Spanyard Discouered*. London: John Charlewood for Richard Smith, 1592. STC 7.

Munday, Anthony. *The Mirrour of Mutabilitie, or Principall Part of the Mirrour for Magistrates*. London: John Allde for Richard Ballard, 1579. STC 18276.

Munday, Anthony. *News from Malta, Written by a Gentleman of that Island*. London: Thomas Creede for John Hippon, 1603. STC 17215.

Munday, Anthony. *The Paine of Pleasure*. London: John Charlewood for Henrie Car, 1580. 2nd ed. London: H. Bynneman, 1583. STC 18277, 18277.5.

Munday, Anthony. *The Strangest Aduenture that euer happened: Containing a Discourse of the King of Portugall Dom Sebastian*. London: Richard Field for Francis Henson, 1601. STC 23864.

Munday, Anthony. *The True Report of the Prosperous Successe Which God Gave unto our English Souldiours in Ireland*. London: John Charlewood for Edward White, 1580. STC 17124.

Munday, Anthony. *A View of Sundry Examples: Reporting Many Straunge Murthers, Sundry Persons Periured, Signes and Tokens of Gods Anger towards Vs.* London: John Charlewood for William Wright, 1580. STC 18281.

Munday, Anthony. *A Watchword to England to Beware of Traytours.* London: John Charlewood for Thomas Hacket, 1584. STC 18282.

Munday, Anthony. *Zelauto: The Fountain of Fame.* London: John Charlewood, 1580. STC 18283.

Nashe, Thomas. *Pierce Penilesse His Supplication to the Diuell.* London: John Charlewood for Richard Ihones, 1592. STC 18371.

Nashe, Thomas. *The Unfortunate Traueller.* London: Thomas Scarlet for Cuthbert Burby, 1594. STC 1380–81.

Ortúñez de Calahorra, Diego. *The First Part of the Mirrour of Princely Deeds and Knighthood,* trans. Margaret Tyler. London: Thomas East, 1580. 2nd ed. London: Thomas East, 1599. STC 18860–61.

Ortúñez de Calahorra, Diego. *The Mirrour of Princely Deedes and Knighthood,* trans. Margaret Tyler. London: Thomas East, 1578. STC 18859.

Ortúñez de Calahorra, Diego. *The Second Part of the First Booke of the Myrrour,* trans. Robert Parke/Parry. London: Thomas East, 1585. 2nd ed. London: Thomas East, 1599. STC 18862–63.

Ortúñez de Calahorra, Diego. *The Third Part of the First Booke of the Mirrour of Knighthood,* trans. Robert Parke/Parry. London: Thomas East, 1586. 2nd ed. London: Thomas East, 1599. STC 18864–65.

Painter, William. *The Palace of Pleasure.* London: Thomas Marshe, 1569. 2nd ed. London: Thomas Marshe, 1575. STC 19122–23.

Painter, William. *The Second Tome of the Palace of Pleasure.* London: Thomas Marshe, 1567. 2nd ed. London: Thomas Marshe, 1580. STC 19125.

Palmerín de Olivia. Salamanca, Spain: Juan de Porras, 1511. IB 16737.

Palmerin d'Oliua, trans. Anthony Munday. London: John Charlewood for William Wright, 1588. 2nd ed. London: Thomas Creede, 1597. 3rd ed. London: Thomas Creede, 1615. 4th ed. London: Bernard Alsop and Thomas Fawcet, 1637. STC 19157–60.

Palmerin d'Oliua, trans. Anthony Munday. Parts 1 and 2. London: Thomas Creede and Bernard Alsop for Richard Higgenbotham, 1616. STC 19159a.

Pasqualigo, Luigi. *Fedele and Fortunio,* trans. Anthony Munday. London: John Charlewood for Thomas Hacket, 1585. STC 19477.

Paynell, Thomas. *Treasurie of Amadis of Fraunce.* London: Henry Bynneman for Thomas Hacket, 1572. STC 545.

Peacham, Henry. *The Garden of Eloquence.* London: H. Jackson, 1577. STC 19497.

Petrarch, Francesco. *Petrarch's Lyric Poems: The Rime Sparse and Other Lyrics,* trans. and ed. Robert M. Durling. Cambridge, MA: Harvard University Press, 1979.

Pettie, George. *A Petite Pallace of Pettie his Pleasure*. London: Richard Watkins, 1576. 2nd. ed. London: Thomas Dawson for Richard Watkins, 1585. STC 19819–20.

Plater, Felix. *A Golden Practice of Physick*. London: Peter Cole, 1662.

Plato. *Axiochus*, trans. Anthony Munday. London: John Charlewood and John Danter for Cuthbert Burby, 1592. STC 19974.6.

Primaleon. Los tres libros del muy esforçado cavallero Primaleon et Polendos su hermano hijos del emperador Palmerin de Oliva. Venice: Giovanni Antonio Nicolini for Giovanni Battista Pederzano, 1534. EDIT 16 32003.

Primaleón (Salamanca, 1512), ed. María del Carmen Marín Pina. Alcalá de Henares, Spain: Centro de Estudios Cervantinos, 1998.

Primaleone, nel quale si narra a pieno l'historia di suoi ualorosi fatti, et di Polendo suo fratello, trans. Mambrino Roseo. Venice: Tramezzino, 1548. 2nd. ed. Venice: Gironimo Giglio, e compagni, 1559. EDIT 16 63465.

Puttenham, George. *Arte of English Poesie*. London: Richard Field, 1589. STC 20519.

Rich, Barnabe. *Riche his Farewell to Militarie Profession*. London: Robert Walley, 1581. STC 20996.

Rich, Barnabe. *The Straunge and Wonderfull Adventures of Don Simonides*. London: John Kingston to Robert Walley, 1581. STC 21002.

Roberts, Henry. *Honours Conquest*. London: Thomas Creede, 1598. STC 21082.

Roberts, Henry. *Pheander: The Mayden Knight*. London: Thomas Creede, 1595. STC 21086.

Ryckes, John. *The True Image of Christian Love*, ed. Anthony Munday. London: John Charlewood, 1587. STC 21801.

San Pedro, Diego de. *Arnalte y Lucenda*. Burgos: Fabrique de Basilea, 1491. IB 17160.

San Pedro, Diego de. *Carcel de amor*. Sevilla: Paulus de Colonia & Juan Pegnitzer & Magno Herbst & Thomas Glockner, 1492. IB 17162.

San Pedro, Diego de. *The Castell of Love*, trans. Johan Bourchier. London: Richard Field for Johan Turke, 1548. 2nd ed. London: Robert Wyer for Richarde Kele, 1552. 3rd ed. London: John King, 1555. STC 21739.5, 21740, 21742.

San Pedro, Diego de. *The Pretie Historie of Arnalt and Lucenda*, trans. Claudius Hollyband. London: Thomas Purfoot, 1575. STC 6758.

The Second Booke of Amadis de Gaule Contaning the Description, Wonders, and Conquest of the Firme-Island: The Triumphs and Troubles of Amadis, trans. Anthony Munday. London: Adam Islip for Cuthbert Burby, 1595. STC 542.

The Second Booke of Primaleon of Greece, trans. Anthony Munday. London: John Danter for Cuthbert Burby, 1596. STC 26366.a.

Shelton, Joseph. *Catalogue of Greek, Latine and English Books both Antient and Modern, on Variety of Subjects Consisting [of] Divinity, History, Law, Mathematicks, Travels, Voyages, Poetry, Romances*. London: Catalogues are distributed Gratis, at Mr. Wades, under the Piazza of the Royal-Exchange; at Mr. William [M]illers at the Acorn, in St. Paul's Church-Yard; at Mr. Collins near Temple-Bar; at Mr. Hartles over against Grays-Inn-Gate, in Holbourn, and at the place of sale, 1692.

Sidney, Sir Philip. *The Major Works*, ed. Katherine Duncan-Jones. Oxford: Oxford University Press, 2002.

Sierra, Pedro de la. *The Second Part of the Myrror of Knighthood*, trans. Robert Parke/Parry. London: Thomas East, 1583. 2nd ed. London: Thomas East, 1598. STC 18866–67.

Spenser, Edmund. "Propospopoia: Or Mother Hubberds Tale," in *Complaints*. London: Thomas Orwin for William Ponsonby, 1591. STC 23078.

Sylvain, Alexander. *The Orator*, trans. Anthony Munday. London: Adam Islip, 1596. STC 4182.

Syr Bevis of Hampton. London: Thomas East, 1585. STC 1990.

Tatius, Achilles. *Clitophon and Leucippe*, trans. William Burton. London: Thomas Creede for William Matts, 1597. STC 90.

Tellin, Guillaume. *Archaioplutos*, trans. Anthony Munday. London: John Charlewood for Richard Smith, 1592. STC 23867.

Treasurie of Amadis of Fraunce, trans. Thomas Paynell. London: Henry Bynneman for Thomas Hacket, 1572. STC 545.

Le Tresor des Amadis. Paris: Jean Ruelle pour Jacques Kerver, 1563. FB 926.

Warner, William. *Pan His Syrinx, or Pipe*. London: Thomas Purfoote, 1584. STC 25086.

Whetstone, George. *An Heptameron of Civill Discourses*. London: Richard Iones, 1582. STC 25337.

Whetstone, George. *The Rocke of Regard*. London: Henry Middleton for Robert Walley, 1576. STC 25348.

Winstanley, William. *The Essex Champion, or, The Famous History of Sir Billy of Billerecay and his Squire Ricardo*. London: Printed for J. Blare, 1699.

Secondary Sources

Adair, Richard. *Courtship, Illegitimacy, and Marriage in Early Modern England*. Manchester: Manchester University Press, 1996.

Álvarez-Recio, Leticia. "Anthony Munday's *Palmendos* (1589) in the Early Modern English Book Trade: Print and Reception." *Atlantis: Journal of the Spanish Association of Anglo-American Studies* 38.1 (2016): 53–69.

Álvarez-Recio, Leticia. "Chapters Translated by Anthony Munday in *The History of Palmendos* (1589): A Long-Standing Error." *Notes and Queries* 62.4 (2015): 549–51.

Álvarez-Recio, Leticia. "La ficción inglesa en prosa a finales del siglo XVII: Las lecturas del Paladín de Essex." In *William Winstanley: El Paladín de Essex*, trans. María Losada Friend, ed. Pedro Javier Pardo. Salamanca, Spain: Ediciones Universidad de Salamanca, 2022. Forthcoming.

Álvarez-Recio, Leticia, ed. *Iberian Chivalric Romance: Translations and Cultural Transmission in Early Modern England.* Toronto: University of Toronto Press, 2021.

Álvarez-Recio, Leticia. "*Palmendos*, 1589–1663." In Sánchez-Martí, *Los libros de caballerías en Inglaterra 1578–1700*, 87–103.

Álvarez-Recio, Leticia. "Provenance and Reception of Iberian Chivalric Books in English from the Seventeenth to the Twentieth Century: The Case of Anthony Munday's *Palmendos* (1589)." *Studies in Medievalism* 30 (2021): 107–28.

Álvarez-Recio, Leticia. "Sir Francis Drake: Conquest and Colonization in Anthony Munday's *Palmendos* (1589)." In Álvarez-Recio, *Iberian Chivalric Romance*, 51–73.

Álvarez-Recio, Leticia. "Spanish Chivalric Romances in English Translation." *Cahiers Élisabéthains* 91.1 (2016): 5–20.

Álvarez-Recio, Leticia. "Translations of Spanish Chivalry Works in the Jacobean Book Trade: Shelton's *Don Quixote* in the Light of Anthony Munday's Publications." *Renaissance Studies* 33.5 (2019): 691–711.

Ames, Joseph. *Typographical Antiquities.* London: Printed by W. Faden and Sold by J. Robinson, 1749.

Arber, Edward, ed. *A Transcript of the Registers of the Company of Stationers of London: 1554–1640.* New York: P. Smith, 1950.

Armstrong, Guyda. "Print, Paratext, and a Seventeenth-Century Sammelband: Boccaccio's *Ninfale Fiesolano* in English Translation." In Barker and Hosington, *Renaissance Cultural Crossroads*, 79–99.

Barker, Sara K. "'Newes Lately Come': European News Books in English Translation." In Barker and Hosington, *Renaissance Cultural Crossroads*, 227–44.

Barker, Sara K. and Brenda M. Hosington, eds. *Renaissance Cultural Crossroads Catalogue: Translation, Print and Culture in Britain, 1473–1640.* Leiden and Boston: Brill, 2013.

Barnes, Geraldine. *Counsel and Strategy in Middle English Romance.* Cambridge, UK: Boydell and Brewer, 1993.

Bartlett, Robert. *Trial by Fire and Water: The Medieval Judicial Ordeal.* Oxford: Clarendon Press, 1986.

Bennett, Henry S. *English Books and Readers.* Vol. 2: *1558–1603.* Cambridge: Cambridge University Press, 1965.

Bloch, R. Howard. *Medieval French Literature and Law.* Berkeley, Los Angeles, and London: University of California Press, 1977.

Bognolo, Anna. "Il Progetto Mambrino. Per una explorazione delle traduzioni e continuazioni italiane dei libros de caballerías." *Rivista de Filologia e Letterature Ispaniche* 6 (2003): 109–202.

Boro, Joyce. "Multilinguism, Romance, and Language Pedagogy; or, Why Were so Many Sentimental Romances Printed as Polyglot Texts." In Schurink, *Tudor Translation*, 18–38.

Boro, Joyce. "Reading Juan de Flores's *Grisel y Mirabella* in Early Modern England." In Barker and Hosington, *Renaissance Cultural Crossroads*, 35–59.

Bovilsky, Lara. *Barbarous Play: Race on the English Renaissance Stage*. Minneapolis: University of Minnesota Press, 2008.

Bowers, Fredson, ed. *The Dramatic Works of Thomas Dekker*. 4 vols. London: Cambridge University Press, 1953–1964.

Braden, Gordon and Stuart Gillespie, eds. *The Oxford History of Literary Translation in English*. Vol. 2: *1550–1660*. Oxford: Oxford University Press, 2010.

Brault, Gerard J. "English Translations of the *Celestina* in the Sixteenth Century." *Hispanic Review* 28.4 (1960): 301–12.

British Book Trade Index. Bodleian Libraries. Oxford: University of Oxford. http://bbti.bodleian.ox.ac.uk/#.

Britton, Dennis Austin. *Becoming Christian: Race, Reformation, and Early Modern English Romance*. New York: Fordham University Press, 2014.

Brumble, H. David. *Classical Myths and Legends in the Middle Ages and Renaissance: A Dictionary of Allegorical Meanings*. New York and London: Routledge, 1998.

Burrow, John A. *Gestures and Looks in Medieval Narrative*. Cambridge Studies in Medieval Literature 48. Cambridge: Cambridge University Press, 2002.

Chiari, Sophie. *Freedom and Censorship in Early Modern English Literature*. New York: Routledge, 2019.

Church, Stephen and Ruth Harvey, eds. *Medieval Knighthood V: Papers from the Sixth Strawberry Hill Conference 1994*. Rochester, NY: Boydell and Brewer, 1995.

Ciapparelli, Lidia. "La relación intertextual entre *Las mil y una noches* y el *Palmerín de Olivia*." In *Actas del II coloquio internacional de literatura comparada "El Cuento."* Vol. 2, 35–38. Buenos Aires: Universidad Católica Argentina, 1995.

Clegg, Cyndia Susan. *Press Censorship in Jacobean England*. Cambridge: Cambridge University Press, 2001.

Clericuzio, Antonio. "Webster, John (1611–1682)." In *Oxford Dictionary of National Biography*, online ed., ed. Lawrence Goldman. Oxford: Oxford University Press, 2004. Accessed July 15, 2021, http://0–www.oxforddnb.com.fama.us.es/view/article/28944.

Collier, John Payne. *Catalogue, Bibliographical and Critical, of Early English Literature Forming a Portion of the Library at Bridgewater House, the Property of the Rt. Hon. Lord Francis Egerton, MP*. London, 1837.

Cooper, Helen. *The English Romance in Time: Transforming Motifs from Geoffrey of Monmouth to the Death of Shakespeare*. Oxford: Oxford University Press, 2004.

Cosman, Madeleine Pelner. *The Education of the Hero in Arthurian Romance*. Chapel Hill: University of North Carolina Press, 1966.

Crane, Ronald S. *The Vogue of Medieval Chivalric Romance during the English Renaissance*. Menasha, WI: George Banta, 1919.

Cruz, Anne J., ed. *Material and Symbolic Circulation between Spain and England, 1554–1604*. Aldershot, UK: Ashgate, 2008.

D'Amico, Jack. *The Moor in English Renaissance Drama*. Tampa: University of South Florida Press, 1991.

Daniels, Marie Cort. *The Function of Humour in the Spanish Romances of Chivalry*. New York and London: Garland, 1992.

Das, Nandini. *Renaissance Romance: The Transformation of English Prose Fiction, 1570–1620*. Farnham, UK and Burlington, VT: Ashgate, 2013.

Davis, Alex. *Chivalry and Romance in the English Renaissance*. Cambridge, UK: D. S. Brewer, 2003.

Dictionnaires d'Autrefois. The ARTFL Project. Department of Romance Languages and Literatures. Chicago: The University of Chicago. http://artfl-project.uchicago.edu/content/dictionnaires-dautrefois.

Dolven, Jeff. *Scenes of Instruction in Renaissance Romance*. Chicago: University of Chicago Press, 2007.

Dunn, Caroline. *Stolen Women in Medieval England: Rape, Abduction, and Adultery, 1100–1500*. Cambridge: Cambridge University Press, 2013.

Ebel, Julia G. "A Numerical Survey of Elizabethan Translations." *The Library* ser. 5, 22.2 (1967): 104–27.

Eisenberg, Daniel. *Castilian Romances of Chivalry in the Sixteenth Century*. London: Grant and Cutler, 1979.

Elmer, Peter. "The Library of Dr. John Webster: The Making of a Seventeenth-Century Radical." *Medical History* 30.6 (1986).

Erickson, Amy L. *Women and Property in Early Modern England*. New York and London: Routledge, 1993.

Espinasse, Francis. "Egerton, John, Second Earl of Bridgewater (1623–1686), rev. Louis A. Knafla." In *Oxford Dictionary of National Biography*, online ed., ed. Lawrence Goldman. Oxford: Oxford University Press, 2007. Accessed July 18, 2021, http://0-www.oxforddnb.com.fama.us.es/view/article/8588.

Farmer, Alan B. and Zachary Lesser. "What Is Print Popularity: A Map of the Elizabethan Book Trade." In *The Elizabethan Top Ten: Defining Print Popularity in Early Modern England*, ed. Andy Kesson and Emma Smith, 19–54. Farnham, UK: Ashgate, 2013.

Feather, Jennifer. *Writing Combat and the Self in Early Modern English Literature*. New York: Palgrave Macmillan, 2011.

Fehrenbach, Robert J. and E. S. Leedham-Greene, eds. *Private Libraries in Renaissance England: A Collection and Catalogue of Tudor and Early Stuart Book-Lists*. 8 vols. Binghamton, NY: Medieval and Renaissance Texts and Studies, 1992–2014.

Fink De Backer, Stephanie. *Widowhood in Early Modern Spain: Protectors, Proprietors, and Patron*. Leiden: Brill, 2010.

Fleming, Juliet. "The Ladies Man and the Age of Elizabeth." In *Sexuality and Gender in Early Modern Europe: Institutions, Texts, Images*, ed. James Grantham Turner, 158–81. Cambridge: Cambridge University Press, 1993.

Furrow, Melissa. *Expectations of Romance: The Reception of a Genre in Medieval England*. Cambridge, UK: D. S. Brewer, 2009.

González, Javier R. "El ave profeta de *Palmerín de Olivia* y *Primaleón*." *Exemplaria: Revista de literatura comparada* 4 (2000): 73–108.

González, Javier R. "El sistema profético en la determinación del *Palmerín-Primaleón* como unidad textual." *Incipit* 20–21 (2000–2001): 81–118.

Goodey, Christopher F. *A History of Intelligence and Intellectual Disability: The Shaping of Psychology in Early Modern Europe*. Burlington, VT: Ashgate, 2011.

Goodman, Jennifer. "European Chivalry in the 1490s." *Comparative Civilizations Review* 26.26 (1992): 43–72.

Goodman, Jennifer R. and Jennifer Robin, eds. *Chivalry and Exploration, 1298–1630*. Woodbridge, UK: The Boydell Press, 1998.

Grafton, Anthony. *The Culture of Correction in Renaissance Europe*. London: British Library, 2011.

Greg, W. W. "The Rationale of Copy-Text." *Studies in Bibliography* 3 (1950–1951): 19–36.

Griffin, Eric. "Copying *The Anti-Spaniard*: Post-Armada Hispanophobia and English Renaissance Drama." In *Representing Imperial Rivalry in the Early Modern Mediterranean*, ed. Barbara Fuchs and Emily Weissbourd, 191–216. Toronto: University of Toronto Press and the UCLA Center for Seventeenth- and Eighteenth-Century Studies, 2015.

Hackett, Helen. *Women and Romance Fiction in the English Renaissance*. Cambridge: Cambridge University Press, 2000.

Hadfield, Andrew. *The Oxford Handbook of English Prose, 1500–1640*. Oxford: Oxford University Press, 2013.

Hagen, Tanya. "An English Renaissance Understanding of the Word 'Tragedy.'" *Early Modern Literary Studies*, Special Issue 1 (1997): 5.1–30. http://purl.oclc.org/emls/si-01/si-01hagen.html.

Hamilton, Donna. *Anthony Munday and the Catholics, 1560–1633*. Aldershot, UK: Ashgate, 2005.

Hamilton, Donna. "Anthony Munday and *The Merchant of Venice*." *Shakespeare Survey* 54 (2001): 89–99.

Hamilton, Donna. "Anthony Munday, Romance Translations, and History Writing: Church Rights, Toleration, and the Unity of Christendom, 1609–1633." In Álvarez-Recio, *Iberian Chivalric Romance*, 181–203.

Hamilton, Donna. "Anthony Munday's Translations of Iberian Chivalric Romances: *Palmerin of England, Part I* as Exemplar." In *Catholic Culture in Early Modern England*, ed. Ronald Corthell, Frances E. Dolan, Christopher Highley, and Arthur F. Marotti, 281–303. Notre Dame, IN: University of Notre Dame Press, 2007.

Hardman, Phillipa. "Popular Romances and Young Readers." In *A Companion to Medieval Popular Romance*, ed. Raluca L. Radulescu and Cory James Rushton, 150–164. Woodbridge, UK: The Boydell Press, 1998.

Hayes, Gerald R. "Anthony Munday's Romances of Chivalry." *The Library* ser. 4, 6.1 (1925): 57–81.

Henderson, Frances. "Clarke, Sir William (1623/4–1666)." In *Oxford Dictionary of National Biography*, online ed., ed. Lawrence Goldman. Oxford: Oxford University Press, 2008. Accessed July 18, 2021, http://0-www.oxforddnb.com.fama.us.es/view/article/5536.

Herrick, Marvin Theodore. *Tragicomedy: Its Origin and Development in Italy, France, and England*. Urbana: University of Illinois Press, 1955.

Highley, Christopher. *Catholics Writing the Nation in Early Modern Britain and Ireland*. Oxford: Oxford University Press, 2008.

Hill, Tracey. *Anthony Munday and Civic Culture: Theatre, History and Power in Early Modern London, 1580–1633*. Manchester and New York: Manchester University Press, 2004.

Hunter, John Paul. *Before Novels: The Cultural Contexts of Eighteenth-Century English Fiction*. New York: Norton, 1990.

Hutson, Lorna. *Thomas Nashe in Context*. Oxford: Clarendon Press, 1989.

Jaritz, Gerhard. "Dress, Jewels, Arms and Coat of Arms: Material Culture and Self-Representation in the Late Middle Ages." Department of Medieval Studies. Budapest: Central European University. Accessed October 5, 2021, web.ceu.hu/medstud/manual/SRM/.

Johnson, Francis R. "Notes on English Retail Book-Prices, 1550–1640." *The Library* ser. 5, 5.2 (1950): 83–112.

Jowett, John. "Notes on Henry Chettle." *Review of English Studies* 45 (1994): 384–88.

Kaeuper, Richard W. and Montgomery Bohna, "War and Chivalry." In *A Companion to Medieval English Literature and Culture, c. 1350–1500*, ed. Peter Brown, 273–91. Malden, MA: Blackwell, 2007.

Kathman, David. "Roberts, James (b. in or before 1540, d. 1618?)." In *Oxford Dictionary of National Biography*, online ed., ed. Lawrence Goldman. Oxford: Oxford University Press, 2006. Accessed July 18, 2021, http://0-www.oxforddnb.com.fama.us.es/view/article/23756.

Keen, Maurice Hugh. *Chivalry*. New Haven, CT and London: Yale University Press, 2005.

Kennedy, Angus J. "The Hermit's Role in French Arthurian Romance (c. 1170–1530)." *Romania* 95 (1974): 54–83.

Kennedy, Elspeth. "Failure in Arthurian Romance." *Medium Ævum* 60.1 (1991): 16–32.

Kesson, Andy. *John Lyly and Early Modern Authorship*. Manchester: Manchester University Press, 2014.

Krause, Virginia. "Serializing the French Amadis in the 1540s." In *Charting Change in France around 1540*, ed. Marian Rothstein, 40–62. Cranbury, NJ: Rosemont, 2006.

Kromm, Jane. *The Art of Frenzy: Public Madness in the Visual Culture of Europe, 1500–1850*. London and New York: Continuum, 2002.

Leitch, Megan G. *Romancing Treason: The Literature of the War of the Roses*. Oxford: Oxford University Press, 2015.

Lexton, Ruth. *Contested Language in Malory's Morte Darthur: The Politics of Romance in Fifteenth-Century England*. New York: Palgrave Macmillan, 2014.

Liebler, Naomi Conn, ed. *Early Modern Prose Fiction: The Cultural Politics of Reading*. New York and London: Routledge, 2006.

List of Catalogues of English Book Sales, 1676–1900: Now in the British Museum. London: British Museum, 1915.

Lockey, Brian C. *Early Modern Catholics, Royalists and Cosmopolitans: English Transnationalism and the Christian Commonwealth*. New York and London: Routledge, 2016.

Lockey, Brian C. *Law and Empire in English Renaissance Literature*. Cambridge: Cambridge University Press, 2006.

Lucas, Caroline. *Writing for Women: The Example of Women as Reader in Elizabethan Romance*. Milton Keynes, UK: Open University Press, 1989.

Mack, Peter. *Elizabethan Rhetoric: Theory and Practice*. Cambridge: Cambridge University Press, 2002.

Maslen, Robert W. *Elizabethan Fictions: Espionage, Counter-Espionage and the Duplicity of Fiction in Early Modern England*. Oxford: Clarendon Press, 1997.

Maslen, Robert W. "Robert Greene." In Hadfield, *The Oxford Handbook of English Prose*, 188–203.

Matar, Nabil. *Turks, Moors, and Englishmen in the Age of Discovery*. New York: Columbia University Press, 1999.

McKerrow, Ronald B. *A Dictionary of Printers and Booksellers in England, Scotland and Ireland, and of Foreign Printers of English Books, 1557–1640*. London: Bibliographical Society, 1910.

McKerrow, Ronald B. *Prolegomena for the Oxford Shakespeare: A Study in Editorial Method*. 1939. Reprint, Oxford: Clarendon Press, 1969.

McSheffrey, Shanon and Julia Pope. "Ravishment, Legal Narratives, and Chivalric Culture in Fifteenth-Century England." *Journal of British Studies* 48.4 (2009): 818–36.

Mentz, Steve. "Day Labor: Thomas Nashe and the Practice of Prose in Early Modern England." In Liebler, *Early Modern Prose Fiction*, 18–32.

Mentz, Steve. *Romance for Sale in Early Modern England: The Rise of Prose Fiction*. New York and London: Routledge, 2017.

Merriam-Webster's Collegiate Encyclopedia. Springfield, MA: Merriam-Webster, 2000.

Meserve, Margaret. *Empires of Islam in Renaissance Historical Thought*. Cambridge, MA: Harvard University Press, 2008.

Moore, Helen. "Ancient and Modern Romance." In Gordon and Gillespie, *The Oxford History of Literary Translation in English*, 333–46.

Moore, Helen. "Barclay's *Argenis* and *Amadis de Gaule*." In Hadfield, *The Oxford Handbook of English Prose*, 59–76.

Moore, Helen. "The Eastern Mediterranean in the English Amadis Cycle Book V." *Yearbook of English Studies* 41.1 (2011): 113–25.

Moore, Helen. "Gathering Fruit: The 'Profitable' Translations of Thomas Paynell." In Schurink, *Tudor Translation*, 39–57.

Moretti, Gabriella. "The Other World and the 'Antipodes': The Myth of the Unknown Countries between Antiquity and the Renaissance." In *The Classical Tradition and the Americas*, ed. Wolfgang Haase and Meyer Reinhold, 241–84. Berlin and New York: De Gruyter, 1994.

Morini, Massimiliano. *Tudor Translation in Theory and Practice*. Aldershot, UK: Ashgate, 2006.

Neri, Stefano. "Cuadro de la difusión europea del ciclo del Amadís de Gaula (siglos XVI–XVII)." In *Amadís de Gaula: Quinientos años después*, ed. José Manuel Lucía Megías and María del Carmen Marín Pina, 565–91. Alcalá de Henares, Spain: Centro de Estudios Cervantinos, 2008.

Neri, Stefano. "El *Progetto Mambrino*. Estado de la cuestión." In *Tus obras los rincones de la tierra descubren*, ed. A. Dotras Bravo, J. M. Lucía Megías, E. Magro García, and J. Montero Reguera, 577–89. Alcalá de Henares, Spain: Centro de Estudios Cervantinos, 2008.

Newcomb, Lori Humphrey. *Reading Popular Romance in Early Modern England*. New York: Columbia University Press, 2002.

Nicholl, Charles. *A Cup of News: The Life of Thomas Nashe*. London: Routledge and Kegan Paul, 1984.

Nicholl, Charles. "Nashe [Nash], Thomas (bap. 1567, d. c. 1601), writer." In *Oxford Dictionary of National Biography*, online ed., ed. Lawrence Goldman. Oxford: Oxford University Press, 2008. Accessed October 8, 2021, http://www.oxforddnb.com/view/10.1093/ref:odnb/9780198614128.001.0001/odnb-9780198614128-e-19790.

Norton, Rictor. "The Homosexual Pastoral Tradition," June 20, 2008. http://rictornorton.co.uk/pastor00.htm.

O'Dell, Sterg. *A Chronological List of Prose Fiction in English Printed in England and Other Countries 1475–1640*. Cambridge, MA: Massachusetts Institute of Technology Press, 1954.

Ortiz-Salamovich, Alejandra. "Anthony Munday's *Palmerin d'Oliva*: Representing Sexual Threat in the Near East." *Sederi: Yearbook of the English Society for English Renaissance Studies* 26 (2016): 67–84.

Outhwaite, R. B. *Clandestine Marriage in England, 1500–1850*. London: Hambledon Press, 1995.

Pane, Remigio Ugo. *English Translations from the Spanish, 1484–1943: A Bibliography*. New Brunswick, NJ: Rutgers University Press, 1944.

Parmelee, Lisa Ferraro. *Good Newes from France: French Anti-League Propaganda in Late Elizabethan England*. Rochester, NY: Rochester University Press, 1996.

Parmelee, Lisa Ferraro. "Printers, Patrons, Readers, and Spies: Importation of French Propaganda in Late Elizabethan England." *Sixteenth Century Journal* 25 (1994): 853–57.

Patchell, Mary. *The Palmerin Romances in Elizabethan Prose Fiction*. New York: AMS Press, 1966.

Peltonen, Markku. *The Duel in Early Modern England: Civility, Politeness and Honour*. Cambridge: Cambridge University Press, 2003.

Pettegree, Andrew. "Translation and the Migration of Texts." In *Borders and Travellers in Early Modern Europe*, ed. Thomas Betteridge, 113–28. Aldershot, UK and Burlington, VT: Ashgate, 2007.

Phillips, Joshua. "Chronicles of Wasted Time: Anthony Munday, Tudor Romance, and Literary Labor." *English Literary History* 73 (2006): 781–803.

Phillips, Joshua. *English Fictions of Communal Identity, 1485–1603*. Farnham, UK and Burlington, VT: Ashgate, 2013.

Phillips, William D. "The Frustrated Unity of Atlantic Europe: The Roles of Spain and England." In Cruz, *Material and Symbolic Circulation between Spain an England, 1554–1604*, 3–12.

Plomer, Henry R. *Dictionary of the Booksellers and Printers Who Were at Work in England, Scotland and Ireland from 1641 to 1667*. London, 1907.

Plomer, Henry R. *English Printers' Ornaments*. London: Grafton and Co. Coptic House, 1924.

Plomer, Henry R. "Some Elizabethan Book Sales." *The Library* ser. 3, 7.28 (1916): 318–29.

Ramey, Lynn. "Medieval Miscegenation: Hybridity and the Anxiety of Inheritance." In *Contextualizing the Muslim Other in Medieval Christian Discourse*, ed. Jerold C. Frakes, 1–19. New York: Palgrave Macmillan, 2011.

Renaissance Cultural Crossroads Catalogue. The Digital Humanities Institute and the Centre for the Study of the Renaissance. Sheffield and Warwick: The

University of Sheffield and the University of Warwick. http://www.dhi.ac.uk/rcc.

Rhodes, Neil. "Italianate Tales: William Painter and George Pettie." In Hadfield, *The Oxford Handbook of English Prose*, 91–105.

Rhodes, Neil, Gordon Kendal, and Louise Wilson, eds. *English Renaissance Translation Theory*. London: Modern Humanities Research Association, 2013.

Rothstein, Marian. *Reading in the Renaissance: Amadis de Gaule and the Lessons of Memory*. Newark: University of Delaware Press, 1999.

Salzman, Paul. *English Prose Fiction, 1558–1700: A Critical History*. Oxford: Clarendon Press, 1985.

Salzman, Paul. "Placing Tudor Fiction." *Yearbook of English Studies* 38 (2008): 136–49.

Sánchez-Martí, Jordi, ed. *A Critical Edition of Anthony Munday's Palmerin d'Oliva. Edited with an Introduction, Critical Apparatus, Notes, and Glossary*. Tempe: Arizona Center for Medieval and Renaissance Studies, 2020.

Sánchez-Martí, Jordi. *Los libros de caballerías en Inglaterra, 1578–1700*. Salamanca, Spain: Ediciones Universidad de Salamanca, 2020.

Sánchez-Martí, Jordi. "The Publication History of Anthony Munday's *Palmerin d'Oliva*." *Gutenberg-Jahrbuch* 89 (2014): 190–207.

Sánchez-Martí, Jordi. "*Zelauto*'s Polinarda and the Palmerin Romances." *Cahiers Élisabéthains* 89.1 (2016): 1–9.

Saunders, Corinne. "Bodily Narratives: Illness, Medicine and Healing in Middle English Romance." In *Boundaries in Medieval Romance*, ed. Neil Cartlidge, 175–90. Cambridge, UK: D. S. Brewer, 2008.

Saunders, Corinne. "A Matter of Consent: Middle English Romance and the Law of Raptus." In *Medieval Women and the Law*, ed. Noël James Menuge, 105–24. Woodbridge, UK: Boydell, 2003.

Scanlon, Paul A. "A Checklist of Prose Romances in English, 1474–1603." *The Library* ser. 5, 33.2 (1978): 143–152.

Schmitt, Charles B., Quentin Skinner, Eckhard Kessler, and Jill Kraye, eds. *The Cambridge History of Renaissance Philosophy*. Cambridge: Cambridge University Press, 1988.

Schoenfeldt, Michael C. *Bodies and Selves in Early Modern England: Physiology and Inwardness in Spenser, Shakespeare, Herbert, and Milton*. Cambridge Studies in Renaissance Literature and Culture 34. Cambridge: Cambridge University Press, 1999.

Schurink, Fred, ed. *Tudor Translation*. Basingstoke, UK: Palgrave Macmillan, 2011.

Scodel, Joshua. *The English Poetic Epitaph*. Ithaca, NY: Cornell University Press, 1991.

Sheehan, Michael M. *Marriage, Family, and Law in Medieval Europe: Collected Studies*, ed. James K. Farge. Toronto: University of Toronto Press, 1996.

Singer, Julie. *Blindness and Therapy in Late Medieval French and Italian Poetry*. Woodbridge, UK: D. S. Brewer, 2011.

Skinner, Quentin. *Visions of Politics*. 3 vols. Cambridge: Cambridge University Press, 2002.

Smith, Charlotte C. "'Depicted with Extraordinary Skill': Ottoman Dress in Sixteenth-Century German Printed Costume Books." *Textile History* 44.1 (2013): 25–50.

Smith, Sara. "A Reattribution of Munday's *The Paine of Pleasure*." *Oxfordian* 5 (2002): 70–99.

Spanish-English Translations, 1500–1640, Database. Department of Spanish and Spanish-American Studies. London: King's College. www.ems.kcl.ac.uk/apps/index.html.

Spenser, Terence. "Shakespeare's Isle of Delphos." *The Modern Language Review* 47.2 (1952): 199–202.

Stanivukovic, Goran. "English Renaissance Romances as Conduct Books for Young Men." In Liebler, *Early Modern Prose Fiction*, 60–78.

Stanivukovic, Goran. "Iberian Chivalric Romance and the Formation of Modern Fiction in Early Modern England." In Álvarez-Recio, *Iberian Chivalric Romance*, 207–32.

Stanivukovic, Goran. *Knights in Arms: Prose Romance, Masculinity, and Eastern Mediterranean Trade in Early Modern England, 1565–1655*. Toronto: University of Toronto Press, 2016.

Starke, Sue P. *The Heroines of English Pastoral Romance*. Studies in Renaissance Literature 20. Rochester, NY: Boydell and Brewer, 2007.

Straznicky, Marta. *Shakespeare's Stationers: Studies in Cultural Bibliography*. Philadelphia: University of Pennsylvania Press, 2012.

Sumillera, Rocío G. "The Rhetoric of Letter Writing: The *Amadís de Gaula* in Translation." In Álvarez-Recio, *Iberian Chivalric Romance*, 115–36.

Tanselle, Thomas. "Some Principles for Editorial Apparatus." *Studies in Bibliography* 25 (1972): 41–89.

Taylor, Barry. "Learning Style from the Spaniards in Sixteenth-Century England." In Barker and Hosington, *Renaissance Cultural Crossroads*, 63–78.

Thomas, Henry. *The Palmerin Romances*. Transactions of the Bibliographical Society 13. London: The Bibliographical Society, 1916.

Thomas, Henry. *Spanish and Portuguese Romances of Chivalry: The Revival of the Romance of Chivalry in the Spanish Peninsula, and Its Extension and Influence Abroad*. Cambridge: Cambridge University Press, 1920.

Thompson, Diane P. *The Trojan War: Literature and Legends from the Bronze Age to the Present*. Jefferson, NC: McFarland and Company, 2003.

Wald, Christina. *The Reformation of Romance: The Eucharist, Disguise and Foreign Fashion in Early Modern Prose Fiction*. Berlin and Boston: De Gruyter, 2014.

Warner, Lyndan. "Widows, Widowers and the Problem of Second Marriage in Sixteenth-Century France." In *Widowhood in Medieval and Early Modern Europe*, ed. Sandra Cavallo and Lyndan Warner, 84–107. London: Longman, 1999.

Wells, Marion. *The Secret Wound: Love-Melancholy and Early Modern Romance*. Stanford, CA: Stanford University Press, 2006.

Werth, Tiffany. *The Fabulous Dark Cloister: Romance in England after the Reformation*. Baltimore: Johns Hopkins University Press, 2011.

Willes, Margaret. *The Making of the English Gardener: Plants, Books and Inspiration, 1550–1660*. New Haven, CT and London: Yale University Press, 2011.

Wilson, J. Dover. "Anthony Munday, Pamphleteer and Pursuivant." *Modern Language Review* 4 (1909): 484–90.

Wilson, Katherine. *Fictions of Authorship in Late Elizabethan Narratives: Euphues in Arcadia*. Oxford: Oxford University Press, 2006.

Wilson, Louise. "'I Marvell Who the Divell Is This Printer': Fictions of Book Production in Anthony Munday and Henry Chettle's Paratexts." In *The Book Trade in Early Modern England: Practices, Perceptions, Connections*, ed. John Hinks and Victoria Gardener, 1–17. New Castle, DE and London: Oak Knoll Press and the British Library.

Wilson, Louise. "Playful Paratexts: The Front Matter of Anthony Munday's Iberian Romance Translations." In *Renaissance Paratexts*, ed. Helen Smith and Louise Wilson, 121–32. Cambridge: Cambridge University Press, 2013.

Wilson, Louise. "The Publication of Iberian Romance in Early Modern Europe." In *Translation and the Book Trade in Early Modern Europe*, ed. José María Pérez Fernández and Edward Wilson-Lee, 201–16. Cambridge: Cambridge University Press, 2014.

Wilson, Louise. "Writing Romance Readers in Early Modern Paratexts." *Swiss Papers in English Language and Literature* 22 (2009): 111–23.

Wunder, Amanda. "Western Travelers, Eastern Antiquities, and the Image of the Turk in Early Modern Europe." *Journal of Early Modern History* 7 (2003): 89–119.

Yalom, Marylin. "Betrothal: Overview." In *The Oxford Encyclopedia of Women in World History*, ed. Bonnie G. Smith, Vol. 1, 220–21. Oxford: Oxford University Press, 2008

TEAMS

VARIA SERIES

The Study of Chivalry: Resources and Approaches, edited by Howell Chickering and Thomas H. Seiler (1988)

Studies in the Harley Manuscript: The Scribes, Contents, and Social Contexts of British Library MS Harley 2253, edited by Susanna Fein (2000)

The Liturgy of the Medieval Church, edited by Thomas J. Heffernan and E. Ann Matter (2001; second edition 2005)

Johannes de Grocheio, *Ars musice*, edited and translated by Constant J. Mews, John N. Crossley, Catherine Jeffreys, Leigh McKinnon, and Carol J. Williams (2011)

Aribo, "De musica" and "Sententiae," edited and translated by T. J. H. McCarthy (2015)

Guy of Saint-Denis, *Tractatus de tonis*, edited and translated by Constant J. Mews, Carol J. Williams, John N. Crossley, and Catherine Jeffreys (2017)

Typeset in Garamond Premier Pro

Medieval Institute Publications
College of Arts and Sciences
Western Michigan University
1903 W. Michigan Avenue
Kalamazoo, MI 49008-5432
http://wmich.edu/medievalpublications

Western Michigan University

9781580444811